Richard C

D1188210

The ROAD *to* H

80C
HV
5822
H4
C47
COP. 5

The ROAD to H

NARCOTICS, DELINQUENCY,
and
SOCIAL POLICY

ISIDOR CHEIN
DONALD·L·GERARD
ROBERT·S·LEE
EVA ROSENFELD

WITH THE COLLABORATION OF
DANIEL M. WILNER

 Basic Books, *Inc.*
PUBLISHERS
NEW YORK / LONDON

Robert Manning Strozier Library

APR 28 1975

Tallahassee, Florida

Second Printing

© 1964 BY BASIC BOOKS, INC., PUBLISHERS

Library of Congress Catalog Card Number: 63–17342

Manufactured in the United States of America

DESIGNED BY VINCENT TORRE

Preface

This book is aimed at those who are seriously concerned with the narcotics problem. Such an audience includes people with a wide variety of professional backgrounds—lawmakers; behavioral scientists; police officers; social case workers; psychiatrists; the personnel of correctional institutions, probation departments, and voluntary social agencies; representatives of local, state, and federal government directly charged with doing something about the problem; and the informed and alert citizenry with no direct contact with the problem but without whose participation in public affairs rational efforts to solve many of our society's ills would be hopeless.

It may be assumed that the majority of such a hoped-for audience is uninformed on technical aspects of research design and statistical data. Despite the fact that most of Part One is based on research, we have been advised to play down these aspects of our work. The typical reader, we have been assured, would be willing to take our technical competence on faith and would want to know *what we have found out,* without being bothered with issues of method or with the details on which our conclusions are based. The typical reader, it is said, is carried along by the dramatic quality of the presentation and is only alienated by the intrusion of evidence expressed in *numbers* and considerations of logic and of the nature, relevance, and limits of evidence.

Perhaps so. Yet, even if we had the competence to write these sections of Part One in a way that would hold the "typical reader" spellbound, we would not be inclined to do so. We have had a number of opportunities to see what happens to our materials when they are worked over by skilled publicists with such "typical readers" in mind. The results, as they have appeared in newspapers and popular magazines, may have made interesting reading, but they have somehow lost their authority—not the pseudoauthority of ascription to eminent professors and years of university-based research nor the pseudoauthority of polysyllabic technical jargon, but the true authority of respect for the reader's intelligence. That sort of authoritative writing presents him with the essential materials in as unbiased a fashion as possible and with the thinking that the investigators have contributed. It gives the reader a fair basis on which to accept or reject the conclusions reached or to form his own.

The worth of research cannot be measured in years of effort or in the reputation of those who carry it out; even professors have been known to bumble along for unproductive years or to wander into unavoidable blind alleys, and the time spent in writing a book may reflect the pressures of other commitments, indecisiveness of thought, and the sheer lack of writing skill or inspiration. The popular articles we have referred to appealed to these false bases of authority and selected from our materials the kinds of statement and fact that would hold the interest of "typical readers," but they were, in fact, no more authoritative than countless other journalistic efforts. If we were to try to emulate the publicists, we could only do worse—we lack the necessary writing skills—and we would only be adding to the reams of paper already devoted to the topic and as quickly forgotten.

Our convictions about the kind of book we should write were strongly reinforced by certain aspects of the topic with which we are dealing and by a related experience that occurred early in the course of our research. The question of what to do about drug use is highly controversial. Certain issues of fact are germane to this controversy. In the past few years, there have been many hearings by various bodies— a committee of the United States Senate, special legislative commissions in various states, and local government agencies. At these hearings, there are always many witnesses to testify on the facts. The experience we have already referred to gave us some perspective on the quality of these facts.

It happened that, toward the end of the first year of our investigations, a major hearing was to focus on the narcotics problem in New York City. It was already widely known that we had been collecting data on drug use in the juvenile population of the city. A few days before the hearing, we began to receive visits from representatives of certain public and private agencies. Each of our visitors had the same request, worded somewhat differently, but, in essence: "I have to testify at the hearing, and I will surely be asked how many addicts there are in the city. I hope you can tell me." We explained the nature of our statistics; they referred to individuals involved with narcotics—most of them known to have taken narcotics, and the bulk of the remainder could be safely assumed to have done likewise. At that time, we took it for granted that a user, if not already addicted, would almost certainly end up an addict; but, even then, we were careful to distinguish between "users" and "addicts" (a distinction which will be discussed at some length in Chapter II).

We are not here concerned, however, with the failure of our visitors to keep the distinction in mind, but with a simpler issue. We pointed out that we were dealing with only three of the five boroughs; that our figures referred to *known* cases; and that, to arrive at the true figures, one would have to multiply our statistics by an unknown factor—perhaps two, or three and one-half, or seven. In the next few days, we were both amused and dismayed by newspaper reports (subsequently verified in the published record) of the testimony given by each of our visitors. The figures they cited differed wildly (we assumed that they arbitrarily chose different multipliers and added a few odd cases to eliminate the imprecision that might be suggested by too rounded numbers); there was no reference to the common source and no indication of the operations they had performed on the figures we had given them. And—this is the crux of the matter—apparently no one thought of asking them how they arrived at the figures.

The facts and figures of one "expert" are seemingly as good as those of another. How the expert arrives at his facts is a matter of technical detail that the ordinary person is not supposed to look into, to say nothing of the question of what the facts are supposed to mean. If the experts disagree, one takes his pick according to his predilections; according to which expert is most articulate; according to what fits best with one's preconceived solution of the problem; or he concludes as we have heard at a recent hearing, that, "in the field of drug addiction, there are no experts." This is what comes from not looking at how the "facts" are obtained.

We simply do not want our facts and figures to be lost in a mass of undocumented assertions. We do not mean to suggest that we are infallible. We do mean that, if someone disagrees with us, then the quality of what he disagrees with ought to be such as to place on him the burden of demonstrating the flaws in our procedures or argument and, perhaps, of producing something better.

We are tired—and we think that the interested public ought to be tired—of conclusions presented with no indication of the grounds on which they were reached. We are also tired of appearing as witnesses at public hearings and as participants in conferences where the sheer number of voices clamoring to be heard precludes any extensive critical examination of what is being said and where those responsible for formulating recommendations all too often show signs of having made up their minds in advance or of being concerned with little more than feeling the pulse of that portion of the public which is sufficiently stirred by the problem to want to be heard.

We do not mean to suggest that most of those who give testimony are uninformed or inexperienced, but only that what they have to say cannot be weighed in any intelligent fashion without going beyond the conclusions to the premises, the data, and the reasoning on which they are based and without going beyond the statistics to the circumstances and procedures under which they were collected and processed and the statistical logic from which their cogency must be inferred.

Nor do we mean to suggest that it is senseless to take action until every loophole in the evidence has been closed, every premise exposed, every argument formulated with unassailable mathematical rigor, and every possible conclusion but one disproved. Far from it. The requirement of absolute certainty, even if it were possible in principle with regard to any issue of action, could only result in paralysis; and there are situations in which doing *something* is so urgent that one may be quite justified in acting blindly, even at the risk of worsening the situation.

Our point is that one should never proceed more blindly than one must. If, in the potential audience that we have envisioned, there are those who, for one reason or another, prefer to do so, this is, of course, their choice. If they open the book at all, they will skip the difficult sections and the discussions of methodological issues in Part One and look for the summary sections; there may even be some entire chapters that will hold their interest. We have, however, felt obliged to tell our story as fully as we could. If there are flaws in the materials of which we are cognizant, we have tried to call attention to them. If there are points at which we have felt that a particular kind of expert would be inclined to lift an eyebrow, we have attempted to acknowledge them. We have not wittingly attempted to conceal weakness for the sake of making a more convincing case for what we advocate.

There may be technical matters that are simply beyond the reach of individuals without relevant specialized training. We have, however, written this book with the conviction that such is not the case with respect to the kinds of material that we have to present and with respect to our potential audience. We are quite willing to give up the "typical readers" in this audience, but we assume that there are enough left who will put in the extra effort required. There must, of course, be many among these who will never have heard of a variance, of a multiple correlation, or perhaps even of a simple correlation coefficient; but we believe that these and other statistical concepts can be made reasonably intelligible as the need for them arises and in the applications that we have made.

We have attempted to make the text self-sufficient, with a minimum of explanation of such concepts, but we have also included somewhat fuller explanations, in terms comprehensible to the statistical laity, in several appendixes and a number of footnotes. Specifically, Appendix C deals at some length with the meaning of correlation coefficients; Appendix E deals similarly with cluster analysis; and Appendix J deals briefly with the logic of statistical inference. In the course of these appendixes, we also deal with a number of other statistical and psychometric or sociometric concepts (e.g., the concept of a standard score) and some special versions of the correlation coefficient (e.g., the tetrachoric correlation).

Throughout, we have designated footnotes concerned with technical statistical points by superscript letters. Thus, we have dealt with some of the basic notions of multiple correlation in such footnotes. These footnotes are intended for the critical reader who may otherwise be puzzled by some point in the text and who is entitled to be informed of special statistical issues as they arise. A small number of such footnotes and Appendix F are also addressed to readers with special statistical training. Such items are concerned, in the main, with points that might otherwise be bothersome to statistically trained readers, but which are not relevant enough to the text to justify detailed exposition.

Ordinary footnotes, containing additional remarks or information relevant to the text, but not incorporated into it, have been designated by superscript numbers. All the appendixes not already mentioned are also of this character. Footnotes to tables have been uniformly designated by asterisks, daggers, etc., although most belong in the present category.

Several chapters of Part One do not deal with statistical data at all, and even those that do devote more space to the clarification of the research issues than to statistics.

In the years since we began our work on drug addiction, the number of agencies and individuals to whom we are indebted has become unmanageably large. We have received active assistance from the various courts of New York City, the probation and parole departments attached to them, the Youth Counsel Bureau, Riverside Hospital, the New York State Training School at Coxsackie, the public school system of New York City, the school system of the Archdiocese of New York, the New York City Youth Board, the New York City Planning Commission, the New York School of Social Work, and the School of Social Work at New York University.

The studies carried out at the Research Center for Human Relations of New York University under the general direction of Isidor Chein, the reports on which constitute the bulk of this book, and the preparation of the first draft of the book were made possible by a series of special grants from the National Institute of Mental Health of the United States Public Health Service.

To attempt to list the many individuals to whom we are indebted would detract from the credit due each of them. We hope that they will not consider us unappreciative of their help.

Two exceptions, however, must be made. One is John A. Clausen, formerly chief of the Laboratory of Socio-Environmental Studies, National Institute of Mental Health, without whose help, advice, and encouragement our work could not have proceeded. The other is Daniel M. Wilner, now at the School of Public Health of the University of California at Los Angeles, who was an active partner in much of our research. Although he has had no part in the actual writing of this book, we have considered it entirely appropriate to list him on the title page as a collaborator.

It should be entirely unnecessary to add that none of the agencies or individuals that have helped us should be considered in any way responsible for the opinions we express and that there is no basis whatever for any assumption that they necessarily share these opinions to any degree.

ISIDOR CHEIN
DONALD L. GERARD
ROBERT S. LEE
EVA ROSENFELD

New York City
November 1963

Contents

CONTENTS

The ROAD *to* H

PART

1

EPIDEMIOLOGY
OF
DRUG USE

I

Introduction

"H" is for heaven; "H" is for hell; "H" is for heroin. In the life of the addict, these three meanings of "H" seem inextricably intertwined.

How and why does addiction happen? What, if anything, should be done about it? These are the basic questions to which this book is addressed. They are complex questions, not merely in the sense that many factors must be taken into account in answering them, but also in the sense that they reach beyond the borders of the intellect and the devices with which one ordinarily tries to find answers to intellectually challenging questions. Although we have attempted to approach these questions as behavioral scientists, bringing to bear many research and analytic techniques and trying to lay bare fundamental facts, we rather doubt that it is possible to answer them dispassionately.

When one tries to answer these questions, he finds himself profoundly implicated. The addict is not simply an alien specimen that can be placed under a microscope, coldly dissected, or otherwise displayed to our disinterested and detached observation. He is a human being; that, in itself, is enough to implicate us. No matter how offensive and destructive we may find his behavior, we cannot regard him as a merely noxious object, an insensate thing, or less than human creature without to some degree dehumanizing ourselves. Moreover, however insufficient the sheer fact of our common humanity may be as a basis of empathic communion, the addict stands before us as a stark model of what the rest of us might have made of ourselves; insofar as we sense in his life story a tragedy of temptation and fall, he serves as a bleak reminder of our own vulnerability to temptation and of our own desperate hope never to be cut off from all possibility of redemption.

Our own inner reverberations when confronted by such unpleasant potentialities of the human image—the arousal of our hidden guilts, fears, awareness of frailties, and, let us face it, our envy of the "freedoms" of irresponsibility and of the esoteric delights that we dare not permit ourselves—all of this may be difficult to bear. We may try to protect ourselves by turning outward and adopting a stance of witness to a drama of the implacable working out of retributive justice. Prometheus, having illicitly brought the heavenly fire to earth, is condemned to a millennium of being eaten alive; Tantalus, having stolen the ambrosia of the gods, suffers a fate that makes his name a symbol of an exquisite form of torture; Icarus, having soared to forbidden heights, suffers the inevitable consequence of plummeting to the depths; and the addict, having trespassed in heaven, has earned his hell.

Alas, it does not take much witnessing to learn that the great drama is nothing but a tawdry parody. Our Promethean-Tantalic-Icaric addict is not a heroic figure, but a miserable wretch. The heaven on which he has trespassed is not the heaven of a normal man's dreams, but an impoverished counterfeit. The hell that he suffers is not the inevitable consequence of impersonal forces or of the will of the gods, but a hell generated by human society. Our stance as witnesses turns out to be a pose designed to mask a petty, punitive, narrowly self-righteous superiority.

Be it a contemporary rendition or a shabby burlesque of the classical tragedy, we are all implicated in the life story of the addict. He is one of us. His character and actions have consequence for us, as ours do for him. As members of a common society, we share in the responsibility for the conditions that have helped make him what he is, insofar as these conditions are subject to human control. The dispositions we make for his treatment help to determine the consequences of his addiction. No matter how low he sinks, he cannot lose his right to justice; the lower he sinks, the greater is his claim to our concern.

There is thus ample occasion for passion in the discussion of addiction. It is not, however, the traditional role of the scientist to display his involvement in his subject matter. If he is involved, it is the style of scientific reporting to carefully conceal that fact. Sentences that would normally be expressed in the first person are, for instance, systematically translated into the third person, neuter gender, passive voice. This is his guarantee of objectivity. Yet, the closer his subject matter to areas of significant human concern, the more is that guarantee a pretentious sham. Or, if he is truly detached, the greater the reason to be suspicious of the quality of his observation; flatness of affect and detachment are common symptoms of psychopathology, and we do not normally trust the mentally sick to be the most accurate observers.

The true characteristics of scientific inquiry are in the steps taken to guarantee the accuracy of the observations, regardless of the state of one's feelings with regard to the outcome; to control for possible sources of error; and, in instances of failure to control, to make express acknowledgment of the failure and to take account of its possible effects. If the personal involvement of the scientist makes more tenable the hypothesis that he is in large measure merely observing that which he wants or expects to observe, then it is all the more his scientific responsibility to acknowledge his personal involvement, not to conceal it. It is his responsibility to keep his feelings from intruding into his determination of the facts; it is not his responsibility to deny himself as a human being by indifference to the facts, and it is only scientific irresponsibility to conceal from his readers the fact that he does have feelings.

As a matter of historical record, we had no axes to grind when we started our investigations, and we still do not have any in the sense of material advantages that might accrue to us or to any agencies with which we are associated from the defense of one position as against another. Neither our own statuses nor those of the agencies for which we work are at stake in the sheer fact of concluding one way or another.

We were also free of any expectations with regard to the substantive aspects of the problem, so that we could not be fairly said to have started with any particular bias. We had no idea whether all strata of society were equally vulnerable or whether some segments were more vulnerable than others. If we had to make a guess, it would have been in the direction of our findings, and we would probably have been surprised if it had turned out that all individuals are equally vulnerable; but we were open to the possibility that the only factor relevant to the spread of drug addiction is the prevalence of inducements to try the drugs and that, once one has partaken of them, there is, subject only to continuation of access, a physiologically inevitable course to addiction.

It was not until we were well into the problem that we began, at first vaguely, to distinguish between users and addicts; and it was not until this book was well under way that it dawned on us that even a person with a history of drug use and physiological dependence on the drug might conceivably not be an addict. Such a person might be lacking in what we now regard as an indispensable characteristic of a true addict—craving, that is, a powerful desire for the drug independent of the degree to which the drug has insinuated itself into the physiological workings of the body. It was not until we were well into the problem that we clearly realized that the factors responsible for drug use might be different from the factors responsible for addiction, given drug use. We started with the common belief that prolonged use of narcotic drugs is intrinsically devastating to the human being, physically and psychically, and it was not until we set to work to prepare a true-false test on information about narcotics that it was brought home to us how completely without any scientific foundation and contrary to fact such a belief is.

When we began our studies, we were, of course, aware that there were laws concerning the possession and sale—and, by implication, the use—of narcotics. We viewed the problem as a special case in the general area of crime and delinquency. We saw the law as setting the framework of the problem, but we did not start with any suspicion that the law might be in any way contributing to the existence of the problem. If we gave the matter any thought at all, we would probably have gone along with the common assumption that the law was a perfectly rational way of meeting a genuine need and with the common-sense view that, if people do something that is dangerous to society or morally reprehensible under the risk of arrest and prosecution, they will be all the more likely to do it if the risk is removed. It did not occur to us at that time to question the fundamental premise of the common-sense view, namely, that the motivation of such actions exists independently of the risk and of the conditions that make these actions risky. It did not occur to us to ask how much drug-taking behavior would not take place were it not for the challenge of the risk; the attractiveness of the forbidden; the glamor of defying authority; the power of self-destructive needs given a socially validated channel of expression; the drawing power of an illicit subsociety to lonely individuals alienated from the main stream and the lure of its ability to confer a sense of belonging, interdependence of fate, and common purpose to individuals who would otherwise feel themselves to be standing alone in a hostile world; and the inducements to drug use motivated by vast profits made possible by the very effectiveness of the law enforcement agencies and the operation of the economic law of supply and demand. We did not, then, have any notion that the most dangerous consequences of addiction to the individual were a direct outcome of the existence and enforcement of the law.

We did, however, eventually reach conclusions—in briefest version, that the problem of addiction is commonly viewed in the most violently distorted perspective and that the efforts of society to cope with the problem are models of irrationality. These are strong conclusions, bound to evoke strong reactions. If this is not enough to alert the reader to proceed with a critical eye, let us add that, although we have disclaimed any initial bias, we are conscious of the all-too-human tendency to develop a personal investment in one's conclusions. There is evidence that, once one has committed oneself to certain conclusions, there is a tendency to hold to them with all the more unshakable conviction, the less solidly they are based. In our own eyes, therefore, if only on this ground, our conclusions are not invulnerable.

If we have, nevertheless, already stated some bald conclusions, perhaps implied some others, and continue this chapter with a bare summary of some of our findings, it is only because such a statement helps to provide an integrative map of the rest of the book. This is where the reader is given a picture of the sort of things he is going to be asked to believe. It is the big picture. We have put it at the beginning rather than in the customary position at the end because this makes easier the reader's job of checking the big picture. By the customary procedure, the reader must fix all of the details in mind before he knows what will be done with them, and it is relatively easy for him to go along with the authors in any distortions they may introduce in the summary, wittingly or unwittingly overlooking conflicting details, over-emphasizing some details, and underemphasizing others. But, if he has the big picture clearly in mind at the outset, then jarring details, insufficiencies of evidence, and the like are more likely to strike him as he goes along. We believe that the big picture we present is faithful to its subject; but that is for the reader to judge.

In our view, grossly exaggerated estimates of the number of addicts is a numbers game. There seem to be two kinds of vested interest at work in establishing the exaggerated statistics as authentic—one benevolent, the other not so.

On the benevolent side are the agencies and individuals who are desperately trying to provide services for the addict. Treatment, rehabilitation, and research resources are so grossly inadequate, however, that these agencies and individuals find themselves in the situation of a person caught in a traffic jam who is trying to estimate the number of cars on the road. It may also be good politics to exaggerate the need in the hope that legislators and other controllers of funds may be moved to approach the level of need. On the whole, however, we think that these individuals are honestly reflecting what they see; it is merely that they are in no position to provide authentic figures. It is also our, perhaps naïve, opinion that it should not be necessary to exaggerate to be able to meet existing human needs. These are acute needs, and there has been scarcely a beginning in meeting them.

On the not-so-benevolent side there is what seems to be an occupational disease of law enforcement agencies. Such agencies are continually frustrated in the discharge of their proper functions by considerations of civil liberties. These frustrations are real, even though they are necessitated by the larger social good. The law enforcement agencies, however, are not charged with maintaining the larger social good, but with law enforcement, and they are quite naturally most concerned with establishing the conditions that will enable them to carry out their responsibilities most effectively. Moreover, the normal course of their relationships with law violators is such as to make it difficult for them to achieve a balanced view of criminals as human beings included among those whom the Bill of Rights was designed to protect. Their constant concern is to outwit and to keep from being outwitted; such a relationship can hardly be expected to generate a desire to protect the rights of others. Finally, there is a phenomenon similar to the traffic-jam effect mentioned in the preceding case; in the experience of the law enforcement agent, the world must be far more densely populated with malefactors than is actually the case.

What does all this have to do with the numbers game? If the addiction problem can be inflated to the proportion of a national menace, then, in terms of the doctrine of clear and present danger, one is justified in calling for ever-harsher punishments, the invocation of more restrictive measures, and more restrictions on the rights of individuals.

There seems to be a trend for law enforcement officials to accept the definition of addiction as a disease, but this trend does not entail much of a change in outlook. The argument goes something like this: The addict is mentally sick and irresponsible. We know that he will commit crimes. It is essential to protect society from his depredations. Therefore, he should be committed to a mental hospital.

No American law enforcement officer, to our knowledge, has ever dared suggest that a person be sentenced to jail for crimes he has not yet committed; but to sentence him to hospital servitude is, after all, thoroughly humanitarian and not a violation of the Bill of Rights at all. It takes panic to make this sort of logic palatable, and numbers are useful in generating panic.

Although we shall present, in later chapters, some data on other subgroups, we shall here limit ourselves to the subgroup we have most intensively studied, the sixteen-to-twenty–year–old male drug-user. All of our data are limited to cases in three boroughs of New York City—Manhattan, the Bronx, and Brooklyn.

From the information available to us, allowing for differences in specific statistics, it can be said that the picture is probably not much different from that of other subgroups and other large cities with large numbers of cases. The major exceptions in at least some important details are the so-called medically addicted cases—that is, individuals introduced to narcotics in the course of medical treatment—the majority of which (excluding terminal cancer cases) currently come from the rural areas of states which still permit nongraduates of medical schools to practice medicine and the cases of individuals addicted exclusively to barbiturates, to so-called tranquilizers, and to one or another of a variety of synthetic drugs.

Every year since 1949, about five hundred young men, give or take a hundred or so, who have not been previously known to be illicitly involved with narcotics have been coming to the attention of the courts, city hospitals, and other interested agencies. The great majority of these have used heroin; only a small proportion are nonusing sellers of heroin or involved exclusively with marijuana. How many of these become addicted is not known, especially since the word "addict" is not used in any standardized way. How many additional cases there might be which do not come to public attention is also not known, but it is unlikely that a habituated individual (that is, one who has been taking at least one daily dose for at least two weeks) can escape attention for long. The count probably includes nearly all those who, for some considerable period during the time span under consideration, may be considered habituated users.

It is not known, however, how many habituated users there are among sixteen-to-twenty–year–old males in the three boroughs on any given day; the number is undoubtedly far less than the total number of cases counted for the statistic cited at the beginning of the preceding paragraph. Some have discontinued use, if only temporarily, by virtue of finding themselves in custody; some have voluntarily, perhaps also temporarily, discontinued use for a variety of reasons; some have left town; many have graduated beyond their teens. It is also not known how many habituated users are to be found, let us say, today in the three boroughs who are known to have become involved there with narcotics prior to their twentieth birthdays; some have died, some have left the area, some have quit temporarily and are clear as of today, some have reduced their level of intake to less than that which we have designated as habituated use and others have never reached that level, and some may have quit permanently.

It is a virtual certainty that only a fraction—an unknown fraction, to be sure—of the 2,950 males in the sixteen-to-twenty age range whom we counted as having become involved with drugs in the period from January 1, 1949, through December 31, 1954, are still alive, residing in New York City, and habituated as of today. This fraction may be greater or smaller than the fraction of those truly addicted, in the sense earlier defined, as of today, since, on the one hand, not all habituated individuals are necessarily addicts and since, on the other, not all true addicts are necessarily habituated on a given day. To be sure, a habituated person with so long a history of continuous involvement with narcotics is very likely to be a true addict; but, for all we know to the contrary, there may be a substantial number of the same individuals who are today habituated but who have had no involvement at all in the interim.

Whatever the actual numbers of juvenile habituates and true addicts may be, drug use among juveniles is most frequently found in the most deprived areas of the city. In the early 1950's, 15 per cent of the census tracts in the three boroughs, containing less than 30 per cent of the sixteen-to-twenty–year–old boys, contributed over 80 per cent of the cases of involvement. The areas of high incidence of drug use are characterized by the high incidence of impoverished families, great concentration of the most discriminated against and least urbanized ethnic groups, and high incidence of disrupted families and other forms of human misery. There is no reason to suppose that this situation has materially changed since then.

The relation of drug use to crime and delinquency is not a simple one. The illegality of the possession of heroin and marijuana, of course, defines the user of these drugs as *ipso facto* a criminal, and he can only obtain the drugs by dealing with criminals. Moreover, the high market cost of heroin makes it impossible for ordinary habituated users, especially juveniles, to maintain their supplies by legitimately obtained financial resources. Habituated use demands financing by illegal means, participation in the sale of narcotics ("pushing") and in other forms of crime that promise cash returns. In areas of high drug use, the increase in the latter is accompanied by an increased proportion of potentially money-making juvenile crime. Still, the increase in drug use does not result in an over-all increase in juvenile crime when the direct violations of the narcotics laws are discounted. Drug use flourishes in areas of disproportionately high delinquency, but it is not the cause of the delinquency (again, of course, discounting the direct violation of the narcotics laws). The increase in crimes of profit is compensated for by a decrease in such crimes as rape, assault, automobile theft, and disorderly conduct. Nor is the prevalence of delinquency in an area a sufficient condition of its hospitability to the spread of drug use. The areas with the highest incidence of drug use are high delinquency areas, but they differ from equally high delinquency areas of much lower drug use in a greater concentration of the kinds and sources of human misery referred to in the preceding paragraph.

The juvenile street gangs that become involved in delinquent activities are not major agencies of the spread of drug use—even in the cases of gangs where the use of marijuana and heroin is more or less common. True, few gang members have strong feelings against the smoking of marijuana, and substantial numbers have no strong objections to moderate and controlled experimentation with heroin. In general, however, delinquent gangs seem to resist the spread of immoderate drug use in their midst. The considerations are not moral, but practical. Drug-users are considered unreliable "on the job," and it is believed that they can get the whole gang into trouble if arrested with others. Individuals with histories of habituated use get to be known to the police and remain under more-or-less continuous scrutiny, thus endangering their not-so-law-abiding associates. Moreover, there are laws of "constructive possession" that imperil the innocent; for instance, all individuals in a car in which narcotics are found are technically liable to prosecution. The interests of the regular users also tend to become limited and specialized so that they form cliques and thereby threaten the cohesiveness of the gang. In consequence, gang leaders who start to use drugs tend to lose or to yield their leadership positions. A gang member who is a pusher will not normally tempt a vulnerable fellow member, for example, a dehabituated addict returned from a period of custody in some hospital or jail; the pusher will, of course, have no hesitation about plying his wares among nonmembers and the members of other gangs.

Also contrary to popular belief, the great majority of juvenile regular users are not initiated into drug use by an adult pusher; even those who are, are not necessarily persuaded by the adult pusher. Some boys seek out even their initial source on their own. Most take their first dose of heroin, free, in the company of one or more boys of their own age—in the home of one of the boys, on the street, on a roof, or in a cellar—rarely on school property. Frequently, the first occasion arises just before a dance or party, probably for the same reason that some of their peers and many adults brace themselves with one or more shots of alcohol, as a source of poise and courage. Ninety per cent or so of habituated users have become so within a year of their first dose.

Already by the eighth grade, about a fifth of the boys in highly deprived areas give evidence of having acquired what we have characterized as a "delinquent" orientation to life. This orientation consists of moods of pessimism, unhappiness, a sense of futility, mistrust, negativism, defiance, and a manipulative and "devil-may-care" attitude on the way to get something out of life. This orientation, particularly prevalent among the greatest social misfits, is generally favorable to experimentation with narcotics. In an area of extremely high drug use, however, the connection of this orientation to attitudes favorable to narcotics is especially marked. Moreover, this connection has two major strands, one emphasizing the dysphoric mood and the other the more active aspects of the delinquent orientation. The first of these strands is particularly tied to a wholesale rejection of many arguments for not taking heroin. In addition, there is, in this area, evidence of a pervasive polarization of attitudes among the eighth-grade boys, more-or-less independent of the issues of the delinquent orientation, that favor or disfavor drug use. That is, there must be a substantial number of individuals in this area whose attitudes are favorable to drug use even though they do not share fully in the delinquent orientation. This generally favorable attitude is also related to direct exposure to the use of narcotics. It does not follow, of course, that attitudes favorable to the use of drugs will be realized in action. If other conditions are also conducive, however, the likelihood of yielding is increased by that much.

The boys in the areas of high drug use who neither become delinquents nor drug-users are actively resistant to sociocultural pressures in these directions. They have a negative attitude toward the "other crowd" and dissociate themselves from it. In their own groups, they find a wider range of stimulating activities than the others ever do. They participate in more active sports, including hiking and camping. They discuss books and current events. Their daydreams are realistically oriented to future work and family life. They stay in school longer and appreciate the importance of learning new skills and improving their minds. They are likely to show interest in and participate in school government, newspapers, or magazines. They do not spend as much time as do the others at the local candy store, going to the movies, or just "goofing off." They are more likely to have stable and intimate friends among their peers.

These boys come from more cohesive families than do the users; but they are not more likely to come from such families than are delinquents who are not users. They are less likely to have confronted the developmental task of adjusting to new families in the course of their lives through the middle teens and are more likely to have continued living with their real fathers through these years. Their extended families are less likely to include individuals with police records, and their immediate families more likely to be regular churchgoers. Most have a father, a teacher, a minister, or priest to whom they can talk about personal matters that bother them. Insofar as they have an ideal which they would like to emulate, it is more likely to include the father; but, in any event, they are more likely to value their ideal for what he *is* (e.g., his courage or kindness) rather than for what he *has* (e.g., his wealth or skills).

The boys who become addicts are clearly related to the delinquent subculture. Even before they started using drugs regularly, most users have had friends who had been in jail, reformatory, or on probation. In their general activities, interests, and attitudes, they resemble the non-using delinquents and are quite unlike the group described in the preceding paragraphs. Their leisure is spent aimlessly, talking about having cars, expensive clothes, pocket money.

Their home life is conducive to the development of disturbed personalities, which they display in abundant measure. Relations between parents are far from ideal, as evidenced by separation, divorce, overt hostility, or lack of warmth. In almost half the cases, there was no father and no other adult male in the household during a significant portion of the boys' early childhood. As children, they tended to be over-indulged or harshly frustrated. The parents were often unclear about the standards of behavior they wanted their sons to adhere to and tended to be inconsistent in their application of disciplinary measures. Their ambitions for their sons were typically unrealistically low, but in other instances they were unrealistically high. Although we had hoped to do some special studies of deviant cases—that is, of addicts coming from psychologically adequate homes and of nondelinquent nonusers coming from psychologically deficient homes—we were frustrated because we did not find such cases; on scales of psychological adequacy of the homes, there was virtually no overlap between the two distributions.

The evidence indicates that all addicts suffer from deep-rooted, major personality disorders. Although psychiatric diagnoses are apt to vary, a particular set of symptoms seems to be common to most juvenile addicts. They are not able to enter prolonged, close, friendly relations with either peers or adults; they have difficulties in assuming a masculine role; they are frequently overcome by a sense of futility, expectation of failure, and general depression; they are easily frustrated and made anxious; and they find both frustration and anxiety intolerable. To such individuals, heroin is functional; it offers relief from strain, and it makes it easy for them to deny and to avoid facing their deep-seated personal problems. Contrary to common belief, the drug does not contribute rich positive pleasures; it merely offers relief from misery.

Let us pause, now, to ask a few questions. Assuming for the moment that the picture we have just drawn can be supported, do such findings support the premise that the paramount objective of the treatment of the addict is to get him off the drug? It seems clear to us that such a premise confounds a relatively minor symptom with the disease. Yet this is the major premise of all public policy in the United States with regard to the problem of addiction. Although some physicians and others have raised courageous voices in protest, it is a premise that dominates even the medical treatment of addiction.

What have we left out of the picture that might justify such a premise? Is it possible that the drug is so inherently dangerous as to make it the

paramount consideration? Overdoses are clearly fatal, but whence comes
the danger of overdosage? Apart from those addicts bent on suicide—
and, needless to say, such people have many alternatives available to
them—the big danger is a direct consequence of our public policy. On
the illegal market, the drug does not come from quality-controlled
manufacturers. The user, therefore, never knows what dosage he is
actually getting, and he has no protection whatever from adulterants,
many of them possibly more dangerous than the drug itself.

Is the drug dangerous in other ways? Strong habituation brings with
it the danger of severe reactions (not as severe, however, as in cases
of habituation to the readily available barbiturates) to abrupt discontinuance. But why should the addict have to confront the necessity of
abrupt discontinuance? In any event, is the addict any worse off than is,
say, the diabetic in his dependence on insulin? And, if the danger of
abrupt discontinuance is our major concern, why is it that this is the
treatment typically imposed on him?

Apart from the dangers of overdosage and abrupt discontinuance,
there are a few other, relatively mild, medical disturbances (such as
severe constipation) commonly associated with prolonged usage. Are
these the dangers that justify the premise? This is, of course, to say
nothing of the neglect of health and sanitary measures into which the
addict is forced by his monomaniacal pursuit of continuance of his supply under present conditions.

Does the drug sap the moral fiber of individuals and produce criminals? In the first place, the question confuses cause and effect. Drug
addicts are not distinguished for their moral fiber prior to their first experience with drugs. People of high moral fiber do not take opiates except under medical instruction and supervision and, even if habituated
under these conditions, do not continue as addicts once they have been
detoxified. The fact that jails are crowded with individuals who have
illicit drug experience proves that criminals are prone to such experience rather than that such experience per se disposes individuals to
crime. Even so, under the conditions dictated by the major premise, the
addict has no alternative to a criminal existence; even if he can afford
the drugs at black market prices, which few can, his uncontrollable craving makes him a criminal because possession per se is defined as a
crime. With all this, there is our own remarkable finding that, at least
among teen-age boys, there is no net increase in the volume of crime,

apart from the direct violations of the narcotics laws, accompanying a marked increase in drug use.

Is it possible, then, that the great danger justifying the major premise is that of the enormous spread of what, apart from the effects of the premise, would be a relatively minor disease? Even a relatively minor disease in epidemic proportions may be taken as a national peril. But is the premise necessary to defense against such a peril? No one, to our knowledge, advocates the utterly uncontrolled distribution of opiate drugs. Suppose, then, that the prescription of drugs were left to the total discretion of the individual physician in his treatment of the individual patient; do we have any reason to believe that the occasional abuse of such a privilege could not be controlled by the internal disciplinary processes of the medical profession? Do the police have to be brought in at all? Suppose, further, that there remains a hard core of addicts who refuse to abide by the discipline of medical control and that there remains a residual black market in opiate drugs; would we be worse off than we are now?

Just for the sake of argument, let us consider what would happen if anyone were free to purchase opiate drugs without presciption in an un-inflated market. Would this bring with it the danger of epidemic? On the available evidence, the danger would be no greater than the prevalence of social and psychological pathology, and this is what should concern us rather than the possible danger of an epidemic of addiction. In any case, we need not speculate on the danger. Prior to the passage of the Harrison Act, there was precisely the condition we are now imagining, with the further complication that many proprietary medicines were loaded with opiates without warning to the user. The evidence, to be reviewed below, is that there were many addicts—most of them probably habituates rather than true addicts and, at that, habituates without any real awareness of their physiological dependence—but the numbers were not cataclysmic.

We are not suggesting that ridding ourselves of the major premise would solve all of our problems; we shall return to this issue. But is there not in all this occasion for anger?

II

The Neighborhood Distribution of Juvenile Drug Use in New York City

No one knows—and the writers of this book are no exception—how many people, under twenty-one or over, illicitly take drugs. The great bulk of available data are based on arrests. Unfortunately, there is no simple relationship between the number of arrests and the number of users. It depends on the amount of police activity. It depends on the adaptability of those who possess drugs to the possibilities of detection and the rate at which law enforcement officials accommodate themselves to current skills and techniques of evading detection. It depends on the kind of police activity.

Thus, if the police are concentrating on primary sources of distribution, we may expect the relative number of arrests to go down, simply because it is a more difficult job to get at the primary sources and takes more man-hours of police energy. Contrariwise, if the police are concentrating on the consumer end of the business, the number of arrests will rise. The easiest way to produce a large number of arrests is to concentrate on the known addicts at large in the community. The number of arrests will also reflect the disposition of cases in the courts, and probably in a curvilinear fashion, at that. Thus, if the courts go hard on the police, the latter can only accommodate themselves by trying to build stronger cases and letting the weaker cases go. On the other hand, if the courts go hard on the persons arrested, the proportion of users in circulation at any given time—and hence the number available for arrest—goes down. But an addict serving a jail sentence is still an addict and, as such, to be counted in the population of users. Our point is that a given user may be represented in the arrest statistics for a given period from zero to many times, depending on what the police and courts are doing in that period. Lest we be misunderstood, let us emphasize that we are talking about *counting* the number of users and not about the effects of law enforcement on the long-range growth or decline of this population.

We have similar problems with hospital admission statistics. Not only will the number of, say, voluntary first admissions vary with the available hospital facilities, but also with the activities of the police and the courts. Thus, it is reasonable to assume that, the more difficult life becomes for the addict, the more likely he is to seek medical assistance. Experience with addicts also indicates that they do not always seek hospitalization with the hope of being cured, but rather with the intention of reducing the habit to more manageable proportions or with the intention of restoring the power of the drug to produce a "kick." The pressure on the hospitals at any given time will, consequently, vary with the numbers of individuals who are finding their habit unmanageable and whose accommodation to the drug has reached a point where it no longer satisfies, but whose physical dependence is such that they cannot, by themselves, abstain. And the availability of hospital facilities is not a simple function of the number of hospital beds devoted to addicts. For a given number of beds, the number of admissions (new or total) varies with the average length of stay of patients, which, in turn, varies in complex ways with hospital policies.

There are other problems and a more general semantic issue involved in the statistics. They may be illustrated by two of the most carefully compiled sets of statistics available. Referring to a carefully compiled list of narcotics-involved individuals drawn from many sources in addition to Police Department arrests and meticulously eliminating duplications of cases, Inspector Joseph L. Coyle (at that time in charge of the Narcotics Squad of the New York City Police Department) wrote: "From July 1, 1952, to February 28, 1958, . . . it shows that there are 22,909 drug addicts in the City of New York. . . ."[1]

Despite the fact that, elsewhere in the same article, Coyle informs us that 7½ per cent of the 4,278 arrests in 1957 were "nonaddict sellers," there is reason to believe that the basic list which produces the "22,909 drug addicts" does not exclude violators of the narcotics laws who do not themselves use narcotics. This is the first problem with the statistics. The law does not make the actual use of narcotics illegal; it makes the illicit possession and transmission of narcotics and the possession of equipment the probable use of which is for taking narcotics illegal.[2] We have reason to believe that no serious errors are introduced on this score into the statistics of juvenile users (under age twenty-one), but we do not know how to evaluate the situation in the case of adults. Coyle's "7½ per cent" may offer a maximum estimate of the error, but it is difficult to evaluate, since it is based on only one year's experience, on arrests rather than on persons, and on total figures that include the cases of juveniles.

A major problem in Coyle's list was that, once a person got on the list, there was no way short of death to get him off it. The list did eliminate the names of cases known to have died, by checking New York City death records. Departures from the city and deaths in other localities presumably could not be checked. If a person has not taken drugs since the last time he has been known to have done so, does he still belong on the list? The issue is not a simple one. If he has been truly addicted, there is reason to believe that the stoppage is only temporary. In such a case, there is likely to be no great error in continuing to list him as a user. Not everyone, however, who has got involved with the law as a consequence of drug usage or who is otherwise known to have been using drugs is an addict. If a nonaddict user stops, there is no reason to

[1] Joseph L. Coyle, "The Illicit Narcotics Problem," *New York Medicine,* 14 (1958), 526–528, 534–538.

[2] In some places, however, what is called "internal possession" is also illegal. In such localities, a person may be arrested for "internal possession" if there is reason to believe that he has taken drugs, but the violation is still in the possession rather than in the use. Such a law invites many abuses and is often hotly debated even in law enforcement circles. There are also problems involved in the proof of "internal possession," including the use of a recently developed drug which neutralizes opium products in the body and can thereby precipitate withdrawal symptoms in an addict.

continue to list him as a user; even if he were to resume at some time, this would require, so to speak, a reinfection.

A somewhat similar procedure on a national scale has been adopted by the Federal Bureau of Narcotics (FBN), beginning January 1, 1953.[3] This list has the virtue of providing some means of transferring a name from it and is not seriously affected by changes of residence within the country, although the removal of the dead is under somewhat less adequate control. Persons who may have been listed as addicts but who have developed some organic pathology that requires narcotic medication are transferred from the active file, since they are considered to be receiving drugs under a physician's supervision. The major basis of transfer from the active file, however, is that the case has not been reported as a user for a period of five years. Cases removed from the active file may, of course, be returned to it if they are again reported as illicit users.

Of special interest is the report by Charles Winick concerning the individuals who were first added to the list during the calendar year 1955 and who were transferred to the inactive file during 1960 on the basis of the five-year lapse—that is, let us emphasize, during the first year in which they could have become eligible for such transfer. There were 7,234 such cases.

Now, it would obviously be desirable to know what proportion these inactivated cases are of the number originally placed on the list in 1955. Unfortunately, the figure is not reported. We are, however, told that 45,391 active addicts were known to the bureau up to the end of 1959 (about 46 per cent of them from New York), and this number must include the 7,234 of the 1955 series of cases, since the latter did not become inactive until 1960. On the assumption that approximately the same number of cases were added each year, there would have been one seventh of 45,391, or 6,485, names added to the list in 1955. That is, on this assumption, more than 100 per cent of those originally on the list became inactive at the first possible opportunity to do so. Since we cannot believe in such remarkable curative effects from being put on a list, we take it that the assumption of equal yearly increments is wrong. It seems obvious, however, that the proportion who become inactive at

[3] U. S. Treasury Department, *Bureau of Narcotics, Prevention and Control of Narcotic Addiction* (Washington, D. C.: 1960). Also, and most germane to the present discussion, C. Winick, "Maturing out of Narcotic Addiction," *Bulletin on Narcotics*, 14 (1962), 1–7.

the first possible opportunity must be astonishingly large; 7,234 is already 16 per cent of the entire seven-year crop of 45,391.[4]

The reason that our assumption of equal yearly increments in the growth of the list was so far off the mark also seems rather obvious. In early years, the file must have been loaded with old-timers. That is, there was a reservoir from which to establish the file. A large proportion of the cases were not really new cases; they had been known to various agencies for a long time and were new only in the sense that they were newly added to a recently established file. Even among our 7,234 inactivated cases, 9 per cent are listed as having been addicted for from fifteen to fifty-six years. But, if the original 1955 list was heavily loaded with hard-core old-timers, then a high proportion of inactivated cases is all the more impressive.

There is another astonishing fact about the 7,234 cases transferred to the inactive file in 1960. More than a third of them are listed as having been addicted for only five years before being transferred. Since, by the FBN classification system, a person is listed as an addict until he has been unreported for five years, we take it that these 2,473 individuals were not only not known to have taken drugs in the five years subsequent to 1955, but also that they had no history of addiction prior to 1955; that is, the five years of "addiction" are the five years during which they had to stay drug-free (at least in the sense of being unreported as users) in order to be transferred to the inactive file. By analogy, a postoperative cancer case who has remained symptom-free for five years after the operation would not be regarded as "cured" until the five years had elapsed. He would still be listed as suffering from cancer for the five years in which he was completely symptom-free. A more familiar way of thinking about this is that such a case is cured by the operation, even though the proof of the cure is not available for five

---

[4] A recent publication by Winick, "The 35 to 40 Age Dropoff." *Proceedings, White House Conference on Narcotic and Drug Abuse* (1962), gives the number of cases entered in the file in 1953 and 1954 as 16,725. As of December 31, 1959, 65 per cent of these had not been reported again—that is, a seven-year period for the 1953 cases and a six-year period for those added to the list in 1954. The number of 1955 entries is still missing. We do not know whether to attach any special significance to the missing number, but it is worth noting that Winick's interest in the paper cited, as in that previously cited, was in the 1955 series. On the assumption that the number of 1955 entries equaled the average of the 1953–1954 entries, 7,234 equals 85 per cent of the 1955 cases. On the assumption that the number of 1955 entries was less than 8,363 (as is likely on the basis of the argument in the next paragraph), the number of nonrepeaters would have to exceed 85 per cent of the 1955 cases.

years. If getting on the list means, as is claimed, that a person was known to have been a regular user of opiates, then these 2,473 individuals were "regular users" only during the course of the year 1955.

In similar fashion, it is common practice to refer to any person who has received treatment in a hospital in connection with a narcotics problem as an "addict," without consideration as to whether he is addicted in any sense other than this. We do not know, however, what proportion of such cases of drug use have relatively minor involvements. Some people have themselves committed, and there is no doubt that they think of themselves as addicted, but this amounts to self-diagnosis without any clear-cut medical criterion. Others may have themselves committed because a frightened parent has persuaded them to do so, even though they may not regard themselves as addicts. Still others accept commitment because a benevolent judge has offered this as an alternative to jail in the light of a first offense and testimony as to their prior good character. Sometimes, a judge will offer the hospitalization alternative to a second or third offender. Such patients are, of course, repeaters; but is sheer repetition sufficient to define addiction? In connection with other crimes, we often interpret repetition in terms of a continuance of the conditions that led to the first violation. Why should we not do likewise here? In any case, it is almost a certainty that the most seriously involved people are more likely to wind up in jail than in a hospital.

Meaning and Varieties of Addiction

There are some important distinctions to be made before we can hope to be clear on the issues involved in the definition of addiction. There are, in the first place, more-or-less regular users. Some unknown proportion of these become physiologically dependent; that is, if they do not get the drug, symptoms of bodily (and, in some instances, psychic) malfunctioning—ranging from perspiration, nausea, and cramps to death—appear. It is likely that individuals differ in their susceptibility to dependence,[5] and we know of individuals who have used heroin for

[5] It is sometimes asserted that anyone will become dependent if he gets a large enough dosage at sufficiently frequent intervals over a sufficiently long period of time. Such a statement is an extrapolation from experience and, although a good axiom, cannot, in its very nature, be proven without subjecting everyone to "large enough" dosages, etc. Obviously, if one accepts the axiom, then a person who has been taking drugs fairly regularly without

several years on a more-or-less regular week-end basis and then, apparently without difficulty, quit.[6]

Dependence is, however, not all there is to addiction. If it were, then it would be easy to treat and cure, for all that would be needed would be to subject the addict to a period of enforced abstinence. Alas, the cure is not so simple. All too often the addict so treated emerges from jail or the hospital purged of his dependence but eager and scarcely able to wait for his first "shot." Some addicts have themselves committed so that they can lose their tolerance (and, more-or-less incidentally, except where a major aim is to make the habit more manageable, their dependence), so that they can once again derive full enjoyment from drugs. The more-or-less periodic cycle of arrests and the associated enforced withdrawal serves a similar function for those who do not have whatever it takes to seek withdrawal on their own.

On the other hand, it is conceivable that a person might become dependent without even knowing that he has been receiving narcotics. This could occur in the course of medical treatment, where the patient might associate the withdrawal symptoms with the illness for which the narcotics were prescribed, recover, and never return to the use of narcotics. It is doubtful whether such a person would be properly called an addict at all, even in the past tense. Prior to the Harrison Act, considerable

---

developing dependence has not been taking enough with great enough frequency or has, perhaps, not been observed over a sufficiently long period of time. Associated with the concept of dependence is that of tolerance: as the body accommodates itself to the drug, it takes more of the drug to produce the same psychic and physiological effects. What has been said of dependence may presumably also be said of tolerance; there are undoubtedly individual differences in the rate at which tolerance develops, but the axiom that everyone would acquire tolerance from sufficiently frequent doses over a sufficiently long period seems a reasonable one. It does not follow, however, that tolerance and dependence develop at the same rate. Hence, it also does not follow that a person who develops tolerance will go on taking increasing doses; that will depend on what psychophysiological functions the drug serves. A person who takes a drug purely for sociability may conceivably be indifferent to the fact that it ceases to have any discernible effects. Moreover, there seem to be variable tolerance levels at which the drug can prevent withdrawal symptoms, but no increase in dosage can restore the desired psychological effects; the only way of restoring the latter is to go through withdrawal and start the process afresh. Addicts do not go on indefinitely increasing their intake.

[6] Whether one could actually find people who have taken heroin in ordinary doses daily over an even shorter period and of whom the same could be said, is problematical. If they exist at all, experience would suggest that they are exceedingly rare.

numbers of individuals must have developed dependence on opiates as a result of their indiscriminate use of proprietary medicines. They must have experienced considerable discomfort when the formulas were changed in response to the new law, but there is no evidence to indicate that many of them did not quickly adjust to the new state of affairs without ever realizing what had been ailing them immediately after they started taking the new formula.

Knowledge of one's dependence and of the role of the drugs in alleviating the distress of withdrawal is, to Lindesmith,[7] an indispensable ingredient of the definition of a true addict. Actually, there are two, or perhaps three, aspects to Lindesmith's criterion: the recognition of dependence; the consequent change in one's self-concept and in preoccupation (the "frantic-junkie" state); and the subsequent assimilation into the addict culture, with a seeking out of others of one's kind and the development of skills, customs, and language necessary to the maintenance of one's supply. Becker[8] has described an essentially similar process involved in the course of becoming a confirmed marijuana user, a drug which does not produce dependence. Hence, the two aspects— the recognition of dependence, on the one hand, and the change in self-definition and the associated, so to speak, switch in subcultural identification, on the other.

The parallel between Becker's analysis of becoming a confirmed marijuana-user and Lindesmith's analysis of opiate addiction suggests that the recognition of dependence is not the important part of Lindesmith's criterion. This is also obvious in the case of an "addict" in a temporarily dependency-free state. Note, also, that the recognition of dependence is possible without any of the rest following; it may facilitate the changed definition of the self and the correspondingly altered pattern of existence, but it is neither a necessary nor a sufficient condition.

Wikler[9] has made a number of observations which seem to have considerable bearing on the Lindesmith criterion. The first again emphasizes the relative unimportance of the recognition of dependence. It is that, under experimental conditions, addicts are quite willing to

[7] A. R. Lindesmith, *Opiate Addiction* (Bloomington, Ind.: Principia Press, 1947).

[8] H. S. Becker, "Becoming a Marijuana User," *American Journal of Sociology*, 59 (1953), 235–242.

[9] A. Wikler, "On the Nature of Addiction and Habituation," *British Journal of Addiction*, 57 (1961), 73–79.

undergo abrupt withdrawal, sometimes with severe withdrawal reactions, for relatively paltry rewards, for instance, the reduction of a long prison sentence by a few days or weeks.

The second was made in the course of a study of a patient during experimental readdiction to morphine. After he had developed a high degree of tolerance so that he could no longer experience the euphoric effects that he had at first achieved, he noted that he was getting another kind of gratification, viz., relief from the abstinence discomfort that developed toward the end of the intervals between injections. The patient himself drew an analogy to the development of appetite in connection with food. He remarked, for instance, that although a steak always tastes good, it tastes even better when one is hungry. "In other words," Wikler comments, "with the development of 'pharmacogenic dependence,' a continuous cycle of drug-induced 'need' and 'gratification' develops which can motivate behaviour in much the same way as the recurrent cycles of hunger, thirst or other 'primary needs' and gratifications thereof, in normal life." Related to this is Wikler's observation that "postaddicts" have sometimes noted the recurrence of withdrawal symptoms long after they have been withdrawn from the drug when they find themselves in situations in which narcotic drugs are readily available. This is analogous to the markedly increased salivation which most people are apt to experience when they think of or see highly appetizing foods even though they may not be at all hungry. The last of Wikler's observations to which we want to refer concerns the preoccupation of narcotic addicts with "hustling" (the activities of the addict aimed at keeping himself supplied with the drug), not merely when they are under pressure to do so, but in their thoughts and conversation in the hospital environment after they have been withdrawn, especially in the presence of other "addicts" and "postaddicts."

One of the present writers has elsewhere elaborated a general theory of motivation and personality structure,[10] some aspects of which are relevant here. The behaving individual, according to this theory, develops enduring concerns with regard to the assurance of the conditions of satisfying recurring needs. These enduring concerns come to play a larger role in the life of the individual than the needs that originally gave

[10] I. Chein, "Personality and Typology," *Journal of Social Psychology*, 18 (1943), 89–109; "The Awareness of Self and the Structure of the Ego," *Psychological Review*, 51 (1944), 304–314; "The Image of Man," *Journal of Social Issues*, 18 (1962), 1–35. A fuller development will be included in *The Image of Man* being prepared for publication by Basic Books, probably in 1964.

rise to them, and indeed they acquire independence of the needs. As concerns with the *conditions* of satisfying motives, they incorporate the individual's conception of the self and of the relevant physical and social environment, and they require the development of relevant knowledges, skills, statuses, and personal relationships. They acquire manifold interdependencies which serve to redefine them. Reflexively or retroflexively, they have bearing on the self. The system that includes the self-image and these interdependent enduring concerns is the personality.

We cannot develop here this interpretation of the nature of personality fully or elaborate in detail its bearing on the observations of Lindesmith and Wikler with regard to addicts. In a word, however, it seems to us that what Lindesmith and Wikler have, between them, described is the emergence of a personality structure built on narcotics, an associated self-image, and a related way of life. Even more briefly, what they have described is a pattern of *total personal involvement* with narcotics.

There is still another aspect of addiction that must be noted. This is the fact of craving, a phenomenon that will be familiar, in lesser degree, to the cigarette-smoker when he is deprived of his customary drug, one that does not produce dependence.[11] The full-blown addict is not content with a maintenance dose that will prevent the withdrawal syndrome. He craves the experience of the "high" and will go to great lengths to achieve it. Again, the familiar experience of cigarettes may help to illustrate the point. It often happens that, because of illness or overindulgence, one loses one's satisfaction in smoking. Many a cigarette-smoker will, under these circumstances, not simply be content with not smoking until he can again experience gratification; he will be actively frustrated and may again and again futilely light a cigarette, hoping against hope. Or sex: the failure to achieve the acme of gratification does not commonly result in a simple loss of interest or an acceptance of the banality of the experience, but often in a frantic preoccupation with, and desperate efforts to achieve, the denied fulfillment. Or, for that mat-

---

[11] Some cigarette-smokers show physical symptoms, e.g., marked tremor, in response to deprivation. Such symptoms are, however, psychological in origin, the correlates of tension and anxiety. True physical withdrawal symptoms related to physiological dependence can be demonstrated in animals. The point does, however, raise an interesting issue: in any particular observed human withdrawal reaction, how much is psychogenic and how much physiogenic is generally indeterminate. In strict logic, therefore, the mere fact of withdrawal symptoms is not sufficient to establish the fact of physiological dependence. This, in turn, complicates the issue of the dosage-frequency-duration combination that will produce dependence in almost anyone.

ter, food: how can one account for the sense of frustration over a meal that assuages hunger, but does not yield the anticipated gratification? Our point is not that these cravings are necessarily of the same nature, but simply that craving involves something beyond the elimination of bodily tensions or the awareness of having done what needed to be done; craving involves the demand for gratification that can be subjectively experienced as something special.

Craving undoubtedly has its ups and downs, not only in relation to the recency of gratification, but to mood cycles and the ups and downs of living. One addict, for instance, known to one agency for many years, apparently has no difficulty in staying away from drugs as long as the daily affairs of living proceed smoothly. As soon as any difficulty develops, however, he goes back on drugs. The phenomenon should be familiar to tobacco-smokers who commonly find themselves in periods of heavier smoking than usual. It is also involved in the relapse of apparently cured addicts who, after relatively long periods of abstention, go back on drugs after a quarrel, an affront, getting a new job, meeting an attractive girl, or the like.

Reviewing these distinctions, it becomes apparent that we have 'described three dimensions of addiction: degree of physiological dependence, degree of total personal involvement with narcotics, and degree of craving. To facilitate the examination of this three-dimensional scheme, let us dichotomize each of the dimensions:

1. Presence versus absence of some significant degree of physiological dependence.
2. Presence versus absence of some significant degree of total personal involvement with narcotics.
3. Presence versus absence of some significant degree of craving—i.e., regardless of the degree of physiological dependence, having intensification of the desire for a "high" experience with the passage of time since the last "high" and/or with increased stress from whatever source.

Compounding these three dimensions, it is obvious that we can conceive of eight types of individuals, seven of them being in some sense "addicted." Or if, as seems more sensible, we were to reduce the first dichotomy to subordinate status because of its shorter-range significance, we would have four types, three of which could be thought of as "addicts": (1) totally involved, but without craving; (2) having craving, but not totally involved; and (3) having both craving and total involvement. Each of these types would include individuals who, at any given time, are dependent and others who are not. To these three "addict" types, we would have to add a fourth "addict" type, that is, individuals who have a history of repeated dependence without indications of either total involvement or craving, again with some of them currently dependent and others not. Note that we have not included as an "addict" type individuals who are currently dependent, but who have no such history and who show no signs of total involvement or craving; nor have we included individuals with one-time history of dependence, but no further recurrence; nor have we included as an "addict" type users with no history of dependence and with no signs of total involvement or craving.

It is a virtual certainty that cases of the first three types actually exist, and it seems extremely likely that there actually are cases of the fourth type. The fact of the matter is that no one has attempted to apply such a typological classification, and there are consequently no data as to the proportion of the total "addict" population that each of the types comprises.

Yet it is perfectly obvious that these types pose differing problems in treatment and that they are likely to have quite different etiological histories and prognoses. Consequently, it is clear that it is meaningless simply to identify an individual as an "addict."

Consider, for instance, the so-called British system of narcotics control.[12] In England, it is discretionary with the individual physician whether to keep an addict on maintenance doses of opiates, i.e., the minimum dosage that will prevent withdrawal reactions. A substantial proportion of British addicts are apparently willing to continue on this basis. Given the fact of tolerance, it is a certainty that these addicts cannot experience a "high" under these conditions. From the point of view of subjective gratification related to the direct pharmacologic effects of the drug, these addicts are getting no returns. From this point of view, they would be just as well off if they underwent some humane form of withdrawal treatment and then simply stayed clear of the drug. Why do they not? It seems clear that they must be getting some other kind of gratification. That is, they must be getting involvement gratifications rather than the satisfaction of cravings. In other words, these must be Type 1 cases.

In the United States, there is a great deal of agitation for the adop-

[12] Edwin M. Schur, *Narcotic Addiction in Britain and America: The Impact of Public Policy* (Bloomington: Indiana University Press, 1962).

tion of the British system, and it is highly likely that, within the next few years, this system will be introduced on an experimental basis. The ultimate decision of whether to adopt the system as general policy will, therefore, hinge on the selection of the experimental cases and on how they behave under this regimen. It thus seems to be important to select Type 1 cases if the experiment is to be successful. By the same token, however, if the experiment is successful, it would not follow that this kind of treatment would work at all in Type 2 and Type 3 cases.

Actually, there is reason to believe that a large proportion of American addicts are Type 1 or Type 4 cases. This follows from the fact that the withdrawal reactions commonly observed are as a rule relatively mild. This fact is usually explained on the assumption that black market heroin is so heavily diluted that the real dosages are too small to develop serious dependency. Again, however, we come up against the fact of tolerance. Continuing on standard available dosages must rather quickly eliminate any true "high." In principle, there is nothing to stop an addict from taking two or three or five or ten "packs" of heroin per "shot" or as many as he needs to give him an adequate "high." That is, the low true dosage per pack does not offer any rational explanation of the relatively low degree of dependency in most addicts. Again, a more plausible explanation is that they are seeking involvement gratifications and have relatively little true craving (Type 1) or that they are getting no gratifications from the drug at all, but are simply unable to resist the pressures of their milieus.

All of this is thoroughly plausible and, to us, convincing. Is it also correct? We will never know until a considerable body of research is available that takes these (or better) distinctions into account. Our own studies did not do so; we did not know enough.

The Number of New Cases in New York City

Desirable as it may be to know how many cases there are at any given time and how many of each type, it does not follow that, lacking this information, there is no point in knowing how many drug-users, not necessarily even addicts, first come to public attention in a given period. Whether or not a new case reforms, continues along lines characteristic of his type, or develops into a more serious type, there can be no doubt that, as time goes on, an increasing proportion of seriously involved cases must come from a reservoir of recent cases. The more we learn about the formation of the reservoir, the better off we are. If we are interested in compiling a list of cases as of their first becoming known, it is because of our concern with the reservoir and not because we think that it can tell us the number of "addicts."

THE DEVELOPMENT OF THE CASE FILE

Our primary sources of cases were the courts and municipal hospitals in the three boroughs of Manhattan, Brooklyn, and the Bronx. The decision to limit the study to these boroughs developed out of early discussions with police and court officials who reported only a negligible drug problem in the boroughs of Queens and Richmond.[13] These discussions also set the starting date for the file; 1949 was the year in which adolescent drug cases began to come to the attention of official agencies in sizable numbers.[14] It was also decided that we would limit ourselves to the category of cases which includes the vast majority of all juvenile users—males from sixteen to twenty-one years of age.[15] Some

[13] In the Police Department file for 1952–1958 (Coyle, *op. cit.*), 67 per cent of the cases came from Manhattan, 15 per cent from Brooklyn, 14 per cent from the Bronx, and 4 per cent from Queens. If there are any cases at all in Richmond, they come to less than .5 per cent. These figures, of course, include adult cases. For the 1949–1952 period, there is reason to believe that there were hardly any juvenile cases in Queens.

[14] 1949 thus marks what may be the beginning of a new period in narcotics use. We do not know to what extent the "natural history" of the adult user who turns to narcotics in his adult years is the same as that of the younger cases, although even in the 1920's and 1930's statistical studies had pointed out that the majority of adult addicts had started to use drugs in their adolescence or early adulthood. The ranks of the adult users certainly include a much larger proportion of innocently caused cases, both because adults are more likely to suffer from ailments that call for the use of opiates and because physicians have become more careful in their administration of these drugs and utilize, whenever possible, more recently developed, less addictive substitutes. There is also some reason to suspect that personal psychopathology currently plays a larger role in the initial flirtation with narcotics among adults than among adolescents. At any rate, for some time to come, increasing proportions of adult users will be individuals who started in their teens.

[15] The reason for this strategy may be described as follows: If females and younger cases are not materially different in relevant aspects of their drug use from males in the sixteen-to-twenty age range, then, in excluding them from the study, we have sacrificed little but the greater precision contributed by a relatively small number of additional cases. If, on the other hand, there are materially relevant differences, including them obfuscates the picture for all. Why not study all groups separately? This is a question of the availability of resources. Additional analysis entails additional expense. Later in the book, we shall report on a small series of female cases, in addition to the statistics presented in this section.

data on girls in the sixteen-to-twenty bracket and on children under sixteen were gathered, however, in order to round out the picture.

Data were collected in two series. The earlier series was for the forty-six–month period beginning January 1, 1949, and the later series for the thirty-six–month period from November 1, 1952, to October 31, 1955.[16] The lists of drug-users and other drug-connected cases were combined into a single file, that is, entries that appeared in several source files or more than once in the files of a single agency were consolidated into a single case listing with a notation as to the earliest known date of drug involvement.

The basic source of our information was the docket books of Magistrates' Courts. Identifying data and home addresses at the time of first contact with the court were copied from Youth Term and Felony Court docket books for youngsters charged with possession or sale of narcotics or of such narcotics paraphernalia as a bent spoon or hypodermic syringe. Those who applied for voluntary commitment and treatment at Riker's Island or Riverside Hospital were added to our list from the records of the Chief Magistrates' Term Court and Narcotics Term Court.

Prior to July, 1952, when Riverside Hospital opened, treatment facilities for youthful drug addicts were in operation at the psychiatric divisions of Bellevue and Kings County hospitals. These facilities account for an estimated 95 per cent of all addicted individuals treated in municipal hospitals during the first period (January 1, 1949, to November 1, 1952) of our study. By adding these cases to our list, we were able to include many self-admissions for whom there was no court record. Subsequent to the opening of Riverside Hospital, juvenile narcotics cases received medical treatment in public facilities only at Riker's Island (for detoxification) or at Riverside Hospital. According to informed opinion, a negligible number of cases, if any, receive private treatment without being known to one or another public agency.

In order to include drug-users appearing before the courts on charges *other* than violation of the narcotics laws, access was obtained to the records of the Probation Department of the Magistrates' Courts and of the Youth Council Bureau, a private organization attached to the dis-

16 We did not learn until shortly before the publication of Coyle's article (*op. cit.*) that the Police Department had started a file as of the beginning of 1952. Actual work on this file presumably did not start until some time after its opening date.

trict attorney's office in each borough. Since January 1, 1949, the Probation Department has been maintaining a separate file of narcotics cases for purposes of study. Similarly, the Youth Council Bureau has also indicated cases of narcotics involvement in its files. Social workers in this bureau attempt to interview every youth under twenty who is arraigned in one of the youth parts of the Magistrates' or higher courts. Until late in 1952, the bureau gave a medical examination to those youths who were arrested on a nonnarcotics charge but suspected of using drugs, as well as to youngsters charged with narcotics violations.[17]

TOTAL NEW CASES

A total of 3,457 new cases of boys in the sixteen-to-twenty age bracket were discovered to be involved with narcotics during the seven-year period. On the average, about five hundred new cases of boys and young men from sixteen to twenty-one have come to the attention of the city courts and hospitals each year between 1949 and 1955. The majority of these youngsters (62 per cent) are from Manhattan. The Bronx accounts for 23 per cent of the cases, whereas only 15 per cent of them are from Brooklyn.[18]

There has been some variation from year to year in the number of cases discovered, particularly for Manhattan (see Figure II-1 and Table II-1). The peak year was 1951, when over 800 new cases appeared in the courts and hospitals. This was almost eight times the number of cases known in 1949, the first year for which we have data. Since the peak year of 1951, there has been a moderate decline in each of

[17] The drug involvement of girls aged sixteen to twenty and children below the age of sixteen was determined from the probation case-file of the Magistrates' Court Probation Department referring to cases appearing in Home Term, Girls' Term and Women's Court (prostitution), the Youth Council Bureau case file, municipal hospital records, and the docket books of Children's Court. These data were collected only for the first series, covering the period from January 1, 1949, to October 31, 1952. Unless otherwise specified, all findings mentioned in this chapter refer to males between sixteen and twenty-one years of age on the date that drug involvement was first officially discovered. Some of the cases in our 1949 series and to a lesser extent in the lists for each succeeding year may, of of course, have been known prior to 1949. "First officially discovered" and "new cases" should therefore be interpreted with this qualification in mind: "since January 1, 1949, they first came to public attention in the year . . ." The total number of such cases, dating back to before 1949, must, however, be quite small.

[18] These figures may be compared to the Police Department figures for all cases as cited in footnote 13. When the latter are adjusted to the three-borough basis, they become: 69.8 per cent in Manhattan, 14.6 per cent in the Bronx, and 15.6 per cent in Brooklyn.

TABLE II-1 *Annual Number of Adolescent Males First Known to Be Involved with Drugs*

| | YEAR FIRST DISCOVERED AS INVOLVED WITH DRUGS | | | | | | | |
	1949	1950	1951	1952	1953	1954	1955*	TOTAL†
Manhattan	53	266	502	317	284	395	314	2,131
Bronx	28	138	166	132	112	118	115	809
Brooklyn	26	57	137	97	55	67	68	507
TOTAL	107	461	805	546	451	580	497	3,447

* Figures for 1955 are estimates based on the number of cases appearing in the first ten months of that year.

† These totals do not include ten cases which were first discovered between 1949–1955 but for which the exact year is not known.

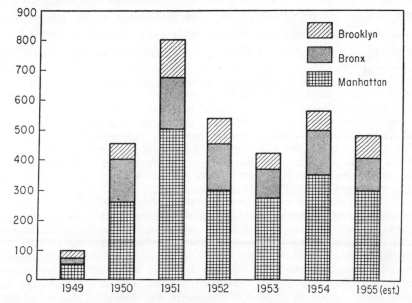

Fig. II-1. Annual Number of Adolescent Males First Known to Be Involved with Drugs

the boroughs, and, since then, the number of new cases seems to have stabilized at about five hundred per year over-all.[19]

[19] Not included in the above figures is a total of 344 girls (aged sixteen to twenty) with narcotics involvement who were known to the courts and hospitals during the period between January 1, 1949, and October 31, 1952. This is slightly more than one-fifth of the number of males appearing during the same period. Many of these cases appeared in the probation files of Women's Court and were prostitutes. The peak year for girls, as for boys, was 1951 in each

These figures suggest that the drug problem has become a chronic one in New York City; there is no indication of a falling off of cases over the long run. Actually, there were probably more cases than we are able to show, particularly for the years 1953–1955, when there was an unavoidable weakening in the efficiency of case-finding procedures compared to the earlier years.[20]

JUVENILE PUSHERS ARE ALSO USERS

Thus far, we have described our cases as *involved with,* rather than as *users* of, drugs. To what extent do actual users occur among the cases we have collected? For the 1,845 cases appearing in our first series, each boy was classified as a known user on the basis of the record if he (1) was given treatment for use at some hospital, (2) confessed to the use of drugs, (3) was charged with possession of equipment used in the injection of narcotics, or (4) was discovered in the course of a special medical examination to have body marks associated with heroin use. All other cases in this series were classified as "use status not

---

borough. Similarly, a large majority of all girls with drug involvement lived in Manhattan, rather than in the Bronx or Brooklyn, at the time of their first narcotics-involved contact with the court or hospital.

In addition, a total of 130 children below the age of sixteen became known to the courts and hospitals during the forty-six–month period covered by our first series. Of these, 106 were boys and 24 girls, the proportion being between 4 and 5 to 1, as was true for the older juveniles. Again, the peak year for these younger children was 1951, and a large majority lived in Manhattan at the time they were discovered to be involved with drugs.

[20] On the death of its physician, the Youth Council Bureau terminated its examinations of youngsters charged with a narcotics violation or suspected as users. Another factor in the relative "weakness" of our second series is that, over the years, Probation Department workers have probably become less diligent in sending in their special reports on narcotics involvement. This would be quite understandable, considering the enormous case load on these investigators and the fact that they were not continually reminded of the need for these special reports to be filled out whenever they discovered that an accused was known to be a drug-user.

The effect of both these factors is that our data for the later period are based almost completely on youngsters actually charged with a narcotics violation. This means that estimates for the later years must be, if anything, relative underestimates in comparison to our figures for the early period.

At a meeting of the Narcotics Committee of the Greater New York Community Council, Inspector Coyle stated that the Police Department list was growing at the rate of four to five thousand cases a year, closer to five than to four. He also stated that from 13 to 15 per cent were cases in the sixteen-through-twenty age range. This would give about 650 new cases per year in this age range, and, allowing for girls and cases under sixteen, the figures agree fairly well with our own.

established." Two-thirds of the cases could clearly be described as users of drugs on the basis of these criteria. In general, the third about whom we were not certain appeared in Magistrates' Court docket books charged with possession or sale of narcotics and did not appear in other consulted sources which gave more detailed information on the use of drugs. The following collateral evidence, however, suggests that, although concrete information is missing, most of the boys in this latter group were probably also users as well as sellers of drugs.

1. The Elmira Reception Center processes and sends to correctional institutions many of the boys under twenty-one who have been found guilty of charges in the New York City courts. The following data from the reception center were made available to us:

Of boys received and found guilty on charges of possession or sale of drugs (mainly from New York City), at least 95 per cent were found on examination to be drug-users. If we may generalize this information to the 609 cases in our file whose drug-use status is uncertain, it is clear that the vast majority of these boys are probably users as well as pushers. Since there is reason to believe that not all drug-users are detected by the time they have left the reception center, the 95 per-cent figure, high as it is, may well be an underestimate.[21]

2. Data from our study of drug use in eighteen streets gangs indicate that 80 per cent of the sellers in these gangs are known to have used heroin and an additional 14 per cent to have used marijuana. Again, almost 95 per cent of the boys who have a history of drug-selling have also been users of drugs.

DRUGS USED

Table II-2 shows the type of drug used when the youth was first discovered to be involved with drugs. In about one-third of the cases, the name of the drug did not appear in the source or sources consulted. In more than 80 per cent of the cases where some drug was specified, heroin was listed.[22] The table also shows that mention of this drug has been rising each year of the series.

[21] Of fifty cases at a state training school to which boys are sent after being processed at Elmira, selected by the authorities as nonusers, four admitted to regular use prior to their commitment and gave enough circumstantial details to our interviewers for the admission to be accepted at face value. This is 8 per cent and suggests a fairly large over-all number of undetected users.

[22] Although Table II-2 does not give borough data, the predominance of heroin involvement also appears in each borough.

TABLE II-2   *Drug Indicated at Time of First Offi-*
cial Listing as Involved with Narcotics
(Males Sixteen to Twenty)

A. Availability of knowledge of drug used (number of cases)

	1949	1950	1951	1952 (TO OCT. 31)	EXACT DATE NOT KNOWN	TOTAL
At least one drug known	28	298	609	273	2	1,210
Drug not known	79	163	196	195	1	634
TOTAL	107	461	805	468	3	1,844

B. Drug used (based on number of individuals for whom one or more drugs are known)*

	1949	1950	1951	1952 (TO OCT. 31)	EXACT DATE NOT KNOWN	TOTAL
	PERCENTAGE					
Heroin	46	80	89	91	(1)	86
Marijuana	57	35	24	18	(1)	26
Other	7	2	2	2	—	2
TOTAL	(28)	(298)	(609)	(273)	(2)	1,210

* Percentages do not add to 100 because more than one drug is reported for some individuals.

For one-quarter of the cases, marijuana was specified; other drugs, such as morphine and cocaine, were only rarely listed.

Some boys were involved with both marijuana and heroin. The figures for marijuana are probably a gross underestimation, since some sources probably listed only the most serious or "current" drug involvement. It also seems likely that involvement with the use of heroin is more likely to be detected than that with marijuana, which is not a dependency-producing drug.

BOROUGH DISTRIBUTION OF CASES IN THE EARLY PERIOD

Rates were calculated for each borough indicating the number of drug cases per 1,000 boys in the sixteen-to-twenty age bracket.[23] Table

[23] Since it is not possible to estimate yearly changes in the size of the base population, we shall have to satisfy ourselves with an over-all comparison of drug rates for the early period of data collection (1949–1952) with estimated rates for the later period (1952–1955). See Appendix A for a detailed description of the computation of drug rates.

TABLE II-3   *Drug Rates by Borough for the Early*
and Later Periods of Data Collection

Estimated number of new cases per 1,000 boys sixteen to twenty years of age*

	EARLY PERIOD (46 MONTHS)	LATER PERIOD (EST. FOR 46 MONTHS)
Manhattan	23.54	28.95
Bronx	9.62	9.35
Brooklyn	3.66	3.84
TOTAL	10.41	11.11

* These rates should be interpreted with caution, since they are relative indexes of drug activity, rather than actual estimates. For example, the rate of 23.5 for Manhattan in the early period does *not mean* that 2.35 per cent of the boys sixteen to twenty used drugs. It does mean that, over the entire screening period of forty-six months, about twenty-four new drug cases per 1,000 boys in this age bracket came to official attention.

II-3 presents these data, which show a marked difference among the boroughs. Manhattan has the highest rate of juvenile drug activity; the Bronx and Brooklyn are far below it in incidence of new cases. It is also apparent that there has been no substantial change over the period we have studied in the rate at which the three boroughs produce new cases.

To summarize, the over-all picture in terms both of numbers of new cases and of borough drug rates has remained fairly constant over the seven-year period, despite efforts to cope with the problem.

Is Drug Use Evenly Distributed?

As everyone knows, a city population is not homogeneously distributed with respect to income, religion, race, nationality, and numerous other characteristics. The various sections of the city also differ in many other ways—in amount of industrial activity, for instance, and rate of population turnover. Hence, if we find that some disease does not strike evenly over a city, we have reason to suspect that clues to the full story of the spread of that disease are to be found in an examination of the differences between the areas where the disease strikes harder and those in which it strikes more lightly. This is true even when a specific agent can be described as the "cause" of the disease. Tuberculosis and syphilis, for instance, are diseases which depend on specific germs; but the full stories of the spread of these and other diseases depend on (1) patterns of personal contact and other conditions which help or prevent the germs' transmission; (2) factors that affect individual resistance to the germs, including constitutional factors and hygienic practices; (3) the availability of hygienic resources; and (4) factors that affect the utilization of resources.

In brief, if pathology (whether physical, psychological, or social) strikes equally in all strata of society, then we have no reason to suspect that factors related to any of the dimensions of social stratification have anything to do with the spread of that pathology. If, contrariwise, the pathology does not strike evenly, then the lines of stratification along which the differentials in incidence occur provide important clues as to factors responsible for the spread.

This, then, was our first question. Is the illicit use of narcotics evenly distributed over the city, or is it unevenly distributed, as has been found to be the case for a variety of forms of pathology ranging from tuberculosis and heart disease, on one extreme, through venereal and mental disease to juvenile delinquency on the other? The answer to these questions is an unequivocal verdict of *unevenly*.

These data refer to the "earlier period" of January 1, 1949, to November 1, 1952. The reason for this restriction is simple. To say that there are more cases in one area than in another does not mean anything unless we also know what the maximum possible numbers of cases are in these areas. Suppose, for instance, there are ten cases in an area which has one hundred boys in the specified age range, sixteen through twenty. Suppose, further, that there are fifteen cases in another area which has one thousand boys in the designated age range. What does it mean to say that there are more cases in the second area than in the first? Though true, such a statement can be extremely misleading. The "disease" obviously strikes much more heavily in the first area, where one boy out of ten is afflicted, than in the second, where the rate is 1.5 per hundred. To compare areas on the degree to which a disease strikes, we need rates, not absolute numbers. But we are dependent on the 1950 census for the base figures on which these rates are calculated; the further we get from the 1950 census, the less certain we can be that the census figures reflect a true state of affairs; hence the need to restrict the time involved. The bulk of the analysis in the following chapter is based on additional census data; the same consideration applies to these data.

Our basic unit of analysis is the census tract. This is the smallest geographic unit—usually, an area of about four to six square blocks in the city—on which the bulk of census information is available.[a] The census tracts are laid out to be as socially homogeneous as possible, although there is some deviation from this principle in order to maintain the historical comparability of census tract information.

Each census tract with three or more cases[24] was colored in on a map. In addition, any tract with one or two cases was also marked if it was adjacent to a tract that had at lease three cases. The result was—except for two isolated tracts in the Bronx which met the primary criterion of three or more cases—a series of sizable "islands" in the three boroughs. These "islands" (including the two tracts just mentioned) we have designated, with some apologies for the emotionally loaded term, "epidemic areas." We do not know how many cases justify the possibly alarmist implications of the word "epidemic." We do not intend any such implications; the reader will have to form his own opinions on this score. We want to convey only that there are clearly more cases in these areas than elsewhere, and the reader will not be misled if he bears our usage in mind. As to the cases not included in the epidemic areas, it is our assumption that they are too sporadically distributed to be much illuminated by the present approach. Preliminary analyses of the data also suggested that the statistical trends do not hold for the areas with sporadically distributed cases.

That there are more cases in these areas in a relative as well as in an absolute sense is evident from Table II-4. For the three boroughs combined, 15 per cent of the tracts, containing 29 per cent of the sixteen-to-twenty–year–old boys, contribute 83 per cent of the cases. Even in Manhattan, where the discrepancies are not nearly so great as in the other two boroughs, one-third of the tracts, containing half the boys, contribute 84 per cent of the cases.

Incidence maps clearly indicate that Harlem was the section with the most drug activity among boys in the sixteen-to-twenty age range. In the Bronx, the south-central (Morrisania) portion of the borough had the highest concentration of drug-involved cases, with some sections within this region reaching the high levels characteristic of Harlem. The pattern in Brooklyn was similar to that of the other boroughs, but the level of drug activity was much lower, even in the areas of relatively high incidence. Most of the areas in Brooklyn had few or no cases. The rela-

---

[24] Let it be here specified that, unless otherwise indicated, a "case" refers to a boy in the sixteen-to-twenty age range who is known to have been involved with narcotics. A given case is counted only once; that is, if the same boy has been involved in more than one offense, he is still counted as only one case.

TABLE II-4   *Number of Census Tracts, Drug Cases,*
and Males Sixteen to Twenty Years
of Age in the Epidemic and
Nonepidemic Areas

	MANHATTAN	BRONX	BROOKLYN	TOTAL
	PERCENTAGE			
Census tracts in epidemic areas	34	10	11	15
Tracts with no cases	54	81	85	78
(Total number of tracts)	(278)	(419)	(861)	(1,558)
Males 16–20 in epidemic areas	50	30	18	39
(Total number males 16–20)	(46,388)	(46,046)	(84,782)	(177,216)
Drug cases in epidemic areas	84	83	77	83
(Total number drug cases)	(1,092)	(443)	(310)	(1,845)

tively high areas formed a belt from Red Hook in the west through the Fort Green and Bedford Stuyvesant areas to Brownsville in the east.

Our first question, then, seems to be answered decisively in favor of the uneven distribution of drug involvement. But can we trust the answer? After all, we have been working only with *known* cases. Is it not possible that there are many unknown cases and that the uneven distribution reflects differences in the detectability of cases? That is, is it not possible that the true distribution is even, but that cases are more readily detected in certain areas than in others? If this possibility were taken seriously, it would certainly put our findings in a quite different light. There are, however, at least five lines of reasoning and evidence that, taken together, seem to us to demonstrate convincingly that the distributions are, in fact, much as we have found them.

DOES THE DETECTION OF CASES BIAS THE DISTRIBUTION?

In the first place, to maintain the hypothesis of even distribution we would have to assume that there is a large number of undetected cases. Even a crude calculation on the basis of the data in Table II-1 shows that there are about 35 cases per thousand in what we have called the epidemic areas. With about 125,000 boys in the nonepidemic areas, there would have to be over 4,000 cases in these areas just to maintain the same average rate. This calculation does not take into account the differences in rate of known cases *within* the epidemic areas. To establish complete homogeneity of rates, we should work from the highest rates in the epidemic areas. At, say, 100 per thousand, we would have to assume about 12,500 cases in the nonepidemic areas plus the undetected cases in the areas of lower known rates within the epidemic areas. Even this would have to be based on the assumption that there are few, if any, undetected cases in the census tracts of the highest known rates, an assumption which we have ample reason to question. From a study to be reported on below, we know that cases which are detected average about two years from their initial trial of heroin to their detection. From another study to be discussed below, we have ninety-four heroin-users in street gangs, two-thirds of whom have been using the drug for two years or longer, and three-fourths of whom have never been picked up. These gangs are in high-use areas. The resulting figures are simply too high to be credible, and we must consequently challenge the assumptions by which they are reached, that is, we must adopt the assumption that the incidence of drug involvement is, in fact, not evenly distributed.

In the second place, drug involvement is not the kind of illicit activity that can be carried on alone or even exclusively in the company of a small number of friends. The case is not comparable, say, to finding a car parked on the street with the key in the ignition and deciding to go for a joy ride. Reefers and packets of heroin are not conveniently parked on the street; nor are they obtainable by the simple process of a few youngsters deciding to raise hell. Access to these drugs presupposes contact with a highly illegal traffic which is a target of vigorous police activity on federal, state, and local levels. It is axiomatic, however, that, the more people involved in the commission of a crime, the more detectable that crime is. It is further axiomatic that, the more frequently a crime is committed, the more likely is it to be detected. Moreover, unlike car theft or statutory rape, the evidence of drug use is apparent after the fact. All of this means that, if our figures are seriously biased, they are biased in the direction of more serious involvement. That is, the more peripherally and the less frequently a youngster is involved, the more likely he is to escape the network of detection.

There simply cannot be a high degree of involvement with narcotics among significant numbers of youngsters without its drawing the attention of the police, school authorities, and others. This finding is reinforced by the patterns of school attendance in the epidemic and nonepidemic areas. Relatively few youngsters leave school at the age of sixteen in the nonepidemic areas, and, consequently, a much higher proportion remain under the surveillance of school authorities.

In the third place, we attempted a direct check on the representativeness of our distributions. This involved a survey of community agencies, recreation and educational centers, private hospitals, and medical clinics throughout the three boroughs. Responsible officials in a total of 175 agencies were asked whether their agencies had had contact since January 1, 1949, with narcotics-involved youths under twenty-one years of age. Of the agencies contacted, 128 answered either by mail or by telephone, and thirty-four reported contact with one or more cases. Of the latter, fourteen agencies functioned city-wide. Two of these agencies furnished the addresses of the 192 cases known to them. The vast majority of these had home addresses in areas of high drug rate, as we had calculated the latter on the basis of our court and public hospital data. Twenty local agencies, serving more limited areas, also reported one or more cases. Half of these agencies were located in tracts in which our estimated drug rate exceeded five per thousand. By contrast, only 15 per cent of the agencies reporting no cases were located in such tracts. In evaluating the latter data, it should be borne in mind that the precise area served by even a local agency is difficult to specify. Hence, in the case of such an agency physically located in a tract of zero drug rate but reporting one or more cases, the cases themselves may have arisen in tracts of some drug incidence according to our original figures. The result of this survey was to reinforce our belief that the distributions we obtained were, in fact, fairly representative of the true state of affairs.

The fourth and fifth lines of evidence involve internal checks on our data. In forming our basic series of cases, we had collected series of females and of children under sixteen. The relative incidence in the three boroughs and the years of smallest and greatest incidence were identical for males aged sixteen to twenty, females in that age range, and children under sixteen. Similarly, there were approximately the same ratios of males to females above and below sixteen. The consistency of these findings for these three groups of individuals who generally come to the attention of public officials under quite different circumstances suggests that our data for the males in the sixteen-to-twenty age group are not seriously distorted by sampling biases.

Finally, we separated from our sixteen-to-twenty male series the 273 cases who first became known as drug-involved to Bellevue or

Kings County hospitals. The remainder were, in the main, cases first known to the police or the courts, although they included a small number of self-commitments to Riker's Island and, after July, 1952, Riverside hospitals. For practical reasons, the latter could not be segregated, but there were not enough of them during the period under study to materially affect the comparisons about to be described.

On the basis of the larger series, we divided the census tracts in which the home addresses were located into three groups—low, medium, and high rates—with approximately one-third of the cases in each group. The 273 hospital-initiated cases were then also tracted, and, as it turned out, virtually the same proportions came from each group of tracts. (See Table II-5.) As one might expect from Table

---

TABLE II-5   *Comparison of Court and Hospital*
Cases
(All boroughs combined)

CENSUS TRACTS GROUPED BY DRUG RATE IN THE THREE BOROUGHS ON THE BASIS OF COURT CASES	COURT CASES	HOSPITAL CASES
	PERCENTAGE	
Low three-borough rate	33	31
Medium three-borough rate	34	36
High three-borough rate	33	34
TOTAL	(1,571)	(273)

II-4, there are interborough differences in the incidence of low-, medium-, and high-rate tracts. We therefore made the same kind of comparison on a within-borough basis (a procedure which has the effect of eliminating the between-borough differences from the comparisons), and, again, the distribution of the two series turned out markedly similar. (See Table II-6.)

On the assumption that there are likely to be quite different selective factors involved in determining whether a case first gets to be known to the hospitals or to the police, we were again confirmed in our belief that the geographic distribution of known cases must conform fairly accurately to the true distribution of all cases. All in all, then, we conclude that our answer to the first question stands.

What about the second period for which we have data, from November 1, 1952, through November 1, 1955? As already indicated, this

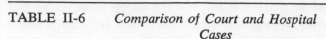

TABLE II-6   *Comparison of Court and Hospital*
Cases
(*Distributed for each borough*
separately and then combined)

CENSUS TRACTS GROUPED BY DRUG RATE WITHIN EACH BOROUGH ON THE BASIS OF COURT CASES	COURT CASES	HOSPITAL CASES
	PERCENTAGE	
Low borough rate	34	39
Medium borough rate	31	30
High borough rate	35	32
TOTAL	(1,571)	(273)

brings us quite far from the base data of the 1950 census. With the help of data kindly made available by the Department of Planning of the City of New York, we were able to estimate the numbers of males in the sixteen-to-twenty age range as of 1954. We could use these estimates as base figures for the later period. These estimates were on a health-area basis, a standard geographical unit established for the compilation of vital statistics; it usually consists of from sixteen to twenty-four square city blocks forming a more-or-less identifiable neighborhood; there are eighty-five health areas in Manhattan, 116 in Brooklyn, and sixty-four in the Bronx. Actually, we made three estimates and averaged them.[25]

THE LATER PERIOD

Health-area drug rates for the later period were calculated on the basis of these estimates, and these were correlated with the rates for the earlier period. The resulting correlations were .84 in Manhattan, .57 in Brooklyn, and .89 in the Bronx.[26] This means that, if health

---

[25] See Appendix C for an explanation of the procedure.

[26] For the benefit of readers unfamiliar with this statistic, a relatively simple explanation is given in Appendix C. This statistic is used extensively in the analysis that follows. In general, the statistic varies from plus 1 to minus 1. A correlation of plus 1 implies a perfectly consistent trend for one variable to increase with the other. A correlation of minus 1 implies a perfectly consistent inverse trend—as one variable goes up, the other goes down. A correlation of zero means that there is no trend—the average on one variable tends to remain the same as the other increases.

areas are arranged in the order of the later-period drug rates, they still tend to be arranged in much the same order as they would be on the basis of the earlier period rates.

The relationships are not perfect, of course; more initially low-rate areas show increases than decreases in rate, and the initially high-rate areas mainly show decreases. Moreover, the amount of change is negatively correlated with initial rate: —.50 and —.52 in Manhattan and the Bronx, respectively, and —.73 in Brooklyn. This means that the health areas with the initially highest rates show the most marked, and those with the initially lowest rates the least marked, changes.

The important point in the investigation of the later-period rates, however, is that the initially high-rate health areas tend to remain high-rate areas and the initially low-rate areas tend to remain low-rate. In other words, if we investigate the socioeconomic correlates of the census-tract drug rates in the earlier period, we are investigating a phenomenon that is probably still with us.[27] Beyond this point, the findings just reported with regard to the later-period rates, cannot be taken too seriously. There may be some substance to them; but they may also be, in whole or in part, statistical artifacts.[b] The section with the most marked increase in drug rate in the three boroughs and presumably the most likely to have really changed is in the lower part of Greenwich Village and the area south of the Village, the section sometimes known as Little Italy.

[27] It should be emphasized that the sheer incidence of *drug use,* regardless of the context in which drugs are used, is not at issue. For example, if we were to investigate the socioeconomic correlates of drug use prior to passage of the Harrison Act, we would probably come up with a quite different picture. But, then, the behavior involved in taking drugs without medical prescription was doubtless also different. Opiates were used quite indiscriminately in proprietary medicines; users did not know what they were taking; they were not involved in illegal activity; the sociocultural factors encouraging and facilitating drug use were quite different; and so on. The question is whether we might not be in a period of radically changing drug use, with associated changes in the nature and meaning of the behavior involved and, consequently, whether we might not be in a period of changing correlates of drug use. It is with this question that the above text has been concerned. If there had been marked change in the distribution of drug use in the two periods, we would have to consider the possibility that, in some way, the nature of the behavior involved had changed. The analyses we report in the subsequent chapter would then become hardly more than a historical curiosity, rather than germane to a pressing contemporary problem.

STATISTICAL FOOTNOTES

a Some census information is tabulated on a block basis. However, because some of the data we wanted are available only on a census tract basis, we had to use the latter to maintain the unity of the analysis. We would have done this in any event. The smaller the geographical unit, the smaller the base number of teen-aged boys. If the base number is quite small, the rate is radically affected by whether, say, one or two cases of drug use are detected. With larger units, errors of detection tend to balance out—i.e., the relative errors vary less from unit to unit—and, because of the larger base numbers, small numbers of undetected cases have relatively little effect on the rates.

b The tendency for initially high-rate tracts to go down and for low-rate tracts to go up may, for instance, be a simple (and statistically expected) consequence of errors of measurement. The statistics we have used are not subject to sampling errors, since we have dealt with specified total populations at specified times. There undoubtedly are, however, errors of measurement. Specifically, with regard to the numerators involved in calculating drug rates (i.e., number of cases), we may define as error any deviation in a given health area or census tract from the over-all proportion of the number of detected cases to the true number of cases. By this definition, errors may be positive or negative and are presumably randomly distributed. In Appendix A, where we describe the method of computing drug rates for the later period, it is noted that the numerators involved in computing later-period drug rates are subject to greater errors than those for the earlier period. As to the denominators (number of boys), not even the census is foolproof, and, in the later period, we are dealing with estimates, not actual counts. In the technical language of measurement theory, the early-period drug rates are assuredly not perfectly reliable, and the later-period rates must be even less so. The effect of unreliability of measurement on correlation coefficients is to produce precisely such "regression" effects as noted in the first sentence of this footnote.

The lower correlation between early- and late-period rates in Brooklyn is also of no special import. The variation in drug rates between health areas in Brooklyn is considerably less than in the other two boroughs, and, as will be explained in the next chapter, this is a condition that leads one to expect lower correlations. The lower variability obtains in both periods—a point that also speaks for the consistency of the data in the two periods.

Finally, it should be acknowledged that statistically sophisticated readers may be inclined to challenge even the main point, on the basis of a statistical artifact known as "spurious index correlation" that sometimes arises in the correlation of rates and produces higher correlation coefficients than are warranted by the true relationships. The issue will be discussed in the next chapter. For the moment, suffice it to say that the possibility need occasion no concern in the present instance; there is no such effect. Given the indicated sources of error, the obtained correlations between the early- and later-period rates are impressively high.

III

Social and Economic
Correlates of
Drug Use

Drug use is, as we have seen, not evenly distributed over the city. This fact, in itself, does not provide many clues to the factors making for drug use. It may be regarded as not so much a fact in its own right as a directive to investigate the lines of neighborhood differentiation corresponding to the differentials in drug use. But there are probably no two neighborhoods—i.e., census tracts, in the present investigation—exactly alike in all respects. In other words, the number of possible differentiations is certainly very large, perhaps even infinite. What lines of possible differentiation shall we, then, select for investigation?

Some suggest themselves by an inspection of the map and an impressionistic acquaintance with the city. Thus, it appears that the areas of highest drug use are areas inhabited, in the main, by certain ethnic groups. This suggests that relevant dimensions of neighborhood differentiation are the proportions of Negroes and of individuals who (and/or whose parents) came to the city from Puerto Rico. Similarly, it appears that the areas of highest drug use include some of the city's worst slums. This suggests that we look at some socioeconomic indexes, such as proportion of low-income families, proportion of households without television, proportion of unemployed males, proportion of employed males employed in so-called lower occupations, proportion of highly crowded dwelling units, and the like.

Some lines suggest themselves on the basis of the general theory of social pathology and studies of other forms of deviant behavior (e.g., juvenile delinquency). To some extent, this basis would lead to the same kinds of variables as those already mentioned, but the focus is quite different and calls attention to additional variables. Thus, we would be concerned with variables related to the potency, stability, pervasiveness, coherence, and need-satisfying sufficiency of social norms; the standards of behavior which individuals learn and internalize through precept and example; the rewards or gains (e.g., parental and other social approval) that come from abiding by them; and the punishments or losses that come from deviating from them.

Uprooted populations tend to show disruption of the normative patterns. This suggests such variables as proportion of the population which has recently changed its places of residence, and it calls attention to such variables as proportions of Negroes and Puerto Ricans because large sections of these populations have migrated in recent years.

Similarly, the intrusion of business and industry into residential areas tends to disrupt the normative patterns, perhaps because it tends to bring with it a floating population and sources of power without roots in the community, social mobility, restlessness, and so on. Hence, the relevance of such variables as the relative number of employees in large establishments and the number of business establishments per block.

The family unit is perhaps the major agent of society for the transmission of social norms, especially in individuals' formative years. This would lead us to expect that areas with high incidence of disrupted normal family living arrangements would also be areas of highly disrupted and relatively impotent normative patterns. Hence, the relevance of such variables as the proportion of married individuals living apart from their spouses, proportion of individuals not living with their families, proportion of married couples not living in their own households, and proportion of women in the labor force. Again, such variables as poverty and migration come into the picture because these variables are not unrelated to the degree to which individuals can establish ideal family living arrangements. Indeed, any variables which can have impact on social norms are relevant from the viewpoint of family arrangements because the family is itself a complex, normatively regulated social institution.

Still another way of looking at the potency, stability, pervasiveness, and coherence of social norms is to determine the degree to which these norms have functionally adaptive values to the individuals governed by them. As Robert Merton has pointed out,[1] if the normative system emphasizes certain goals (e.g., owning a car, having an attractively furnished home, a prestigeful occupation, and so on) and there is, at the same time, an insufficiency of legitimate means of attaining these goals, then one may anticipate a variety of forms of breakdown of the normative system. This directs attention to such variables as poverty and to the minority groups which are especially underprivileged by virtue of the discriminatory practices they encounter in housing, employment, education, and other matters.

Another possibly relevant line of social differentiation is suggested by the age group we are studying. This is the "density" of the male adolescent population. The greater the density of the male adolescent population, the greater is the probability, other things being equal, of a multiplicity of contacts among teen-aged boys and mutual reinforcement in their behavior patterns. If this happens, it is not unreasonable to assume that there may be a corresponding decrease in the average degree of adult control over teen-age behavior. That is, it is possible that, the greater the density of the male adolescent population, the more autonomous does the behavior world of the teen-aged boy tend to become. Also, the spread of teen-age fads (of which experimentation with drugs may be an example) may be facilitated by the density of the teen-aged population.

Another possibly relevant line of social differentiation was suggested by the psychological study of drug addicts. Addicts have been described as having passive personalities and, even more to the point, being confused with regard to their masculine roles. We thought it possible that a preponderance of females in the environment might, if not cause such personality orientations in the first place, at least contribute to their maintenance. Hence we felt it desirable to investigate the ratios of females to males.

Final decisions as to the lines of social differentiation to be investigated had to be based on the availability of data. The list of twenty-four

[1] R. K. Merton, "Social Structure and Anomie: Continuities," in *Social Theory and Social Structure* (Glencoe, Ill.: The Free Press, 1957).

variables we finally selected, along with their precise definitions, are given in Appendix B.

Three points should be made clear before proceeding with the analysis. First, in comparing the epidemic and nonepidemic areas with respect to the selected social variables, it should be borne in mind that the latter are, in the main, based on the 1950 census, whereas the primary distinction is based on events (incidents of narcotics involvement) that took place between January 1, 1949, and October 31, 1952.[2] We are assuming that the state of affairs revealed by the census holds reasonably true for this entire period and for some time prior to it.

Second, by whatever process of thinking we may have come to a variable, the interpretation of a relation between the incidence of cases and that variable is not necessarily limited to that channel of thought. Thus, if we find a greater ratio of females to males in the epidemic than in the nonepidemic areas, it does not necessarily follow that an excess of females in the environment tends to maintain passive orientation or confusion with regard to masculine roles in teen-aged boys. Our initial reasoning, at best, suggests a hypothesis to account for the observed relation. It does not preclude other interpretations or even the possibility that the observed relation may be accidental, in the sense that there is no direct relation. In other words, the excess of females may have nothing to do with the incidence of drug cases, but be related to another variable which does. The findings should, therefore, be interpreted with caution.

Third, the reader should bear in mind that we are investigating the characteristics of neighborhoods, not those of individual boys. Thus, if we find the anticipated relation of excess of females to incidence of drug use, it does not follow from these data that individual drug-users tend to be surrounded in their intimate circles by a preponderance of females. Nor does a relation between proportion of low-income families and drug use necessarily imply that the drug-users come from the most impoverished families. Nor does it follow, if high-drug-use areas tend to be heavily populated by Negroes, that the Negroes in these areas are more likely to become drug-users than the whites. The variables we are considering are likely to be reflected in, or to

---

[2] Because of the availability of the data on a census-tract basis, the greater reliability of the early-period drug rates and the fact that the additional data drawn from the census become increasingly inaccurate as we go further from the base year of the census (1950), we have restricted the analysis in this chapter to the early period.

be indicators of, the cultural climate and the ethos of the neighborhoods; the degree of vulnerability to drugs is at least partly determined by the cultural climate and the ethos.

An analogy may be helpful. People living in a rat- or vermin-infested environment are more vulnerable to diseases spread by rats or vermin, regardless of their personal habits. In the same way, people living in areas where the dignity of human beings is of little worth are likely to develop corresponding attitudes, even though they may not themselves have experienced direct assaults. People living in areas where they are surrounded by disrupted family life may develop certain attitudes which would not be at all justified by their personal family experiences. Members of discriminated-against minority groups do not have to experience discrimination personally for it to become a major fact in their lives; and members of majority groups in the same areas learn in many ways that such ideals as that of the equality of all men regardless of social position and that of the brotherhood of man are not always taken seriously in practice.

We are trying to get a view of the kind of environment in which the use of narcotics by teen-aged boys spreads. We assume that the factors which most sharply differentiate the epidemic from the nonepidemic areas contribute, directly or indirectly, to the vulnerability of the boys in the epidemic areas, or that these factors are in some way related to aspects of the sociocultural climate which have this effect.

Table III-1 presents, in the order of the magnitude of the relative differences between the epidemic and the nonepidemic areas, the comparative data on twenty-four lines of social differentiation examined. The absolute differences, though of interest in their own right, are not comparable to one another. Thus, the difference of more than 30 per cent in the proportion of Negroes in the two kinds of areas is impressive and, perhaps, tells us a great deal about the difference between the two worlds. This difference, however, cannot be directly compared to the difference of not quite 8 per cent in the proportions of Puerto Ricans. The 1950 census counted 240,730 Puerto Ricans in the three boroughs, in comparison with 690,712 Negroes (exclusive of nonwhite Puerto Ricans). The relatively small total number of Puerto Ricans means that areas of high Puerto Rican concentration must be quite small and these constitute only a fraction of the epidemic areas. If we want to consider the absolute percentages, in this respect, the significant point is to be found in the column for the nonepidemic

TABLE III-1 *Social and Economic Characteristics of the Epidemic and Nonepidemic Areas in Manhattan, the Bronx, and Brooklyn*

VARIABLE	EPI-DEMIC AREAS	NON-EPI-DEMIC AREAS	DIF-FER-ENCE	RELA-TIVE DIF-FER-ENCE*
20. Percentage of population that is Negro	33.2	1.7	31.5	2.88
21. Percentage of population that is of Puerto Rican origin	9.5	1.6	7.9	2.02
5. Percentage of wives separated from husbands	16.7	5.9	10.8	1.24
23. Percentage excess of females over males (15–19 age group)	12.0	4.2	7.8	1.21
8. Average number of male adolescents per block	24.7	11.4	13.3	1.00
6. Percentage of husbands separated from wives	12.2	5.4	6.8	.83
22. Percentage excess of females over males (21-and-over age group)	14.9	7.7	7.2	.76
16. Average number of vacant dwelling units per block	4.4	2.5	1.9	.64
7. Percentage of married couples not living in own homes	14.2	8.1	6.1	.63
1. Percentage of population in hotels and large boarding houses	6.2	3.8	2.4	.56
12. Percentage of income units earning $2,000 or less in 1949	44.8	27.6	17.2	.53
13. Percentage of dwelling units that are highly crowded	7.3	4.6	2.7	.53
14. Percentage of men employed in "lower" occupations	51.9	34.0	17.9	.47
15. Percentage of adults with fewer than eight years of schooling	36.4	24.6	11.8	.42
11. Percentage of unemployed men	10.7	7.4	3.3	.39
18. Average number of business establishments per block	15.4	11.9	3.5	.37
2. Percentage of individuals not living with a relative	13.3	9.7	3.6	.34
3. Percentage of working women	39.8	33.6	6.2	.18
17. Percentage of dwelling units without television	81.3	69.7	11.6	.16

VARIABLE	EPI-DEMIC AREAS	NON-EPI-DEMIC AREAS	DIF-FER-ENCE	RELA-TIVE DIF-FER-ENCE*
9. Average number of male adolescents per adult	0.043	0.038	0.005	.13
4. Percentage of divorceés and widows	21.3	19.0	2.3	.11
10. Percentage of male adolescents	3.1	2.8	0.3	.09
24. Percentage of population living at a new address	7.1	7.2	−0.1	−.01
19. Number of local employees per resident	.13	.34	−0.21	−.73

* The relative difference is the difference divided by the corresponding index for all areas combined. It expresses the difference relative to the over-all value of the variable. Thus, relative to the over-all percentage of Puerto Ricans, the obtained difference is quite large—in fact, twice as large. The percentage of Puerto Ricans in the total area is 3.9; the difference between the percentages in the epidemic and nonepidemic areas is 7.9, and 7.9 divided by 3.9 is 2.02, the relative difference. The figures for the combined area are not given in the table.

areas: these have very low concentrations of either Negroes or Puerto Ricans.

In order to provide some degree of comparability of the between-area contrasts provided by the various indexes, we have computed and recorded in the last column of Table III-1 the relative difference between the two areas for each index. This is the absolute difference expressed in terms that are relative to the corresponding index for the three boroughs taken as a unit. Thus, the difference between the epidemic and nonepidemic areas with respect to the average number of male adolescents per block is of the same magnitude as the total three-borough average; the difference with respect to percentages of individuals not living with a relative is about one third as large as the corresponding three-borough percentage; the difference in percentages of wives separated from their husbands is about one-fourth again as large as the over-all percentage; and so on.

Apart from certain purely statistical problems in the interpretation of either the absolute or the relative differences, there is another way in which the information given in Table III-1 can be misleading. We do not know anything about the comparative *perceptible impacts* of the differences. Consider, for instance, the difference of 17 per cent in the proportions of income units earning $2,000 or less as compared to the difference of 6 per cent in the proportions of working women; in relative terms, the former is almost three times as great as the latter. Yet, for all we know to the contrary, it is conceivable that the latter has much greater consequence in the lives of the youngsters in these areas than does the former.

In general, therefore, the significant fact to be learned from Table III-1 is that virtually all of the differences are in the expected direction —expected, that is, on the basis of the reasoning that led us to examine these lines of social differentiation in the first place. In all of these respects, the epidemic areas are "worse off" than the nonepidemic areas.

The two noteworthy exceptions probably have little bearing on this conclusion. The percentages of the populations living at a new address show virtually no difference, and this in the "wrong" direction. We had, however, taken this measure, with some trepidation, as an index of population instability—the proportion of the population that had not been living in the same place long enough to sink roots in the community —and we were interested in population instability only because it might serve as an indicator of the extent of rootlessness in the population. If we had a satisfactory measure of population instability, negative results would not necessarily upset the underlying hypothesis that rootless populations are vulnerable to the spread of narcotics; it is conceivable that stable populations may, for reasons other than geographic mobility, nevertheless fail to develop a sense of rootedness in a community. As is, however, we do not even know how the comparison would have gone had we had the data to compare the relative proportions of people who had been living in the same neighborhoods (rather than at the same addresses) over a longer period than one year.[3]

As to the second exception—and, if taken seriously, it is a marked contradiction of our expectations—it is not unlikely that it involves a statistical artifact. Establishments employing twelve or more people tend to be concentrated in nonresidential areas. If these happen to be nonepidemic areas, they would markedly raise the index for the nonepidemic areas as a whole; but the index would be quite atypical for the great bulk of the neighborhoods included in the nonepidemic areas.[4]

Comparisons similar to those given in Table III-1 were made between the epidemic and nonepidemic areas in each of the boroughs. Six of the variables showed reversals in Manhattan with respect to the anticipated direction of the findings. With respect to only one, however,

[3] We shall be able to throw some additional light, below, on what went "wrong" with this variable as measured.

[4] This objection to the index is not relevant to the primary purpose for which we intended it and to which we shall return—the comparison of individual census tracts.

was the difference large enough to suggest that the epidemic areas are markedly "better off," ("better off," that is, in terms of the reasoning that led us to examine the variable in the first place) than the non-epidemic areas, there being, on the average, more than twice as many business establishments per block in the latter areas as in the former. The next largest difference favoring the epidemic areas, of almost 5 per cent, was found with respect to individuals not living with a relative. The third largest reversed difference, of almost 3 per cent, occurred with respect to the number of individuals who had changed their place of residence in the preceding year. There was, on the average, one extra vacant dwelling unit per block in the nonepidemic areas of Manhattan as compared to the epidemic areas.

There was only one reversal in the Bronx and only one in Brooklyn. In both cases, the same variable was involved, with one extra local employee per resident in the nonepidemic areas of the Bronx and almost two in Brooklyn.

Eliminating all variables that did not support the initial reasoning in the over-all comparison or in any of the boroughs and eliminating, in addition, any variable with respect to which the epidemic areas of at least one of the boroughs was not more badly off than the combined nonepidemic areas of the three boroughs[a] leaves us with the following variables that consistently distinguish the epidemic areas:

20. Percentage of population that is Negro
21. Percentage of population that is of Puerto Rican origin
5. Percentage of wives separated from husbands
8. Average number of male adolescents per block
6. Percentage of husbands separated from wives
22. Percentage excess of adult females over males
7. Percentage of married couples not living in own homes
12. Percentage of income units earning less than $2,000 in 1949
13. Percentage of dwelling units that are highly crowded
14. Percentage of men employed in "lower" occupations
15. Percentage of adults with fewer than eight years of schooling
11. Percentage of unemployed men
3. Percentage of working women
17. Percentage of dwelling units without television

The epidemic areas are, on the average, areas of relatively concentrated settlement of underprivileged minority groups, of poverty and low economic status, of low educational attainment, of disrupted family

evidence in the other. We have no way of evaluating the relative weight of the two types of error.

No attempt was made to eliminate case duplications—i.e., instances in which the same case is brought to court more than once—since we are primarily interested in the number and variety of delinquent acts discovered and brought to court from various neighborhoods.

There were 10,025 delinquency charges of all kinds in our age group in the two Manhattan courts from January 1, 1949, to December 31, 1952. Within each court and for each year separately, we took a 23 per-cent random sample of the docket charges on the basis of a table of random numbers. All charges involving narcotics violations, females, and individuals with addresses outside the borough were eliminated. This left us with 1,514 charges against males in the sixteen-to-twenty age range and involving other-than-narcotics violations. The addresses of the alleged offenders were classified on a health-area basis, and health-area delinquency rates were computed. These were compared to the corresponding health-area drug rates.

If one plots drug rate against delinquency rate on a graph, there is

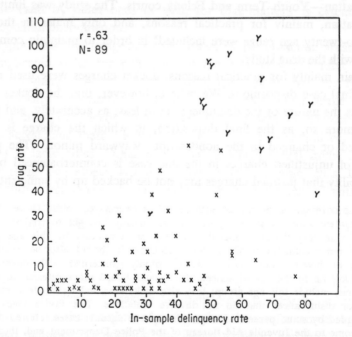

Fig. III-1. Scattergram of Health-Area Drug and Delinquency Rates (Areas with 70 per cent or more Negroes and Puerto Ricans indicated by "y")

a clear trend (see Figure III-1): the drug rate tends to increase with the delinquency rate. Expressed differently, health areas with higher delinquency rates have, on the average, higher drug rates. The degree of relationship between the two rates may be expressed by a moderately high correlation coefficient of .63. The true relationship, however, is more complex than would be evident from this statement. There are actually two kinds of high-delinquency health areas; some are quite high in drug rate, and some relatively low. Thus, among the twenty-nine health areas with delinquency indexes of 40[b] or more, seven have drug rates of less than 10, and another six of less than 20. Then there is a large gap. Another two of this group of health areas fall in the drug-rate class of from 38 to 40, and the remaining fourteen run from drug rates of over 50 to over 100. By contrast, none of the health areas with delinquency rates of less than 40 have drug rates of 50 or more; two (with delinquency rates over 30) have drug rates of 38 and 48, respectively; seven (all with delinquency rates over 15, and five of them over 20) have drug rates ranging from 20 to 33; five (also all with delinquency rates over 15) have drug rates of from 10 to 20; and forty-seven (running the gamut of delinquency rates from zero to 40) have drug rates of less than 10 .

Of the fourteen health areas with drug rates over 40, twelve have populations of 70 per cent or more Negroes and Puerto Ricans. There are only two other health areas in Manhattan which are so heavily segregated with respect to these minority groups. One of these, with the highest delinquency rate in the borough, has a drug rate of 38; the other has drug and delinquency rates of about 30. The highly segregated health areas are, however, distinguished by more than segregation, high delinquency rates, and high incidence of juvenile drug involvement. Only two less-segregated health areas have as many families with 1949 incomes of less than $2,000; from almost 40 to almost 60 per cent of the families in the highly segregated areas have such incomes (See Figure III-2). One of the less-segregated areas in this income group has a drug rate of 57, but the other has one of less than 5. The remaining two areas with drug rates over 40 have more than 30 per cent of their families in this low-income bracket. The health-area correlation between drug rate and percentage of families with 1949 incomes under $2,000 is .76.[c] The health-area correlation between delinquency rate and poverty index is less: .68.

The high correlation between drug use and delinquency fits well with a stereotype of narcotics as a cause of crime. The years 1949–1952

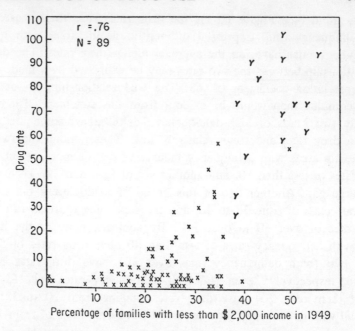

Fig. III-2. Scattergram of Health-Area Poverty and Drug Rates (Areas with 70 per cent or more Negroes and Puerto Ricans indicated by "y")

saw a marked increase in juvenile drug use; they were also years of increasing delinquency. The year 1949 contributed 20 per cent of the delinquencies in our sample; 1950 contributed 22 per cent; and 1951 and 1952 each contributed 29 per cent. The simultaneous increase of the two types of violations is consistent with the stereotype. There are, however, facts which sharply contradict it.

In the first place, the increase was at the level of minor violations. The number of felonies remained virtually constant over this four-year period. At the very least, then, there is no support here for the notion of the most serious crimes being associated with the taking of drugs,[6] at least among the males under twenty-one. The virtual constancy in the number of felonies also raises a serious question about the nature of the "crime wave." The period was one in which there was not

[6] It should be recalled that direct violations of narcotics laws have been systematically excluded from the series of delinquency charges. This does not, however, exclude the possibility of crimes carried out for the sake of obtaining drugs, crimes committed in the course of the withdrawal syndrome, or crimes committed in sufficiently mild states of narcotic intoxication. In other words, the finding and the corresponding inference are not artifacts of the procedure.

merely an increase in delinquency charges, but one in which many voices were being raised about the "alarming" increase in juvenile delinquency. The constancy of the incidence of felonies, however, gives one pause. The distinction between a felony and a misdemeanor may be a relatively sharp one in legal terms; it cannot be so in behavioral terms. Consequently, if there had been a real increase in misdemeanors, one would expect, although perhaps not in constant ratio, increases all along the behavioral gradient of severity of offense, and, hence, one would also expect an increase in number of felonies. The fact that such an increase does not occur suggests that the "crime wave" is most plausibly interpreted in terms of police activity. Specifically, if there were no real increase at all, but if cases were more readily brought to court for offenses which would have formerly been ignored or dismissed by the police officer with a warning, we would get exactly the kind of curves we do get.

In the second place, if the use of narcotics is a major cause of other types of crime, one would expect the most marked changes in the high-drug-use areas. That this is not the case may be seen from Table III-2.

In the third place, our data suggest that, though drug use has no marked effect on the relative incidence of delinquency (exclusive, of

---

TABLE III-2   *Percentage of Total Delinquencies by*
*Year for Each Type of Drug Area**

| | | DRUG-USE AREAS | | | |
YEAR	NONE	LOW	MEDIUM	HIGH	TOTAL
		PERCENTAGE			
1949	21	20	20	19	20
1950	19	25	22	23	22
1951	26	28	30	30	29
1952	34	27	28	28	29
TOTAL	100	100	100	100	100
	(265)	(219)	(269)	(509)	(1,262)

* Classification based on census-tract drug rates. Low: 1–9.9. Medium: 10–54.5. High: 55 and over. These cutting points were selected to divide the male sixteen-to-twenty population into as nearly equal parts as possible. There are forty-two tracts in the "none" category, with 10,379 males in the indicated age range; thirty-three tracts in the "low," with 9,342 males; twenty-nine tracts in the "medium," with 8,371; and twenty-six in the "high," with 9,175 males. Census tracts with fewer than 150 males in the sixteen-to-twenty range were eliminated from consideration in order to increase the reliability of census tract drug rates. This accounts for the decreased total number of delinquencies dealt with in the table. The loss of these cases has no effect on the distribution of the combined totals by year. In addition, the present analysis does not include tracts which had cases neither in our series of delinquency charges nor in our series of drug-involved cases.

course, of the narcotics violations), it does affect the type of delinquency committed; it tends to be associated with a larger proportion of utilitarian violations than crimes of violence or other behavior disturbance. This flies directly in the face of the stereotype.

The relative distributions of the various types of charges are given in Table III-3. It may be noted that relatively—i.e., in comparison to the "no"- and "low"-drug-use areas—small proportions of the charges in the "medium"- and "high"-drug-use areas involve assault, disorderly conduct, or auto theft. Relatively high proportions involve robbery or rape. The other categories do not show any clear trends.

In order to get a clearer picture of what is happening in the various types of area, the delinquent acts were further classified into two inclusive categories: (1) potentially profit-yielding and (2) others. The following groups of charges were classified as potentially profit-yielding: robbery, jostling (attempted pickpocketing), procuring or pimping, unlawful entry, burglary, larceny.

Possession of a dangerous weapon was not included in either category since, according to officials in the Probation Department, about equal numbers of charges of this type come from roundups of delinquent gangs engaged in or preparing for street warfare and from boys who probably possessed these weapons for purposes of robbery. The exclusion of this category from the following analysis, if anything, militates against the point we are about to make; as we shall see in a later chapter, drug-using gangs tend to cut out street warfare.

Similarly, the assignment of rape to the second category probably also militates against the point we are about to make. In the high-drug-use areas, many statutory rape charges are probably an indirect consequence of the "fund-raising" activity that is a necessary condition of much drug use. The adolescent female drug-user characteristically obtains money for drugs by means of prostitution, and it is not unreasonable to expect a large number of rape charges in neighborhoods with many prostitutes who are legally minors. When these girls are arrested, they are often persuaded to reveal the identities of their clients, who automatically become subject to charges of statutory rape.

At any rate, whatever may be said of the crudeness of the procedure, the result of the analysis is interesting. This result is given in Table III-4. There was no over-all change from the two-year period 1949–1950 to the two-year period 1951–1952 in the proportion of charges involving potentially "profit-making" delinquent acts, and there was

TABLE III-3* *Distributions of Charges by Cate-*
gories of Delinquent Acts for
Each Type of Drug Area

DRUG-USE AREAS

CATEGORY OF DELINQUENT ACT	NONE	LOW	MEDIUM	HIGH	TOTAL
	PERCENTAGE				
Burglary	23	26	28	22	24
Larceny	19	14	15	20	18
Robbery	13	13	16	16	15
Assault	16	13	11	11	12
Rape (including statutory)	4	5	7	11	8
Disorderly conduct (exclusive of jostling and degeneracy)	9	9	6	5	7
Possession of a dangerous weapon	3	7	6	7	6
Auto theft	7	4	3	2	4
Nonrape sex offense	3	4	3	2	3
Jostling	†	1	2	1	1
Unlawful entry	†	†	1	†	1
Procuring or pimping	†	†	†	†	†
Miscellaneous	2	5	3	3	3
TOTAL	100	100	100	100	100‡
	(265)	(219)	(269)	(509)	(1,262)

* See notes to Table III-2.
† Less than 0.5 per cent.
‡ The columns do not add to 100 per cent because of rounding errors.

very little change—a decrease—in the "no"-drug-use area. The "low"- and "medium"-drug-use areas, however, showed marked decreases in this respect; but the high-drug-use area showed a marked increase. In other words, whereas the delinquents in other areas showed an increased inclination to turn to what might be described as behavior-disturbance types of delinquency, the delinquents in the high-drug-use area showed an increased concentration on potentially money-making delinquencies.

To be sure, there is no assurance that such crimes as robbery may not be primarily crimes of aggression, with relatively little interest in the financial return. We have only examined gross statistics, not individual motivation, and we do not know from these data the dis-

TABLE III-4 *Proportions of Charges Involving Potentially "Profit-making" Delinquencies in 1949–1950 and in 1951–1952, by Types of Drug-use Area*

		DRUG-USE AREAS				
YEARS		NONE	LOW	MEDIUM	HIGH	TOTAL
1949–1950		60	66	71	60	64
1951–1952		58	57	65	70	64
	CHANGE	−2	−9	−6	+10	0

tribution of the motivations toward delinquent acts. Still, the findings make sense. Heroin is a tranquilizer—perhaps the most effective tranquilizer known—but it comes in expensive doses.

We began this section with a question about the nature of the phenomenon we seek to explain. Is drug use simply another expression of lawlessness? Is the distribution of drug use simply a manifestation of the general distribution of lawlessness, and is the explanation of the distribution of drug use to be found in the explanation of the distribution of lawlessness? It turns out that the two do tend to go together, but not always. There are areas of high delinquency with relatively little drug use—hardly an astounding finding, since we did have delinquency before drug use, but it does indicate that high-delinquency areas can remain resistant to drug use when the latter does arrive on the scene.

Which high-delinquency areas succumb most readily? We have explored only two dimensions of differentiation. The high-delinquency areas most vulnerable to the spread of drug use are the ones that are most heavily populated by the two most deprived and discriminated-against minority groups in the city, and they are the areas with the highest poverty rates. If we had explored other lines of differentiation, the differences between the two kinds of high-delinquency areas would undoubtedly parallel the other differences we have already found between the epidemic and nonepidemic areas; these dimensions are not independent, but highly correlated. In other words, the high-delinquency areas that are most vulnerable are the ones that are "worst off" in a variety of respects.

On the other hand, the highest-drug-rate areas are all high-delinquency areas. Is delinquency in these areas a consequence of drug use? The evidence is that it is not, except in the sense that the varieties of delinquency tend to change to those most functional for drug use; the total amount of delinquency is independent of the drug use.

Socioeconomic Correlates of Drug Use in the "Epidemic" Areas

The comparison of epidemic and nonepidemic areas has given us a picture of the kind of social world in which the use of narcotics by older boys and young men thrives. The question now before us is whether we can disentangle among the social differentiae of the two worlds those most relevant to the spread of this type of deviant behavior.

Do poverty and squalor establish a hopelessness from which one can seek refuge only in the serenity of a chemically induced state of nirvana?[7] Does the widespread disruption of family life induce or sustain the sense of aloneness in the individual from which he seeks escape in a drug-induced illusion of oneness with the universe? Is the turning to narcotics a desperate effort of "emasculated" males in a world inundated by females to assert their independence? Is the hospitality of the social climate to drug use simply an exaggeration of normal teenage conformity and an exacerbation of normal tendencies of adolescent boys to mutually induced states of social intoxication in which they undertake deeds of reckless derring-do and rash bravado—grim realizations of the potentials of teen-age coexistence, generated by excessive numbers of teen-agers in close proximity to one another? Is it some combination of factors, say, a breakdown of adult authority confronted by adolescent rebelliousness, as evidenced by the major significance of excessive numbers of teen-agers in a world of disrupted family life?

To be sure, these questions may be fancifully put in the light of the kind of evidence that we can marshal. There is, for example, quite a gap between a prosaic "percentage of income units earning less than

[7] "Nirvana" is a concept in Hindu and Buddhist philosophy that designates fulfillment of all desire through the conquest of desire. The term has come into common use in contemporary psychological literature in a somewhat broadened meaning. The term "conquest" implies the exercise of discipline; in psychological usage, the sense of fulfillment associated with the cessation of desire is designated by the same term regardless of how the condition comes about—most commonly as a short-lasting aftermath of gratification.

$2,000" and related variables, on the one hand, and "a hopelessness from which one can seek refuge only in the serenity of a chemically induced state of nirvana," on the other. Yet, if it were to turn out that these are the only variables of major significance, such an interpretation may not be far-fetched. Similarly, other possible outcomes of the analysis might suggest the interpretation implicit in one or another of the questions. Still other outcomes may tell a story not anticipated by any of the questions; they were not intended to be more than an illustrative listing of possibilities.

How, then, disentangle the roles of the variables? To begin, it seems reasonable to suppose that the place to study these roles is where drug use occurs. That is, we are concerned with the islands designated as epidemic areas and the immediately adjacent census tracts. Within these regions, there is considerable variation in census-tract drug rates, despite the fact that there are drug markets available to all. Or, to pursue a different analogy, all are reasonably close to the sources of infection; if there is nevertheless variation in the intensity of contamination, this variation is likely to be directly related to differences in vulnerability. The further we get from these critical areas, the less certain we can be that the absence of signs of contamination may not be due simply to distance from the centers of contagion rather than to resistance.

In the second place, a well-developed technique for studying the roles of variables in relation to a selected one involves correlational analysis. The result of the application of this technique is not unequivocal; the correlation coefficient is itself ambiguous from the viewpoint of causality,[8] and hence any results based on the examination of correlation coefficients must also be ambiguous.

In principle, the only way of studying causal relationships without ambiguity is by direct experimentation. Applied to the present case, this would call for the following: Census tracts in which there is no drug use would be divided into homogeneous groups (i.e., the census tracts in each group would be selected so that each tract in the group resembles every other one with respect to what are assumed to be the relevant significant variables). From each group, we would randomly select one or more tracts for experimental treatment and one or more

[8] For a discussion of the many ways in which correlation can arise between variables and, hence, of the many possible interpretations of correlations, see Appendix C.

tracts for purposes of control. The experiment would consist of trying to seduce the youth of these tracts into drug use. How much could be learned from such an experiment would depend on further details of the experimental design, but, needless to say, not even the most primitive experiment calling for such measures could be carried out. Even if one could find trained personnel willing to try, the social and, hence, the behavioral meaning of drug use would necessarily change so that we would be studying a quite different phenomenon from the one which concerns us—the illicit and heavily prosecuted use of narcotics.

The most that we can hope for, therefore, is that, once the basic correlational facts are clear, they will lend themselves to sensible interpretation. If the interpretations turn out to be debatable, they (and whatever alternatives may be suggested) will nevertheless be based on a foundation of sounder information than guesses based on no information at all.

One statistical point should be explained before we proceed with the analysis—the relation between the correlation coefficient and the variances of the variables involved. Variance is one of a large number of measures of the variability of scores in a distribution.[d] It can be shown that the square of the correlation coefficient gives the proportion of the variance of one variable that can be statistically accounted for in terms of the other.[e]

To illustrate this point concretely: The correlation between drug rate and the percentage of Negroes is .77 in the Manhattan epidemic and border areas. On the basis of this relationship, we can calculate the drug rate that would be expected from the over-all trend for the particular percentage of Negroes in a given census tract in the designated area. This gives us one component of the drug rate, a component that can be "accounted for" by the percentage of Negroes in the tract and the known correlation between drug rate and percentage of Negroes. If we subtract this "expected" drug rate from the actual drug rate (and, since the "expected" rate may be larger or smaller than the actual rate, this may leave us with either a positive or negative number), we are left with a second component of drug rate, one that cannot be "accounted" for on the same basis. The words "accounted" and "expected" have been surrounded by quotation marks to emphasize that the accounting and expectation involved are on a statistical and not necessarily a causal basis. If we were to compute the "expected" drug rates for each of the tracts, the variance of the "expected" components would turn out to be 59 per cent (.77 squared times 100) of the variance of the actual drug rates, and, in this sense, we would have accounted for 59 per cent of the variance of the drug rates. The variance of the left-over components would turn out to be 41 per cent of the variance of the actual drug rates.[f] Stated differently, if we were to hold the percentage of Negroes statistically constant, the variance of the drug rates would go down to 41 per cent of their original variance.

The correlations between each of the variables that we investigated and the drug rate are given in Table III-5. The correlations were calculated separately for each of the boroughs and, as previously explained, are based on only the census tracts in the epidemic areas and those immediately adjacent to them.[g] Alongside each coefficient, in parentheses, is given the percentage of the drug-rate variance that can be "accounted for" by that variable.

The three variables that stand out most in all three boroughs in terms of their respective abilities to account for the variance in drug rates are percentage of Negroes, percentage of low-income units, and percentage of males in "lower" occupations. No particular significance should be attached to the fact that the correlations in Brooklyn are considerably lower than those in Manhattan and the Bronx. The variance in drug rates in Brooklyn is considerably smaller than the variances in the other two boroughs (about two-thirds of that in Manhattan and four-fifths of that in the Bronx), and accounting for a small portion of a small variance is, in an absolute sense, not necessarily a poorer accounting job than accounting for a larger part of a larger variance. Over a comparable range of drug rates, the discrepancies between drug rates and, say, percentage of Negroes may be of the same order in the two cases.

To put the same point differently, relative to the degree of dispersion of scores (and this is what counts in computing the correlation coefficient), a small absolute difference between two scores may loom large if the variance is small and be quite trivial if the variance is large.[h] For this reason, we are mainly interested in the order of the relationships. On this basis, the three variables mentioned at the beginning of the preceding paragraph are most closely related to drug rates in each of the three boroughs.

In the case of some of the variables, the correlations with drug rates are quite different, even in ordinal terms, in the three boroughs. The

most extreme case involves the percentage of people living at a new
address; this variable yields the fourth highest positive correlation in
the Bronx, but the most marked negative correlation in Manhattan.
We have already noted that this variable cannot be interpreted as we
had originally hoped; that is, we cannot take it as a satisfactory measure
of possible rootlessness. Its quite different behavior in the three
boroughs in relation to drug rate is also associated with markedly different patterns of recent residential change. In the Bronx, most of the
moving has been into census tracts of high unemployment, low occupa-

TABLE III-5   *Correlations* with Drug Rates by*
Census Tracts in Epidemic and
Border Zones

VARIABLES (Number of census tracts)	CORRELATION WITH DRUG RATES		
	MANHATTAN (132)	BRONX (66)	BROOKLYN (179)
20. Percentage of population that is Negro	.77 (59)	.63 (40)	.45 (20)
12. Percentage of income units earning $2,000 or less in 1949	.65 (42)	.66 (44)	.43 (18)
14. Percentage of men employed in "lower" occupations	.63 (40)	.62 (38)	.41 (17)
17. Percentage of dwelling units without television	.48 (23)	.53 (28)	.40 (16)
13. Percentage of dwelling units that are highly crowded	.45 (20)	.56 (31)	.32 (10)
15. Percentage of adults with fewer than eight years of schooling	.44 (19)	.42 (18)	.07 (—) †
— Delinquency rate	.43 (18)	‡	‡
22. Percentage excess of females over males (21-and-over age group)	.35 (12)	.44 (19)	.37 (14)
23. Percentage excess of females over males (age 15–19)	.34 (12)	.50 (25)	.10 (1)
19. Number of local employees per resident	.31 (10)	.24 (6)	.17 (3)
A. Index of disrupted family living arrangements	.30 (9)	.56 (31)	.30 (9)

VARIABLES (Number of census tracts)	MANHATTAN (132)	BRONX (66)	BROOKLYN (179)
11. Percentage of unemployed men	.29 (8)	.52 (27)	.22 (5)
B. Index of density of male adolescent population	.28 (8)	.22 (5)	.01 (—) †
21. Percentage of population that is of Puerto Rican origin	−.04 (—) †	.47 (22)	.08 (1)
18. Average number of business establishments per block	−.10 (1)	.07 (—) †	−.08 (1)
16. Average number of vacant dwelling units per block	−.21 (4)	.08 (1)	.23 (5)
24. Percentage of population living at a new address	−.33 (10)	.60 (36)	.17 (3)

* Parenthetical entries are squares of correlation coefficients expressed as percentages; for explanation, see text.

† Less than 1 per cent.

‡ Not computed.

tions, disrupted family life, relatively high concentrations of Puerto Ricans, and low incomes; the correlations with these variables are, respectively, .74, .71, .68, .65, and .62. In Manhattan, the trends are less marked, but, such as they are, the tendency has been for moving into areas of higher occupations, higher educational levels, lower density of male adolescent population, and fewer Negroes; the correlations are, respectively, −.46, −.41, −.40, and −.37. In Brooklyn, the pattern is again different, but, in character, more like that in the Bronx. The highest correlations are with percentage of families without television (.44), percentage of Negroes (.42), crowded dwelling units (.41), disrupted families (.41), vacant dwelling units (.40), and low incomes (.39). Clearly, this variable has no consistent meaning, so that its varying behavior with respect to drug rate is not remarkable.[1]

In general, the varying behavior of the mobility variable with respect to drug rates in the three boroughs is related to the differing relationships among the variables themselves. The second most noteworthy case of a variable with markedly varying relationships to drug rate—percentage of Puerto Ricans—merits some special comment. If drug rates are plotted against this variable, the line which best marks the trend turns out to be far from straight; it is, in fact, a markedly U-shaped curve. That is, drug rates are highest in the tracts where the percentages of Puerto Ricans are relatively low and also where they are relatively high; they are lowest for intermediate ranges of percentages of Puerto Ricans. If one were to add the excluded tracts without any Puerto Ricans, the curve would be even more remarkable, for all the tracts excluded from the analysis have zero or nearly zero drug rates.

In other words, the full curve would tell the following story. There is no known drug use among teen-aged boys where there are no Puerto Ricans. But, as we move into tracts with low concentrations of Puerto Ricans, drug use jumps to very high levels. As we go on to tracts with higher concentrations of Puerto Ricans, drug rates fall markedly. But, as we continue into tracts with still higher concentrations of Puerto Ricans, the drug rates again mount to very high levels.

The key to the puzzle is that, in the epidemic areas, census tracts with high concentrations of Negroes—a state of affairs that almost necessarily implies low concentrations of Puerto Ricans—have high drug rates. But, as we move into tracts with relatively low concentrations of Negroes, there is an almost linear increase in drug rate with increasing concentrations of Puerto Ricans. If we had had the foresight to define the Puerto Rican variable in terms of the percentage of Puerto Ricans in the non-Negro population, the relationship of this variable to drug rate would undoubtedly have been not greatly different from that obtained for percentage of Negroes. The wisdom of hindsight is assuredly impressive, but it still leaves us with a virtually useless variable for the purposes of the remaining analysis of these data. Suffice it to say that it is hardly likely that the condition of being of Puerto Rican origin is per se conducive to the use of narcotics by teen-aged boys. The true story of the segregated Puerto Rican neighborhoods in relation to juvenile drug use is doubtless not very different, except perhaps in minor details, from the story of the segregated Negro neighborhoods.

It may be noted that, for all of the differential behavior of some of the variables in relation to drug rate in the three boroughs, the general order of the relationships is fairly consistent from borough to borough. The rank-difference correlation[9] between the correlation coefficients of the sixteen variables is .60 for Manhattan and the Bronx, .72 for Manhattan and Brooklyn, and .75 for the Bronx and Brooklyn; if the

[9] The rank-difference correlation is a variant of the usual correlation coefficient, the only difference being that we take the rank position as the score. Thus, percentage of Negroes has a rank of one in all three boroughs. The correlation between delinquency rate and drug rate is, of course, not included in these rank-difference correlations or in the ranking of the coefficients in Manhattan, since its value was not determined for the other boroughs.

four most "misbehaving" variables (i.e., the ones yielding the most variable correlations with drug rate) are eliminated, these become, respectively, .83, .92, and .93. The variables are listed in Table III-5 in the order of the magnitude of the correlations with drug rate in Manhattan, the borough with, by far, the greatest drug problem. Except for a minor inversion involving first and second place in the Bronx, the first six variables in the list are in the identical order in the other two boroughs. The major story that they have to tell is that the incidence of drug use among teen-aged boys is one of segregated slum areas.

If one were to add the percentages of accountable drug rate variance in any of the columns of Table III-5, it is obvious that they would add up to considerably more than 100 per cent. The reason for this is not difficult to find. These variables are correlated with one another as well as with drug rate. Consequently, the portion of drug-rate variance that can be accounted for by one of them overlaps with the portion that can be accounted for by another. By certain advanced techniques of correlational analysis, it is possible to straighten out the picture of the collective relationship. Thus, by means of what is called multiple-correlation anaylsis, it is possible to eliminate the duplication in the accounts.[j]

Table III-6 gives the multiple correlations of selected combinations of variables with drug rate, along with percentages of accountable drug-rate variances. The Puerto Rican variable was not included in any of the combinations because of the already noted deceptive character of the correlation coefficients involved.

As might be expected, combinations of variables do a better job of accounting for the drug-rate variances than do the individual variables. Even so, substantial portions are not accounted for, most notably so in Brooklyn. It does not follow, however, that the addition of other variables to the set would markedly improve the picture. We have already noted that there are undoubtedly errors of measurement in these data. Insofar as there are such errors in the drug rates, this would account for a portion of the drug-rate variance; and, where the absolute drug-rate variance is small, as in Brooklyn, even small errors would loom relatively large.[k] Insofar as there are errors in the other variables (e.g., related to errors of enumeration in the census), they cannot be expected to do a perfect accounting job. In the light of these considerations (and the restrictions on the correlations due to the excluded

TABLE III-6   *Multiple Correlations* of Selected*
Combinations of Variables with Drug
Rates in Epidemic and Border Zones

	MULTIPLE CORRELATION WITH DRUG RATES		
COMBINATION OF VARIABLES	MANHATTAN	BRONX	BROOKLYN
Percentage less than $2,000, percentage in low occupations	.68 (46)	.69 (48)	.50 (25)
Percentage Negro, percentage less than $2,000, percentage in "lower" occupations	.79 (62)	.69 (48)	.50 (25)
Percentage Negro, percentage less than $2,000, percentage in low occupations, percentage without television, percentage of crowded dwelling units	.81 (66)	.74 (54)	.52 (27)
All but percentage Negro and percentage Puerto Rican	.82 (67)	.83 (69)	.63 (40)
All but percentage Puerto Rican	.86 (74)	.83 (69)	.63 (40)

* Percentages of accountable drug-rate variance in terms of the given combination of variables are given in parentheses next to each correlation coefficient.

census tracts), the proportions of accounted-for drug-rate variance are well above our initial expectations.

A second point to be noted in Table III-6 is that the percentage of Negroes adds nothing to the accounting of the drug-rate variance given by percentage of low incomes and percentage of males in "lower" occupations in the Bronx and Brooklyn. If it still accounts for 16 per cent more of the variance in Manhattan than do the latter two variables jointly, this special contribution of percentage of Negroes to the accounting has shrunk to less than half of that amount by the time we introduce the other variables into the accounting system. This still leaves us with 7 per cent of the Manhattan drug-rate variance associated with degree of Negro segregation that is not otherwise accounted for by any of the other variables that we have considered.

What is special about the Negro slum areas of Manhattan that makes their teen-aged boys vulnerable to the lure of narcotics, we do not know. That it is not the sheer fact of Negro population seems obvious in the light of the Bronx and Brooklyn findings. It is possible that the cumulative impact of many unwholesome conditions produces a surplus of vulnerability beyond the net sum of the impacts of the individual conditions. We have not, however, provided for the testing of such a possibility in our system of accounts.[1]

Finally, it may be noted that two variables, percentage of low incomes and percentage of men in "lower" occupations, account for 62 per cent of the portion of the drug-rate variance in Manhattan that can be accounted for by the entire set of variables, 70 per cent in the Bronx, and 63 per cent in Brooklyn. When percentage of Negroes is added, this figure shoots up to 84 per cent in Manhattan, but remains unchanged in the Bronx and in Brooklyn. When percentage of families without television and percentage of crowded dwelling units are added to the preceding trio of variables, the corresponding figures become 89, 78, and 68 per cent. Although not included in Table III-6, if the last of the economic variables we have examined—percentage of unemployed males—is added to the set, the figures become 93 per cent, 80 per cent, and the last remains the same.

As far as the social environment is concerned, the vulnerability of teen-aged males in New York City to the lure of narcotics is in the main associated in some fashion with living in areas of economic squalor, but other unwholesome aspects of the social environment also contribute in substantial measure. That is, conditions of economic squalor dominate the picture, but virtually the entire complex of unwholesome factors plays a contributory role. We had hoped, but not really expected, to discover one or two clear-cut factors that could account for the lure of narcotics; but, as usual, social causation is a complex affair.

STATISTICAL FOOTNOTES

[a] Actually, only one variable was eliminated solely on the latter basis: the epidemic areas of Brooklyn showed an excess of 6.3 per cent in number of adolescent girls as compared to an excess of 7.7 per cent for the combined nonepidemic areas. The nonepidemic areas of Manhattan showed an excess of 9.0 per cent, less than did the epidemic areas (16.1 per cent), but almost as high as the epidemic areas of the Bronx (11.2 per cent) and higher than the epidemic areas of Brooklyn. Within each borough, the difference was in the expected direction.

[b] The delinquency rates are based on the sample. Since the sample includes only 23 per cent of the charges, they should be multiplied by 4.3 to give an estimate of the actual total number of charges per 1,000 boys. The numbers

are, in any event, not directly comparable to the drug rates; the latter concern *persons,* the former, *acts.*

c Even this high correlation underestimates the relationship. It describes a linear trend, whereas the actual trend is clearly curvilinear. For the health areas with fewer than a fourth of their families in the indicated plight, there is a slowly increasing drug rate as one ascends the poverty scale; for the health areas with from about 25 to 40 per cent of their families in this plight, there is a very rapid climb in drug rate; beyond the 40 per-cent point, the rate of increase in drug rate decreases markedly.

d To the nonstatistician, one of the most obvious ones is the *average deviation;* that is, for each score, we calculate how much it differs from the mean of the distribution, and then we average the differences. The more scores differ from one another, the greater the value of the average deviation. In calculating the *variance,* we average the *squared* deviations from the mean; that is, for each score we calculate how much it differs from the mean. Then, instead of proceeding as for the average deviation, we square each of the differences and average the squares. The square root of the variance is known as the *standard deviation.* A major advantage to the use of variances rather than other measures of variability is that variances can be analytically subdivided. Specifically, if the scores are subdivided into a number of independent components, then the variance of the whole scores equals the sums of the variances of the components. One of the many applications of this principle is dealt with in the text.

e It is sometimes stated that the use of the correlation coefficient presupposes that both variables are normally distributed (i.e., that they have a distribution which is sometimes referred to as "bell-shaped"; see Appendix C, Note f). Though true of some applications, this assumption is not involved in either the derivation of the formula for the correlation coefficient or in the relationship described above.

f In the same way, the drug rates "account for" 59 per cent of the variance of percentage of Negroes and leave 41 per cent of the variances "unaccounted for." In this case, the accounting is quite obviously not causal.

g These correlation coefficients are, in most cases, lower than they would have been if all the tracts were included, particularly so in relation to the variables at the top of the list in Table III-1. This follows from the facts that all of the tracts that were not included have zero (or very close to zero) drug rates and that they tend to differ markedly and in the "right" direction from the epidemic-area tracts with respect to the second variable involved in a particular correlation.

h The issue is, of course, further complicated by the variance of the second set of scores involved in a correlation. These are generally smallest in the Bronx and greatest in Manhattan.

i The different patterns of correlation of change of address provide a clue as to why this variable has a quite different meaning in the three boroughs. The patterns are consistent with certain commonly recognized population-mobility trends. Better-off families with children commonly move into the suburbs and newer city residential areas—mostly in Queens and to some extent in Brooklyn— making way for relatively worse-off families. This migration trend is apparently most marked in the Bronx. On the other hand, suburbanites whose children are grown commonly move back into the newer and more expensive city apartments

—mainly in Manhattan. What we really need are age-group-specific mobility rates.

ʲ To illustrate with a simple case, consider drug rate in relation to only two other variables, say, percentage of Negroes and percentage of low incomes. We first split drug rate into two components, one which can be "accounted for" in terms of percentage of Negroes and a second which is unrelated to the latter. We similarly split percentage of low incomes into two components, one related to percentage of Negroes and a second unrelated to the latter. We then split the second component of drug rate into two components, one related to the second component of percentage of low incomes and a second unrelated to the latter. We have thus split drug rates into three components: a component which can be "accounted for" by the percentage of Negroes, a component which can be "accounted for" by the component of percentage of low incomes which is unrelated to percentage of Negroes, and a component which is unrelated to either percentage of Negroes or percentage of low incomes. We can compute the variance of each of these components, and the sum of these three variances will equal the total variance in drug rate. The proportion of the total drug-rate variance contributed by the first component plus the proportion contributed by the second equals the square of the coefficient of multiple correlation; or, equivalently, the coefficient of multiple correlation is the square root of 1 minus the proportion of the total variance contributed by the third component. Alternatively, we could, with the same result, split drug rate into the following three components: one related to the percentage of low incomes, one related to the component of percentage of Negroes which is unrelated to percentage of low incomes, and a third which is unrelated either to percentage of Negroes or to percentage of low incomes. If we were now to add still another variable to the set, we would first derive a component of the latter which is unrelated either to percentage of Negroes or percentage of low incomes and split the third component of drug rate into one which is related and one which is unrelated to the derived component of the last variable, and so on as we add still other variables. The coefficient of multiple correlation is always the square root of 1 minus the proportion of the total drug-rate variance contributed by the component of drug rate that is unrelated to any of the other variables under consideration. The actual computation of the coefficient of multiple correlation abbreviates the procedure just described, but even so one cannot go on adding variables without rather quickly running into the need for electronic computers.

ᵏ The point is that one may think of error as a component of a score. On this basis, the earlier representation of the decomposition of drug rates into a number of components was oversimplified. A closer approximation to a correct description would be as follows. The *true* component of any given obtained drug rate is decomposed into components that can be accounted for on the basis of the other variables and a component that cannot be so accounted for. The total variance of the obtained drug rates equals the sum of the variances of these components plus the variance of the error component. Insofar as the absolute errors in drug rates are of comparable magnitude in the three boroughs, the variances of the error components would also be approximately equal; but, if the total variance of the drug rate is smaller in one borough than in the others, the proportion of the total variance taken up by the error variance must be larger in the first instance than in the others.

It is to be noted that the errors we are discussing are real errors, rather than conceptual constructs, such as are involved in some discussions of psychological test scores, where the "true" score is conceived of as the average of the test scores obtained by a person in an infinite number of replications of testing under identical conditions. Also to be noted is the assumption that the errors of measurement are randomly distributed, an assumption that is reasonable in the light of the arguments and evidence we have adduced for taking the obtained distribution of drug rates seriously.

[1] A simple score based on the number of unwholesome conditions (an "unwholesome condition" being defined as, say, being in the top quarter or third of the census tracts with respect to a given variable) would have helped to clarify the issue if added to the set of variables. This, however, is also a matter of hindsight, although we had used such a variable in a preliminary analysis of the data. Unfortunately, this analysis is not in a form that can be brought to bear here. It is our impression that the Negro slums of Manhattan are worse off in this respect than those in the Bronx and Brooklyn.

IV

The Cultural Context

We have already established that juvenile drug use is not randomly distributed over New York City. It is heavily concentrated in certain neighborhoods. These are not a cross-section of the city's neighborhoods, but rather they are the ones which are economically and socially most deprived. Even within the relatively few tracts in which we found the vast majority of cases, the tracts of highest drug use can be distinguished from those with lower rates of juvenile drug use by a variety of social and economic indexes. The tracts with the greatest amount of drug use are those with the highest proportions of certain minority groups, the highest poverty rates, the most crowded dwelling units, the highest incidence of disrupted family living arrangements, and so on for a number of additional related indexes.

Now, we can think of no good reason why economic squalor per se should lead teen-aged boys and young men to use drugs. Presumably, the effects are indirect, mediated by certain attitudes and values which are generated in such environments and which, in turn, predispose the youth to experiment with narcotics. In the preceding chapter, for instance, we suggested that conditions of economic squalor may generate a sense of hopelessness from which narcotics offer at least a temporary, if illusory, escape. Yet, such an hypothesis sounds naïve, even to us, as applied to the youths.

It might be credible if applied to adults who, after years of futile struggle, simply give up. But what can a youngster have known of futile struggle against the misery of economic deprivation? He may have known the misery itself. He may have shed bitter tears in the extremity of his wants, he may have protested and demanded in vain efforts to bring the world to his terms; he may have, without thought of right or wrong, taken things that attracted him but to which he had no right, only to learn that such taking is likely to bring with it dreaded punishment. But why should he have already given up? Why should he not have been persuaded by the implicit and explicit teachings in his school review of American history of the reality of the American Dream? Why should he not have been persuaded by the glimpses of a better life in the movies and on television, by the sheer volume of beckoning advertisements, by the store displays, by the evidences of conspicuous consumption, and so on that these things are available to him if he but strives hard enough?

If he is oppressed by a sense of futility, where can he get it but from the culture around him, a culture that is more powerful in the concreteness and immediacy of its lessons than the shadowy glimpses and the idealized verbalizations of the achievability of a better life? Where but from his vicarious experiences, the evidences of frustration and failure and of the acceptance of defeat that impinge on his senses? Where but from the expectations and evaluations expressed by those about him who speak with the authority of participation in the world of his direct experience?

He does not need to have himself worn away a lifetime of days in futility to be convinced of its reality. And, if the eloquence of his school books and teachers and the dramatizations of the mass media and their appeals nevertheless bring the American Dream into his life space, is it not *as* dream? Is it not as reality for others, but as a fantasy world for him and others like him? What better foundation can be laid for a willingness to experiment with the alchemical stuff that offers the promise of transforming the fantasy, for a while at least, into an isotope of reality?

These remarks on the sense of futility are intended only as an illustration of how the relation between economic squalor and drug use might be mediated by a process of attitude formation. If they sound convincing, we still cannot but pause and wonder whether they are true. Plausibility is not a satisfying substitute for evidence. If the conditions we have reported as associated with drug use actually are mediated by the formation of certain attitudes and values, we ought to be able to demonstrate the latter directly. We wanted to know whether there was anything about the social climate, the culture, the ethos—

call it what you will—that might make one neighborhood more hospitable to experimentation with narcotics than another.

Practical considerations made us curb our ambitions. We had to limit ourselves to three comparable neighborhoods differing in the known incidence of juvenile drug use—one very high, one medium, and one relatively low but where drug use is reputedly increasing.[1] We also limited ourselves to all of the eighth-grade boys attending the four junior high schools and the seven parochial schools servicing our three neighborhoods.[2] This decision was guided by the reasoning that, on the one hand, the elementary and junior high schools provide easiest access to a relatively unbiased population (the lower the grade level, the more unbiased) and that, on the other hand, eighth-grade boys are approaching the age at which we had found that significant numbers of teen-agers begin to try drugs. Our working hypothesis was that at this level we would already find constellations of attitudes, values, and information or misinformation about narcotics that would help to explain why differing proportions of these boys will, in a few years, probably be willing to try drugs.

It should be apparent, however, from what has already been said about neighborhoods which differ in incidence of drug use, that, though

[1] To avoid redundancy, we shall refer to these neighborhoods as "High," "Medium," and "Low," respectively.

[2] There were 442 boys in High, 212 in Medium, and 271 in Low, respectively. The data are given in Table IV-1. There are also a number of Jewish day schools (the Jewish equivalent of the parochial school) in Low. These were not included in the study for practical reasons (e.g., the absence of any central administration with which to deal) and on theoretical grounds: relatively few Jewish boys nowadays become involved in delinquency and even fewer with narcotics, and the ones who attend the day schools in this area are particularly likely to be isolated from the surrounding neighborhood culture. These schools are, by their very nature, segregated—not only from Gentiles (and this, of course, includes Negroes and Puerto Ricans), but also from Jews of less religiously Orthodox background, who are more likely to mingle freely with other elements of the community. The children spend many more hours in school and, hence, are less free, even if so inclined, to participate in the street culture. Even more fundamentally, from our point of view, many come from other parts of the city and, in some instances, from outside the city; they cannot, therefore, be said to be representatives of some facet of the neighborhood culture. The Jewish boys in the neighborhood public schools were included in the sample, both because there was no way of excluding them and because they were in much closer contact with the neighborhood culture than were those attending the day schools. They probably constitute a substantial proportion of the boys in Low, but very negligible proportions of the boys in the other two neighborhoods.

TABLE IV-1   *Location of Areas and Distribution of Subjects*

ETHNIC GROUP	LOWER EAST SIDE (East River, Rivington Street, the Bowery, New Chambers Street)			MANHATTANVILLE (116th Street, St. Nicholas Avenue, 145th Street, Hudson River)			CENTRAL HARLEM (112th Street, Park Avenue, 131st Street, St. Nicholas Avenue)		
	PUBLIC SCHOOL	PAROCHIAL SCHOOL	TOTAL	PUBLIC SCHOOL	PAROCHIAL SCHOOL	TOTAL	PUBLIC SCHOOL	PAROCHIAL SCHOOL	TOTAL
	PERCENTAGE*								
Negro	7	0	6	52	6	37	91	76	90
White	67	100	71	6	65	25	†	8	1
Spanish-speaking	26	0	23	43	29	38	9	16	9
	(237)	(34)	(271)	(143)	(69)	(212)	(417)	(25)	(442)

LOCATION (Approximate boundaries)

* Do not add to 100 per cent because of rounding errors.
† Less than .5 per cent.

our three neighborhoods may be relatively comparable—e.g., all three are lower-class neighborhoods—they nevertheless differ markedly in many respects: average income, ethnic composition, and so on. High has higher delinquency rates than Low, but all three neighborhoods have quite high delinquency rates.[3]

We used a questionnaire tapping a variety of attitude, value, and information areas that we thought relevant to our problem. Fifty-one items had no specific reference to drug use. Eleven of these called for certain background information, for instance, whether the respondent was living with his father. The remaining forty ranged over the following topics: attitudes toward police, attitudes toward parents, agreement or disagreement with certain middle-class standards of behavior, personal feelings of optimism, evaluation of certain life goals, and adaptations of the items used by Srole[4] in his scale of *anomie*. The *anomie* items try to get at a lack of trust in people, a pessimistic outlook toward the future, and a sense of futility. Forty-five items were explicitly related to narcotics and were divided among the following topics: attitudes toward the use of drugs, image of the drug-user, action orientation with regard to the drug-user, evaluation of arguments against using heroin, information or beliefs about drugs, and personal exposure to the use of heroin.

The questions were cast in as simple a form as possible because we had to meet the reading level of the poorest students. As an added precaution, the questionnaire was administered item by item, the teacher reading the items one at a time to each class. Responses consisted of checking one of two or, in some instances, one of three alternatives. The replies were anonymous. The questionnaire was administered in two parts in two class sessions.[5]

[3] According to New York City Youth Board statistics, Medium is on a par with High, whereas, according to our own data (collected from other sources and with other criteria; for instance, as was indicated in the preceding chapter, to separate as far as possible the drug-use variable from other types of delinquency, we did not include drug violations in the delinquency counts, and we did not include certain behavior disturbances which to our minds do not represent delinquencies but which were included in the Youth Board figures because they were called to the attention of the Juvenile Aid Bureau of the Police Department for one reason or another), it is on a par with Low.

[4] L. Srole, "Social Integration and Certain Corollaries: An Exploratory Study," *American Sociological Review,* 21, (December 1956) 709–716.

[5] The two parts of the questionnaire, labeled respectively "Form F" and "Form G," are given in Appendix D. The background questions were intended mainly to make it possible to put together the two parts answered by a given individual. Since the questionnaires were separated by classes, the birthday

We made several checks on the answers the boys gave, and we are satisfied that they are not random and that they are not merely socially approved responses.

If the boys simply gave approved responses, we would expect that high proportions of the subjects would consistently give what seemed the desired responses to the items. This, in general, was not the case. Not only do the proportions of "right" responses, let us call them, vary considerably from item to item, but, surprisingly (from some points of view, distressingly), high proportions give the "wrong" responses to many of the items.

Thus, two of the items ask what should be done if "you find out that one of the boys on your block is using heroin." In nine of the eleven subgroups formed when we classified the boys by neighborhood, ethnic or racial identification, type of school attended, and type of class[6]—in nine of these eleven subgroups, about 40 per cent agreed with the statement: "Nobody should do anything. It is his own private business." In one subgroup, the proportion agreeing with this statement was as high as 57 per cent and, in one subgroup, only 13 per cent. In all eleven subgroups, about 47 per cent did not agree that one should "tell the school or the police about him."

Similarly, from about 43 per cent to 63 per cent of the respondents in the various subgroups agreed with the statement that "the police usually let their friends get away with things." And from 33 to 83 per cent agreed that "most policemen can be paid off." Or, to take still another illustration, about 39 per cent of the boys in each of the subgroups in High said "Yes" to the question, "Did you ever see anybody taking heroin?" The corresponding figure for Medium was 24 per cent and, for Low, 13 per cent. Forty-five per cent of the respondents in

---

proved sufficient for this purpose. When the second part was being collected, one of the boys suddenly realized that he could be identified by his birthday and tore his paper up. We wanted the ethnic identifications of the boys, but could not ask this directly. We instead gave each teacher a list of the birthdays of the children; from this, she could identify the children and give us the desired information, but she never saw the filled-out questionnaires. On the other hand, we never saw the names of the children. As soon as the two parts were collated and the ethnic information added, the papers were sorted into eleven subgroups, as described below. Within these subgroups, the particular class that a given questionnaire was in could no longer be determined. In this way, the pledge of anonymity was fulfilled.

[6] In High public school, there were, in addition to the regular classes, what were designated "adjustment classes." These classes contained boys who were not mentally retarded but who presented educational and/or behavior problems.

High claimed personal acquaintance with a heroin-user, 32 per cent in Medium, and 17 per cent in Low.[7]

One may, of course, suppose that there is a considerable bloc of pupils who gave what they conceived as "proper" answers and possibly a second bloc who mischievously took advantage of anonymity by giving "improper" answers whenever they spotted an opportunity to do so. The effect of such blocs would be to make for fairly high correlations among the items. This, in general, did not prove to be the case.

We must anticipate somewhat to explain the data. We computed tetrachoric correlations[a] among the items separately for the three neighborhoods. In a few instances, several items with related content were combined into indexes in order to avoid extreme marginal breaks[b] or for other reasons; the distributions for these indexes were dichotomized and the resultant dichotomies used in the computation of tetrachoric coefficients. Counting these indexes as individual items and dropping some of the personal data items, we were left with seventy-two items among which all of the intercorrelations were computed—2,556 correlation coefficients for each neighborhood.

About 20 per cent of the correlations in Medium were statistically significant,[c] about 25 per cent in Low, and about 30 per cent in High. In other words, from about 70 to 80 per cent of the correlations were not statistically significant, a finding which is hardly compatible with the hypothesis of blocs of consistently conventional and consistently unconventional respondents.

This finding, however, may seem to support the possibility that the responses are random. Actually, the figures just quoted would be sufficient to controvert this hypothesis, since the numbers of statistically significant correlations, though small, are nevertheless considerably greater than could reasonably be expected by chance. It should be remembered, in this connection, that the questionnaire was designed to cover a wide variety of attitudes, values, and information. On this basis, it would be surprising indeed (and probably explicable only by some such hypothesis as the one we have already discarded) if a very high proportion of the interitem correlations proved significant. Apart from the sheer number of significant correlations, we are in a position to make a minimum estimate of the reliabilities of the individual items.[d] Such a minimum estimate can be obtained by taking the highest correlation between a given item and any other item as a measure of that item's reliability. When this is done, we find that the median item reliability in

[7] These figures will be evaluated below for their accuracy.

the low-drug-use neighborhood is above .50 and, in the other two neighborhoods, above .55—a high order of reliability for single items and quite incompatible with the random-response hypothesis.

Finally, we may mention that we computed for another purpose[e] the correlations between the correlational profiles of the items. That is, a given item will correlate relatively high with some items, relatively low with others, negatively with still others, and so on; a second item may have a similar correlation profile or one that is quite different. The degree of similarity between profiles can be measured by the correlation between them. The general level of these second-order correlations runs considerably higher than the tetrachoric correlations we have been discussing. Such a result would indicate an underlying structure to the patterns of response, some aspects of which we will discuss below. Of immediate relevance, however, is the fact that this structure is a meaningful one, and meaningful structures are hardly likely to appear if responses to items are arbitrary or capricious.

Granted, however, that the boys have, by and large, taken the questionnaire seriously and attempted to set down in response to each item their true thoughts and feelings, it still does not follow that we can take these responses at face value. The process of communication is replete with ambiguities and sources of mutual misunderstanding even under the best of circumstances—when people are talking to one another face to face, in a position to respond to facial and bodily expressions and to vocal intonations as well as to words, when the content of the communications can be amplified or repeatedly paraphrased as one person senses the needs of another, and when the continuation of the process itself provides checks and cues as to the messages that get across. In a questionnaire situation, none of these conditions exist,[8] and what looks like a simple "yes" or "no" to what looks like a simply

[8] It should be said, however, that the questions were carefully reviewed, both as to wording and format, by a committee of teachers in the school with the most serious reading problems. This invaluable help is gratefully acknowledged. In addition, the questions were pretested in face-to-face interviews with boys in a somewhat comparable neighborhood, and question wordings were revised as sources of ambiguity became apparent. The interviews were explicitly aimed at the meaning of the items rather than at getting answers. Special words like "heroin" and "marijuana" were explained in the course of the administration, and colloquial synonyms were written on the blackboard. It has already been noted that the questionnaires were administered item by item, the teachers pausing after each item to make sure that everyone understood. In the parochial schools, members of the research staff substituted for the teachers. In brief, every measure that we could think of was taken to make sure that our end of the communication process was as clear as it could be under the circumstances.

worded item may be an extremely complex psychological event. Consider, for example, the following item: G 26. "Most addicts who take the cure never go back on drugs again." The respondents were asked to check, "True," "False," or "I don't know." The second is factually correct,[9] and this item was one of a series designed to get a measure of the prevailing level of information in each of our three neighborhoods on matters pertaining to drugs.

Let us note that no eighth-grade boy can be expected to *know* the correct answer to this item in the same sense that, say, a psychiatrist who has been trying to treat addicts for many years may be expected to know it. At best, our young respondent will have heard relevant statements from sources to which he reacts as more-or-less credible; he may have direct personal knowledge of a case or two. He will have accepted the correct version with more-or-less assurance and will therefore be more-or-less inclined to say "false" to the item as presented.

But many other influences may bear on the determination of the response that he finally makes. He is, for instance, more-or-less confident that his inclination is correct. How confident must he be to draw a dividing line between "I don't know" and one of the definite responses? Individuals differ in this respect. Some will doubtless readily convert a pure guess into an unhesitating, assured response; others will cautiously conceal much more supported opinions behind an "I don't know." That is, we have here a temperamental, or personality, variable in addition to an information variable.

Various attitudes also have bearing on the determination of the response. Take the following item, by way of illustration: G 3. "Heroin is probably not as bad for a person as some people say." At the moment, all that concerns us is the bearing of the reaction to this item on the response to the preceding one. Suppose that a person has come to feel that the effects of heroin are so catastrophic that no one can exaggerate its dangers. With such an attitude, a person who has never considered or heard anything about the effectiveness of the treatment of addiction may, nevertheless, be inclined to assume the worst. To the extent that this is so, choosing the correct response to Item G 26 would be an expression of an attitude rather than of information.

Other determinants of the response have nothing to do with the con-

[9] Experts will, of course, be confronted by difficulties stemming from ambiguities in "take the cure" and "never go back on drugs again." These ambiguities may be assumed to be too subtle to bother our respondents.

tent of the item, but with the formal properties of the wording. It is known, for instance, that individuals differ with respect to what may be called "gullibility," or "acquiescent tendencies." Some find it relatively difficult to resist definitely worded statements and are inclined to assent to them; others are relatively negativistic, critical, or suspicious of definitely worded statements and, other factors being equal, are inclined to disagree. Moreover, consider a person who is inclined to disagree with such statements. Suppose that, by the time he has gotten to the item we are considering, he has already been confronted with a series of items with respect to which he had little to go by other than this no-saying tendency. By the time he has reached our item, his no-saying tendency may have been thoroughly satiated, and he may have developed quite a tension to say "yes" to something—and our item reaps the benefit. It may be assumed that individuals differ in the readiness with which their yes- (or no-) saying tendencies are satiated; and, even if we could select individuals who are exactly alike in this respect, it seems likely that any specific series of items would produce individual differences in the satiation rates.

There are a number of other factors which can affect how a person answers a particular item at a particular time. The actual answer may be a result of many influences, some of which lead the respondent to agree, some to disagree, and some—if the alternative is available—to say, "I don't know."

It seems clear that, given only the response of a particular person to a specific item, we can know very little about the meaning of the response. Even if we have the responses of many individuals to the same item, we are still in no position to disentangle the individual meanings. We can say how many selected each of the alternatives, but we cannot say whether or in what respect those who selected a given response have responded to the same aspect of the item or given expression to the same aspect of themselves.

As the number of items that comes within our purview increases, however, our situation changes; for, from the way that the responses to many items cohere, we can say something about the prevailing structure of the determinants.

Suppose, for example, that the addiction-cure item, G 26, hangs together with other items designed to get at information; that is, suppose that the answers to this item tend to be related to the answers given to many other items in the same way that the other information items are.

This would support the assumption that the item does, indeed, tend to get at information. In the existence of a cluster of such items, we would have a basis for concluding that there exists an information current in the cultural atmosphere. Some individuals may be more-or-less in the current, some more-or-less out of it. But there is something that brings these diverse items of information together, that makes them relatively equivalent one to another, that establishes them in a functional unity. The nature of the "something" we do not know, and, at this juncture, we do not particular care; what interests us is the existence of the current.

Suppose, by way of contrast, that the information items do not cohere and that the addiction-cure item does cohere with certain attitude items. We might then conclude that the outlook on the cure of addiction tends to be shaped by an attitudinal, rather than an informational, current in the cultural atmosphere. The particular alternatives selected by individuals in responding to the addiction-cure item would tend to be determined by where they stand with respect to the attitudinal complex or to the forces that shape this complex.

We might, of course, find that the addiction-cure item coheres with both information and attitude items, an outcome that would give us still another picture of the bearing of the cultural atmosphere on attitude toward the cure of addiction. Or we might find that the addiction-cure item does not hang together with any others, an outcome that would suggest that the outlook on the cure of addiction is shaped by highly idiosyncratic influences or by cultural influences untapped by our questionnaire.

We have been focusing on a particular item for purposes of illustration. Our interest lies, however, in the identification of the broad currents in the cultural atmospheres of our three neighborhoods, as evidenced by the coherence, or clustering, of the items.

The meaning of item clusters is discussed in some detail in Appendix E, and our reasons for preferring this form of analysis to a more popular type are given in Appendix F. For present purposes, it may be sufficient to indicate that a cluster consists of a number of items, each of which has a pattern of correlation with all the other items that is similar to the patterns shown by the other items in the cluster. The items in a cluster may be said to have similar or closely related implications to the respondents.

Instead of thinking in terms of cultural currents, we may think of a cluster as a group of items providing a crude map of a cultural channel through which certain ideational, attitudinal, and/or valuational issues become linked so that the position that one takes with regard to one or more of these issues is related to the positions that one takes with regard to the others. Issues may become so linked because of their common content; e.g., dislike of the police and tolerance of lawlessness may become linked because they have in common a belief that laws are made for the benefit of others. They may become linked by processes of direct causal interaction; e.g., the perception of police venality may breed disrespect for law, which, in turn, may contribute to selective perception of police activities. They may be linked by historical contingencies—e.g., a minority group may be impressed by its political impotence and regard law as an expression of the will of the majority group (regardless of the merits of the laws per se)—and, at the same time, perceive that most members of the police force are members of the majority group; in this case, the linkage would be a function of the minority-group situation and the crystallization of attitudes and beliefs relevant to this situation.

The linkage in the preceding illustrations between liking or disliking of police and intolerance or tolerance of lawlessness is purely hypothetical, as are the alternate bases of the linkage described. That the conditions of the linkage postulated in these illustrations are not sufficient ought to be clear from the compatibility of these conditions with reversals of the linkage or of their bases. The belief that laws have been enacted for the benefit of others need not be accompanied by tolerance of lawlessness. Many Southerners, for instance, who believe that the Supreme Court decisions on segregation are expressions of Northern and international politics and inappropriate for the South, nevertheless accept the decision as the law of the land and believe that, as long as this is so, it should be observed. One may disapprove of a law, but still respect law enforcement officers for trying to do a good job. The observation of police corruption may serve only to heighten one's sense of the importance of preserving law and order. With respect to minority groups, Kurt Lewin has described the complex phenomenon of self-hatred (and one may also think, in this connection, of the phenomena that Freud has described as identification with the successful rival and identification with the aggressor), in terms of which minority-group members may come to respect the law and its enforcement officials all the more, precisely because they represent the majority group.

Nor is the particular linkage itself, in whichever direction, necessary;

one may have an attitude toward lawlessness without ever bringing attitudes toward the police into the same context; or toward the police, without ever thinking in the same context of the importance or unimportance of the preservation of law and order in general and without either condemning or condoning particular instances of lawbreaking in particular. Attitudes toward the law and/or its enforcement officers may or may not be linked to the perception and evaluation of status differentials in society, to other authoritarian or egalitarian attitudes, to religious attitudes, or to whatever. Attitudes toward particular regulations (e.g., those governing automobile traffic or the filing of truthful income tax returns) may or may not be isolated from attitudes toward law in general.

The point is that the conditions governing the linkages of ideas, attitudes, values, and the like are extremely complex. The question of how particular linkages come about may be worthy of intensive research or may constitute fertile ground for learned or entertaining speculation. But, however they may come about, the discovery of linkages in a society or subsociety tells us something about the prevailing culture and the patterns of thought and the like which characterize it. Moreover, once they do come about, they tend to become self-sustaining, regardless of how they may have originated, for they constitute part of the objective basis of the experience of the participants in the culture. In a sense, these linkages are as much an aspect of the geography of the behavioral environments of individuals as the streets, alleyways, and bridges are of their physical environments. They offer familiar and convenient channels of association and thought and thereby help the individual to interpret and evaluate the things he experiences.

The linkages need not be consciously articulated or put into words. They are implicit in the course of the conversations that one overhears, in the things that people take for granted as they draw inferences, in the choice of figures of speech, and in the patterns of events and the classes of objects that elicit similar reactions—the occasions for laughter, incredulity, cynicism, optimism or pessimism, cursing, blaming, admiring, and so on. The process of internalizing the linkage in one's psychic structure may, of course, be facilitated by the recurrence of conditions that originally gave rise to them or by new conditions that contribute to the same end.

A person who finds himself on one side of an issue is likely to find himself on the corresponding sides of other issues linked to it, even with regard to issues that he may never before have encountered as such. All that he needs are enough cues to place the new issues in his psychic map of the cultural terrain. If unearned sensuous gratification is evil, then, even though he may never have confronted the issue of narcotics before, he need but sense that the taking of narcotics is a means of achieving unearned gratification, and this practice, too, will be tainted with evil. If, on the other hand, the practice of smoking tobacco is already firmly linked to other contexts—say, manliness or the sheer exercise of habit—and there are not enough cues to place tobacco in the context of unearned gratification, then to the same person smoking will not be tainted with evil, even though the man from Mars may find it difficult to distinguish between the two practices.

Needless to say, we cannot hope to explore every aspect of the cultural terrain of the eighth-grade boys in our three neighborhoods. At the most—and this is what we attempted to do in the questionnaire— we can sample from strategically selected sets of issues and try to explore the linkages that exist. The linkages are inferred from the statistical behavior of the items, not so much from the direct correlations between items as from the relationships of each item to all the remaining ones.[f]

The Delinquent's World View

Turning now to the actual data, we shall first consider the appearance of four clusters, one each in Low and Medium and two in High, which suggest the widespread consolidation of attitudes and values in an outlook favorable to delinquency.

These are sixteen items[g] common to the four clusters. For convenience, we shall refer to the items by their questionnaire numbers and brief descriptions or paraphrases, wording the latter in the direction of the scoring. Each of the sixteen items correlated positively with each of the others. Similarly, the correlation profile of each item correlated positively with the correlation profiles of each of the others.

Two of the sixteen items expressed attitudes unfavorable to parents:
    F 2, 16, 21: Compound item
    F 24: Parents always looking to nag
Four of the items expressed attitudes unfavorable to the police:
    F 6: Police open to bribes
    F 17: Police practice racial discrimination
    F 19: Police pick on people
    F 23: Police favor their friends

Two of the items expressed rejection of middle-class rules of deportment:

F 7, 13, 26: Compound item

F 9: Shouldn't always treat girls nice

Two of the items involved issues of major values:

F 29: Value power over people

F 39: Value thrills and taking chances

Three items expressed attitudes of profound pessimism and alienation:

F 4: Not much chance for a better world

F 22: Most people better off not born

F 25: Everybody really out for himself; nobody cares

Finally, there are three items which express "wrong" attitudes on issues involving narcotics:

G 1: Heroin use a strictly private affair

G 3, 4, 5: Agree with at least one of the following: heroin not so harmful as people say; taking a little heroin once in a while doesn't hurt; it is OK to smoke marijuana at parties

G 8: Heroin OK if you don't get hooked

A common theme of many of these items is that people do not respect other people, that they are mean and arbitrary in the pursuit of their private ends. If this is the premise, it is not difficult to conclude that a major value is the achievement of power and getting other people to do what one wants, that the outlook for most people is indeed bleak, that no one should interfere if people are engaged in illicit or self-destructive behavior, that socially set rules of deportment do not make much sense, and that the most sensible thing a person can do is to seek pleasure and gratification where he can find them.

This is perhaps to put an overly rationalistic construction on this grouping of items, but it seems reasonable to assume that the items cohere on some such basis; they are expressive of a reasonably integrated world outlook.

It does not follow, of course, that everyone in these three neighborhoods shares this philosophy, but that substantial numbers of individuals wittingly or unwittingly orient themselves with respect to such a philosophy. Some accept, some reject, and some waver. If our interpretation of the meaning of a cluster is correct, however, the existence of such a philosophy is an objective fact in the lives of the youngsters of the three neighborhoods.

A rough index of how thoroughly such views have seeped into our eighth-grade populations may be obtained by treating the set of items as a test. If each item were scored 1 or zero, the resulting distributions are given in Table IV-2. Forty-seven per cent of the eighth-grade boys in

---

TABLE IV-2   *Percentage Distributions of Scores*
on Sixteen Items Expressive
of an Outlook Favorable
to Delinquency

RELATIVE LEVELS OF DRUG USE IN NEIGHBORHOOD

SCORES	LOW	MEDIUM	HIGH	TOTAL
8 or more	23	24	28	25
4–7	45	41	45	45
3 or less	32	35	27	30
	(271)	(212)	(442)	(925)
6 or more	42	38	51	47

Type of school in high-drug-use neighborhood

	PUBLIC		PAROCHIAL
	ADJUSTMENT CLASSES	REGULAR CLASSES	
8 or more	40	23	28
4–7	50	45	48
3 or less	10	32	24
	(101)	(316)	(25)

---

the three neighborhoods scored 6 or more, and one-fourth scored 8 or more. There were neighborhood differences, however. High (and it will be recalled that this neighborhood is also highest of the three in juvenile delinquency) stood out, with more than half scoring 6 or more and 28 per cent scoring 8 or more. In contrast, 42 and 38 per cent, respectively, in Low and Medium scored 6 or more, and less than one-fourth scored 8 or more. At the low ends of the distributions, there were fewer boys in High than in the other two neighborhoods who scored 3 or less. The disproportionate numbers of boys scoring 8 or more and 3 or less in High, however, came mainly from the adjustment classes,[10] as may be seen from the lower portion of Table IV-2.

[10] As explained in an earlier note, these are special classes for children with reading problems and/or other behavior problems; they do not include children classified as mentally retarded. It is, perhaps, noteworthy that almost one-fourth of the boys in High are assigned to such classes. There are no comparable classes in the other two neighborhoods.

We have referred to the outlook represented by these items as one that is favorable to delinquency. We have not meant to imply that children who absorb such a philosophy will necessarily become delinquents or that those who do not will not. Delinquency in the legal sense has many causes, ranging from the thoughtless impulsiveness of the moment to profound personality disturbances and including youngsters who are simply carried along—whether innocently, by threat, by a process of what has been described as group intoxication, or by simple conformity —in the delinquent activities of others. Similarly, there are many constraints, ranging from the absence of opportunity through timidity to the influence of associates. What we meant was quite literally that such an outlook is one that could be expected to be favorable to delinquency; whether it materializes in action would have to depend on other factors.[11]

It may be of some interest to examine the sixteen items in the light of what Albert Cohen has described as the delinquent subculture. Cohen describes the normative strands of this subculture as nonutilitarian (e.g., "There is no accounting in rational and utilitarian terms for the effort expended and the danger run in stealing things which are often discarded, destroyed or casually given away."); malicious (". . . an enjoyment in the discomfiture of others, a delight in the defiance of taboos itself"); negativistic ("The delinquent's conduct is right by the standards

---

[11] Even so, there is some evidence that children who share this philosophy are more likely than others to get into trouble. The high scores of the boys in the adjustment classes are, of course, germane. In a doctoral thesis in the Sociology Department at New York University, Janet Leckie reports the results of administering fourteen of the twenty-two items we have been discussing (counting the components of the compound items as separate items) to 292 girls in a vocational high school in New York City. The drug items and the two value items were not included. Forty of the girls were classified as "trouble-makers" by school authorities, and twenty as "outstanding" children. Three-fifths of the "trouble-makers" were in the high-scoring third of the children as compared to 15 per cent of the "outstanding" girls; and about one-fifth of the "trouble-makers" were in the low-scoring third, as compared to more than half the "outstanding" girls. More than half the "trouble-makers" scored 6 or more on the fourteen items, as compared to only one of the "outstanding" girls. Considering that the population on which Miss Leckie tried these items out is so different from the population in which they were selected (older and female as compared to younger and male), this indication that the items measure something that is likely to be reflected in behavior seems remarkable. We had interpreted the set of items as yielding an index of "delinquency orientation" before we asked Miss Leckie to include it in her battery of measures.

of his subculture *because* it is wrong by the norms of the larger culture"); concerned with the pleasures of the moment rather than with long-range goals; versatile in the variety of outlets for the expression of these attitudes; and intolerant of restraints except for those informal pressures emanating from the group itself.[12] With the exception of versatility (and this possibly because we did not have the foresight to include a variety of such items in the questionnaire), all of these strands seem to be reflected in our sixteen items. One questionnaire item (F 33) that is missing from our set of sixteen items, perhaps because it does not include the qualification of conformity to the group, does express the value placed on freedom from restraint; but it is found in two of the four clusters from which the sixteen items were selected. The one major aspect of our items that is not explicitly included by Cohen in his description of the delinquent subculture but is not unrelated to Cohen's discussion of the dynamic roots of this subculture is the sense of pessimism, futility, and of the lack of real concern of human beings for one another's welfare.

Despite the evidence of the scores on the items to the effect that the outlook we have been discussing is most pervasive in the high-delinquency, high-drug-use, high-poverty, and otherwise highly deprived neighborhood and that it is quite pervasive in the other two relatively high-delinquency neighborhoods, it may be that we have been making too much of these sixteen items. We do not know, for instance, whether these items would also be linked in better-off sections of the city or, for that matter, whether the implied philosophy of life might not be a major current of the entirety of our civilization. Lacking this essential background, it could be a mistake to place much emphasis on what is implied by these items as something related to the causal context of the vulnerability of neighborhoods to the spread of drug use. Our major interest, therefore, is in the balance of the four clusters to which these sixteen items were common, and on the differentiations implied by the differences in the clusters.

THE LOW-DRUG-USE NEIGHBORHOOD

In the neighborhood with relatively low drug rates, the most striking features of the delinquency-orientation cluster are that the two items involving claims of personal contact with heroin use (G 48: "Saw someone take heroin" and G 49: "Know at least one user") are tied

12 A. Cohen, *Delinquent Boys* (Glencoe, Ill.: The Free Press, 1955), pp. 26–28.

to the delinquent outlook and that this outlook is associated with correct answers and few "don't know" responses to information items. This sort of clustering is not found in the other neighborhoods. One may say that, in this neighborhood, the youngsters who tend to develop a philosophy of life favorable to delinquency are also those who tend to "know the score" with regard to narcotics. Specifically, we find the following items in the cluster:

    G 16–30: Fewer than seven "don't knows" on fifteen information items

    G 19: Most addicts did not start before they were thirteen

    G 20, 28: Right on both legal items

    G 22: Heroin costs more than one dollar a shot

    G 26: Addicts are not permanently cured

    G 27: It is not true that more girls than boys use heroin

Closely related to the two personal-contact items and also included in the cluster is Item G 47 ("Most information about drugs picked up on streets"). This item is, however, common to three of the four clusters we are discussing. The cluster also includes several attitude items related to drugs:

    G 2: Should not tell authorities about user

    G 6: Smoking marijuana is not the worst thing I can think of

    G 7: Taking heroin is sometimes excusable

    G 9: Users do not have fewer brains

    G 11: Users are not more poorly dressed

In addition, there is an item that fits with the basic delinquent-philosophy cluster, one reflecting an attitude of social alienation, F 10 ("You are a fool to believe what most people tell you"). Finally, we find what, in the context of the rest of the cluster, we can regard only as "whistling in the dark," Item F 1 ("I'm a very lucky person").[13] Items G 2, G 6, G 7, and G 11 are also found in one of the two delinquency-orientation clusters in High, and Item G 9 in the corresponding cluster in Medium.

One may be inclined to assume a causal connection between direct

[13] Interestingly enough, apart from considerations of clustering, this item received the highest proportion of assent in the most deprived of the three neighborhoods. About 74 per cent of the Negro boys (both in the regular and in the adjustment classes) agreed with this item, and the over-all percentage of agreement in High was 70. In Low, about 58 per cent of the boys agreed with the item.

personal contact with heroin use, on the one hand, and correct information and favorable attitudes toward narcotics, on the other. We must then ask, why did we not find a similar constellation in the other two neighborhoods?

Actually, we did find a similar cluster in Medium,[14] but this cluster was not tied to the delinquency-orientation cluster, and it does not include the three drug-related items of that cluster, probably the most favorable to drug use in the questionnaire. We also find a cluster of contact and information items in High,[15] but this is also not tied to the delinquency-orientation cluster, and it is virtually devoid of items favorable to drug use. The one exception is Item G 6, which denies that "just the idea of smoking marijuana is the worst thing I can think of"—an attitude which the authors of this volume share.

Thus, there seems to be ample ground for assuming that contact with drug use[16] is tied to relevant information. The question, however, is why contact and information are tied to favorable attitudes toward drug use and generally to a delinquent philosophy of life in Low—and not so in the other two neighborhoods. The answer seems to lie in the very issue of the extensiveness of drug use. It seems reasonable to assume that in Low the only individuals likely to be exposed are the delinquents and potential delinquents, i.e., those who share the delinquent philosophy. In the other neighborhoods, by contrast, exposure is so much more common and the availability of information so much greater that contact and information have no other significance.

It is consistent with this interpretation that considerably fewer of the boys in Low claim to know a heroin-user—17 per cent, as compared to 32 per cent in Medium and 45 per cent in High. Similarly,

[14] This cluster includes items G 6, G 7, G 11, G 16–30, G 19, G 20, G 28, G 22, G 26, G 27, G 47, G 48, and G 49. In addition, it includes two more information items, G 16 ("Heroin not from same plant as marijuana") and G 29 ("Marijuana costs less than heroin"). The rest of this cluster consists of F 17 ("Police practice racial discrimination"), F 30 ("Values being popular and respected"), and F 31 ("Values ease and comfort"). Still another distinguishable cluster consists of the same drug-related items, except for G 7 and G 11, and three more information items, G 18, G 23, and G 30; there are no other items in this cluster.

[15] This cluster consists of items G 6, G 16, G 16–30, G 18, G 19, G 20, G 28, G 21, G 22, G 23, G 27, G 29, G 47, G 48, and G 49.

[16] The very fact that items G 48 and G 49 cohere with information suggests that the answers to these items are apt to have at least some truth. We shall, however, return to the issue of how seriously to take the answers to items G 48 and G 49 in Appendix H.

considerably fewer claim to have seen someone taking heroin—13 per cent, as compared to 24 and 39 per cent.

The picture with regard to accurate information is not so clear. Low is not consistently the neighborhood with the lowest percentage of correct answers. The issue is, however, confused by the fact that the subgroup with by far the lowest percentage of correct answers, and consistently so on almost every information item, consists of the boys in the adjustment classes in High. One may guess that these boys are generally poor learners, not merely at school. At any rate, the effect is that High does poorly, rather than that Low does relatively well on the information items.

We based a score on the six information items that clustered together in all three neighborhoods, not including the "don't know" index, but scoring G 20 and G 28 separately. Fifty-seven per cent of the boys failed to give correct responses to four or more of the six items. The corresponding figures for High and Low were 61 and 62 per cent, respectively; for Medium, it was 43 per cent.

These findings are not inconsistent with the hypothesis that the kind of information represented by these items goes with exposure. The cluster analyses were carried out separately for each neighborhood. This means that the relationship between exposure and correct information were studied by the neighborhoods' own standards of information. The level of accurate information in High seems to be quite low— mainly, as we have noted, because of the adjustment-class boys—but the relationship nevertheless appears. The level of accurate information in Low is equally low, and the relationship also appears. The level of accurate information is considerably higher in Medium, and the relationship again appears.

To summarize: Certain kinds of information go along with exposure to the use of narcotics. In Low, such exposure tends to be limited to the boys whose outlook on life is favorable to delinquency. Consequently, the exposure and information items are drawn into the delinquency-orientation cluster. Attitudes favorable to drug use may be interpreted as an expression of the delinquent philosophy of life.

THE MEDIUM-DRUG-USE NEIGHBORHOOD

In Medium, we found eleven items added to the common delinquency-orientation cluster. One rejected an additional middle-class standard of deportment (F 3: "Loudness around the house is OK"). One expressed self-confidence (F 15: "Nothing can stop me"); this may be regarded as an aggressive counterpart of the "I-am-a-lucky-person" item found in the Low constellation. Two are concerned with values—one (F 33) accepting the value of freedom to do what one wants and not be held back by other people, the other (F 34) rejecting the value of being of service to people regardless of credit.

Seven of the items are related to narcotics. One (G 23) involves misinformation to the effect that it is legal to *give* heroin or marijuana as long as one does not sell it. Three of the items involve rejection of arguments against taking heroin:

G 32: Hurting people close to you is not a main reason
G 36: Not having real friends is not a main reason
G 39: Becoming too different is not a main reason

Three of the items involve the image of the heroin-user:

G 9: Users do not have fewer brains
G 12: Users do not get fewer kicks out of life
G 13: Users do not have fewer close friends they can trust

If the general delinquent-philosophy cluster seems to express pessimism and futility, the boys in this neighborhood who share the outlook seem to be adding, "But I won't let it get me down." The orienting combination of ideas is explicitly antisocial and aggressively self-sufficient. One sees this trend in the non-drug-related items (F 15, F33, and F 34), as well as in the rejection of the particular reasons against drug use that are tied to the cluster.

To be sure, G 36 may follow from G 13; if one perceives heroin-users as not having fewer close friends they can trust, then one cannot consistently accept the lack of real friends as a major reason for not taking heroin. We may note, however, that a high valuation on close friendship (Item F 27) is not included in the cluster and wonder why G 13 and G 36 should be salient enough to these boys to get into the cluster at all. We may note, further, that G 13 does not get into the delinquency-orientation clusters of the other neighborhoods, wonder why this neighborhood should differ in this respect, and note that G 36 gets into one of the high delinquency-orientation clusters without the support of G 13. We may note, finally, that another construction can be placed on the conjunction of the two items which is more consistent with the cluster as a whole: people in general do not have close friends they can trust; users can, therefore, be no worse off than anyone else, and the argument of loss of friends can hardly be taken seriously as a deterrent to anything. By this construction, the two items get into the cluster precisely because of the centrality of the issue that one must stand on his own and do whatever will get him what he wants. If this interpretation is correct, it seems reasonable to interpret all six of the drug-related items as an expression of this central outlook, rather than as an expression of favorableness toward drug use per se.

Of special interest is the remaining drug-related item in the cluster, G 23. This is the neighborhood that makes the best record on the information items. The appearance of one item of misinformation in the cluster—and on so important a point—comes, therefore, as a surprise. We have already noted, however, that, at best, such items can be said to measure information in only a limited sense—that of being sufficiently *au courant* for the correct alternative to seem the most reasonable—and that the responses may reflect attitudes rather than information per se, a situation that would be evidenced by a tie-in of an information item with attitude items. This is such an instance, and it seems likely that the item does reflect an attitude.

Consider the precise wording of the item: "It is against the law to sell heroin or marijuana, but they can't touch a person if he gives it away." Who are "they?" The police, the defenders of law and order, the representatives of the mores of the larger society, the out-group? The item as a whole suggests that there is a loophole in the law, a breach in the defenses of the detested out-group, a way of beating *them*. To one who holds to an aggressively delinquent philosophy of life, the contemplation of such a breach may be so delightful as to make it difficult to resist; the wish, we suggest, is the father of the response. There are many loopholes in the law, and finding them must be an ideal expression of a delinquent philosophy, a violation of the spirit of the law with a minimum of risk, a malicious thumbing of one's nose at respectability with an assured get-away. Loopholes do exist; why not this one?

To summarize: The boys in the medium-drug-use neighborhood who share in the delinquent orientation do so with an emphasis on rugged individualism, on the principle that one must stand on his own and do whatever will get him what he wants, regardless of whom it may hurt. In its generic and its specific aspects, the delinquent philosophy carries with it certain attitudes favorable to drug use.

THE HIGH-DRUG-USE NEIGHBORHOOD

We have spoken of two delinquency-orientation clusters in the neighborhood with the highest drug rates. In addition to the sixteen items of the general delinquency-orientation cluster, the two clusters have five items in common—or a total of twenty-one of the thirty-six items involved. Moreover, ten of the fifteen items not common to the two clusters fall in one of them, so that the second cluster has only five of its twenty-six items unique to itself. This raises the question of why we bother to distinguish the second cluster at all. Or, alternatively, why not content ourselves with one twenty-one–item cluster, rejecting the other items as behaving in a statistically suspicious manner?

To explain the issue, we must refer to our procedures in discovering clusters. As is explained in Appendix E, we began by isolating what we call "prime clusters," adding additional items to identify what we have been referring to as clusters. For the distinction between prime clusters and the more inclusive clusters and for the rationale of the following statement, the reader is referred to Appendix E. For present purposes, it may be sufficient to assert that the essential character of a cluster is most clearly defined by scrutinizing the items in the prime cluster.[17]

Each of the prime clusters in the two clusters we are discussing consists of six items,[h] five of them members of the general delinquency-orientation cluster. The complete cluster developed around each of the prime clusters, of course, includes the remaining items of the general delinquency-orientation cluster.

The items of the first prime cluster are:

F 4: Not much chance for a better world
F 6: Police open to bribes
F 22: Most people better off not born
F 24: Parents always looking to nag
F 25: Everybody really out for himself; nobody cares
F 18: Live for today rather than try to plan for tomorrow

The last item is not in the general delinquency-orientation cluster, nor is it in the second cluster.

The items of the second prime cluster are:

F 9: Shouldn't always treat girls nice
F 7, 13, 26: Reject middle-class rules of deportment
F 17: Police pick on people
F 19: Police practice racial discrimination
F 23: Police favor their friends
F 10: Fool to believe what most people try to tell you

[17] We have not referred to the prime clusters in the preceding presentation because they did not seem to tell any different story than was obtainable in greater detail from a consideration of the more inclusive clusters. In the present instance, the consideration of the prime clusters does make a difference.

Again, the last item in the list is not in the delinquency-orientation cluster; it is, however, a member of the first cluster. This item also happens to be the weakest member of the second prime cluster.[1]

It is clear that the first prime cluster has picked up all of the items of the general delinquency-orientation cluster emphasizing the mood of pessimism, social isolation, and futility and, so to speak, underscored the selection by adding another emphasizing the undependability of the future. The second prime cluster, on the other hand, has picked up the items reflecting negative attitudes toward the representatives of social authority and the rejection of accepted standards of deportment in middle-class society. The police item in the first speaks of the corruption and selfishness of human beings; the police items in the second and perhaps the last item, too, speak of their meanness. The first prime cluster spells hopelessness; the second, negativism.

Even so, we might not be inclined to make much of these differences were it not for additional differences in the augmented clusters and for the bearing on attitudes toward narcotics.

We have already mentioned that there are ten items in the first cluster which are absent from the other. One of these, already mentioned, is in the prime cluster. The other nine are all concerned with the arguments against using heroin. These are:

G 31–41: Accepts less than nine of the eleven arguments[18]

G 31: Becoming a slave to heroin not a main reason

G 33: Having to continue even when kick wears off not a main reason

G 34: Becoming a helpless tool of pushers not a main reason

G 36: Not having real friends not a main reason

G 37: Losing chances of steady income not a main reason

G 38: Never being safe from the police not a main reason

G 39: Becoming too different not a main reason

G 40: Losing ability to work well and be good at sports not a main reason

Another argument (G 32: "Hurting people close to you not a main reason") also appears in this cluster, but it also appears in the second cluster. The only argument items not appearing in the cluster are G 35 ("People will look down on you") and one that was not included in

[18] Approximately half (47 per cent) of the boys in the three neighborhoods combined accepted nine or more of the arguments as "one of the main reasons that would keep you from taking heroin."

the cluster analysis.[j] This does not mean that the latter are accepted, but merely that their acceptance or rejection does not tend to hang together with the other items in the cluster.

By contrast, the five items appearing in the second cluster but not in the first are:

F 3: Loudness around the house is OK

F 33: Values freedom from restraint

F 6: Smoking marijuana is not worst thing I can think of

G 7: Taking heroin is sometimes excusable

G 11: Heroin-users are not more poorly dressed

The first two of the latter five items carry on the theme of the prime cluster, and the three drug-related attitudes are simply consistent with the general outlook expressed. That is, as in the delinquency-orientation clusters in the other two neighborhoods, we have no indication of anything here that would move youngsters toward narcotics other than the convention-challenging aspect of the delinquency orientation itself.

In the case of the first cluster, however, we do seem to have something quite different. The connection between the delinquency-orientation complex and attitudes favorable to experimentation with drugs cannot be interpreted simply in terms of reckless bravado in the face of a hostile world. Here, we come much closer to an attitude of surrender, a mood of "What difference does it make anyhow?" When one is in this mood, hardly any argument against heroin use is convincing, and most tend to be rejected outright. The point of greatest danger seems to be right here. When one is in a mood of defiance of convention, the sheer act of taking the drug may give some measure of gratification, but not inherently more so than other convention-defying activities; the psychopharmacological effects of the drug are irrelevant. When one is in a mood of hopelessness and futility, however, the psychopharmacological effects of the drug are directly relevant; they provide a chemical balm to a sorely depressed spirit. It is not surprising, therefore, that the prodrug items of the general delinquency-orientation cluster are more closely linked to the first cluster than to the second.

Thus, Item G 1 ("Drug use is a private affair") has an average profile correlation of .44 with the items of the first prime cluster, as compared to one of .40 with the items of the second, and an average tetrachoric of .17, as compared to .14. Items G 3, 4, 5 (agreeing with at least one: "Heroin not so harmful as people say"; "Taking a little heroin once in a while doesn't hurt"; "Smoking marijuana at parties

OK) has an average profile correlation with the first prime cluster of .67, as compared to .58 with the second; and an average tetrachoric of .31 with the first, as compared to one of .21 with the second. Item G 8 ("Using heroin is OK if you make sure you don't get hooked") has corresponding profile correlations of .54, as against .42, and tetrachorics of .18, as against .07.

To complete the record on the two clusters we have been discussing, the three items that have not yet been mentioned which are not in the general delinquency-orientation cluster but which are common to the two clusters[19] are:

F 5: I can get away with things

G 2: Shouldn't tell authorities about user

G 47: Information about drugs from streets

The only noteworthy point about these items is the contrast between F 5 and the "I'm a very lucky person" of the low-drug-use neighborhood delinquency-orientation cluster and the "Nothing can stop me" of the medium-drug-use neighborhood cluster. Like its counterparts in the other two neighborhoods, F 5 rings the one optimistic note of the two delinquency-orientation clusters; but, unlike its other-neighborhood counterparts, F 5 is focused much more on the illicit.

Before closing this review of the delinquency-orientation clusters in the high-drug-use neighborhood, we must note still a third cluster that is related to the first two.[k]

The third cluster includes thirty-nine items, thirty of which are found in the first or second clusters. It includes twelve of the sixteen items of the general delinquency-orientation cluster. Except for the four items missing from the latter group, it includes all of the first cluster and, with one additional exception, all of the second cluster. Two of the missing items from the general delinquency-orientation cluster are in the first and second prime clusters—one in each, of course. These items are, from the first prime cluster, F 22 ("Most people better off not born") and, from the second prime cluster, F 9 ("Shouldn't always treat girls nice"). The other two missing items are the compound item F 2, 16, 21 ("Unfavorable to parents") and F 29 ("Values power"). The fifth item present in the second cluster but not in the third is one of the second-prime-cluster items, F 10 ("Fool to believe what most people try to tell you").

[19] The two other such items are F 10 and G 32.

There are six items in the third prime cluster, all drug-related. These items are:

G 3, 4, 5: Agree with at least one of following: Heroin not so harmful as people say; taking a little heroin once in a while doesn't hurt; smoking marijuana at parties is OK

G 6: Smoking marijuana is not the worst thing I can think of

G 7: Taking heroin is sometimes excusable

G 8: Heroin OK if you don't get hooked

G 11: Users not more poorly dressed

G 47: Information from streets

The nine items in the cluster which are not present in either the first or the second are:

G 9: Users don't have fewer brains

G 12: Users don't have fewer kicks out of life

G 13: Users don't have fewer friends

G 16–30: "Don't know" to fewer than seven of fifteen information items

G 26: Addicts not permanently cured

G 29: Marijuana less costly than heroin

G 48: Saw someone taking heroin

G 49: Knows one or more heroin-users

This cluster, then, is centered on narcotics. It draws in many of the items of the delinquent philosophy of life, both in its general form and in its specific varieties, but some of the themes characteristic of this philosophy are muted. One may say that there is a lack of full conviction about the delinquent outlook. What seems to have happened is that the drug-using subculture has been absorbed and, along with it, aspects of the associated delinquent outlook. Attitudes toward narcotics do not flow from the delinquent orientation; the philosophy of delinquency is rather a by-product of the absorption of attitudes toward narcotics.

As might be expected from the nature of the cluster, the items in the general delinquency cluster that involve drugs are more closely related to the third than to the first two prime clusters, the rejection of arguments more closely related to the third than to the first, the narcotics-related items of the second cluster more closely related to the third than to the second prime cluster.[1] In brief, at every point where a comparison can be made, the drug-involved items are more closely related to the third prime cluster than to the first or second.

To summarize: In the neighborhood with the highest drug rates and also with the highest delinquency rates, we have found two strands in the delinquent orientation—one giving emphasis to the negativistic aspects, one to the sense of futility. Both draw in attitudes that are favorable to the use of narcotics, but the second in a more dangerous form; not only is the second associated with the rejection of reasons that might serve as deterrents, but its basic mood is one that can be relieved by the psychopharmacological effects of narcotics. In addition, we have found evidence of a third strand of the neighborhood culture, one that absorbs the drug-using subculture and much of the delinquency orientation that goes with it. The three strands are interwoven.

STATISTICAL FOOTNOTES

[a] An explanation of tetrachoric correlation is given in Appendix C. along with a general explanation of the meaning of correlation coefficients. Briefly, the tetrachoric correlation is computed from dichotomous (two-valued) variables and provides an estimate of what the correlation would be if it were computed from corresponding many-valued variables, the distributions of which have been normalized.

[b] The formula for computing tetrachoric correlations is very involved, so we used an approximation procedure which is sufficiently accurate for most purposes if the dichotomies do not break more extremely than 80–20; for more extreme breaks, the procedure becomes increasingly inaccurate. In some instances, we formed compound items. In some instances, however, there were no other items with which such items could be sensibly combined. One such item (see Note j) was G 41 (i.e., Item 41 in the Form-G questionnaire; the questionnaires are reprinted in full in Appendix D), which dealt with one reason for not taking heroin. A number of other items were also omitted from the cluster analysis on the same grounds. Three were concerned with the image of the heroin-user: G 10 ("Nonusers more fun to be with"), with percentages of 83, 91, and 92 in Low, Medium, and High, respectively; G 14 ("Nonusers get along better on their own"), with percentages of 80, 92, and 83; and G 15 ("Nonusers better able to take care of themselves"), with percentages of 84, 95, and 86. One was concerned with exposure to heroin: G 50 ("Had a chance to take heroin"), with percentages of 6, 10, and 10. In addition, there were F 20 ("Sometimes think people like me hardly good for anything"), with percentages of 17, 21, and 23; and F 35 ("Value job one can count on and knowing one can always get along"), with percentages of 89, 92, and 93.

[c] Strictly speaking, the idea of statistical significance is not relevant. When computing correlations in a random sample of cases from a larger population, the sample may differ from the population, and the correlations may, as a

consequence, differ from the correlations that would have been obtained if the entire population had been utilized. Because of certain mathematical relationships involved, it is possible to estimate the range within which the "true" correlation probably lies with any specified odds—generally taken as 19 to 1. If this range does not include zero, the correlation is said to be "significantly greater than zero," or simply "significant." In the present instance, however, we are dealing with virtually total (i.e., total except for absentees) specified populations at a specified time, not random samples of much larger populations. It is sometimes convenient, however, to provide a crude guide to how large a correlation to take seriously by pretending that the population studied is a random sample of a fictitious, much larger population and applying the test of statistical significance to the obtained correlation. It is in this sense that we speak of statistical significance above. Although tests of the statistical significance of correlation only take into direct account the possibilities of sampling errors, they take indirectly into account random measurement errors (e.g., accidental misreading or misinterpretation of items because of a momentary set or accidental markings of unintended answers) as well. This follows from the fact noted elsewhere that, the greater the measurement errors, the more difficult it is to obtain statistically significant correlations.

d The smaller the role that chance plays in determining responses to an item (whether the chance factors are related to ambiguities of wording—it being a matter of chance which meaning the respondent happens to seize upon on a particular occasion—or whether the chance factors enter in a variety of other ways), the more reliable the item is said to be. The measurement of reliability hinges on the fact that substantial correlations are not likely by pure chance. In the present instance, we speak of minimum estimates because we have not met the optimal conditions for measuring item reliabilities. A final point to be made in the matter of item reliabilities is that the correlations of correlational profiles described in the following paragraph are remarkably high. To those familiar with psychometric theory, it will be clear that item communalities must also be very high, and it will be recalled that communalities also provide minimum bound estimates of reliability.

e The cluster analyses described below.

f See Appendix E for the rationale of this procedure. In the preceding chapter, we referred to the pattern of correlations involving a variable in a reversed application. There we argued that the percentage of the population living at a new address cannot have the same meaning in the three boroughs. The patterns of correlations between this and the other variables were too radically different from borough to borough for the variable to be measuring the same thing. Here we are asserting that different variables with similar correlational patterns probably have related meanings.

g Three of these are actually compound items, each, as it happens, being composed of three items. Thus, for the purpose of computing tetrachoric correlations, items 2, 16, and 21 of the first part of the questionnaire were combined into a single item. This item was scored 1 if the respondent gave an answer unfavorable to parents on one or more of the three component items; it was scored zero if the respondent answered favorably to parents on all three items. Similarly, three items involving issues of what we have labeled middle-class manners—items 7, 13, and 16 of the first part of the questionnaire—are scored in the same way for rejection of middle-class rules of deportment.

Finally, items 3, 4, and 5 of the second part of the questionnaire were combined and scored in the same way for favorableness to drugs. These combinations were made in order to avoid extreme marginal breaks. See Note b, *supra*.

The average of the profile correlations of the sixteen items with one another was .56 in both Low and High, and it was .60 in Medium. The average tetrachoric correlation was also the same in Low and High, .23, and in Medium it was .26.

[h] The average profile correlation of the items in the first prime cluster with one another is .67, and the average of the tetrachoric correlations of these items with one another is .29. The corresponding averages for the second cluster are .71 and .32. The average profile correlation of the items in the first with the items in the second is .54, and the average of the tetrachoric correlations of the items in the first with those of the second is .18. Each of these prime clusters is more closely related to the other, by the test either of the average-profile correlation or the average tetrachoric correlation, than it is to any other cluster.

[i] Its average profile correlation with the other items in the prime cluster is .63; the item with the next lowest average profile correlation is F 17, with an average of .70. Its average tetrachoric correlation with the other items in the prime cluster is .24; the item with the next lowest average tetrachoric correlation is F 19, with an average of .31. Without this item, the average profile correlation of the remaining items with one another is .73, and the average tetrachoric is .34.

[j] The item is G 41 ("Health will be ruined and life will be full of worries and troubles"); the percentages of agreement that this is one of the main reasons for not taking heroin are 87 in Low, 88 in Medium, and 91 in High.

[k] The average profile correlation of the items in the first prime cluster with those in the third is .46, and the average tetrachoric is .12. The corresponding figures for the second and third are .48 and .14. The average profile correlation of the items in the third prime cluster with one another is .71, and the average tetrachoric is .30.

[l] The statistics on the three items in the general delinquency cluster are, giving in each case the average profile correlation first and then the average tetrachoric correlation with the items of the third prime cluster: G 1—.52, .53; G 3, 4, 5—.74, .36; G 8—.72, .38. These may be compared to the figures already cited for the first and second clusters. On the arguments, the third cluster draws in item G 35, with statistics of .60, .13; for the arguments in the first cluster, the comparisons, giving the statistics for the correlations with the third prime cluster first, are: G 31–41—.63, .18 versus .47, .07; G 31—.48, .10 versus .47, .10; G 32—.65, .12 versus .57, .11; G 33—.50, .04 versus .40, .00; G 34—.54, .12 versus .43, .10; G 36—.68, .21 versus .49, .09; G 37—.58, .12 versus .49, .06; G 38—.65, .19 versus .43, .01; G 39—.60, .14 versus .45, .04; G 40—.65, .22 versus .47, .07. On the drug-involved items of the second cluster: G 2—.56, .21 versus .49, .16; G 6—.72, .28 versus .53, .19; G 7—.69, .30 versus .54, .17; G 11—.68, .24 versus .41, .09; G 47—.68, .26 versus .41, .09.

V

The Individual Environment

Thus far, we have considered only the differentiating characteristics of regions within which drug use thrives. In these very environments, however, there are individuals who succumb and others who do not. We turn now to the question of whether we can find differences in the specific environmental backgrounds of these two classes that might help to explain why some do and some do not.

Our first look at the personal environment of the user-to-be is at certain gross characteristics of his personal history, his family, and his peer associations and is, by design, panoramic. A more sharply focused, minute investigation of the family background of individuals who become addicted as these backgrounds relate to their personalities and psychopathologies will be found in chapters X and XI. At the moment, we wish to explore the possibility that the personal experiences of the users included some obvious major deprivations that were either unique for them as a group or which they shared wth the nonusing delinquents but not with those youths in the same neighborhoods who became neither users nor otherwise delinquent.

The study which was designed to explore these questions compared the personal backgrounds of four groups of boys in the age range from sixteen through twenty (the median age was nineteen) from neighborhoods similar in delinquency and drug rates. The study dealt with fifty-nine institutionalized drug-users who were not otherwise delinquent

TABLE V-1   *Comparative Data on Four Groups*

of Subjects

	PERCENTAGE			
	NONUSERS		USERS	
	NON-DELIN-QUENTS	DELIN-QUENTS	NON-DELIN-QUENTS	DELIN-QUENTS
1. Ethnic group				
Negroes	42	40	41	39
Puerto Ricans	29	30	32	29
Whites	29	30	27	32
TOTAL	100	100	100	100
2. Age				
19–22 years old as of April 1, 1953	31	38	59	51
3. Neighborhood characteristics at "critical age"*				
Living in health areas where drug rate was forty or more per 1,000 boys aged 16–20	63	18	44	41
Living in health areas where delinquency rate was fifty or more per 1,000 adolescents	67	52	54	51
Living in census tracts where median family income was less than $2,000 in 1949	60	26	49	34
Living in census tracts where median education was less than eight years	33	14	25	17
(Number of cases)	(52)	(50)	(59)	(41)
(Number from Riverside)		(0)	(0)	(38)	(12)
(Number from state training school)		(0)	(50)	(21)	(29)

* "Critical age" was defined as that at which regular drug use started in the case of users, as age sixteen in the case of nonusers (see text). Drug rates were computed as explained in Chapter II. Delinquency rates were taken from statistics compiled by the New York City Youth Board for the period March 1, 1951, to March 1, 1952; a given individual was counted only once. The drug-rate difference is significant by the chi-square test at the .05 level, as is the difference in neighborhood income. The other differences do not meet this criterion of significance. When the neighborhood characteristics are taken as scores for the individuals who live in them, the average health-area delinquency rate was 54.8 for the controls and 48.8 for the

before they started to use drugs (we shall refer to them as "non-delinquent users"); forty-one institutionalized users who *were* otherwise delinquent prior to onset of drug use (to be referred to as "delinquent users"); fifty institutionalized delinquents who were not heroin-users ("delinquent nonusers"); and fifty-two controls ("non-delinquent nonusers") from the same types of neighborhood.

These four groups of boys were not selected with an eye to any characteristics other than those specified above, except that we tried to get, for each group, equal proportions of white, Negro, and Puerto Rican boys who came from health areas that are comparable with respect to the incidence of drug use and who were of the same age levels.[a] Some comparative data on the four groups are given in Table V-1.

In the original design, we had planned to take fifty cases from Riverside Hospital, naïvely assuming that these would all have been nondelinquents prior to their involvement with drugs; fifty cases of users from the New York State Vocational Institution at West Coxsackie, N. Y., again naïvely assuming that these would all have had histories of delinquency; fifty cases of nonusers from the training school at West Coxsackie, again (although this time excusably so) naïvely assuming that users who have undergone arrest, trial, processing at a reception center, and final allocation to the institution where we contacted them would have been detected as such before we picked them; and fifty control cases with no history of either drug use or any other kind of delinquency.

As might be expected from our use of the term "naïvely" and as is evident from Table 1, these plans went astray. The departures from our expectations were, however, instructive.

We first interviewed the boys of the three deviant groups in 1953–1954. The control group was interviewed in the following year. We picked the boys in the control group by the following procedure: We first selected five junior high schools, one of them a parochial school, in areas of relatively high drug use. We then picked the graduating classes that, so we thought, would place the graduates in the age range

other three groups combined, a difference that is significant at the .01 level. The age differences between the two user groups and between the two nonuser groups are both significant at the .05 level. Between the combined user and nonuser groups, the difference is significant at .01. The controls are, on the average, the youngest, and the nonusing delinquents are also, on the average, younger than the boys in either of the user groups. The delinquent users are, on the average, younger than the nondelinquent users.

characteristic of our first three groups. From the lists of the graduates, we then selected a large random sample of boys. We checked with the school authorities for any history of having been seriously suspected of chronic antisocial behavior (e.g., fighting, truancy), drug use, or other forms of delinquency, eliminating the boys with any such history. The remaining individuals were cleared through the Social Service Exchange to determine whether they or their families were known to any of the social agencies in the city. If they were, we checked with these agencies for any history of the boys' having been suspected of behavior that would disqualify them from the control group. We also checked with the Juvenile Court. In some instances, the social agencies to which the families were known refused to cooperate and, in such cases, the boys were automatically disqualified.[b]

Letters were sent to all the boys whose names were cleared before we had completed the intended number of interviews. The letters explained that we were studying the experiences of boys in neighborhoods where many of the boys get into trouble with the law; that we had found out that the recipient had never been in such trouble (even so, we received a number of phone calls from anxious parents); that we would like to talk to him; and that we would give him $5 for his time.[c] Eventually, ninety of the 425 boys answered the letter. Of these, twenty-six did not keep their appointments. Of the remainder who were interviewed, five were eliminated because the interviews gave rise to suspicions of delinquency or drug use (one of these, for stealing $5 from the interviewer) and seven because they were clearly under age. This left us with the fifty-two control cases.

It is quite clear that we had grossly underestimated the degree of educational retardation among the delinquents and drug-users. The differences in age between the controls and the other groups would be even more marked if we had included the seven cases eliminated because of age.

It is also evident from Table V-1 that a history of delinquency prior to drug use is not nearly so determinative as we had supposed of whether a case will be found at Riverside Hospital or in a state reform school, although the difference ran in the expected direction. More than a fourth of our final sample of delinquent users turned up at Riverside, and over 35 per cent of the final sample of users without previous delinquency turned up at the training school. At any rate, this—to us unexpected—situation accounts for the facts that our sample of delinquent users was smaller than we had planned and that the sample of nondelinquent users was larger. A second sample of fifty Riverside cases, taken a year later and about which more will be said below, was more in line with our initial expectations, including only three with histories of prior delinquency.[d]

Not evident in the table is the fact that four of the first fifty interviewed subjects who were designated as nonusers at the training school asserted that they had been using heroin regularly prior to their incarceration and provided enough circumstantial detail for us to believe them. They were assimilated to our samples of users. Note, incidentally, that, if marked withdrawal symptoms are a criterion of addiction, these boys could not have been addicts; but they were regular users, nonetheless.[1]

The most striking feature of the table is the large difference between the delinquent and nondelinquent nonusers in the percentage of subjects coming from areas of very high drug use. Since we were trying to fill the sample with cases coming from such areas, the very low percentage of such cases in the delinquent nonuser group strongly suggests that, at least at the time of the study, delinquents from such areas were extremely likely to be users. It is, of course, possible that delinquent nonusers from high-use areas were being sent to another institution; but this conjecture is inconsistent with what we know of assignment policies, and we find it impossible to imagine an assignment policy which might result as an incidental consequence in the kind of pattern we found,

---

[1] In retrospect, the only thing surprising about this is that the boys should have admitted to drug use, a point that attests to the confidence aroused by our interviewers. It has been commonly observed that the withdrawal symptoms of young users are rather mild. See, for instance, Gamso and Mason, *op. cit.* They attribute the mildness of the symptoms to "the facts that the Riverside patients are young and rarely have any organic disabilities, that the percentage of pure drugs in a 'fix' is small, that *many of these patients use drugs irregularly, and that the total period of addiction is often short.*" We have italicized one of the clauses in this quotation to emphasize the point that even many of the patients admitted to a "Hospital for Adolescent Drug Addicts" are "addicts" in only a relatively loose sense of the term, especially when the irregularity of usage is taken in conjunction with the mildness of withdrawal symptoms. It has also been asserted that, even among older users, withdrawal symptoms of the intensity that were commonly observed in the early days of Lexington Hospital are quite rare in recent years. A relevant possibility is that the typical addict seeks relief from the tolerance levels he has achieved and/or police vigilance accomplishes the same effect for him at an earlier point in the addiction cycle; see, in this respect, the discussion of types of addicts in Chapter II.

delinquent and nondelinquent users and nondelinquent nonusers all being found in ample supply.

On the other hand, in taking our controls from predesignated schools in high-use areas, we have obviously unduly restricted this sample to boys coming from such areas. One can draw no inference from the plenitude of such cases, since, even in the areas of the highest drug and delinquency rates, the majority of boys have no known history of delinquency or drug use. The restriction does imply that the typical control case labored under a greater neighborhood-environmental handicap than did the typical cases in the other three groups.

We do not know, however, to what extent the control cases may have been atypical of the nondelinquent nonusing boys of the same neighborhoods. To a considerable extent, they were self-selected. They were the boys who were sufficiently attracted by the lure of $5 and/or the nature of the study to return the post card indicating their willingness to participate; they had to have enough self-assurance and willingness to talk about themselves not to be frightened off by the prospect of being interviewed; they had to be willing to earn their reward by giving up the time needed to get to our offices as well as that required by the interview itself; they had to be willing to engage in an individual enterprise that necessitated leaving their familiar haunts to report for the interview; they had to be sufficiently impressed by the university letterhead and/or not be sufficiently repelled by the prospect of talking to "professors"; they had to trust that they would actually get the promised reward; and they had to have enough responsibility to keep their appointments. It would not be in the least surprising if they were, indeed, an atypical group of boys.

The interviews lasted from one and one-half to two and one-half hours. The current status of the institutionalized respondents and their relative inaccessibility made it impractical to attempt more extensive investigation. The time restrictions compelled us to limit the scope of the interview. There was also another compelling reason for such a limitation—we were concerned with past events and situations and necessarily had to rely on recall. It may be taken as axiomatic that, even though we were to credit the respondents with the utmost candor, the further into the past that one seeks to probe, the less reliable is recall as an indicator of historical fact. We therefore limited ourselves to the relatively recent past: "the time just before [you] started using heroin regularly" in the case of the users and the age of sixteen (which we expected and, in fact, found[2] to be the median age at which the users shifted from occasional to regular use) in the case of the nonusers.

The interviews were conducted in a relatively free style from the point of view of the order and exact wording of the questions. The interviewers, however, had before them detailed schedules of questions which they filled out as the interviews proceeded. All the interviewers were highly skilled in intensive interviewing. Most were advanced graduate psychology students or social workers, but the group included several Ph.D.'s in psychology and one in anthropology.

The interviews were designed to explore the nature and extent of drug use, relevant experiences, the home and family situation, education, friendships and leisure-time activities, orientation to the present and the future, attitudes toward drugs, and related matters.

In the cases of the drug-users and delinquents, it was possible to check many of the answers against available records, discussion with case workers or parole officers, and, in all of the Riverside and some of the training school cases, against the results of interviews with a parent. Data from all these sources were entered in the interview schedules. We computed a "reliability score" for each boy in terms of items of objective information that could be checked. A small number of interviews were rejected for an apparent lack of truthfulness or marked inaccuracy on the part of the boy; these cases were, of course, not included in this report. For the remaining cases, in instances of apparent contradiction by other information, we first checked each source for internal consistency on the point at issue and resolved the contradiction in accordance with predetermined principles for assessing credibility on particular points. On the whole, however, we had no reason to question the impression of the interviewers that the boys were sincerely cooperative and trying to report as accurately as they could. When the boys themselves were asked how they felt "about all this questioning," only 5 per cent gave negative reactions, as against 46 per cent who gave decidedly positive responses; the rest gave mixed reactions or something that could not be classified as favorable or unfavorable.

One other point is relevant with respect to the group comparisons reported below. We have already mentioned that the interviews were,

[2] Gamso and Mason, in their report on the first seven years of Riverside Hospital, *op. cit.*, also indicate sixteen as the median age at which regular drug use by the hospital's patients began.

in the main, focused on the time immediately preceding the "critical age" and that this age was defined somewhat differently for users and nonusers. For the users, it was defined as the age when regular drug use began, and, as it turned out, this varied from age thirteen to eighteen. For the nonusers, the "critical age" was arbitrarily set at sixteen (questions were put in terms of the time "just before you were sixteen"), and this was, of course, uniform for all nonusers. The answers of users and nonusers to such questions are, hence, not strictly comparable, since the time reference is not exactly the same.

By the time we interviewed the control group, we had thought of a number of areas that we wanted to explore which were not covered in the original interviews. About thirty new questions were added to the interview schedule, dealing with the boys' reference groups, the constructive activities in which they engaged, and a variety of matters relevant to the transition from adolescence to maturity. In order to provide some comparison data on these questions, we took a second sample of fifty Riverside cases. The interviews with this second set of cases were much briefer than those of the preceding year, dealing in the main with the new questions, although some of the original questions were retained.

We have already mentioned one difference between the first and second Riverside samples, namely, that the second included only three subjects with histories of delinquency before they turned to drugs; for all practical purposes, this group may be regarded as nondelinquent users. Apart from this, the only other statistically significant difference between the two Riverside samples, on items for which we had comparative data, was that somewhat more of the second sample answered a question about things they wanted but could not get in their critical year with some reference to a different way of life (e.g., getting out of the neighborhood). Such differences as were found are consistent with the description of the second sample as essentially one of nondelinquent users.[3]

[3] Thus, 47 per cent of the second Riverside sample, as compared to 38 per cent of the first, came from health areas with drug rates of 40 or more; reference to Table V-1 shows that 44 per cent of the nondelinquent users, as compared to 41 per cent of the delinquent users, came from such areas. Similarly, 49 per cent of the second Riverside sample, as compared to 38 per cent of the first, came from census tracts with median family incomes less than $2,000; again, Table V-1 shows that 49 per cent of the nondelinquent users came from such tracts, as compared to 34 per cent of the delinquent users.

Some Socializing Influences

Both drug use and juvenile delinquency are socially deviant forms of behavior. Their very existence indicates that the standards which society seeks to impose on all have failed to take sufficient hold.

Since the family is the primary agency for the transmission of standards of behavior, we shall compare the four groups of boys in terms of some aspects of their family backgrounds.

We constructed an index of the cohesiveness of the families with which the boys lived longest from their tenth to the critical year. The index was based on the answers to seven questions concerning quarrels among family members and various family practices and customs with respect to the celebration of holidays and birthdays, mealtimes, joint activities, and behavior when someone in the family was ill. Each answer was given a value of zero, 1, or 2—the higher value indicating a more frequent or more marked cohesive practice. For instance, if the family usually had dinner together, the family was credited with two points; if the boy said that the family had dinner together several times a week, the family was credited with one point; and if having dinner together was a rare occurence, the family did not get any points. By adding the total number of points on the seven questions, we got a score for each of our respondents that could serve as a rough indicator of the degree to which the members of his family stuck together.[4]

We assume that, the more cohesive the family, the more effectively it can function in transmitting the basic values of society to the developing child. It is, no doubt, possible that the values which a particular family transmits may themselves be deviant, and, from the point of view of the conservation of the social order, one may be inclined to wish that the families were less effective in such instances. Whatever standards of behavior the family may sponsor, a cohesive family (in the sense implied by our index) gives a child his first taste of the virtues of social discipline, a feeling of the need for human beings to accommodate themselves to one another, a sense of mutuality and "to-

[4] Fuller details concerning the index of family cohesiveness are given in Appendix I. It is, of course, possible to define family cohesiveness in other terms, e.g., a family in which each member normally pursues his own merry way, but which presents a united front against a hostile world in times of trouble may be thought of as a very cohesive family. Alternative definitions of cohesiveness would, however, strike at different issues than the ones we are considering.

getherness." This kind of feeling is, to our minds, the most basic of social values. It is that in terms of which the acceptance of social standards as one's own is a consistent elaboration on one's experience.

There are other grounds on which one may internalize social standards, the most noteworthy being fear; but, in this case, the internalized standards remain essentially ego-alien and a source of frustration, and the self-imposed compliance makes it likely that reactions to frustration will be turned against oneself.[5]

We are not asserting that a child who is deprived of the experience of a cohesive family cannot acquire a sense of mutuality in other ways; we think it less likely that he will. Nor are we asserting that the years from ten to sixteen or thereabouts are the most critical years for such development; actually, there is reason to believe that the foundations are laid much earlier. In going back as far as the tenth year, however, we felt that we were already stretching the reliability of our informants to its utmost limits, and we were willing to assume that what happened in these later years would probably be indicative of what had gone on earlier or that, at the very least, the later experience would reinforce or to some extent negate the effects of the earlier.

Nor are we asserting that family togetherness is necessarily a virtue. We take it for granted, for instance, that excess can transform any virtue into a vice. A harsh discipline that holds the members of a family to common activity against the will of its members can be intensely frustrating and teach lessons that are quite contrary to those we attribute to a cohesive family. We do not think it likely, however, that such a family could earn a high score on our index. We would expect, for instance, that the physical togetherness would be marred by constant bickering, that the family would break up as quickly as the formalities are over, and so on. Moreover, we would expect the interviews to have picked up evidence of the ritualistic, enforced character of such togetherness, and, if they seemed important enough, we would have modified our index accordingly.

At any rate, it should be borne in mind that the comparisons we are making are statistical. We need not assume that the index functioned

[5] It may be a coincidence, but the two user groups have a higher incidence of serious accidents (e.g., a broken leg) than either of the nonuser groups, with the control group reporting the smallest number. More than half the boys in each of the user groups reported that they had had such accidents, as compared to 42 per cent of the delinquent nonusers and 31 per cent of the controls. The issue of serious accidents as forms of aggression against oneself is, however, too complex to discuss here.

perfectly in every instance, only that it is good enough for our purposes.

Figure V-1 shows how the four groups compare in terms of their average scores on the index. The striking finding is that the users scored

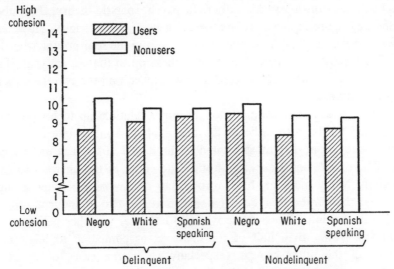

Fig. V-1. Mean Scores of Users and Nonusers in All Subgroups on the Family Cohesion Index

significantly lower than the nonusers, and this result held within each of the ethnic groups.[e]

It may be recalled that the data just described refer to the family with which the boy resided for the longest time between his tenth and his critical year. The question raises the possibility that the boy lived in more than one household during this period. Whatever the degree of cohesiveness of any of the families involved, the fact of tearing up one's family roots and having to find a place in another family is probably a trying experience to a child and one which may well undermine his sense of confidence in the dependability of other human beings. Our data on this are for the entire lifetimes of the boys up to the critical year. The differences between the groups are mainly along the lines of delinquency and only secondarily along those of drug use.[6] Fewer of the nondelinquents, regardless of whether they were users, had to withstand the trauma of shifting families. If we compare the controls with the

[6] The most favored group in this respect is the control group, with only 15 per cent of the boys having undergone such an experience; the nondelinquent users, with 20 per cent, run a close second. Twenty-six per cent of the delinquent nonusers and 34 per cent of the delinquent users have had similar experiences.

nondelinquent users and the delinquent nonusers with the delinquent users, however, in both cases more of the users had been confronted with the task of adjusting to new families.

An important aspect of the stability of the family is the continuity of the boy's relationship to his father. In psychoanalytic theory, the father is the key figure in the development of a boy's moral sense. There are marked differences in the proportions of boys in the four groups who did not live together with their biological fathers up to the critical year. The control group is the most favored in this respect, and the two delinquent groups, least so.[7]

A related issue is the quality of the boy's relationship to his parents. We asked the boys to indicate the one adult person, among all whom they knew, whom they most wanted to think well of them at the critical age. There were some striking group differences in the answers to this question. Many more of the controls than of any of the other groups specified their fathers or both parents, and the two delinquent groups lagged far behind.[8] When those who did not refer to either parent were excluded,[9] fewer than half of the controls, as compared to large majorities of the other groups (especially so in the cases of the two delinquent groups), specified the mother alone.[10]

What of the values transmitted by the families apart from those im-

[7] Twenty-three per cent of the controls did not live with their fathers throughout this period, as compared to 37 per cent of the nondelinquent users, 51 per cent of the delinquent users, and 62 per cent of the delinquent nonusers. These figures may be compared to figures obtained in another study that will be described in chapters X and XI. In the latter study, we compared cases known to be addicted, in the full sense of the term, with a set of controls selected in the same manner as the control group in the present study. The figures are not perfectly comparable because the question was put somewhat differently (the question in the latter study concerned the presence in the household of the father or of a male adult playing the father role, i.e., a father figure); the issue was only raised with reference to the early childhood period, and the addicts were not distinguished by histories of delinquency. The figures are, however, sufficiently similar to the ones just reported to justify the reference here. A father figure was absent from the household for some significant portion of the boy's early childhood in 48 per cent of the addict cases, as compared to 17 per cent of the controls.

[8] Forty-two per cent of the controls, 22 per cent of the nondelinquent users, 15 per cent of the delinquent users, and 10 per cent of the delinquent nonusers.

[9] Twelve per cent of the delinquent users, 21 per cent of the controls, 24 per cent of the delinquent nonusers, and 34 per cent of the nondelinquent users.

[10] Forty-eight per cent of the controls, 67 per cent of the nondelinquent users, 85 per cent of the delinquent users, and 90 per cent of the delinquent nonusers.

plicit in the experience of a stable and cohesive family? We have several kinds of data bearing on this question.

We may begin by assuming that a family which includes individuals who are drug-users, alcoholics, or who have been in serious trouble with the law is apt to encounter some special difficulties in impressing on its youngsters the importance of abiding by the standards of society. The differences between the groups were, in general, consistent with such an expectation, although not all were statistically significant. The most impressive difference involved individuals with a police record (i.e., having been sentenced to jail or a reformatory or placed on probation). The families of controls again clearly had the best record on this score, and the nondelinquent users came out second best; the delinquent users, however, came out better than the delinquent nonusers.[11] The safest generalization is that the controls are better off than the other three groups; if any other generalization is warranted, it is that nondelinquents, whether or not users, have the advantage over delinquents.

On the issue of drug-users in the family, each of the user groups came out somewhat worse than either of the nonuser groups, but none of the differences were large enough to justify generalization.[12] With regard to alcoholism, the division was, if anything, along the lines of delinquency, each of the delinquent groups reporting a larger proportion of families with alcoholics than either of the nondelinquent groups.[13]

At the opposite end of the behavior spectrum, one may get some

[11] On this and the following two comparisons, the reference is to the extended families (i.e., including family members not in the immediate household). The statistics on police records are: 10 per cent of the control families include individuals with such records, 25 per cent of the nondelinquent users, 30 per cent of the delinquent users, and 40 per cent of the delinquent nonusers. Another comparison not mentioned in the text concerns the percentages of families that include reportedly insane members. The delinquent nonusers come out best, with 8 per cent; the delinquent users next, with 10 per cent; the controls third, with 12 per cent; and the nondelinquent users worst, with 15 per cent. The differences are not large enough to warrant generalization.

[12] The statistics are: 10 per cent of the families of delinquent nonusers are reported to include drug-users, 12 per cent of the controls, 15 per cent of the delinquent users, and 17 per cent of the nondelinquent users. Even if we were to take the differences seriously, the incidence of drug-users in the family is not great enough to justify the conclusion that intrafamilial contagion is a major factor in the spread of drug use, especially when we note that such differences can be just as readily interpreted by the hypothesis that the kinds of families which breed some drug-users are also more likely to breed others.

[13] The statistics: 8 per cent of the families of nondelinquent users are reported to include alcoholics, 12 per cent of the controls, 20 per cent of the delinquent users, and 27 per cent of the delinquent nonusers.

indication of the values fostered by the families from the reported regularity of church attendance. The control families were clearly the most churchgoing, with more than three-fifths reported as attending regularly, and only 2 per cent attending seldom or never. By contrast, about half the families in each of the delinquent groups were said to attend regularly, and about one-third seldom or never. About two-fifths of the families of the nondelinquent users were described as regular attenders, and the same number as nonattenders. The statistics for the boys themselves during the critical year paralleled those reported for their families; but, in all four groups, the boys described themselves as less frequent churchgoers than their families.[14]

The presence of deviant individuals in a family is only one of many possible indexes to difficulty in imbuing the young with respect for social norms. We investigated the possibility that the failure of the users and delinquents to abide by conventional standards was related to the fact that their families were less well equipped for teaching their sons the socially acceptable "know-how" because they themselves might have been ignorant of conventional norms, either because they were immigrants or otherwise strangers to the community through geographic or social mobility. This hypothesis was, if anything, contradicted by the evidence.

The proportion of sons of immigrants was highest in the control group.[15] In the same vein, the boys who were themselves born abroad (there are twenty-one of them) were found primarily in the control group and in the group of delinquent nonusers; very few boys in the two user groups were foreign-born.[16]

There remain the native-born boys. Some lived all their lives in New York City. Others had "high mobility";[17] they experienced a more-or-less drastic change of environment involving at least a move from one large city to another and, for some, a move from a rural area

[14] The statistics: 46 per cent of the controls attended regularly, and 10 per cent seldom or never. In the two delinquent groups, about 30 per cent attended regularly, and about one-third seldom or never. In the nondelinquent user group, only 12 per cent attended regularly, and 61 per cent seldom or never.

[15] Fathers born outside continental U.S.A.: controls, 71 per cent; delinquent users, 51 per cent; nondelinquent users, 51 per cent; delinquent nonusers, 43 per cent. Mothers born outside continental U.S.A.: controls 63 per cent; delinquent users, 48 per cent; nondelinquent users, 47 per cent; delinquent nonusers, 30 per cent.

[16] Controls, 15 per cent; delinquent nonusers 14 per cent; nondelinquent users, 8 per cent; delinquent users, 2 per cent.

[17] See Appendix I for index of high mobility.

to a large city. The two delinquent groups showed the greatest proportion of boys whose mobility was high; the control group was least mobile; and the nondelinquent users fell in between.[18] The differences were, however, not large enough to warrant generalization.

Several related data may be gleaned from the study of the families of addicts which is reported in chapters X and XI.[19] The families of addicts were residents of New York City for a significantly longer time than were the families of control cases. It does not, therefore, seem likely that the "cultural shock" which recent arrivals to the city might be experiencing is any more conducive to producing a juvenile addict in the family than long residence in a deprived urban area. There was also no difference between addict and control families in the extent of social participation with friends, neighbors, or relatives, in the use of community resources, or in participation in formal organizations.

One final set of data has some bearing on the matters discussed in this section. This concerns the orientation of the families to the future.

There were no differences among the groups in the proportions[20] of families in which one or more persons saved money, for whatever purpose. Nor were there any differences in the proportions[21] of families in which one or more persons were described by our respondents as having actively planned for the future. Nor in the proportions[22] of families in which the plans of the boys for the future were discussed.[23]

The one striking difference between the groups was the frequency with which the boys' plans were discussed. Hardly any of the controls described their parents as nagging or said that these matters were discussed very frequently, as compared to a third or more in the other groups.[24] This does not mean that the parents of the controls were less

[18] Controls, 14 per cent with high mobility; nondelinquent users, 20 per cent; delinquent users, 27 per cent; delinquent nonusers, 28 per cent.

[19] The findings here reported emerged in the course of a separate analysis of the family study data by four of the interviewers who participated in that study. See the joint Masters thesis in the Department of Social Services at New York University, "The Relationship between Drug Addiction and Social Integration," Valerie Crump, Adele Gellert, Lucy Lieberfeld, Doris Yarber, May 1955.

[20] About 85 per cent in each group.

[21] About 45 per cent in each group.

[22] About 80 per cent in each group.

[23] In three of the four groups, the mother was the most likely to discuss these matters with her son, from 60 to 70 per cent of the mothers doing so, as compared to 40 to 50 per cent of the fathers. In the group of delinquent users, the likelihood was reversed—65 per cent of the fathers, as compared to 45 per cent of the mothers. We can think of no plausible explanation for this difference.

[24] Five per cent of the controls, 32 per cent of the delinquent users, 40 per cent of the nondelinquent users, and 40 per cent of the delinquent nonusers.

interested in their sons' futures. The difference can be easily explained in terms of occasion for concern. As will be seen later, more of the control boys had definite plans for the immediate future, and there were a number of other characteristics (e.g., a continued interest in schooling) that would occasion less concern over where they were bound. By the same token, the fact that their own plans were consistent with their parents' aspirations for them would tend to eliminate any flavor of nagging from conversations about such matters, and even frequent discussions would not seem so frequent because there would be no *issue* made of the future. On the other hand, the common planlessness of the boys in the other groups, their lack of interest in education, and their disinclination to seek or to prepare themselves for steady jobs would provide ample grounds for the issue to arise frequently, and to arise in a way that would make the boys feel that they were being constantly harrassed.

An associated difference between the groups, involving the substantive aspects of the discussion of the boys' futures, undoubtedly has the same explanation. Although most of the parents in all of the groups were mainly concerned in these conversations with the problem of what the boys would do occupationally, there were nevertheless significantly fewer of the control parents who focused on this aspect of the matter, and there were more of them who focused on educational matters.[25]

To summarize: With respect to most of the factors that might be expected to help generate a family climate that would instill in the young respect for societal standards of behavior or that might be expected to have the opposite effect, the controls come out in the most advantaged position and the delinquents in the most disadvantaged position. In other words, most of these factors are, at best, relevant to deviancy in

[25] On occupation: 77 per cent of the controls and 83 to 84 per cent of each of the other groups. On education: 50 per cent of the controls, 42 per cent of nondelinquent users, 39 per cent of delinquent users, and 32 per cent of delinquent nonusers. Primary emphasis on education with an occupational goal can, of course, be—and was—classified both ways, so that corresponding figures add up to more than 100 per cent. The differences in educational emphasis are not statistically significant, but, in view of the lesser occasion for concern and the probably lesser degree of tension associated with these discussions, the real interest of the families of the controls in education may well be underestimated. A related datum involving a comparison of the controls with the second Riverside sample supports such a conclusion. Only 23 per cent of the controls, as compared to 42 per cent of the latter sample, said that there were less than twenty-five books at home.

general or to delinquency in particular; they do not suggest any specific clues to factors in drug use. Contrary to our expectations, for instance, the experience of a relatively prolonged deprivation of contact with the father and the choice of the mother as the person whose opinion of oneself one values most are factors most closely associated with delinquency, rather than with drug use.

On two factors that might be expected to be disruptive of the normative system—the immigrant status of the parents or of the boys themselves—our controls actually come out worse than the other three groups; for the boys born in this country, however, a high degree of geographic mobility was associated with delinquency, not with drug use.

Two factors which primarily distinguish delinquents from nondelinquents do have a possible adjunctive role in drug use. When we hold delinquency status constant—i.e., when we compare the users with the nonusers among the delinquents and, similarly, among the nondelinquents—more of the extended families of the users in the sample do include individuals with police records, and more of the users have had the experience of living with different families.

The one factor we have found to be distinctly related to drug use and apparently unrelated to delinquency per se is the experience of living with a relatively cohesive family. The users have, on the average, been more deprived, in this respect, than the nonusers. We have interpreted the value of living with a cohesive family as a contribution to a sense of mutuality.

Material Deprivation

One may argue that social and economic deprivation in the family can be perceived by a child as failure in the legitimate world, as a proof that one cannot win in legitimate ways. One would accordingly expect the two groups of users and the delinquent nonusers to be more deprived in this sense than the controls. Indeed, studies of juvenile delinquents have repeatedly shown that, in comparison to nondelinquents, they tend to belong to socially and economically underprivileged strata in disorganized areas often bordering on "respectable," high-income neighborhoods.[26]

[26] The most systematic investigation of background factors is reported by Sheldon and Eleanor Glueck in *Unraveling Juvenile Delinquency* (New York: The Commonwealth Foundation, 1950). Almost without exception, other studies show that, where juvenile delinquency flourishes in big cities, it is most highly con-

Does the same hold for drug-users? We already know that they live in the most deprived areas of the city and that, the greater the neighborhood poverty, the greater the *rate* of juvenile users, even in a generally deprived area. But, in comparison to other youths who have also grown up in deprived neighborhoods but who have not become heroin-users, do the *individual* users come from the most deprived homes?

We compared the four groups on an index[27] of socioeconomic deprivation based on three items: the dependence of the family on outside financial help; the level of the breadwinner's occupation; and the quality of housing facilities. Index scores range from zero (where all these conditions are favorable) to 3 (where they are all unfavorable). The results for all the subgroups in our sample are given in Figure V-2.

The delinquents are consistently more deprived than the nondelinquents in terms of the index. These findings not only corroborate the work of the Gluecks, but extend their general results to another city at a later period and to three ethnic categories.

There is, however, no correspondingly clear-cut difference in this respect between the users and nonusers; here, the three ethnic groups present varying pictures. Although the Negro users are more deprived than nonusers, the situation is reversed among both whites and Puerto

---

centrated in "interstitial areas"; in minority-group ghettos; or in ethnically mixed disorganized areas (see, for instance, B. Lander, *Towards an Understanding of Juvenile Delinquency* (New York: Columbia University Press, 1954).

[27] See Appendix I.

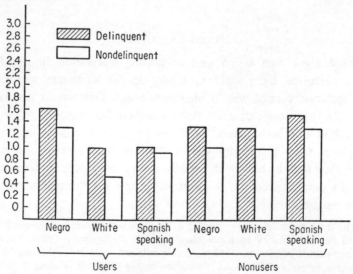

Fig. V-2. Mean Scores of Subgroups on Index of Socioeconomic Deprivation

Ricans; the users come from homes of better socioeconomic circumstances than do the nonusers.[f] (See Figure V-3.) We can advance no explanation of the differing patterns that is both plausible and simple.

The finding should, however, give pause to one inclined to interpret the correlation between neighborhood poverty and the incidence of drug use as signifying that poverty per se is conducive to drug use. It may be recalled that we have interpreted the correlation not in terms of the direct impact of poverty on the youth, but in those of the community atmosphere. The youngsters react to the values and practices they experience and not simply to the material deprivations from which they suffer. The most vulnerable are, at least among the whites and the Puerto Ricans, not those from the poorest families in their neighborhoods.

It may be that there is something particularly pathogenic about the somewhat better-off family which stays in the deteriorated neighborhood

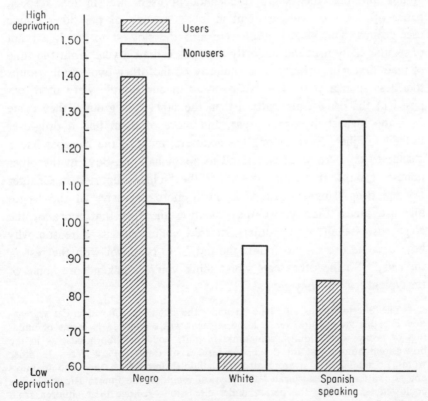

Fig. V-3. Index of Socioeconomic Deprivation among Users and Nonusers
in the Three Ethnic Groups

voluntarily—*what,* if anything, we do not know. If this were the case, it would not be relevant to the Negroes who experienced extraordinary difficulties in breaking out of the Negro ghettos.[28] If such an explanation were sufficient, however, we would expect that there would simply be no relationship among the Negroes between the material circumstances of the family and drug use, rather than the definite relationship that was found.

It is, of course, also possible that there is something special about the group of Negro users, and, in fact, there are a number of reasons that lead us to take this possibility seriously. First, it may be noted that the index of socioeconomic deprivation is highest for the Negro users, but we also suspect that there is among them much less personal psychopathology conductive to drug use. Reference to Figure V-1, for instance, shows that the gap between the Negro users and nonusers with respect to family cohesiveness is smaller than that for any of the other groups and that the Negro nondelinquent users are, in this respect, better off, on the average, than members of any of the other ethnic user groups. The Negro users were also the slowest to reach a point of regular daily use; the majority took more than a year from the time of their first trial, whereas the majority of the other two ethnic groups took less than a year. The Negro users in our sample were more exposed to the drug-using pattern than the other two groups; they came from the highest drug-rate areas, and more of them had a drug-user in their families. Even among the nonusers, most of the Negroes had a chance to try heroin, as compared to about half the boys in the other nonuser groups. If we may generalize the findings reported in Chapter IV, the drug-using subculture is much more pervasive in the Negro high-use areas. Finally, we may mention the fact that more of the Negro users than of the others stressed conformity as a reason why boys become users—"to follow the fad," "to be down with the rest of the cats," "so the other cats won't think you're chicken" are some of the typical reasons they gave.

[28] The Puerto Ricans also labored under the handicaps of residential segregation. For this group, however, a large segment was segregated in terms of buildings or groups of buildings, sometimes in quite good neighborhoods, as in the brownstone houses just off the upper reaches of Central Park West. In other words, no matter how overcrowded the buildings into which they had to move and no matter how deteriorated the physical facilities, the Puerto Rican families could—at least during the period under discussion—remove their children from the ghettoized slum.

In other words, we are suggesting that, whether the users have a history of prior delinquency or not, drug use among the Negro members of our sample is most closely linked to factors conducive to delinquency rather than to drug use as such.[29]

To recapitulate the rather tortuous and, at best, incomplete explanation of the differing relationships between the index of socioeconomic deprivation and drug use: The families of the white and Puerto Rican users do have considerably greater freedom than do the families of the Negroes to move away from the unwholesome neighborhoods in which the children are growing up, and their materially better circumstances put them in a better position to do so. The fact that they do not suggests that there may be other things wrong with these families that have not been tapped by our investigation—perhaps that they are little concerned with the welfare of their children—and that are particularly associated with vulnerability to drug use. The Negroes, however, are immobilized by residential segregation so that the failure of the better-off families to move away can have no possible diagnostic significance. On the other hand, drug use among Negroes is more intimately related to delinquency and accompanies more marked socioeconomic deprivation, just as does delinquency.

Adolescent Stress

Adolescence is a transition from childhood to maturity, and the stresses peculiar to it stem from problems of transition. The adolescent wants, in many ways, to be treated as an adult and, in others, to retain the relationships of childhood. The adult world also wants him to act as an adult in certain ways and as a child in others. Trouble arises from the facts that, where the teen-ager wants to be adult, the adult wants him to be a child and, where the adult wants him to be adult, he wants to be a child.

The teen-ager, for instance, typically wants the freedom that is to him the essence of adult status—freedom to come and go as he pleases, freedom to engage in sexual relations, freedom from the need to give an accounting of his actions, freedom from the supervisory eyes of

[29] For additional data supporting such an interpretation, see the ethnic comparisons reported in Stanley Schiff, "A Self-Theory Investigation of Drug Addiction in Relation to Age of Onset," doctoral dissertation, New York University, 1959.

adults—but he is not ready to accept, and often does not appreciate, the responsibilities that go with such freedom. The adult, on the other hand, wants the teen-ager to act with increasing responsibility, but he is not willing to grant the youth the freedom he craves.

It is not that people—adolescents, adults, or both—are contrary. The adolescent is impelled by his maturation, the emergence of his sexuality, the widening of his horizons, the incitations of his fellow teen-agers, the imminence of the time when he must stand on his own feet, the very urgings of the adults around him to act as a grownup. The adult, on the other hand, is all too aware of the dangers that go with freedom —dangers to which, he is with some justification convinced, the young-sters cannot be fully sensitive and dangers which are enhanced by the impulsiveness and inexperience of youth. Even apart from their own emotional investments in the welfare of their children, adults retain legal responsibility or social accountability for the actions of their children.

Nor is the conflict entirely between the teen-ager and the adult. To a considerable degree, a similar conflict goes on within the adolescent himself. Freedom, as Erich Fromm has noted,[30] can be terrifying if it is not accompanied by assured competence and clarity of destination. The teen-ager, therefore, counts on the adult to keep him within bounds and on a safe course, and the very controls against which he so vigor-ously rebels are essential to his sense of security. His burgeoning im-pulses impel him to defy restraints, but they also threaten the integrity of his selfhood, for the very vigor and inchoateness of his impulsive life threaten to engulf him and sweep him into depths in which, for all he knows to the contrary, he may never be able to resume control.

Moreover, with the imminence of the time when he must stand on his own, the issues of the *self*—who and what am I? where do I be-long? what shall I be? what goals, what restrictions, what behavior am I to accept as appropriate for me and what am I to reject as not fitting? —become extraordinarily acute. The adolescent is impelled to define a distinctive identity for himself and is, at the same time, full of too many conflicting possibilities to be able to commit himself to one *identity*. He needs the shelter and the restraint of an understanding adult to give him the freedom to experiment with personal identities and the assurance that no one act or series of acts necessarily represents the final com-

[30] Erich Fromm, *Escape from Freedom* (New York: Rinehart, 1941).

mitment.[31] To the observing adult, he may seem immersed in a struggle to seize (prematurely, from the adult's viewpoint) the requisites of the adult status, but, consciously or unconsciously, he dreads being abandoned to adulthood.

The stresses of transition are, of course, not equally grave or intense for all adolescents. The factors, internal and external, that give rise to the teen-ager's bids for adult status do not impinge on every individual at the same rate or with equal force, nor do they find all equally unprepared to cope with them. The suddenness with which he is confronted by his budding sexuality, for instance, and the effectiveness with which he has dealt with the problems of earlier stages of development are only two of the things that make a difference in the teen-ager's readiness to take on the new problems of adolescence. Moreover, the adults with whom the teen-agers have to deal are not equally flexible and understanding, equally concerned with the welfare of their children, equally prone to project their own unresolved anxieties onto their children or to treat them as instrumentalities of their own efforts at adjustment.

The current environment of the adolescent may also make the transition more or less difficult. It may provide support or add unnecessary frustration. It may clarify or confuse, help or obstruct. The five major factors identified by Cottrell[32] as facilitating the adolescent transition are, in the main, aspects of the concurrent environment. The factors identified by Cottrell are: (1) the presence of a male adult who acts both as an ideal and as a guide and interpreter, (2) imaginary or actual rehearsal for adult roles, (3) opportunities for respite from tensions, (4) consistency of expectations, and (5) provision of adequate paraphernalia of adulthood. Note that all but the second refer to some aspect of the adolescent's environment and that, even with respect to the second, it is largely the current environment that instigates the daydreams that constitute the imaginative rehearsals for adult roles and that contributes the stuff of which these dreams are made.

[31] Compare Erik H. Erikson's discussions of adolescence as the period of identity crisis and of the need for a psychosocial moratorium for adolescents, *Childhood and Society* (New York: Norton, 1950), and in H. Witmer and R. Kotinsky, eds., *New Perspectives for Research on Juvenile Delinquency* (Washington, D.C.: U.S. Government Printing Office, Children's Bureau Publication No. 356, 1956).

[32] Leonard S. Cottrell, Jr., "The Adjustment of the Individual to His Age and Sex Roles," *American Sociological Review*, 7 (1942), 617–620.

We did not think of inquiring into these matters until after the two user groups and the delinquent nonusers had already been interviewed. We did, however, raise the issues with the controls and with the second sample of Riverside cases. The questions all concerned the critical year.

ADULT FIGURE IN BOY'S LIFE

The differences we found between the two groups are limited to rather subtle aspects of the boy-adult relationship. In general, both groups are alike in that roughly one-half of each group said that they knew, or knew of, some grownup whom they wished to be like. Of the latter, about 15 per cent said that this person was their father, about a fifth mentioned some other related male, and the rest referred to public figures in the world of sports or music, or to teachers, ministers, older friends, and the like.

The boys in the two groups who designated some ideal adult differed, however, in what it is about the latter which they wish they could emulate. The control group mentioned personality attributes (such as kindness or courage) much more often than did the user group;[33] the users tended to mention more often attributes with material implications, such as wealth or skills.[34]

Similarly, there is no difference in the proportion of boys in each group who voluntarily sought out some adult to discuss a personal problem—about two-thirds in each group. However, in the control group this was more often the boy's own father or teacher or priest; in the user group, slightly more boys mentioned older brothers.[35]

Most of the boys in both groups who sought out an adult felt that they "could really be open" with this person, and most of them claimed that they "usually felt better" after a talk with him. They talked mainly about school problems (the control group mentioned this more often than did users),[36] sex, work, and future education. A few also dis-

[33] Forty-one per cent, versus 9 per cent of the boys who specified an ideal adult.

[34] On the individual categories, the differences are not large enough to warrant generalization. Of those specifying an ideal adult, 21 per cent of the controls mentioned skills, as compared to 35 per cent of the users; 14 per cent of the controls mentioned wealth, as compared to 26 per cent of the users.

[35] Of those seeking out an adult: seeking out father, 44 per cent, versus 20 per cent; seeking out teacher or priest, 24 per cent, versus 0 per cent; seeking out older brother, 3 per cent, versus 20 per cent. The last-named difference is not quite large enough to warrant generalization.

[36] Thirty-six per cent, versus 20 per cent of those seeking out an adult. The difference is not statistically significant.

cussed family problems, and there were small numbers discussing a host of other matters, such as the draft, how to deal with people, immediate financial difficulty, and so on.

The help given by the adult to the users consisted largely of advice. The boys in the control group also mentioned receiving advice, but less frequently,[37] and a few mentioned other forms of help, such as the adult encouraging their decisions or being helpful by showing understanding.

RESPITE FROM TENSIONS

The boys were asked: "Was there any place where you felt especially easy and relaxed and free from worries?" More of the users than of the controls said that they had such a place.[38] Of those who had such a place of escape, twice as many users had a club or other specific place where they met with friends. Even so, most of the boys in both groups usually whiled the "blues" away outdoors, at home, or at the movies, without, however, indicating whether they were with friends; only a small minority specified that they sought refuge in solitude.

On the face of it, the advantage lies with the users; but it is also likely that more of them needed a special place in which to relax. Much of the data already reviewed from the four-group comparisons (e.g., the data on family cohesiveness) suggest that home was a more comfortable place for the controls. Another datum that points in the same direction is the fact that many more of the controls' parents approved of their sons' friends whom they brought home.[39] Similarly, fewer of the nonusers reported that they were "yelled at" at home or punished by rejection —ordered out of the house, locked up, ignored.[40] Another factor that points to the relative unimportance of a *place* of refuge, also from the four-group comparisons, is the quality of the boys' friendships. The control group reported more stable and intimate friendships.[41] Thus,

[37] Sixty-seven per cent, versus 87 per cent of those seeking out an adult.

[38] Sixty-seven per cent of the controls, versus 80 per cent of the users.

[39] Fifty-eight per cent of the controls, as compared to 41 per cent of the nondelinquent users, 40 per cent of the delinquent nonusers, and 29 per cent of the delinquent users.

[40] "Yelled at": 73 per cent of controls, 84 per cent of delinquent nonusers, and 90 per cent of each of the two user groups. Punished by rejection: 4 per cent of delinquent nonusers, 8 per cent of controls, 13 per cent of delinquent users, and 15 per cent of nondelinquent users.

[41] Stability of friendships: 83 per cent of controls said that they had known their friends "for years," as compared to 73 per cent of nondelinquent users, 61 per cent of delinquent users, and 60 per cent of delinquent nonusers. Intimacy:

the significance of the finding seems to be in the fact that more of the users could identify a *particular* place where they could relax, rather than the apparent relative deprivation of the controls in not having such a place.

CONSISTENCY AND TIMING OF EXPECTATIONS

We asked the controls and the boys in the second Riverside sample how old they were when their families "started treating you as a man— you know, expecting you to be independent and make your own decisions and make your own living." Since the age at which the users became seriously involved with narcotics might make a difference in this respect, we compared the controls (for whom the critical age was, by definition, sixteen) only with those users for whom the critical age was also sixteen (there were twenty such). The users reported having been treated as adults considerably earlier than the controls.[42]

We also compared users and controls, matched on a person-to-person basis for age at the time of the interview, since age at the time of reporting might make a difference in the retrospective dating. On this basis, we had twenty-four cases in each group. Again, the users placed the age at which they were first treated as adults considerably earlier than did the controls.[43]

It is, of course, possible that the users were exaggerating their youthfulness at the point of achieving "maturity" (or exaggerating more than did the controls); some dated the event at fourteen and even earlier. The difference between the two groups shrank below the level of statistical significance, however, when we added the question of whether

---

63 per cent of controls said that they had intimate friends at the critical age, 56 per cent of delinquent nonusers, 41 per cent of nondelinquent users, and 40 per cent of delinquent users. Note that the latter finding is not simply a reflection of the patterns of friendship in juvenile street gangs. Only 17 per cent of the nondelinquent users belonged to regular gangs, as compared to 33 per cent of the delinquent users. That gang membership tends to be associated with delinquency rather than with drug use per se becomes evident when we add the statistics for the other two groups: 19 per cent of the controls, 29 per cent of the delinquent nonusers. A study of drug use in street gangs is reported in Chapter VII, below.

[42] "Treated as adults" by the time they were sixteen, 29 per cent of the controls, versus 50 per cent of the users; still "treated as kids" at this age, 54 per cent of the controls, versus 40 per cent of the users; mixed treatment, 17 per cent of controls, versus 10 per cent of users.

[43] Fifty-four per cent of controls *not* "treated as adults" before they were seventeen or eighteen, versus 26 per cent of users.

they were also treated as adults by others outside their families (e.g., by teachers or tradesmen).[44]

If we were to take these findings at face value, it would seem that, in terms of the adolescent's striving for independence, the user finds the transition to adult status easier than the control. There is, however, also the other side of the issue—responsibility—and the question places heavy emphasis on this aspect. In fact, expecting such youngsters to make their own living is carrying the "privileges" of adulthood to a rather extreme point. We may, therefore, suspect (still taking the findings at face value) that the earlier age of achieving adult status represents a desire on the part of the parents to shirk their parental responsibilities rather than a genuine respect for the maturation of their sons. On this interpretation, the premature granting of adult status is an act of rejection rather than one of affirmation.

This speculative interpretation is in line with the findings of a lesser degree of cohesiveness in the users' families. It is also in line with an associated finding. The granting of adult status is more likely to be associated with some other objective status change among the controls than among the users,[45] as in connection with graduating from school, getting a job, moving out of the house, or the like. The control is apparently more likely to win his maturity by, so to speak, passing a test; he has in some sense proved himself. The user, by contrast, is more likely to have won his maturity for no obvious reason—an indication that his parents may not have cared enough to withhold it from him.

Even so, and despite the apparent delay, more of the controls were ready to confess that they did not greet the adult status, when it did come, with unalloyed joy. More of them said that they did not "feel up to it all the time," and more of them would have preferred to be still treated as a child most of the time.[46] Thus, it would seem that, at least for the boys in the sample, the controls were more likely to experience subjective difficulty in the transition to the adult status than were the users. In this sense, they may be said to have matured less rapidly. It seems likely, however, that, if this is in fact the case, it is so because the

---

[44] Twenty-one per cent of the controls and 40 per cent of the addicts claimed that they were treated as adults by the time they were sixteen both by their parents and by others.

[45] Thirty-seven per cent of the controls, versus 14 per cent of the addicts.

[46] Not up to it all the time: controls, 29 per cent; users, 20 per cent. Preferred being treated as a child most of the time: controls, 10 per cent; users, 2 per cent. These differences are not, individually, significant.

users were already accustomed to being left on their own. It does not mean that the users were actually better prepared to assume adult roles. The sheer fact of their involvement with narcotics stands as testimony to the contrary.

As we have already indicated, the ambiguities of the adolescent status are not arbitrary impositions on the developing youth. They are, to some degree, necessary counterparts of maturation. The process may be eased by tolerant understanding on the part of the parents and by the graduated character of their expectations. The process cannot be eased, although it may be curtailed or aborted, by the parents' abandonment of their roles and the ejection of the child from their concerns into a world which offers no support, guidance, or love on which, if need be, the fledgling might fall back. The users may not have felt the transition so keenly, but the indications are that this is not because the transition was easier for them; it was, in large measure, because they were *deprived* of the transition.

In other words, we are suggesting that, if more of the users than of the controls described themselves as content with the transition, this is only because discontent was to them a normal state of affairs and because they had no image of the possibilities of greater contentment. That this is the case is also suggested by another set of data.

We asked the boys, in a probing, direct way, about their life in the critical year: "Did anything unusual or special happen to you at that time? Was there anything that was bothering you or worrying you? Did you have any discouraging experiences or experiences that were very exciting? Was there something that you especially wanted but couldn't get?"

In general, the boys mentioned various unfulfilled desires as things that bothered them; and a fair number mentioned events that signified maturity, such as graduating from school or getting a job, as exciting events. The users differed from nonusers in two respects: over half the delinquent users[47] had been "in trouble with the law" during the year; and about a fourth of both user groups had experienced some radical change in their situation—such as moving to another neighborhood, separation from or death in family, shotgun marriage—as compared to only 4 per cent in the control group.

This last difference supported our expectation that, at least for a

[47] On some of these questions, we also have answers from the two original groups of delinquent and nondelinquent users.

large number of the youths, the onset of habitual intake of heroin was accompanied by greatly upsetting events and inner strain. Yet, when we asked the boys, "How would you describe your life in [that year], in just a few words?" and "Would you say that you were happy, fairly happy, or very unhappy?"—the users showed a tendency to deny that the critical year was difficult or painful.

A majority of the boys said that their life at the critical age was "good"—carefree, active, or just in general good—the users slightly more often than controls. Very few said that it was a bad year. Similarly, in answer to the second question, most boys said that they had not been unhappy that year; but whereas the controls tended to say "fairly happy," the users tended to describe that year as "very happy." Note that the users did not deny the stressful experiences, nor did they paint a particularly rosy picture of the happy experiences of that year. They simply seemed to have a defective sense of what it means to be "very happy."

The differing rates at which the users and the controls are projected into adult status are manifested in many ways. Despite the later age at which they said they were expected to act like adults, less than half as many of the controls as of the users described themselves as financially independent at that point.[48] Most were still in school. Correspondingly fewer felt that they had enough spending money.[49] Still another indication of the impulsion to assume adult roles for which they were not well prepared is the larger proportion of users with "steady" girl friends at the transitional age.[50] The point is especially significant because, as will be seen in later chapters, one of the most characteristic problems of addicts is precisely in the confusion over their masculine identities. In other words, their taking steady girl friends at an earlier age occurs despite their lesser readiness for normal heterosexual relationships.

The Environment of Peers

The adolescent does not, of course, live in a world composed of, and defined by, adults. A major feature of his environment is the peer group. This group is an important source of influence and constraint in the choice of patterns of behavior. It provides cues and miscues to oppor-

[48] Nineteen per cent of the controls, versus 40 per cent of the users.
[49] Sixty per cent of the controls, versus 86 per cent of the users.
[50] Forty-two per cent of the controls, versus 60 per cent of the users.

(over 80 per cent) had left school by the time they were sixteen. There was little talk among them about planning for their future; in fact, most of them did not know anyone who planned or saved for the future. But they did know people—friends or family—who believed that "a person should get as much fun as he can now and let the future take care of itself"; most of the people around them were of that sort.

Although, at that age, only about a third of the boys had some plans for following a specific occupation in the future, even these plans and their ideas as to their implementation were vague or conditional on some uncontrollable events.

On the other hand, most wanted things in the immediate future—mainly clothes, a car, other possessions, or just money; a few wished for a different way of life and travel.

About a third of these delinquent boys had belonged to regular gangs; but mostly they "went around" with one or two close friends.

The style of life of youths observed in the natural gang setting[52] fits into this picture, with the addition of special types of activities typical of delinquent gangs. Although there is much variation among the eighteen gangs observed, certain preoccupations are typical. There is gambling (averaging about once a week); sexual delinquency (about once in six months), usually lineups, that is, successive intercourse of a group of boys with the same girl; group-organized robberies or burglaries (about twice a month); vandalism and general hell-raising (about once a month); gang warfare (about once in three months). The gangs typically also organize house parties (about twice a month) or dances (once a month), engage in active sports (once a week), and watch sports events.

But most of the time the boys "hang around." Even though all these gangs were among the most troublesome and each had a Youth Board group worker assigned to it, five of the gangs were described by the worker as not having interest in anything, being in constant search to avoid boredom, suffering from a sense of "not having anything to do or place to go." This search commonly leads to an interest in "kicks" and a readiness to try anything for a kick.[53]

About 10 to 20 per cent of the 305 boys in the eighteen gangs we studied were heavy drinkers of wine, whiskey, or both. Most had neu-

[52] See Chapter VII for a fuller account of the life style of antisocial boys.

[53] In the delinquent gang, this may be an indication of the failure of the delinquent style of life as a permanent solution to the growth problems of adolescents in deprived areas; more about this in Chapter VII.

tral, tolerant, or positive attitudes toward the use of marijuana, and a large proportion were quite tolerant about those among them who occasionally used heroin.

In Chapter VII, we give fuller consideration to the position of the heroin-user in the delinquent gang. Here, the only factor we want to emphasize is that the delinquent subculture in general and the delinquent gang in particular are hospitable to experimentation with any new, exciting activity, including the taking of addictive drugs.

However, this hospitability should not be taken to imply a strong pressure to try drugs. Most youths who belonged to delinquent subgroups have opportunities to try the drug, but not all do try.

Of the fifty delinquents we interviewed who were not opiate-users, two-thirds had had an opportunity to try such drugs, usually in a group or through a friend, mostly when they were about sixteen years old; however, only four tried. These four did not continue, because, at best, they felt "no kick" or, at worst, they felt "sick" after they tried.

THOSE WHO "STAY OUT OF TROUBLE"—THE "SQUARES"

Our knowledge of the life style and attitudes of the nondelinquent subcultures in the deprived areas is based on interviews with the controls. As already noted, these boys grew up in extremely deprived areas,[54] but stayed out of trouble; they did not become court delinquents or chronic truants or chronically acting-out "trouble-makers," and they were not habitual users of any drugs, including marijuana.

One feature of their life which probably greatly influences their activities and interests is their schooling. Only five had left school before they were sixteen (in contrast to the delinquents, almost all of whom left school that early),[55] and almost all had more than ten years of school-

[54] It will be recalled that the areas these boys came from were somewhat worse in all respects than the areas from which our delinquents and users came.

[55] The fact that so many boys claim to have left school by the time they were sixteen is puzzling in view of the compulsory school-attendance law which requires attendance until the sixteenth birthday and subsequent attendance, if the child elects to drop out, at a continuation school until the seventeenth. The boys clearly do not count the latter as continuing in school. The puzzle, however, concerns leaving before the sixteenth birthday. It is possible that some of the delinquents were in the toils of the law during this period, and a prolonged illness may account for some others, but neither of these factors can account for the relatively large numbers. One must conclude that there was a systematic distortion in recall or a failure in communication between interviewers and respondents or that the law is not effectively enforced in these neighborhoods. We have obviously considered the latter explanation sufficiently plausible to justify taking the statements of the boys seriously.

ing (in contrast to only one-fourth of the delinquents); in fact, one-third went to college, although only two stayed beyond the second year. Almost all held some job after sixteen and managed to stay on the job at least half a year. In consequence of all this, they had much less time to "goof off" and "hang around" when they were sixteen (the "critical" year); only a third mentioned "goofing off" with friends (compared to two-thirds of the delinquents) and less than half mentioned "hanging around a candy store" (compared to about three-fourths of the delinquents). For half of them, the most common way of spending leisure time with friends was to engage in active sports; others mentioned going to community centers, parks, and beaches. Although, like the delinquents, most had one or two intimate friends, they also tended to belong to small cliques, rather than to large, organized gangs; most had known their friends for many years.

Half the boys had definite short-range plans, mostly concerning preparation for an occupation (the delinquent boys' plans had been mostly vague, and a sizable proportion planned merely to enter the Army or to get married).

Though many wanted things they could not get at the time, very few wanted merely clothes and a car (as did the delinquents); over a third wished for a different way of life and over half wished for a variety of special possessions (bicycles, cameras, and the like). Among their friends, most of the boys said, there was not much talk about wanting a car, clothes, or much money.[56]

About three-fourths said that they read books and enjoyed reading (half, very much so); a large majority used the public library; they read up to five books a month; most said that they occasionally discussed books among friends, though few claimed that they did much of that.

About half the boys were interested in extracurricular activities, and most of these took active part in such activities.

Though most of the youths dreamed of traveling, most realized that their chances for travel at that time were slight and admitted that they hoped rather than planned to travel; their friends did not talk much about travel.

In summing up their life in the critical year, most control youths said that it had been a good year or an average one; most said that they

[56] This and the following questions were asked only of the controls and of the second sample of users. We have, therefore, no basis for comparison here between the controls and the delinquent nonusers.

were fairly happy at that time. Asked to tell us about the important events in their life that year, one-third of the boys mentioned having learned some new skill; hardly any of the delinquents mentioned this.

The picture that emerges is a very rough profile, yet one that is in very sharp contrast to the delinquent profile. These boys are not at odds with the major institutions; they do not drop out of school, and many manage to hold a job. Their general orientation at sixteen was reasonably realistic in that they had some sort of definite plan for the immediate future, and they did not wish for things they knew they could not possibly get. Their relation to their environment was positive in the sense that they were interested in and able to utilize available opportunities, such as extracurricular activities, to their enjoyment and benefit.

The boys were quite familiar with such addictive drugs as heroin. By the time they were sixteen years old, most had heard about such drugs (a third, when they were fourteen or less). By sixteen, most had also seen someone use heroin and had certain beliefs about addictive drugs—of the kind that would make one hesitate before using drugs. Most mentioned that drugs impair health and the mind, that they are costly, or that they create dependency. (It is striking that the delinquent boys mentioned the same reasons in almost identical proportions.)

Forty per cent (compared to two-thirds in the group of delinquent nonusers) had a chance to try heroin, in the main when they were sixteen years old. The opportunity was usually presented by a peer who offered to give or sell the drug; the offer took place on the street, at a party, or at school. None of the boys tried the drug. The main reasons for refusing were a sense of wrong in taking drugs; belief that drug use is bad for one's health; and fear of getting into trouble with the law. Two boys said that someone else had urged them not to try it at the time they had the opportunity, and they listened. Eight of the control boys did have a try at smoking marijuana, mostly in a group, at a party; but they never smoked it regularly.

What is important for us here is that the subculture of those youths who "stayed away from trouble" was not hospitable to experimentation with addictive drugs; in fact, drug use does not seem to have had a meaningful place in these boys' current lives and future plans. Opportunities to try heroin arose less often than among delinquents, and the boys were not likely to give heroin even one try.

Before we look at the position the users occupied in their peer subcultures and try to establish a connection between the nature of peer associations and the first step toward addiction—experimentation—it may be of interest to examine the interaction between the clearly delinquent and "square" subgroups, the pull and push, attraction and repulsion that goes on between them.

HOW THE TWO SUBCULTURES VIEW EACH OTHER

The "cats" and the "squares" live side by side on every block of the slum area. In answer to our question, "What kind of guys were there in your neighborhood?" most of the controls[57] gave a picture of rather well organized and strongly differentiated groups of adolescents. They mentioned ethnic groupings and degree of organization (gangs and bunches). But, most importantly, one-third mentioned "tough" gangs, and another third, "tough guys," as opposed to those who "kept away from trouble."

The over-all pressure of street associations seems to be in the direction of alignment with the "fast crowd" of noisy, aggressive "toughs," or "cats."[58] The dominance of the "fast crowd" in the street culture was strikingly described by one of the "square" boys who said that, "in a neighborhood like ours, it's never convenient to carry books. . . . One of my friends quit high school because he didn't want to be seen with books." This may be a gross exaggeration of an actual event, it may represent a local myth which the narrator believes so strongly that he offers himself as a personal witness to emphasize its truth, or it may actually have happened, albeit as an extreme case; in any event, it stands as testimony to the "squares' " perception of the streets as dominated by the "toughs."

The "squares' " position in the street culture may be described as "contact but not involvement." Most of the control group had some friends who had been in jail, reformatory, or on probation. However, only a sixth had intimate friends of this kind, compared to half of the delinquents. In answer to our question, "How did you feel about these different groups?" over half the control group expressed negative (dep-

[57] Again, we do not have comparable information on the delinquents, since these were some of the questions asked only of the control group and the second sample of users.

[58] Thus, for example, in answer to our question about the "real reasons why kids take to drugs," 39 per cent of the control sample mentioned some form of pressure for conformity—"to be down with the cats," "to follow the crowd," "not to be called chicken." Delinquents gave this type of answer even more often—60 per cent.

recating, hostile, or both) attitudes to the "others" among their peers who were not their close friends; the rest were largely indifferent. Often this rejecting attitude was expressed with a great deal of affect. In the words of one: "I just passed them up. Didn't want to associate with those little dirty-mouthed bums. They were headed for trouble." A majority spontaneously mentioned that, at the critical age of sixteen, they had no contact with the "others," that they made it a point to stay away; the association was dangerous. As one youth put it: "You are afraid of them—not physically, but because being with them can get you in trouble if you are close to them. I couldn't endure no penitentiary."

The control group's sharper awareness of the presence of the "toughs" in their neighborhoods and the effort to dissociate themselves from those who were "headed for trouble" is also reflected in a more purposeful selection of friends. In answer to our question, "How did you happen to fit in with [those] guys rather than the others?" a majority indicated that they picked their associates for common interests, for protection, or for other specific reasons.

Whether this dissociation from the "toughs," so firmly asserted by the bulk of those who managed to "stay away from trouble," indicates that the values, interests, and activities of the delinquent subgroup had no meaning or negative meaning for them or merely that they were more aware and apprehensive of the risks entailed by such associations, we cannot say. It is sufficient to say that in the deteriorated areas where drug use flourishes, there are subgroups of "tough" adolescents whose alienated style of life is hospitable to experimentation with drugs; there are other subgroups that stay clear from the "toughs" and in general steer away from trouble with what one senses is grim determination. Our main interest is, of course, in the drug-users; where do they fit, by virtue of their preferences, interests, and capacities?

The Future Users: Preferences, Interests, and Associations

An examination of the users' interests and general style of life in the year preceding onset of drug use[59] reveals more similarity to the "tough" subgroups than to the "square" ones. For one thing, the users made

[59] Questions concerning use of opportunities were asked only of the second user sample.

less use of libraries, extracurricular activities, and some of the less common leisure activities than did the control group. They left school earlier, and fewer of them received on-the-job training. Table V-2 shows the differences between users and controls in extent of utilization of constructive opportunities.

TABLE V-2   *Use of Constructive Opportunities by Users and Controls*

	CONTROLS	USERS
	PERCENTAGE	
Used library or book club	63	28
Liked to read books on "how to improve yourself" (explicit mention in answer to open-ended question)	17	4
Was interested in extracurricular activities	50	21
Was active in extracurricular activities	40	6
Went on camping trips, etc.	22	5
Stayed in school at least until age sixteen	88	27
TOTAL CASES	(50)	(50)

These differences between the users and controls are relevant here not as indicators of health or pathology but, rather, in their implied consequences. The "squares" explored certain avenues where the users seldom ventured; there would be, consequently, less likelihood for the users to meet the "squares" on some common ground outside school.

On the other hand, the future users' mode of spending leisure time was likely to bring them into frequent contact with "those who were headed for trouble"; like the delinquents, the users often mentioned going to movies; hanging around candy stores;[60] goofing off; and going to "sets," or parties and dances.

In the second sample of users, one-fifth reported that their life at the critical age was inactive; hardly any of the control group gave this response.

Concerning their wishes and interests at the critical age, all users were similar to the delinquents in their frequent mention of a desire for better clothes. However, the users do not appear to have perceived themselves as closer to the "toughs" than to the "squares." In fact, they seemed equally distant from both.

Their distance from both extremes is evident in their attitudes to the

[60] In this respect, the delinquent users differ also from the nondelinquent users, who mention this less often.

"different types and groups" in the neighborhoods in which they lived at the time they started using drugs. Following the question about what "different types and groups" were to be found in their neighborhood, we asked the boys, "Where did you fit in?" and then, "How did you feel about these different groups (the 'others')?" The reader will recall that the control group, which tended to mention more of the anti-social groups and individuals than "respectable" groups and individuals, expressed negative feelings toward the "others," who, as is clear from their comments, were usually the "tough" ones. The controls also indicated, in a variety of ways, a determined effort to stay away from those "others" who might "get them into trouble." Nearly half the users, on the other hand, expressed neutral or even friendly feelings toward the "others," and few expressed distinctly negative feelings. It is clear from the comments accompanying their statements of feeling toward the "others" that, for the users, the "others" were the "respectable" groups, the "tough" ones, or, in some cases, both. Their positive attitudes expressed a detached tolerance of them all. In fact, the most common answer was: "They were O.K. I got along with them all."

This nonpartisan, passive attitude was also reflected in the way they selected their friends. Whereas the majority of controls claimed that they selected their friends for one or another reason, few users mentioned *picking* friends; the great majority said that their friends were boys with whom they just happened to grow up in the neighborhood or met at school.

The users' description of the boys they went with differs from that given by the controls in the direction typical of the delinquent orientation. A majority of the users, but only a minority of controls, reported that, among the "fellows they went with" at the critical age, there was "a lot" of talk about "real expensive clothes" and that their friends talked "a lot" about wanting to have a car and pocket money.

On the other hand, when asked, "Among the fellows you went with, was there talk about guys who knew a lot about current events, books, art, and such things?" a majority of the users, compared to only a fourth of the controls, said: "No, never." When asked, "Did the fellows you went with talk about the things they read?" over half the users, compared to a third of the controls, said "Never."

In all these statements, the users show their friends to be consistently aligned with the kinds of activity and concern that was shown earlier · in this chapter to be typical of the delinquent subculture. These were the boys they went with before they started using drugs regularly. As we examine, in the next chapter, the process of becoming a habitual user, we shall see that the first step is usually taken in casual association with peers who condoned experimentation with drugs for "kicks."

STATISTICAL FOOTNOTES

[a] See Appendix J.

[b] Disqualified "for cause" were 13 per cent of the Negro boys, 13 per cent of the Puerto Ricans, and 7 per cent of the whites; the variation was not, however, significant at the .05 level by the chi-square test. Disqualified because of non-cooperation by social agencies were 10 per cent of the Negroes, 11 per cent of the Puerto Ricans, and 5 per cent of the whites.

[c] Of the 425 letters sent, eighty-eight were returned as undeliverable, i.e., the family had moved and left no forwarding address. There was a significant difference in this respect between the three ethnic groups—40 per cent of the Puerto Ricans, 22 per cent of the Negroes, and 11 per cent of the whites.

[d] The difference between the two Riverside samples is statistically significant. There are other indications that policies affecting admissions to Riverside Hospital have not remained constant. (There are actually a number of interacting factors involved—the readiness of judges to refer cases to Riverside; the hospital admission policies; and the readiness of family, friends, social agencies, and the patient himself to seek commitment.) For example, the changes over the years in the ethnic distribution of first admissions is not consistent with what one would expect on the basis of the neighborhood distribution of newly discovered cases of boys involved with narcotics. The following table has been adapted from R. R. Gamso and P. Mason, "A Hospital for Adolescent Drug Addicts," *The Psychiatric Quarterly Supplement* (1958), Part 1.

First Admissions of Three Ethnic Groups to Riverside Hospital

	PERCENTAGE						
	1952	1953	1954	1955	1956	1957	1958
White	19	21	27	43	38	33	34
Negro	72	62	36	26	19	31	27
Puerto Rican	10	18	37	32	43	35	38

The figures do not always add to 100 per cent because of rounding of decimal places.

[e] In the statistical evaluation of this and other scores, we used a three-way analysis of variance—delinquency by drug use by ethnic group. Since the number of cases was not exactly equal, we used the approximation method suggested by G. W. Snedecor in *Statistical Methods* (5th ed.; Ames, Iowa: Iowa State College Press, 1956), p. 385. If, in the presentation of such data, a main or interaction effect is not mentioned, the reader may take it that it was not significant.

[f] In other words, the delinquency effect and the user by ethnic interaction are both significant; the other main effects and interactions are not.

VI

Becoming an Addict

In asking the boys to reconstruct the process of becoming involved with narcotics, we distinguished four stages: experimentation, occasional use, regular or habitual use, and efforts to break the habit.

A user may go through all these stages, but he may stop at any stage. There is reason to believe that there are significant differences among the four "types": those who experiment but do not repeat, those who use heroin occasionally but never become habituated, those who become regular users but succeed in their effort to break the habit, and those who are firmly "hooked." We shall follow the path of those who became addicts and note the critical stages at which some stopped and others went on.

The findings presented here are those of the interview study of users, delinquents, and controls and of the study of gangs.

Experimentation

At the time of our interview study in 1953, experimentation with heroin typically followed a period of smoking marijuana cigarettes; eighty-three of the ninety-six heroin-users who answered this question had smoked marijuana, forty of them regularly, before they began using heroin. In the street-gang study, however, it developed that there were many juvenile heroin-users not known to have started with marijuana. The boys were introduced to marijuana at school, dances, or parties and were usually given "cigarettes" by friends; the "reefers" were often passed around a group, like an Indian peace pipe. A few had their first smoke as early as age ten or eleven, but the most common age was fifteen.

Marijuana is undoubtedly in much more common use than heroin. For instance, 15 per cent of the controls had had some experience with marijuana. Even so, we may take it as axiomatic that at least the regular smoking of marijuana is, as a rule, associated with participation of the smoker in a deviant subgroup of peers.[1] On this basis and owing to the common pattern of starting drug use with marijuana, we would expect that the first use of heroin was, for most boys in our sample, an experience which accorded with the general atmosphere of their social groups; at any rate, it was not likely to be a shock. This was, indeed, the case.

Most of the users had heard about heroin for some time before they actually had a chance to try it, usually at the age of about fifteen; by that age, most of them had also seen someone inject or snort heroin. In most cases, the first chance to actually try the drug came when they were about sixteen or seventeen years old, but a sizable proportion were much younger at the time; a fifth were fourteen or less.[2]

The first opportunitiy came about in a simple, casual way. About a third of the boys were offered a "shot" or a "snort" by a youthful friend, and, in about another third, the opportunity developed in a group setting and at the initiative of the group. Very few actively sought the first opportunity, and a few others were offered drugs by members

[1] See Howard S. Becker, "Marijuana Use and Social Control," *Social Problems* (1955), 35–44.

[2] This is by their own dating. The interviews from which these data were obtained were conducted in 1953. It will be recalled (cf. Chapter II) that a marked upsurge of juvenile cases was noted in 1949. Allowing about two years for these cases to come to public attention and an average of about five hundred *new* cases per year since then, opportunities for exposure to heroin use must have been increasing since about 1947. It is interesting to compare the dating of first chance to try among this group of users with data obtained one year later in our study of all the male eighth-grade populations in three neighborhoods differing in incidence of juvenile drug use (this study is reported in detail in Chapter IV and Appendixes G and H), including, of course, the minority who may later have become users. It may be recalled that, in the neighborhood with very high drug rates, close to 40 per cent of the eighth graders (age thirteen to fourteen) claimed to have seen someone taking heroin, 45 per cent claimed acquaintance with one or more heroin-users, and 10 per cent claimed that they had already had the opportunity to try it themselves. The credibility of these claims is discussed in Appendix H. It seems reasonable to assume that, if we could identify those who eventually became users, the percentages would be considerably higher in this subgroup.

of their families or unrelated adults. In most cases, the heroin was obtained easily and without cost; in only 10 per cent of the cases did the boy pay for his first dose. The decision to try drugs and the transaction usually took place on the street, on a roof, in a cellar, in a private house, or often at or before a dance or some other large party. In a few cases, the event took place at school; in another few, in a bar, a poolroom, or some other public establishment. The "second chance," for those who did not take the first offer, occurred under similar circumstances. Typical situations of the first try are described in the boys' own words.

> It was raining, and I was tired. I was standing in a doorway when this friend of mine came by. He said, "Want a pick-up?" I said "Sure," so we popped.

> I was at a party. Everybody was having a good time. I wanted to be one of the crowd. I thought, if it didn't hurt them it wouldn't hurt me. That started the ball rolling. They were sniffing it that time. Two or three pulled out a few caps; said, "Here, if you want to, try." I accepted. They weren't trying to addict me; they just gave it to me.

> It was in school. At that time, all the boys were using it. A friend offered me some. Said it was something different. He had just started using it himself, and he wanted me to try.

Other accounts of the first experience with heroin convey more clearly the easy and "natural" manner in which the mood of the social situation produced or was hospitable to the suggestion to try heroin.

> One of the seamen I knew, knew I smoked reefers and thought I ought to try heroin sometime. Hanging around the block, there were a couple of fellows who were new around the block. They were going down to the cellar to snort the stuff. They asked me to join them. I was a little leery at first, but then I went with them. They offered me a little, and I snorted it.

> Some of us was in a car. We was going to town one night, so one of the guys said, "Let's take off [use drugs] before we start." I said, "Not me; I don't want any." But one of the guys owed me $2, so he said: "Come on. I'll give you four pills, and we'll call it even." So I tried. That was just skin-popping. The next day I was

with this same guy, and he was mainlining. Wanted me to try it. I tried two pills at once that time.

I was going down town with a guy. He wanted to borrow $1.25. (He had money, but no change.) He went and got a bag, or a deck. It was nice stuff. Would have cost anybody else $12. He asked if I wanted some. I said no, but, being as I had put some money into it, I changed my mind and sniffed some.

Bunch of fellows my age were down on the corner. Someone said, "Let's try some." No one knew where to buy it then, but we made a contact. So we went up on the roof and snorted.

At a party. A fellow had some. He was one of my friends, and I figured he was straight. He suggested it, so we snorted.

I was on the corner one night alone. Fellows came up. Some friends of mine said, "Let's go to a party." I said, "Hell, no." One of them said that a fellow at the party had some heroin. So I was curious, and I went along. We snorted.

There were three of us. Someone said, "Let's buy some horse." One of them went and got some works. So I skin-popped.

The social situation in which the suggestion was made to try heroin was free from any overt conflict or constraining pressure. Unless the boy had his own doubts about taking the drug, it was not likely that some other member of the group would demur or question the suggestion. The transition from knowing about heroin and its "pickup" attributes to becoming familiar with the mechanics of buying a "deck" to knowing heroin-users more-or-less casually to personal participation —this transition appears smooth and natural in the types of social group and situation described by most of our sample of users.

The absence of constraint in the situation was matched by absence of inner restraints; three-quarters of those who eventually became addicted tried heroin at their first opportunity.

How representative are these experiments with heroin of the exposure to heroin among all adolescent boys in the high-drug-use areas? The answer is, not at all. The situations described above are typical only of some subgroups in the neighborhood; the easy acceptance of the drug is typical only of some boys.

Even though knowledge of heroin is widespread—most of the non-users had heard about it by the time they were fifteen or sixteen years old—there are subgroups where the suggestion and the opportunity to try drugs never arise; there are youths who refuse to try the drug even when it is offered to them.

Of the fifty nonusing delinquents, two-thirds had had an opportunity to try, but only four did—not continuing, of course. Of the controls, 40 per cent had a chance to try heroin, but none of them did. The first opportunity came when they were in their fifteenth to seventeenth year.

WHY DO THEY REFUSE TO TRY?

Several easily ascertainable factors seem to be related to the readiness to try heroin when the opportunity arises: the boy's age, some deterrent information on the drug, and, less clearly, his interpretation of the attitudes of significant adults toward drug use.

Age. Among the delinquents and users, sixteen seems to be the age most susceptible to experimentation with drugs. For one thing, boys who get their first chance to try drugs at this age are more likely to try on this occasion than boys who are either younger or older at the time of first opportunity. Those who got their first chance when they were under sixteen were least likely to try immediately.

TABLE VI-1   *Boy's Age at First Chance and Decision to Try Heroin*

	12–15	16	17–20	TOTAL*
		PERCENTAGE		
Tried on first chance	47	73	61	58
Tried on later chance	26	6	23	20
Never tried	26	21	16	22
TOTAL CASES	(57)	(33)	(43)	(133)

* Thirty-three nonusing delinquents who had an opportunity to try heroin are included in this and the following table. Twenty of the fifty-two controls also had a chance to try heroin (none did), but there are so many other differences between them and the users that the comparisons would be less meaningful if they were included in the table. Fifty-five per cent of the delinquent nonusers had their first chance when they were younger than sixteen, as compared to 39 per cent of the users. The difference is not statistically significant. There is a five-point difference in the percentages of those whose first chance came at sixteen.

Further, boys who got their first chance at the age of fifteen or sixteen typically reported that this happened on the initiative of a friend in a face-to-face situation, whereas most of the boys who were either younger or older at the time typically reported that they took the drug in a group. The first exposure on the boy's own initiative was also most frequent among the sixteen-year-olds.

Finally, the balance of individuals with favorable, as compared to

TABLE VI-2   *Age at First Chance and Type*
of Initiator

	12–14	15	16	17–20	TOTAL
	PERCENTAGE				
Boy himself	3	8	18	9	10
Boy's peer	26	62	49	35	41
A group of peers	55	15	24	37	34
Other (adult, relative)	16	15	9	19	15
TOTAL CASES	(31)	(26)	(33)	(43)	(133)

those with unfavorable, reactions to the first try was negative (i.e., there were more with unfavorable than with favorable reactions) for those who had their first try at the age of thirteen, but this balance changes rapidly so that it is only slightly negative at fifteen and becomes positive at sixteen. At sixteen, there are more boys with definite positive than with definite negative reactions. By age seventeen, this excess increases to 50 per cent, but for the eighteen-year-olds and over it drops very markedly.[3]

Thus it appears that, among those given the opportunity, the six-teen- and seventeen-year-old boy is more likely to try heroin on the first chance than either the younger or the older boy, is more likely even to initiate the first try, and is more likely to experience a positive reaction to his first intake of heroin. One might venture to say that there is a lowered resistance to the unique temptation and unique satisfactions that heroin offers at that age. It is not difficult to speculate on the reasons. Sixteen is the age of transition from childhood to adulthood. It is the minimal legal age for leaving school and for obtaining working papers. And, in general, it is perceived in our society as an age when the youth is no longer a child. One can assume that a youth who feels in-adequate and insecure, whose self-confidence and self-esteem are low, will experience the demands for maturity that accompany his sixteenth year with increased discomfort. When the need for surcease, for peace of mind, for the quelling of self-doubt is intensely felt, one expects that whatever resistances the youth has to experimentation will become less effective.

Deterrent Information. The hope is often expressed that effective in-

[3] We should probably take these age trends cautiously in view of the relatively small number of cases at each age level. A more conservative analysis shows that, under sixteen, 45 per cent of the reactions were negative, as compared to 30 per cent positive, whereas at sixteen and over, only 18 per cent are negative, as compared to 52 per cent positive.

formation on the dangers of addiction may act as a deterrent to drug use. Some of the statements made by the users we interviewed supported such hopes. One of them said:

> If I had known that it would blow up everything. . . . Those kids just passed it around like it was nothing. Everybody was taking it, just sniffing it, didn't know anything about it. If I had known about it, I never would have tried the junk. I tried it because I didn't know anything about it. No one in my neighborhood knows anything about it. That's what they need—education—so that kids know what the stuff can do. It can blow everything up in your face.

We asked the boys what they had ever learned which might make them "hesitate and think twice" before taking a drug and how old they were when they learned each item of information that they mentioned. We then coded the boys' answers separately for "learned deterrent information before critical age" and "after." Hardly any of the users (only 17 per cent) said that they learned anything cautionary about drugs "before," whereas most delinquent nonusers (79 per cent) said that they did so before they were sixteen (which, as has been mentioned, corresponds to the median critical age for the users).

Although much of this difference might be discounted because of retrospective falsification by the users of events which took place prior to their use of drugs, the difference is too great to be entirely dismissed. It is consistent with the view that such information does, in fact, deter at least some youths. It is, however, also consistent with the possibility that the kinds of boys who become users are more resistant (emotionally and/or intellectually) to such information and with the possibility that the acquisition of such information is a more-or-less incidental correlate of other factors that differentiate the two groups.

What was the nature of the deterrent information? The main thing, mentioned by three-fourths of all delinquent nonusers as well as users, was that drugs were bad for health or dangerous to life.

> It makes your veins collapse, gives you yellow jaundice or abscesses, or you get an overdose and die.

> It will mess you up physically. You get sick, your eyes keep running, you lose a lot of weight.

> You might kick [die] from using too much. Don't take a shot from your friend. He'll give you a hot shot; try to kill you and take it all for himself. I saw it happen to a girl; she died.

Second in frequency of mention (60 per cent) is the fact that the cost of drugs forces users to resort to illegal activities.

When you need drugs, it'll make you go out and steal. Everytime you get a dollar, you'll use it or set it aside until you do need it for drugs.

Makes you do illegal things; makes you steal and peddle.

Finally, about half the users said that they had learned that the drug habit leads to deterioration of character.

Can't get nowhere. Anywhere you go, you go down. Can't hold a job, can't keep money.

You just lay around and do nothing. It changes your character, makes you snobbish, irritable, untidy.

It makes you cranky. Sometimes you lose friends. You lose interest in everything. You like nothing but drugs.

It changes you completely; you become dishonest, like stealing from your mother. I never got to that; I broke in and took things. I know when I was running the dice game, you could trust people and leave the game, but with junkies, you have to watch them every minute.

This information was supposedly obtained predominantly from "own observation" or "own experience" and from friends. Only a few said that they gained information from reading, and a negligible number, from adults (parents, teachers, and the like). The delinquent nonusers had acquired the same type of deterrent information and from the same sources (except, of course, own experience).

Social Pressure. Most of the boys we interviewed (from 60 to 80 per cent in each of the four groups) did have, at the critical age, some friends whose opinion "meant the most" to them. But when we asked what these friends felt about heroin-, marijuana-, and drug-users, only the control group gave unequivocal answers: nearly all the friends who mattered to them had negative feelings about drugs and users. The users and delinquent nonusers claimed mostly that they *did not know* what their friends' feelings about drugs had been. Of the twenty-eight users who "knew," eight said that their friends' feelings about the drugs had been positive or accepting, and sixteen said, negative. Only one of the seven delinquent nonusers who could answer this question associ-

ated positive feelings with his friends, and the other six attributed negative attitudes to their friends. The number of answers is, of course, too
small to bear any weight as evidence, even though the trend is in the
expected direction.

The data are even less discriminating with respect to the one *adult*
person whom the boy would most like to think well of him. Almost all
boys said that there was such an adult in their lives at the critical age.
In the control group, this was usually the father or both parents; in the
other three groups, it was usually the mother.[4] The reported attitude of
this adult to heroin and its users had been overwhelmingly negative in
all four groups we interviewed, and most boys knew or felt that they
could surmise this person's attitude.[5]

Let us return now to those who do try the drug. Why are some of the
youths capable of "playing around with" heroin, sometimes for long
stretches of time, but do not become habituated, whereas others proceed
rather quickly to incontinent use and habituation?

OCCASIONAL USE

Most of the users on the first try "snorted" (sniffed) the drug. Their
reactions ranged from extreme euphoria to nausea, feeling sick, feeling
"bad," or depression. Nearly half experienced definitely pleasant reactions, and about a third, negative reactions. Some reported mixed sensations or no sensation at all, explaining that, "If you don't know about it,
you don't know how the kick goes."

These are descriptions of the positive feeling after the first try:

> It gave me like a sense of peace of mind. Nothing bothered me; it
> felt good.

> Felt above everyone else—ready for Freddie—great.

> I felt all right and more sure of myself.

[4] Forty-two per cent of the controls said "father" or "both parents," as compared to 36 per cent who said "mother." Forty-seven per cent of the nondelinquent users, 62 per cent of the delinquent users, and 69 per cent of the delinquent nonusers said "mother." In the last three groups, the percentages designat-
ing "father" or "both parents" were, respectively, 22, 15, and 10 per cent.

[5] An interesting feature of this part of our inquiry was the difference in the
reported image of the user supposedly held by the important adult at the boys'
critical age. In the main, the image is of a mentally sick person; an unfortunate
person (victim of circumstances); or a stupid person, a "sucker" who should
know better. Most of the control group attribute to their important adult the
image of a drug-user as "unfortunate"; most of the delinquent nonusers, as
"stupid" (the users are similar to the controls in this respect).

I got real sleepy. I went in to lay on the bed. . . . I thought, this is for me! And I never missed a day since, until now.

I felt I always wanted to feel the same way as I felt then.

I felt above everything. I felt I knew everything. I talked to people about interesting things.

Felt like heat was coming through my body and head. It made me forget all things. Felt like nobody existed but me, like I was by myself.

It is, of course, difficult to assess the truthfulness of these accounts. Even with best intentions, the users, at the time of the interview, might have retrospectively endowed their first experience, which took place two to three years before, with the glow of the "high" feeling they later experienced. But there is no reason otherwise to doubt their reports of euphoric reaction on first try. Laboratory experiments[6] have produced positive reactions to first intake of opiates. And, although some users claimed that they felt nothing until they knew what feeling to expect, this need not be universal.[7]

Reaction to the first trial helped to determine the timing of subsequent use. Two-thirds of the boys whose reactions were favorable continued immediately, compared to only two-fifths of the boys whose first reaction was unfavorable. The remainder did not resume until a somewhat later period. In any event, 90 per cent of the users were using regularly within a year of the first trial,[8] the rest within two years.

FROM OCCASIONAL TO REGULAR USE

The distinction between occasional or weekend use of heroin and regular use of at least one intake daily is basic. For one thing, occasional use does not necessitate the urgent quest for contacts and money

[6] Cf., among others, John M. von Felsinger, Louis Lasagna, and Henry K. Beecher, "Drug-induced Mood Changes in Man," *Journal of the American Medical Association,* 157 (1955), 1006–1020, 1113–1118.

[7] Howard S. Becker claims that it is universal with regard to marijuana; Cf. "Becoming a Marijuana User," *American Journal of Sociology,* 59 (1953), 235–242. However, the general effect of marijuana is much milder.

[8] It should be kept in mind that these are boys who became confirmed users. It does not follow that, in the general population, all those who take a first shot or snort continue using. It may be of interest to note here that, of the fifty delinquent nonusers, thirty-three had a chance to try heroin; twenty-nine never tried; three tried on first chance and one on a later chance; but none continued. Of the fifty nondelinquent nonusers, twenty had an opportunity to try heroin, but not one of them did.

to procure the drug. For another, it does not necessarily precipitate the changes in interests, mood, and leisure activities which, as we shall see, characterize the regular user's life. Rather, occasional intake of heroin at parties, on week ends, or at times of feeling low, serve a supportive and pleasurable function as a rule, with no negative side effects; this is sometimes referred to as "the honeymoon stage."

What makes for increased frequency and regularity of intake? The sheer addictive properties of heroin are certainly not sufficient to account for the change, for heroin has no universal addictive impact, and certainly not if taken in intervals of more than a day.[9] Furthermore, there is some evidence that many youths go on using heroin on a more-or-less irregular basis—e.g., week-end and party use—for several years and eventually stop altogether. In our study of heroin use in gangs, we found that, of the eighty current heroin-users, less than half were using daily or more often and that fourteen boys who had used heroin in the past had stopped completely.

This is the one point in our findings to which at least one expert has reacted with total incredulity. He has, on numerous occasions, stated that, in his experience, no teen-ager has ever started to use heroin without going the whole way and that, though there are regular adult users who have been known to stop, no adolescent has, in his experience, ever been known to do so. We referred to the existence of such a point of contradiction in the first part of Chapter V and promised to return to it. The contradiction may be accounted for in large measure by the nature of the agency this expert—modestly, he insists that there are no experts in the field of drug addiction—has created and directs. It is a helping agency; the clients come to it because they are in trouble owing to their involvement with narcotics. Boys who do not get into trouble because of narcotics have no reason to come to the agency. The boys who do come have a strong need to confirm the belief in the irreversibility of the path, since it not only gives them an alibi for continuing use, but also helps to maintain their self-esteem (and, incidentally, makes it more difficult to treat them) by its implication that, basically, they are no different from anyone else. In other words, the testimony of the boys who do come to the agency would be affected by a strong motivation to agree with the belief in irreversibility, along with solemn promises to try to stop.

In part, the contradiction can be accounted for by how one reads the agency's data. One of the cases, for instance, with which the agency has

[9] Harris Isbell, personal communication to Donald L. Gerard.

dealt for many years has been known to abstain voluntarily for relatively long periods of time. He always comes back, however. If one places the emphasis on the relapses, this case is consistent with the hypothesis of irreversibility. If one considers the long periods of voluntary abstention, it definitely is not.

We do not know how many other such cases have come to the attention of this agency. In principle, however, we would expect at least two varieties, not counting the varieties that do not come to the agency. The first is exemplified by the case just mentioned. This young man abstains successfully as long as life is proceeding smoothly for him, but he quickly relapses under conditions of stress. We are, of course, aware that his own self-destructive needs may help to generate that stress. This does not gainsay the fact that there are conditions under whch he can voluntarily abstain. It is consistent with the belief that there is no sharp dividing line between the nonaddicted user and the hopelessly chronic addict; and it is consistent with the fact that there do not seem to be any sharp discontinuities in the distribution of individual differences, no matter which dimension of individual differences is under consideration. Even in the anatomical differentiation of the sexes, one finds intermediate cases.

In Chapter II, we described four varieties of addicts, two of which we described as truly addicted; the essential criterion is that such cases involve craving. The patient described in the preceding paragraph meets this criterion even though his craving for the drug is not continuous. When a person craves a drug, he needs it as a means of alleviating the distress of frustration, anxiety, or pain; it seems clear that this patient does rely on the psychopharmacological effects of the drug as a coping mechanism. On the assumption that his periods of abstention are not completely free of stress, this case does emphasize the fact that craving is not an all-or-none phenomenon, that is, that even true addicts differ in the readiness with which they fall back on this coping mechanism. Parallels are readily found in phenomena related to drug addiction. For instance, alcoholics, thumb-suckers, and overeaters differ in how much stress they can take before they, respectively, feel impelled to drink themselves into oblivion, take their thumbs into their mouths, or "narcotize" themselves with food.

The second variety of recurrent user who can voluntarily abstain under certain conditions belongs, to our minds, in the ranks of users who are not truly addicted. (We make no reference in the present discussion to the first of the not-truly-addicted types discussed in Chapter II—total personal involvement, but without craving—because we are not certain whether there are intermittent users of this type. It is conceivable, however, that some individuals habitually fall back on involvement with narcotics and with the drug-using subculture as a means of filling temporary voids in their lives.) In principle, we would expect that there are many such cases. Such a person is never truly "hooked," although he may go through periods of physiological dependence and experience the withdrawal syndrome. Even after hospitalization or imprisonment, he goes back to drugs, sooner or later, because he returns to the same circumstances in which he succumbed to the impulse to experiment in the first place. These are cases of recurrent "infection," not of continuing addiction. If one does not distinguish between a recurrently induced impulse to indulge and a more-or-less chronic craving for the intoxicated state, such cases would reinforce a belief in the inevitability of the transition from experimentation to addiction.

Again, in terms of the principle of relative continuity in the distribution of individual differences, we would expect that there are many cases of mixed type of the two varieties we have just distinguished, that is, individuals whose craving varies more-or-less consistently with variations in the stress of their situations, whose impulses to indulge are more-or-less strongly induced by their environment, and whose thresholds of stress and resistance to craving are lowered by the effects of indulgence.

At any rate, it is clear that not all youths who experiment do go on. What, then, makes some youths who have experimented with heroin switch from occasional to frequent, regular use? We formulate this question thus—in terms of incontinent use rather than in those of addiction—because, as just noted, the category of regular users is more inclusive than the category of addicts. Only some of the regular users will go on to become full-blown addicts. In other words, from the viewpoint of causation, there is a logically, if not chronologically, intervening step between experimentation and addiction, and this is the step that we now explore.

Let us distinguish between the force of the growing *appetite* and the capacity to maintain *control* over it. Let us also assume that those who develop an increasing appetite are those for whom the effects of the drug are especially gratifying: they meet some strong need. And let us assume that a normal response to the awareness of a strange new impulse—especially one that is commonly known to be dangerous—is not to indulge but to try to control it, to hold it back.

It would follow that those who proceed from experimentation to regular use are either those who experience an exceptionally strong need for the effects of narcotics or those who have little wish or capacity to control the impulses. We consider the issues of need and control in later chapters. For the moment, however, let us note that the need for support may be intensified by objectively greater environmental stress at the time of experimentation. In the preceding chapter, some evidence was presented suggesting that users had experienced, at the time of onset of regular heroin use, some stress in their personal lives or family environment. There were indications that the users came from families that were less cohesive than those of their nonusing peers. There were indications that the users were thrust prematurely into adult roles. Many of them (about a fourth, compared to only one or two controls) experienced some radical change in their lives during the critical year—shift in family occupation, move to another neighborhood, and the like—which may have created special difficulties.

In the following chapter, we shall see that many gang members turn to narcotics when the gang is beginning to break up, withdrawing a feeling of solidarity and of belonging that may serve to make up for the failures of the home. We shall note, too, that this point in the life of the gang comes when the other boys are becoming seriously concerned with settling down to adult responsibilities, selecting a permanent career and a permanent mate; in other words, at a point where it becomes increasingly difficult to pretend that one is living up to an adult role simply because one does not have to account for oneself to parents and because one is earning the money for immediate needs in odd or dead-end jobs. This is the point at which many are confronted by the fact that they are not really ready for adulthood.

In other words, regular use comes at a point when, whatever the intensity of certain needs and whatever the vigor of the inner control system, most of the boys are in a particularly weakened state because they are trying to cope with exceptional stress.

Life Style of Habitual Users

Let us now turn to the youth who, after a year or two of occasional use of heroin, finds himself relying on regular (at least once-a-day) doses of the drug to stand off states of intense misery. This sets what is often called the "frantic-junkie" stage. With the realization of constant need for heroin and anticipation of the depression or even the pain of withdrawal should he fail to obtain a "deck," comes the intense, continuous preoccupation with the means of obtaining the drug and the necessary money. This preoccupation becomes a central motive in the young addict's life, and it colors his behavior, interests, values, relation to his family and friends—in short, his whole life style.

Once regularly on the drug, most of the one hundred users we interviewed took at least one dose daily; two-thirds, two a day or more.

TABLE VI-3   *The Process of Habituation among*
                Delinquent and Nondelinquent Users

	DELINQUENT USERS	NONDELINQUENT USERS
	PERCENTAGE	
Took two or more doses daily	57	76
Spontaneously reported mood changes		
General dysphoria	35	59
Concern over feeling hostile	5	24
Made efforts to break the habit	67	81
TOTAL CASES	(41)	(59)

Almost all the regular users "mainlined"; twelve "sniffed," three "skin-popped," and one, reluctant to "skin-pop" and in order to avoid nasal irritation, sprinkled heroin on his food. Half the users spent more than $30 weekly on the drug; one-third spent between $20 and $30.[10] Since

---

[10] Interviews were conducted in 1953, and this weekly cost probably reflects prices of heroin in 1952. Since that time, heroin "decks" have become more diluted, and the addict consequently must spend more money to obtain the same effect from intake, that is, if the psychopharmacological effect per se matters to the user. That the psychopharmacological effect is not of great moment to many regular users is evidenced by the well-known fact that severe withdrawal reactions are nowadays comparatively rare. That is, despite the development of tolerance (the need for increased drug intake to produce discernible effects), users do not markedly increase their intake to a point that will, as an incidental consequence, produce severe withdrawal reactions. They continue taking the drug despite the absence of any discernible effect and despite the fact that, in the absence of effect, they would be just as well off ridding themselves of the habit at the cost of relatively mild withdrawal discomfort. That they continue taking the drug implies that they are getting some kind of return other than the effect of the drug. We have suggested that this return is in the form of involvement which offers them meaningful associations, a line of activity to which they

most of them were not regularly employed, the necessity to procure the money became one important factor in their lives.

CHANGES IN MOOD

Another change the users reported was in mood and "character." Some of the changes in mood varied, depending on whether they were "on" the drug, "off," or in search of "a fix." The question we asked was: "Tell me something about your life after you started taking drugs. . . ." Only twelve of the one hundred users spontaneously mentioned positive changes, apparently referring to their "on-drug" personality: greater social poise, "smoother" manners, ease of social interaction. Even fewer said that their over-all mood had become a happier one. Most, however, spoke of their "off-drug" self. Half spontaneously reported general dysphoria—"feeling cranky and mean all the time" was the most common response. Some noticed an increase in aggressiveness —"seems like I got more heart to go out and hurt people." About one-fifth mentioned constant worry about the habit as a specific source of unhappiness. Whether they were aware of changes in their character or not, the actual off-drug mood of the habitual users was depressed, pessimistic, cynical.

In their general values and attitudes, the habitual users were strikingly identified with the delinquency-orientation cluster described in Chapter IV. We administered the Form F questionnaire to a group of twenty-nine Riverside patients (most of whom may be safely assumed to be nondelinquent users) and compared their answers to those of the controls. On eleven of the forty attitude-value items, the Riverside group was (1) significantly different from the control group; and (2) the modal response of each group on a given item was the opposite of the modal response of the other group (i.e., if the majority of the users said "yes," the majority of the controls said "no," and vice versa). Six of these items are part of the delinquency-orientation cluster and reflect an attitude of futility, suspicion, *anomie*.

Table VI-4 shows the eleven items and the responses of controls and users. Every boy was scored on the number of "square" responses he

---

can feel committed, a definite status in society, and so on. There are, of course, addicts for whom periodic abstention associated with lack of access to the drug or with voluntary withdrawal serves the function of reducing the tolerance level. If this happens often enough for long enough periods, they can continue to experience the effects of the drug in the intervening periods of use without becoming sufficiently habituated to run the risk of severe withdrawal reactions.

TABLE VI-4   *Differentiating Items in the Form F Questionnaire**

ITEM NO.	ITEMS	CONTROLS' ("SQUARE") RESPONSE	USERS' ("DELINQUENT") RESPONSE
D 6	Most policemen can be paid off.	Disagree	Agree
D 17	Most policemen treat people of all races the same.	Agree	Disagree
D 19	The police often pick on people for no good reason.	Disagree	Agree
10	You're a fool if you believe what most people try to tell you.	Disagree	Agree
14	I am sure that most of my friends would stand by me no matter what kind of trouble I got into.	Agree	Disagree
18	The thing to do is to live for today rather than to try to plan for tomorrow.	Disagree	Agree
D 22	The way things look for the future, most people would be better off if they were never born.	Disagree	Agree
D 25	Everybody is just out for himself. Nobody really cares about anybody else.	Disagree	Agree

Do you want this much more than almost anything else in the world?

28	To be always doing a lot of new and exciting things— never to be bored.	No	Yes
D 29	To be able to get other people to do what you want.	No	Yes
31	To be able to take things easy and not have to work hard.	No	Yes

* The items preceded by "D" are a part of the delinquency-orientation cluster. Since the Form G questionnaire (i.e., the portion containing the drug-related items) was not administered, the drug-related items in this cluster could not, of course, appear in the above list. It is a reasonably safe assumption that these items, along with most and perhaps all of the Form G items, would have appeared in the above list if this part of the questionnaire had been administered.

gave, the actual range from zero to 11. As would be expected from the manner in which these items were selected, the users were very low on the "square" index, the control group very high.

CHANGES IN ACTIVITIES

Changes in the habitual users' activities reflect their mood and attitudes. Nearly half the one hundred users spontaneously reported loss of vitality—laziness, drowsiness, apathy, loss of appetite, sexual impotence. A few mentioned loss of interest in social interaction and a wish to be left alone. Some reported becoming careless about their appearance. There were corresponding changes in their leisure activities. Whereas more than a third spontaneously reported active sports as "the thing they did most often" with friends before they started using drugs, active sports were mentioned by only four of the one hundred users as a major activity after the onset of drug use, and some mentioned constant preoccupation with drugs as their main "leisure activity." Eighty per cent said that they "goofed more time away" after they started taking drugs.

Another evidence of their general detachment from life was the high proportion of users (two-thirds) who, in answer to probing, said that they "gave up responsibilities, such as quitting a regular job, quitting school, and the like." Only one-third said that they took on such new responsibilities as getting married, fathering a baby, taking a higher type job, and the like. We know, however, from clinical studies, that taking on new responsibilities is not equivalent, for a juvenile user, to carrying them on with a sense of responsibility; their marriages (and, among girls, pregnancies) are, as a rule, irresponsible ventures. Four-fifths of the one hundred juvenile users we interviewed said, in answer to probing, that they "started doing things against the law."

In our study of delinquent gangs, reports of Youth Board group workers revealed a similar change in interests and activities of users and nonusing members of the gangs. Fewer users tend to participate in intergang warfare ("rumbles"), dances, house parties, joint trips to movies or sporting events, and active sports. On the other hand, more of them participate in gang-organized robbery and burglary.[11]

The association of drug use with crime for profit has been demonstrated also in other ways, both in New York and in Chicago. In New

[11] It may be of interest to note that more of them also participate in gang-organized sexual delinquencies (mainly "lineups"); this might reflect a loss of sexual interest, rather than the opposite, but the interpretation is speculative.

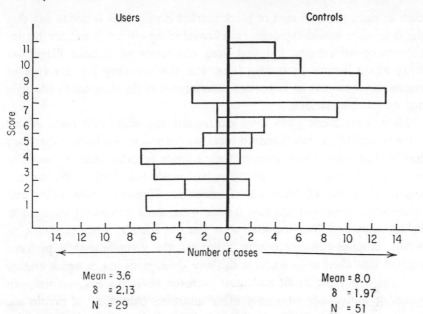

Three of the users are at and none are above the median of the control group. Two of the controls are below the median of the user group.

Fig. VI-1. Distribution of "Squareness" Index Scores for Users and Controls

York City, the proportion of delinquencies likely to result in financial gain (e.g., robbery, jostling, burglary, larceny, procuring, unlawful entry) was substantially greater in areas of high drug use than in those of low or no drug use. Offences against persons and nonprofit rule-breaking (e.g., rape, assault, disorderly conduct, auto theft) were less prevalent.[12] Similarly, a comparison of offenses committed in 1951 by adult and juvenile drug-users handled by the Narcotics Bureau in Chicago and the population handled by the Chicago Police Department revealed that "the number of arrests for non-violent, property crimes was proportionately higher among addicts. In contrast, however, the number of arrests of addicts for violent offenses against the person, such as rape and aggravated assault, was only a fraction of the proportion constituted by such arrests among the population at large."[13]

The evidence is thus clear that the user, juvenile or adult, engages in the illegal activities in which he does become involved, not for "pleasure" or because of any basic depravity, but mainly because he needs the

[12] See Chapter III for a fuller report on that study.

[13] Harold Finestone, "Narcotics and Criminality," *Law and Contemporary Problems*, 22 (1957), 71.

cash to meet the high cost of black market drugs. This is not to say that the drug-user would typically be a law-abiding citizen if not for his involvement with drugs, but that drug use tends to channel illegal activity along income-producing lines. But the necessity for this type of criminality becomes an important determinant of the drug-user's life style and of his associations.

Most users break away from old friends and make new ones. About three in five of the one hundred users we interviewed admitted that they had broken away from some of their friends or other intimate associations, and four in five said that they had made new friends. We did not study the nature of these new friendships. However, from other evidence we believe that the new friends were more commonly engaged in delinquency and drug use than were the old friends. Since juveniles, as a rule, commit delinquent acts in groups, the juvenile user is perforce pushed into close association with those delinquent gangs which engage in delinquency for profit and must perforce sever his associations with gangs or individuals who have other interests. Our study of heroin use in gangs gave clear evidence that this process does, indeed, take place.

Efforts to Break the Habit

It is difficult to assess the relative importance of the various types of pressures and to discern the most important motive for making an effort to "lay off" the drug temporarily or to break the habit. When we asked the seventy-six of the one hundred users who had made at least one such effort to tell us "Why [did you] lay off heroin for a while?" we got more than two hundred answers, an average of almost three reasons by each user. Four reasons were spontaneously mentioned most often, each by about one-third of the boys: they felt it was wrong, they worried about the money they had to get, the heroin made them feel "sick," and they worried about becoming really "hooked." On probing, the first two reasons were again mentioned most frequently, and, in addition, the boys admitted a fear of being arrested and that "somebody worked on [them] to lay off." Other fears mentioned by a smaller number of boys were of "losing my mind"; of becoming sexually impotent; of being killed by an overdose or an "air bubble" or of being poisoned by someone; and concern over the changes in their behavior and character, such as loss of interest in activities, inability to hold a job, inability to "get along with people," and the like. One reason given by many nondelinquent users and almost never by delinquent users involved perception of deterioration of character—laziness, withdrawal, aggressiveness.

> I wasn't myself. I became arrogant, sarcastic, wanted to better myself. Didn't want people to think my family wasn't raising me right. Didn't want to be around a bunch of lousy guys.

> I just felt myself going down, losing interest in everything. I figured it was bad for my health. Then, too, I started pawning clothes and stealing.

Findings from other studies give independent evidence that these reasons are probably genuine, at least on a conscious level. Clinical evidence indicates that their social relations with nonusing peers and their family relations become even more strained than before the onset of drug use, that some of them really feel guilty about drug use, and that heroin makes some "sick."[14] Fears of impotence and of being killed by an overdose are reasonable in view of the properties of the drug and the variability of the adulterants and of the concentration of heroin in the "decks"; so is concern over loss of vitality. The urgent quest for money is evident in the increased criminal activity described above. Fear of arrest is also realistic.

Our study of heroin use in gangs also produced evidence that the users were worried about their addiction. About half of the ninety-four users expressed concern about their habit to their group worker.

But the road from concern and worry to success in abstaining is not an easy one. Three-fourths of the one hundred users we interviewed said that they had made at least one effort to stop using heroin; half had made more than one effort. Of the ninety-four users in the gangs we studied, almost three in five were known to have made some effort to cut down or stop using altogether. At the time of the study, only fourteen had succeeded, and an additional twenty had reduced their intake.

WHAT ARE THE EFFORTS?

Some "efforts" consisted merely of good resolutions. Some, especially among the members of gangs, consisted of the avoidance of contacts with other users and increased contacts with the Youth Board worker and with those members who did not use drugs. In this, some

[14] See Chapter IX for a fuller account of these changes.

users received warm support from their nonusing friends who stayed close to them and, in an earnest effort to be helpful, treated them to food, wine, or marijuana.

Two-fifths of the one hundred users reported that they had been urged, mostly by parents, to "lay off." Yet the actual help proferred by parents does not appear impressive. In about three-fourths of the seventy-one cases on which information is available, parents did nothing at all. If they tried to do something, their action was likely to be authoritarian in approach; they ordered the boy out of the house, took him forcibly to court, beat him, rather than undertaking some program of joint action with the boy. In general, parents seemed little aware of anything effective that could be done to help their children help themselves.[15]

Few who wished to break the habit sought medical help. Of the ninety-four users in the gangs we studied, only one-fifth received any medical attention, and most of those not voluntarily but following an overdose or arrest. Even at Riverside Hospital, although many of the patients are there "voluntarily," very few are voluntary in more than a technical sense.

WHO MAKES THE EFFORT?

Several factors seem to be related to the efforts made by the users to free themselves from the habit: family cohesion, the attitude of important others toward drugs, age at first try, and, in gangs, the composition of gang membership.

Family Cohesion. The more cohesive the young user's family, the more likely he was to make frequent efforts to break the habit. However, this was so only among the nondelinquent users. Seventy-one per cent of those nondelinquent users who came from the more cohesive families made more than one effort to lay off drugs, compared to only 37 per cent of those from the less cohesive families. Delinquent users showed no difference in this respect.

Attitudes of Important Others. Another factor in the boys' efforts to discontinue drug use was the general attitude toward drugs of the adult whom they identified as the one whose opinion was the most important to them. Of the fifty-eight cases who described the attitude toward drugs of this "most important person" as extremely negative, three-fourths made one or more efforts to "lay off"; of the forty-six

---

[15] This is not intended as criticism; it may rather be taken as a measure of the paucity of available help.

TABLE VI-5

Family Cohesion and Boy's Effort to Stop Using Drugs
(Delinquent and Nondelinquent Users)

	NONDELINQUENT USERS		DELINQUENT USERS		TOTAL
	LOW COHESION INDEX (4–9)	HIGH COHESION INDEX (10–14)	LOW COHESION INDEX (4–9)	HIGH COHESION INDEX (10–14)	
	PERCENTAGE				
No effort	30	10	36	29	25
One effort	33	19	18	24	24
More than one effort	37	71	46	47	52
TOTAL CASES	(27)	(31)	(22)	(17)	(97)*

* Three subjects did not answer. The difference between the two subgroups of nondelinquent users is statistically significant.

cases where this adult's attitude was described as less extreme or indeterminate, only two-thirds made such efforts. Also, the attitude toward drugs of the boy's peers was related to his efforts to discontinue; the more negative it was, the greater the chance that the boy would make efforts to stop using drugs. One must, of course, note that this information is not fully trustworthy; it may be that boys who tried to stop were readier to admit to the negative attitudes of significant others, and they may have been readier to accept as significant others individuals whose attitudes to drug use were negative.

The Role of the Gang. What we have learned about the patterns of drug use in gangs confirms the importance of the gang in controlling drug use among its members. In the popular mind, the delinquent gang is a source of pressure for incontinent use of drugs. This is far from true. Experimentation with drugs may be a part of the delinquent culture, but habituation is not. Group workers in our gang study reported many instances where gang members tried to influence, and exerted strong pressure on, using members to cut down or discontinue the use of heroin. Pressures not to use heroin were mentioned by several workers as permeating the whole gang. Even users were more likely to behave in this manner toward their fellow members than to try to influence them to use. This finding held for every gang with more than one or two users. Some of the accounts of such influences against heroin use are illustrative.[16]

In one high-use gang, very permissive toward drug use and with a possible recent increase, the worker reported: "Shorty [a drug pusher] began telling the nonusers about the evils of drug use. . . . He won't sell them horse, only pot."

In another high-use gang, more active efforts were made.

> One key figure known to me stated that he had held a series of informal talks with one of the club members who began to use drugs and as a result of these talks got him off the kick.

> Art, an old user and respected by Frank, took it upon himself to talk periodically with Frank, pointing out the disadvantage of drug usage, and persuaded Frank to drop the kick.

[16] We should mention that, because of their servicing by the New York City Youth Board, these gangs may not be representative of other adolescent street gangs in the city. Yet some of these are highly contaminated gangs; it is our feeling that the attitude toward habituation is probably negative in most juvenile gangs.

In one high-use gang, paradoxically quite hostile toward use and unsympathetic toward users, the following is reported:

> Allie has spoken to Paul individually, telling him that he was much better off before he used drugs; he talked about how much better off he was mentally and physically. Allie sought to get the worker to assist Paul also.

One of the most interesting situations is reported in a very high-use gang with little drug permissiveness and much recent decrease in drug use.

> Members try to get others to cut down use of horse, especially when one member uses a great deal. This takes the form of individuals' or cliques' warning the fellow to get off the stuff, cut down, take more pot. The fear is that the fellow will take an overdose or get really sick. Sometimes the procedure of getting someone to take less stuff takes the form of treating to food or treating to pot.

In one gang, the group attitude toward the sole user was so hostile that he went to other gangs for drug activity; he is now off drugs.

Age. We have already discussed the importance of age as a factor in experimentation and habituation, and we discussed the greatly increased vulnerability to the effects of heroin at the ages of sixteen and seventeen. We also found that those youths who started using heroin regularly at the age of sixteen subsequently made less effort at stopping than those who had begun at either a younger or older age.[17]

HOW SUCCESSFUL ARE THE EFFORTS?[18]

Some of the efforts were apparently successful. Of the fifty-three users in gangs who made efforts to discontinue use, fourteen had stopped using, and twenty had, in the judgment of the group workers, decreased their intake at the time of our study. It is important to stress

[17] Of nineteen subjects who became regular users before they were sixteen, 68 per cent made more than one effort to stop; of the forty-nine who became regular users after sixteen, 52 per cent made more than one effort to stop; of the thirty-three who became regular users at sixteen, 36 per cent made more than one effort to stop. Of the last group, 46 per cent made no effort at all, as compared to 16 and 19 per cent, respectively, of the first two groups.

[18] On the basis of the method of selection, there was little point in getting data on the success of efforts to abstain by the one hundred users who were interviewed.

that not all of those fourteen who stopped completely were merely beginners or week-end users; seven had been taking at least one dose of heroin daily for some time before they "broke the habit."

Nineteen gang users received medical attention in connection with their drug involvement; however, none of these stopped using the drug, although four have decreased their intake.

Thus, while heroin addiction is not necessarily permanent, it is not easy for many to give it up, nor do most young users earnestly attempt to do so.

The great majority who continue with their habit almost automatically enter the category of "junkies" known to the police. At this point, the users have become young adults living in the criminal world. Since all our studies were focused on users under twenty-one years old, we do not have a complete picture of the young adult user. Apparently they continue their drug-centered existence and periodically appear in courts, jails, and hospitals.[a]

Summary

Most youths in high-drug-use areas had heard of heroin at the time they were fifteen years old, and some had seen others take the drug. We have no evidence of group pressure to experiment with drugs. The first try of heroin was a casual, social experience with peers.

The readiness to try the drug appears related to age; those who were sixteen and seventeen were especially susceptible. Descriptions of positive reactions to the first try suggest a sense of surcease, of the lifting of a weight, of peace and rising self-confidence. Most of the boys who had this positive reaction continued to use heroin as an occasional relief and prop. The others did not try again or tried only after some time.

Of those who became regular users, most went on taking heroin occasionally for a year or two. Once a habitual user of heroin, the youth underwent a drastic change in his life style. He became involved in criminal activities to obtain the drug and to procure the money he needed for it. His leisure pursuits became money-getting ones. His mood varied; when on drugs, he was "smoother" in social interactions, more poised. When off drugs, he felt "mean and cranky," worried, depressed, helpless, incompetent, hopeless, apathetic, lazy, indifferent.

Many quit school, gave up jobs, lost contact with old friends. They "goofed their time away."

Fear of arrest, worry about the habit, and a sense of guilt and shame prompted most of them to make some effort to break the habit. Those nondelinquent users who came from cohesive families were more likely to make such efforts. Some tightly knit gangs exerted strong pressure on their members to stop using heroin. Those users who started using heroin regularly when they were sixteen made least effort; those who started at a younger age made most effort.

Some of these self-help efforts were apparently quite successful, but most were half-hearted and not at all earnest. In time, the juvenile user becomes an adult "junkie" with a police record, his progress marked by the revolving doors of prisons and hospitals.

DELINQUENT AND NONDELINQUENT USERS

The process of habituation to heroin appears to differ among the delinquent and nondelinquent users. Most of the boys in both groups tried heroin on the first opportunity; about half had a positive reaction on first try. But, whereas the majority of the delinquents continued to use the drug more-or-less regularly after the first try, about half the nondelinquents resumed heroin use only after some time—a few weeks or more—after having experienced a more positive reaction on the second try. Yet, in spite of this greater initial hesitation at continuing heroin use, the nondelinquents ended up more heavily addicted. They took more doses daily, and they spent more money on heroin (the median weekly expenditure was $42, compared to $28 among delinquents).

The nondelinquents were also more conscious of the impact of the drug on their behavior. More spontaneously reported general dysphoria as an after-effect and concern over feelings of hostility. A somewhat greater proportion of nondelinquents had made efforts to "lay off" drugs, and fully one-fourth spontaneously mentioned that one reason for their making such efforts was the change they noticed in their own character; only one delinquent mentioned this reason. We have already noted that nondelinquents from more cohesive families made significantly greater efforts to free themselves of the habit; among delinquents, there was no relationship between family cohesion and the efforts made to "kick the habit." This might mean that they were less responsive to family influences.

STATISTICAL FOOTNOTES

[a] Cf. "A Study of Two-Hundred Self Committed Drug Addicts in the New York City Magistrates' Courts," a mimeographed report prepared by Max Blaustein (no date, c. 1955). From February, 1954, to May, 1954, 253 addicts appeared voluntarily at Chief Magistrate Term Court for commitment to Riker's Island or (the women) to the House of Detention. Of the 200 who had been interviewed at intake, 42 per cent were twenty-one to twenty-nine years old; 5 per cent were younger; and the rest, older. The twenty-to-twenty-nine age group included a large proportion of adolescents who became drug-users in 1949 and 1950, when the recent wave of juvenile use started. The bulk had been involved with drugs for about four years, but twenty-five had been on drugs for more than five years. Although the data presented in the study of those 200 addicts are based only on unverified statements obtained on intake interview, we present the information about those addicts as an approximately true picture of their life.

Of the eighty-four addicts aged twenty-one to twenty-nine, all but three were males. Sixty-four were Negroes, nine Puerto Ricans, and eight white. Seventy-four were unemployed, and, of those, fifty-five had been without work for more than a month, twenty-five for more than three months. Twenty had committed themselves at least once before to the same court; sixteen had been to Lexington Hospital; one, to Riverside Hospital. Fifty-one had previous court records.

VII

Heroin Use in the Delinquent Gang

At the time of our studies, there was widespread opinion that street gangs were the centers of narcotics activity.[1] It was often said that street gangs were centers of organized selling of narcotic drugs; that the gang population itself used drugs heavily; and that using members, by various means of persuasion, recruited users among hitherto nonusing boys. Actually, according to the experience of staff members, only a minority of the patients at Riverside Hospital belonged to organized gangs. This does not, however, reduce the possibility that the gangs do play the role attributed to them in the cases of gang members. It seemed desirable, therefore, to investigate the role of gangs in drug use. A study was undertaken of all the delinquent gangs in New York City that were at the time (1954) serviced by Youth Board "detached" group workers.[2] Facts on drug activity in the gangs and related information were obtained from these detached group workers.

For some years, the Youth Board has been conducting a program of social therapeutic and preventive group work with antisocial gangs in New York City. In this program, a group worker makes informal contact with a gang and attempts to develop a close relationship with

[1] Cf. Dale Kramer and Madeline Karr, *Teen-age Gangs* (New York: Henry Holt, 1953).

[2] Cf. *Reaching the Unreached* (New York: New York City Youth Board, 1954). The word "detached" does not refer to a state of mind, but to the fact that the worker's center of operations is outside the agency plant.

its members. He spends most of his time with them and is available in emergencies at all times. He participates in their legitimate activities; tries to help in planning such activities; sometimes suggests them; and, if necessary, tries to get help in procuring the resources needed to carry out such activities. He stands up for the boys in court, finds jobs for some, and obtains case-work assistance for the families of others. For all, he is available for guidance in difficult periods. Most important, and perhaps most difficult, he demonstrates that he wants to work *with,* rather than *on,* them. His approach is that of a realist, rather than a moralist. He does not preach to them. He is permissive and demonstrates that his major concern is with their individual welfare. He may advise, but he does not withdraw or display hostility or annoyance if his advice is not followed. He discourages confidences that would make him an accomplice in illegal activity, but he establishes the facts that he is not a police agent and that he can be trusted with all kinds of information. His relations with the gang members are usually highly intimate.

The group worker thus gets to know gang members well. He keeps voluminous records on the boys and their activities. These data, supplemented by the worker's general knowledge of the boys, constitute the source of all the findings reported here and in earlier references to the gang study. Each of the workers filled out a detailed questionnaire about his gang and each of its members. Some of the questions applied to the entire gang—its history, activities, structure. Specifically, we asked the size and nature of groups of boys who used drugs together, where they gathered, and, most important, whether there was any identifiable personal influence or group pressure to use or not to use drugs. Other questions were for each boy—to determine who used drugs, which drugs, amounts used, trend of use, arrests for drug use, history of treatment, efforts to stop use, attitudes toward drugs, and so on. We also asked questions about the boy's background and position in the gang. The complete set of questionnaires took from fifteen to thirty hours of each group worker's time to fill out.

In all, we obtained reports on eighteen gangs, ranging in size from five to twenty-six members—altogether, 305 boys. Most of these gangs were subdivisions, based on age or special interests, of larger gangs. The median age of the boys was eighteen; most were over sixteen and under twenty. The Youth Board selected the gangs for special attention because they had an exceptionally high rate of participation in gang warfare. One measure of the chronic character of their antisocial behavior is the fact that at the time of our study they had been serviced by the Youth Board for several years. More than two-thirds of the boys had habitually participated in delinquent behavior, more than half had been arrested at least once (almost all of these having received at least probationary treatment following arrest), and about one-quarter had served sentences in institutions for delinquents. They are precisely such high-delinquency gangs as one might expect to be involved in drug use and selling (See Table K-2[3]).

The gangs were located in three areas of the city which had very high incidence of delinquency and drug use. Eight were in Manhattan's East Harlem, four in or near the Red Hook section of Brooklyn, and six in the Bedford-Stuyvesant neighborhood in Brooklyn. In modal ethnic composition, seven were Puerto Rican, six Negro, two Italian, one Irish, and two Irish-Italian.

Extent of Use

Heroin use was not common in all eighteen gangs. In four gangs, there was no heroin use at all (let us call them "drug-free gangs"); in eight, less than half the members used heroin ("low-use gangs"); and in six "high-use" gangs, more than half the member were users.

Practically the only drugs in illegal use were heroin and marijuana. Of the 305 gang members, ninety-four used heroin more-or-less regularly, eighty still using it at the time of the study. About half the heroin-users also smoked marijuana. About eighty used or had used only marijuana (these were exclusively Negro and Puerto Rican boys). What follows concerns only users of heroin. Not all the heroin-users were habitual users, even though most had been using heroin for two or three years. Less than half took one or more doses of heroin daily (Table K-1b). The rest took the drug two or three times a week or even less often, and many remained occasional users, even though some injected directly into a vein. Most of the habitual users took the drug intravenously; most of the occasional users sniffed; a few injected it subcutaneously.

DRUG USE AND GANG STRUCTURE

Drug-taking is a clique or solitary activity, not a total gang activity. The group workers, asked whether drug use was usually individual,

[3] References are to the summary tables in Appendix K.

with other club members, or with outsiders also, told us that, in the nine gangs with the largest number of users, most heroin use involved a couple or a clique in the gang; outsiders were not in general involved. In the remaining gangs, in which at most two or three members were users, heroin was used on a solitary basis.

These are typical examples of club or clique participation (from the group workers' reports):[4]

> A clique of three boys, following a burglary, went to one of the member's rooms and took horse.

> A clique of four met in a hallway following a gang fight and took horse—skin-popping.

> At a public dance, groups of four or more go off to corners or toilets to smoke pot or sniff horse.

> Howie says he has some good stuff. He gets Irv and Harry to go up to his house to snort up.

> Eddie, George, Everett, and Shorty said that they were going to the movies to get high. They were going to snort some horse in the balcony. . . . Those not wanting to get high stayed on the block.

This tendency for heroin-users to separate into cliques seems to have serious effects on the cohesiveness of the gang.

The group workers also described other major activities (involving more than half the membership) besides drug use that were carried out on a clique basis. It thus became possible to classify clubs as either "dispersed" (two or more major activities carried out on a clique basis) or "cohesive" (fewer than two major activities carried out on a clique basis). Only one of the six high-use gangs fell into the cohesive category, but three of the eight low-use gangs and three of the four drug-free gangs were "cohesive" (Table K-5k). This suggests that, as the proportion of drug-users in a gang increases, the group splits into cliques, or subgroups.

As the gang breaks into cliques, its leaders become less important, decision-making is less structured, and there is some question as to

---

[4] Before filling out the questionnaires, each of the group workers made a list of the gang members about whom he had information. Next to each name, he entered a pseudonym which was consistently used in referring to that individual. We had no occasion to see the true names.

who the leaders are and what the process of decision-making and of carrying out orders is. In fact, the group workers had some difficulty in answering questions on the group structure in high-use gangs. At the same time, the whole gang becomes less active, more apathetic. In examining the group workers' general comments on the predominant interests of the gangs, we found that some were described as "not having anything to do or place to go," or "avoid boredom," or "no interest in anything." Such gangs were classified as generally "apathetic." These apathetic gangs were found only among the low- and high-use gangs; none of the drug-free gangs were "apathetic" (Table K-5j).

This general lowering of activities and narrowing of interests reached almost all types of usual gang pursuits. The more drug-users in the gang, the fewer gang members engaged frequently in gang fights, vandalism and hell-raising, sexual delinquency, gambling, or active sports. However, in all gangs, similar proportions participated in robberies and burglaries, organized dances and house parties, and watched sports events (Table K-4).

The shift in the social structure, activities, and general mood of the gang was apparently noticed by the nonusing members and apparently resented. And, in general, the nonusers' feelings about users were also negative.

ATTITUDES OF NONUSING MEMBERS TOWARD HEROIN

As one would expect, attitudes toward heroin use and users were much more negative among the nonusers in low-use gangs than in the high-use gangs (Table K-3). In the low-use gangs, most of the 114 nonusers opposed the use of heroin; some had mixed feelings about it; very few thought that occasional use was all right; and only 2 per cent gave unqualified approval of heroin use. Even the smoking of marijuana was rejected; a majority were in outright opposition to it, the rest had mixed feelings on the matter, and some accepted only occasional smoking of "reefers."

The nonusers' feelings about heroin-users and smokers of marijuana was, correspondingly, hostile or derogatory. About half were hostile or derogatory about habitual heroin-users and about a fifth expressed mixed feelings; only about a quarter were tolerant. Feelings about occasional heroin-users were somewhat milder, as were those about smokers of marijuana; but even toward the occasional user nearly half expressed hostile or derogatory feelings. Occasional smokers of marijuana were treated with somewhat more tolerance.

The twenty-six nonusers in the high-use gangs were much more tolerant of heroin use and users (Table K-3). Thus, for example, more of them approved of occasional heroin use, were tolerant of habitual heroin-users, and were tolerant of occasional heroin-users. Similarly, larger proportions than in low-use gangs were tolerant of smoking of marijuana. Correspondingly, smaller proportions opposed the use of heroin and expressed hostile or derogatory feelings toward heroin-users and smokers of marijuana.

The leadership status of users was another indication of the nonusing members' attitudes toward them. In the high-use gangs, it was the nonusing minority that provided most of the leadership; the users were predominantly rank and file. In the low-use gangs, the users appeared to be a special subgroup. Most of them spent little time with the gang (Table K-2k), and yet they contributed proportionately more leaders than the nonusing majority (Table K-3). But those who were leaders were mostly recent users; the boys who had been using drugs for two years or more were mostly rank and file. In both types of gangs, however, members who started using heroin tended to lose their leadership status; and, conversely, as they decreased the intake or stopped using altogether, they gained in leadership (Table K-2n). Drug use apparently does not go well with leadership in a delinquent gang. This fact can be understood only in the light of our findings concerning the behavior, interests, and life style of the user.

For one thing, drug-using activity tends either to split the gang into cliques or to take drug-using members away from the gang into solitary activity. In the high-use gangs, the users tended to snort or inject heroin together, in cliques; if there was no apartment available, they gathered in hallways, toilets, or movie balconies. Users in low-use gangs went off by themselves or with drug-using nonmembers. For another thing, although only slightly more of the users in both high- and low-use gangs showed a persistent pattern of delinquency apart from the use or sale of drugs (Table K-2d), significantly more users had been arrested for such non-drug-related delinquent acts (Table K-2e) and, when arrested, were apparently more likely to be sent to an institution than were nonusers. This finding gives an objective basis to the group workers' general statement that actively delinquent gangs dislike drug-users because they are unreliable "on the job" and can get the gang into trouble if arrested.

Finally, let us remember the differences we have already noted in the users' participation in gang activities: by the selective pattern of their interests and preoccupations, the users set themselves apart from the rest of the gang. All this helps explain the loss of leadership among users.

In general, the actual balance of group pressures seems to be against, rather than for, habitual use of heroin. In not a single case did the group worker report that a gang, as a unit, exerted pressure on its members to use drugs; whatever influence to use is reported derived from a few individuals. In fact, we had very few reports of efforts to influence non-users in their own gangs to start using heroin, even though about half the users (and a fourth of the nonusers) in the high-use gangs peddled drugs. Most often, users enticed other users to continue, or they re-introduced a former user after he had stopped for a while, particularly after he had been imprisoned or hospitalized.

But there were far more reports of influence and pressure against the use of heroin, especially to cut down or stop use. Even users were more likely to behave in this manner. This finding holds for every gang with more than one or two users. Pressures not to use were, in several cases, mentioned as permeating the whole group. This was true of high- as well as low-use gangs, of drug-using gangs with a generally permissive atmosphere as well as of those with much hostility toward drug use. In one high-use gang, for instance, with little drug permissiveness and much recent decrease in drug use, members tried to get others to cut down the use of heroin—especially when one member used it a great deal—warning the boy to get off the stuff, to cut down, or to take more "pot" instead. They feared that the boy would take an overdose or get "real sick." Sometimes, getting someone to reduce the dose took the form of treating him to food, marijuana, or alcohol. "Stay with us," say the nonusers; "we'll watch over you; drink with us, it's better than junk." If habitual heroin use does not appear endemic to or especially compatible with gang life, the question arises: What is it about some gangs that allows for the spread of this habit, and what in the general climate of a gang offers effective resistance to it?

A comparison of the drug-free, low-, and high-use gangs may help throw some light on this question.

DELINQUENT GANGS WITHOUT USERS

We found, first of all, that members of the drug-free gangs were several years younger than the other gangs (Table K-2a). The boys in the drug-free gangs differed from the low- and high-use gangs in many respects which may be related primarily to their being younger. Many were still attending school, whereas most boys in the older gangs were out of school. Also, only about half the boys were habitual delinquents, compared to a majority in the other gangs (Table K-2d). More of the drug-free gangs were very active in sports, and, unlike the others, all engaged in frequent gang fights (Table K-5a, i). Most carried on activities with the whole group, rather than in cliques. A larger proportion of their members participated in such gang-organized activities as sports, expeditions of vandalism, and general hell-raising (Table K-4). Although they seldom organized dances, more of their members participated whenever the gang did organize a dance. None of the drug-free gangs were described as "apathetic," as were five of the low- and high-use gangs (Table K-5j).

In general, members of drug-free gangs showed little concern over the use of heroin. Group workers had some difficulty in ascertaining attitudes toward drug use among the seventy-one members in drug-free gangs; they could give us no information concerning the attitudes of about one-third of the boys and even less information on their attitudes toward marijuana (Table K-3). A large proportion of the forty-nine members whose attitudes to heroin use were known had mixed feelings; the others were less hostile and more tolerant of the habitual user than were the nonusers in the low-use gangs, but not so tolerant as those in the high-use gangs. The generally more tolerant feelings about drug use in drug-free gangs probably reflects less concern about the problem and less awareness of danger from drugs than the nonusers in low-use gangs experience.

Whether any of the members of the four drug-free gangs we investigated would, as they grew older, become involved with drugs we could not, of course, predict.[5] But a closer look at the low-use gangs can give us an approximate picture of the spread of drug use in a de-

[5] A check with the group work supervisor in February, 1956—two years after the original data were collected—brought us the information that, in only one of those four gangs, did a splinter group form in which heroin was used by some members. Since these gangs remained under the supervision of a Youth Board group worker, this course of events cannot be taken to be representative of a natural group process.

linquent gang and of the reaction of the nonusing members to the appearance of users among them.

DELINQUENT GANGS IN WHICH USE BEGINS TO SPREAD

The pattern of activities in the low-use gangs was more similar to that in the drug-free gangs—even though the latter were younger—than to the same-age high-use gangs. More of the low-use gangs tended to engage frequently in sports (active and spectator), vandalism, and hell-raising, and more of them were cohesive. In addition, they engaged more than high-use gangs in robberies, burglaries, gambling, and club-organized sex delinquency (line-ups) (Table K-5). The picture one gets is of a comparatively more lively, active, cohesive pattern.

On the face of it, we cannot say whether the comparatively smaller number of heroin-users in these low-use gangs and the greater antipathy to drug use is a function of their greater liveliness and cohesiveness and will, consequently, continue to remain small or whether the relation is reverse; it may be that the reason these gangs are more lively and cohesive is that drug use is only beginning to spread there and that, as the number of users increases, the pattern of activities will change in the direction of high-use gangs.

The only way to discover the relations between age, activities, and spread of drug use or resistance to it would be to follow the gangs more closely from the time of onset of drug use. Our study was not designed to obtain an intensive, dynamic picture of the gang's role in the spread of drug use. But we do have some descriptive, historical information for individual gangs which is sufficiently suggestive to warrant mention. Let us consider a few brief case histories of the low-use gangs where the pattern of using drugs is either in its early stages or has remained arrested and limited to a minority.

> *Low-use gang No. 12.* This group began as a football team, developed hostility to rival teams, and engaged in gang fights. In the past few years, the boys, all of whom are now over eighteen, became interested in marriage, army service, jobs, adjustment after institutionalization. Some members once tried smoking marijuana, got sick, and never tried again. A peddler trying to sell drugs was beaten up by command of the leader and told never to come back. One boy used drugs, but the attitude of the others was so hostile to it that he used to go to other gangs for drug activity. He is now off drugs. The group participates in team sports, trips away

from home, and other constructive program activities (initiated by the youth worker).

Low-use gang No. 13. This group also began as a ball team and was active in street fights. In time, the group fragmented. Some members got jobs and became self-supporting and independent. A small group got to use drugs, especially following periods of anxiety. They have their own leader. The group's main leader is an intelligent, dominating youngster who resents the influence of the drug clique's leader but cannot counteract a pervasive climate of boredom—"nothing to do and nowhere to go."

Low-use gang No. 19. This fighting group began, in the past few years, to lose interest in bopping. The group appears to be generally disorganized. Since gang fighting declined, drug use seems to have risen. Those members who use drugs do it individually, not as a clique. Others speak out openly against the use of heroin.

Low-use gang No. 8. This group organized five years ago for self-protection against other fighting groups in the area. Recently, as the majority grew cool to bopping, a group of three boys broke off in open conflict with the president; soon after, these three started using heroin and acting "down with the cats." They continue making efforts to get the gang back to fights, but the majority of the members remain loyal to their president. The gang is doing well without fights. The three users are still out, and it is unlikely that they will be readmitted.

Piecing together all of our data and some of the descriptive, historical information for individual gangs, we offer the following speculation on how gang activities and changes in the gang may play a role in the spread of drug use or resistance to it. There appear to be two developmental stages in which the gang assumes differing roles with regard to drug use. In the adolescent stage (roughly under age eighteen), the street culture favors "acting out" on a gang basis. Rumbles, fights, hell-raising, and competitive sports are an appropriate expression for this age. Even if the gang includes a large proportion of anxious, inadequately functioning boys of the type we consider prone to drug use, the activities of the gang offer a measure of shared status and security and a sense of belonging. The boys do not have to face life alone; the group protects them. Escape into drugs is not yet necessary.

But, as the group grows older, two things happen. Sports, hell-raising, and gang fights become "kid stuff" and are given up. In the normal course of events, the youthful preoccupations are replaced by individual concerns with work, future, a steady girl, and the like. If most of the gang members are sufficiently healthy to face these new personal needs and social demands and engage in the new activities appropriate to their age, drugs will not attract their interest.

But, for those gang members who are too disturbed emotionally to face the future as adults, the passing of adolescent hell-raising leaves emptiness, boredom, apathy, and restless anxiety. In a gang where there are many such disturbed members, experimentation with drugs for "kicks" is likely to lead to frequent and, later, habitual use; cliques of users will grow quickly. Enmeshed in the activities revolving around the purchase, sale, and use of drugs and the delinquent efforts to get money to meet the exorbitant cost of heroin, the young users can comfortably forget about girls, careers, status, and recognition by the society at large. Their sexual drive is diminished, they maintain a sense of belonging in the limited world of the addict, they remain children forever. They may give up all sense of personal responsibility for their lives and conveniently project the blame for their shiftless existence on "the habit."

In other gangs, where drugs are not experimented with, the disturbed members are likely to turn at this stage to overt homosexuality, sometimes accompanied by transvestitism.[6] Either life pattern—as drug-user or as homosexual—serves the function of establishing distance from the real-life demands of young adulthood.

In 1957, the director of another agency reported to the writers that a gang with which it had been working had been persuaded to give up narcotics. She did not, however, regard this as an unqualified success, since the gang reverted to a "bopping"—i.e., a fighting and generally hell-raising—pattern. From our present point of view, the significant point is that, if one regards the bopping and drug-using as successive but dynamically unrelated events, this should not have happened. On the independent-event hypothesis, the boys in this gang had already outgrown the bopping phase of the teen-age subculture

[6] This information was obtained from Youth Board workers in an informal communication.

when they turned to drugs. When they left the latter phase, however, there was no reason, on this hypothesis, for reverting to the earlier one. According to our hypothesis, on the other hand, that the late adolescent's turning to drugs is, in part, a defensive maneuver against the necessity of undertaking an adult role for which he does not feel equipped, the reversion may not be predictable, but it is at least understandable. The drugs are a means of deferring the transition to adult responsibility. When this means is abandoned, the boys revert to a frankly adolescent pattern.

Narcotics come into the life of the juvenile street gang as one of the means whereby the maladjusted and inadequate youth evades the full assumption of an adult role. If he does not take to drugs to accomplish this goal, he will find some other means. If the selection of this means is, for other reasons, an easy one (e.g., because of the availability of the drug or a social climate and attitudes favorable to experimentation with it), it is likely to be chosen.

In brief, insofar as habitual drug use makes inroads into the life of the gang, there develops a distinct subculture of drug-users within the normal delinquent gang. The two are not compatible. The delinquent subgroup often contains large proportions of comparatively well integrated and adequately functioning youths for whom antisocial acting out seemingly serves only a transitional, developmental need and who, approaching adulthood, become interested in legitimate pursuits and able to give up delinquent activities. These may be described as relatively "adequate" or "reality-oriented" youths; they look down at the users who fear, and wish to escape from, reality. The conflict between these two subgroups is basic; it comes to a head as the bulk of members reach the age of eighteen and nineteen. At this age, some face the mainstream of life, others turn from it.

Narcotics and Self-Esteem

That the turning to narcotics is at least temporarily effective in preserving self-esteem in the face of inadequacy for adult roles is strikingly underscored by a doctoral dissertation of Stanley M. Schiff,[7] conducted under the supervision of one of the writers. The features of the design of Dr. Schiff's study most germane to the present discussion are as follows:

[7] Stanley M. Schiff, "A Self-Theory Investigation of Drug Addiction in Relation to Age of Onset" (New York University, 1959).

Five groups of subjects were selected from a prison population. All groups were matched or found to be equivalent with respect to education, intelligence, ethnic composition, and neighborhoods of residence. Two of the groups consisted of individuals under twenty-one years of age, one being composed of habitual drug-users and the other of nonusers. The remaining three groups consisted of individuals over twenty-one years of age—one of nonusers, one of habitual users who had become habituated during their teens, and one of habitual users who did not begin to use drugs before their twenty-first birthdays. The two younger and the three older groups were, respectively, matched for age. All subjects had, of course, been sentenced to varying prison terms for diverse violations.

The level of self-esteem of each subject was assessed by a technique known as a Q-sort.[8] In its essence, the technique requires that the subject rank a series of items according to a specified criterion. (The technique can, depending on the criterion, be adapted to many purposes, not merely the measurement of self-esteem.)

After careful review by a group of psychologists familiar with the population, eighty items were selected from an initial set of two hundred, each item describing some personal attribute. The review was concerned with the relevance(i.e., to make certain that the possession or lack of the attribute was likely to make a difference to the kinds of individuals being studied), with the comprehensiveness of the items (i.e., to make certain that the various facets of a personality were represented and that the set was not overloaded with items involving any particular aspect of a person), and, finally, to ensure the intelligibility of the items. Each item was typed on a separate card. For the benefit of Spanish-speaking subjects, a set of cards with the items in Spanish translation was used.

The items dealt with sexual identification and roles, attitudes toward authority, educational values, views on moral issues, passivity, aggressiveness, impulse control, relation to others, feelings of dependence and independence, feelings of personal adequacy, level of aspiration, emotional maturity, and level of frustration. The initial items submitted for review were drawn from existing personality scales, other studies employing the Q-sort technique, statements by drug-users and nonusers to prison psychologists, and suggestions by some of the prisoners. Some sample items from the set finally used were:

---

[8] An elaborate internal check established that the subjects were able to follow the seemingly complicated instructions.

I think that there's something wrong with me.

I like money, and I want lots of it.

I want to have someone love me.

I feel down in the dumps a lot.

I feel relaxed when I pass by a cop.

I stand for what I believe is right.

I think that life is one big rat race.

I think I satisfy the girl when I have sex.

I think that I'm as smart as the next person.

I wish people would stop telling me what to do.

The subject first selected the items which were most aptly descriptive of himself, then a set of items that were next most aptly descriptive of himself, and so on until he got to the items least descriptive of what he thought he was like. When he was through with this task, he again sorted the items, but this time the criterion for sorting was the kind of person he would most like to be. When he was through with the second task, he once again sorted the items, but this time in terms of the kind of person his parents would like him to be. A fourth sort was based on the kind of person his friends would like him to be. A final sort required that he first select the one from a series of categories of individuals—e.g., minister, businessman, and the like— whose opinion of the subject made the most difference to him and that he then sort the items in terms of the kind of person this individual or class of individuals would like him to be. The five Q-sorts were carried out in two sessions.

A comparison of how the items were sorted in the self-description task and how they were sorted in each of the succeeding tasks yields a series of measures of how the subject's self-image falls short of various ideals. The larger the discrepancies—or, equivalently, the lower the correlations—between the self-descriptive sort and each of the others, the more he falls short of his various ideals. For purposes of analysis, the discrepancies between the first and each of the last three sorts were averaged. The procedure thus yielded two scores—a measure of the discrepancy between a person's perceived self and his own description of his ideal and a measure of the discrepancy between his perceived self and the ideals that he attributes to significant others. Schiff also considered two derived scores—one which consisted simply of whichever of the first two scores put the perceived self in the most favorable light and the second, of whichever put the perceived self in the least favorable light. Except for the last score, which yielded no dependable results, it does not make any difference which of the scores is taken as the measure of self-esteem; the results are the same. Table K-6 presents the averages of the first two scores.

With respect to level of self-esteem, the two younger groups did not differ from each other, and they did not differ from the adult users who had become habituated to drugs in their teens. These three groups did, however, differ from the other two adult groups; their level of self-esteem was much higher.

The picture would have been somewhat clearer if Schiff had also been able to study comparable individuals who did not get into trouble. He was not able to do so, and it is not certain that the Q-sort items he used would have been equally appropriate. It is conceivable, but it seems to us most unlikely, that normal late adolescents would also not differ from the two teen-age groups that Schiff studied; we would expect them to show higher levels of self-esteem. It is also conceivable that the comparable normal teen-agers would show higher self-esteem scores than comparable normal adults. It is, finally, conceivable—and this again seems to us to be most unlikely—that, if the latter were to turn out to be the case, the drop in self-esteem from the normal teen-age to the normal adult group would be of the same magnitude as that found by Schiff; we would expect that, if a drop occurred at all, it would be smaller. Schiff argues, quite reasonably, that, if anything, the change in the normal population should go the other way; adolescents have ample grounds for questioning their personal worth.

If our expectations for the comparable normal population are taken seriously, it becomes difficult indeed to escape the conclusions of Schiff's findings that: (1) for the kinds of inadequate individuals who become involved in crime and/or narcotics use, the transition to adult status is, in fact, traumatic, with a resultant sharp drop in self-esteem; and (2) turning to narcotics before the transition is made prevents or markedly delays this development. Note that, in the off-drug personality, at least, the act of turning to narcotics does not restore self-esteem to its adolescent levels. This is implicit in Schiff's finding that the adult users who had started to use narcotics after they had become adults were no different, in this respect, from the nonusing adults. The key fact in Schiff's finding is that the adults who had become habituated as teen-agers apparently remained like the comparable teen-agers in level of self-esteem.

It thus appears that, to the inadequate individual, the postponement of adulthood is not merely a defensive maneuver; it is an adaptive one as well.

Summary

If we may trust the experience of those staff members of Riverside Hospital with whom we have discussed this issue, only a minority of the cases who become seriously enough involved to be committed to the hospital ever belonged to organized gangs. On the face of it, therefore, street gangs cannot be considered a major factor in the spread of heroin use. Even for those who do belong to gangs, the weight of the evidence is that the gangs merely provide an arena in which the use of narcotics can develop. If anything, the gangs play an inhibiting role with respect to the incontinent use of drugs. They not only tend to discourage incontinent use, but they also satisfy needs which may otherwise lead to earlier use. They offer a sense of solidarity and belonging, and they provide inadequate individuals with channels of achievement and recognition that enable such boys to avoid confronting their own inadequacy in the normal channels of legitimate competitive endeavor. It is apparently precisely at the point where the gangs become relatively inadequate in satisfying such needs and at the point where the threatening onset of adulthood becomes imminent that many of these individuals turn to narcotics. The Schiff study indicates that, for such individuals, the use of narcotics helps to preserve their self-esteem, presumably by freeing them of the obligation to confront their responsibilities as adults. "A monkey on my back" is a convincing alibi for a lone, lost soul.

VIII

Personality and Addiction: A Structural Perspective

As we pointed out in Chapter I, the role of personality disorder in adolescent opiate addiction was an open question when we began our research. We began without theoretical predispositions about the strength of one or another set of factors; we wished to explore the problem from the perspective of various behavioral sciences, to take a fresh look at it through our own clinical experience and systematic interdisciplinary study, formulating our concepts as our data and experience developed.

The generalizations in this chapter and Chapter IX draw on the psychiatric experience of one of the writers with adolescent addicts in the community or hospitalized at the United States Public Health Service Hospital in Lexington, Kentucky, and at the Riverside Hospital in New York City. They also draw on clinical reports from hospitals and clinics that have dealt extensively with adolescent addicts in recent years. They are considerably influenced by the findings of a systematic study of adolescent addicts and control cases that will be described below and by relevant findings in the studies we have already reported above. Diverse as the sources may be, they do point to a remarkably coherent characterization of the teen-aged addict.[1] In this and the following chapter, we attempt to develop this characterization systematically, largely within the framework of psychoanalytic theory. We start, however, with two major propositions which, it seems to us, help to put the manifold characteristics of the addict in clear perspective.

I.   The addiction of the adolescents we have studied was an extension of, or a development out of, long-lasting, severe, personality disturbance and maladjustment.

II.   The addiction of the adolescents we have studied was adaptive, functional, and dynamic.

These two propositions are in themselves answers to the orienting questions of this aspect of our study: what kinds of person are the adolescent addicts, and why do they use drugs? Though these questions may be separated for purposes of exposition, in reality they cannot be dissociated. As we discuss those clinically most relevant facets of the addicts' personality—their pathologic structure, as it were—we observe and perforce must discuss how this pathological structure relates to the how and why of their drug use. Conversely, to answer why they use drugs, we have had to focus in some detail on aspects of what they are like; here, as elsewhere in life, structure and function interpenetrate.

I. Personality Disturbance and Adjustment

There are many levels at which the personality and psychopathology of a clinical population can be described, from the tabulation of individual symptoms or behavior traits to the presentation of case histories in which each patient is described in his rich uniqueness and

[1] The reader is reminded that the generalizations which follow are based on study of addicts and need not apply to nonaddicted users of opiate drugs. It should also be emphasized that the relevant experience and data were accumulated before the classification of addicts described in Chapter II was developed. Insofar as there are systematic personality differences among the four types, the failure to make the distinctions would tend to result in a blurring of the image of the addict. In retrospect, we think that the characterization which follows most clearly applies to addicts who have both craving and personal involvement. It would probably also apply fairly well to the other three types, but we would expect much more individual variation from the modal picture; and there may be variation among the four types in the salience of various characteristics, as well as of characteristics of individual types that would have emerged if we had known enough to keep them separate. This is, of course, a matter for future research.

complexity. The clinical population we are describing in these two chapters are male adolescent opiate addicts. We mean addicts and not users; they have used opiates long enough and consistently enough to have histories of dependence on these drugs, they have become tolerant enough to them so that they have had to raise the dosage in order to continue to obtain the effects, and they have experienced some degree of craving for opiates while not physically dependent. The generalizations which follow, then, are limited to such young addicts; they need not pertain to any adolescent who ever used opiates. The distribution and range of personality psychopathology may differ from those of a population of young addicts seen in a jail. There may, for instance, be crucial forces in the police and legal handling of young addicts which selectively place differing kinds of young addicts in jail and in a hospital. However, from the variety seen in hospitals, we would speculate that, although the frequency distribution of various psychiatric diagnostic groups might vary from jail to hospital, no type would be entirely excluded from one or the other institutional setting.

The psychiatric diagnosis is useful for the general description of a clinical population, so long as it is recognized that the diagnostic classifications are of limited reliability and that they are convenient labels which do not do justice to the individual differences among the cases. Nevertheless, they do have some value in indicating the extent and severity of psychopathology. We have found it convenient to describe the major varieties of adolescent opiate addicts in terms of the following schema, and our experience is that others working with adolescent addicts find this schema appropriate to their own clinical experience. To fill the picture out a bit, a brief description is appended to each classification.

1. *Overt schizophrenia.* These patients were not hallucinated or psychotically destructive. However, they displayed flattened affect, severe thinking disorders, delusions of reference and grandeur, and withdrawn social behavior.

2. *Incipient schizophrenia, or "borderline," status.* These patients were struggling against an actively disorganizing and disruptive process in which they experienced extreme anxiety related to feelings of inadequacy and lowered self-esteem. Paranoid trends and early thinking-disturbances were noted. Though moralistic, struggling toward conventional goals in work, marriage, and education, they were unable to carry out the required roles and relationships. Their hold on reality was tenu-

ous. In situations which put them under stress, they became unrealistic and confused. They strove to maintain intellectual control and to avoid situations requiring emotional participation.

3. *Delinquency-dominated character disorders.* These patients were extremely hostile, defensive, provocative, demanding, and manipulative. They could be divided into two types which, though not mutually exclusive, nevertheless permitted the classification of most of the patients as predominantly of one or the other pattern.

a. PSEUDOPSYCHOPATHIC DELINQUENTS. These patients attempted to deny and repress underlying wishes for passivity and dependency by adopting roles in which they defined themselves (and were usually responded to) as dangerous, criminal, and strong men. They had been involved in serious delinquencies (e.g., gang fights, robbery, assault), and, both prior to and during their drug use, they described these activities as pleasurable.

b. ORAL CHARACTERS. The predominant role systems these patients attempted to establish were those in which they were nurtured and cared for. They reacted with rage and anxiety to situations in which nurturance was refused. They were easily upset by, and reacted excessively to, frustration. The petty delinquencies in which they were involved, both prior to and in the course of their drug use, were intended to punish and control significant figures. At times, they almost said in so many words: "If you don't do what I want, then I'll be a bad boy, and then you'll be sorry."

4. *Inadequate personalities.* These patients showed a paucity of interests and goals and an impoverishment of thinking and emotional expression. They were neither "good" delinquents nor "good" schizophrenics. They were successful in establishing role systems in which people responded to them almost as if they were just "not there."

It is evident from the above that, at least as far as psychiatric classification goes, there is no single type or syndrome of maladjustment specific to the adolescent opiate addict. Similarly, we have not been able to discern any single deep-lying need or conflict common to, or specific for, opiate addiction. This is not to say that there is no basis for discussing the adolescent opiate addicts collectively, but rather that such discussion cannot, in terms of our clinical experience, be meaningfully focused on some unitary characteristic. We have found it useful to generalize the personality characteristics of adolescent addicts in the framework of four concepts from psychoanalytic psychology:

A. ego pathology
B. narcissism
C. problems of sexual identification
D. superego pathology

We use the term "framework" advisably, since none of these concepts are nuclear or elementary; they are themselves highly complex rubrics, beneath which a number of subsidiary ideas are to be considered.

A. Ego Pathology

The term "ego" refers to certain aspects of the psychic structure which regulate or govern, as it were, the relationship between the world outside the person and the drives, impulses, demands, values, and goals within him. Many ego functions can be distinguished; each can be regarded as a resultant of the important life experiences and relationships in interaction with biologically conditioned, autonomous, "conflict-free" mental organizations or capacities for organization. The ego apparatus is probably formed in early childhood or infancy, conditioning the perception of, and reaction to, the experiences of later childhood and later life. We have observed insufficiencies in three major areas of ego function among adolescent opiate addicts. These are: response scope, synthesis, and purposeful action.

1. *Response scope*. As a group, the adolescent addicts are relatively unresponsive to the world outside them and to their own creative urges. In our clinical experience and from what they tell us about their interests and activities, we note that their interests are meager and the range of their activities limited. When they are exposed to special opportunities for learning or acquiring work or recreational skills, they respond slowly or not at all. Though such attitudes as suspicion play some role in this reaction, our impression has been that this unresponsiveness reflects a general lack of interest, a blunting of curiosity, a narrowing of the inlet of experience.

School teachers at the Riverside Hospital, working with small classes in a highly flexible, individually oriented school program, have told us about the (often friendly) indifference of the adolescent addict students to the school program. It is not that the adolescent addicts are devoid of talent or skills; like any group of adolescents, there are those who can paint or draw or make things with ceramics. Indeed, a distorted view of their potential creativity is obtained from the fact that a teacher may succeed in getting them interested in any of a variety of activities (e.g., both art and ceramic work were favorite activities) so that the discrepancy between the student's current production and his prior level of interest and productivity makes it seem that there is an untapped well of talent and creativity. In general, however, the relation between the teacher and the student addict's level of interest is dependent on the teacher's efforts and enthusiasm; as soon as the teacher stops pushing the addict patient, the latter ceases to perceive or to respond to this aspect of his environment.

These observations are supported by some data from the study reported in Chapter V. As already indicated, adolescent users were aware of fewer opportunities for supportive, enriching experiences or situations than actually existed in their communities. They participated in a smaller range of leisure activities than did their peers; they showed little interest in extracurricular programs, in any aspects of the political situation, or indeed in anything outside their immediate lives. These clinical observations and social-psychological data illustrate our thesis, namely, that the response scope of the adolescent addict is limited. Further evidence bearing on this point may be drawn from a study by Gerard and Kornetsky.[2]

The addicts in this study were thirty-two consecutive admissions of male patients under twenty-one years of age at the United States Public Health Service Hospital at Lexington, Kentucky. The controls were twenty-three cases meeting specified criteria who were indicated as friends by patients at Riverside Hospital.[3]

The subjects were given psychiatric interviews and several psycho-

[2] D. L. Gerard and C. Kornetsky, "Adolescent Opiate Addiction: A Study of Control and Addict Subjects." *Psychiatric Quarterly*, 29 (1955) 457–486. This study was conducted while its authors were commissioned officers in the United States Public Health Service, working with the Laboratory for Socio-environmental Studies of the National Institute of Mental Health. Although a close working relationship between these investigators and the N. Y. U. group began late in 1952, when Gerard and Kornetsky began to assemble their control subjects, Dr. Gerard did not join the N.Y.U. group until 1954.

[3] The criteria for selection were: residence in a high-drug-rate census tract in New York City, in the sixteen–to–twenty-one age range, not attending college, no history of opiate addiction, no current drug use, and no record of delinquency. A history of nonaddictive use terminating six or more months before they were contacted did not preclude the inclusion of such individuals as controls. In addition, the restriction was introduced that the control sample should as nearly as possible match the addict sample for ethnic composition. Controls were paid $5 an hour for participating, and each gave at least three hours.

logical tests.[4] Of immediate interest are the findings of the Rorschach test.[5] On the basis of this test, the addicts were characterized by a more meager affective life and a more shallow and stereotyped fantasy life.[a] After the standard administration of the test, it was administered again with the instruction to produce new responses.[6] The addicts were far less successful than the controls.[b] As judged by performance on the Rorschach test, therefore, the addicts show up, at least on the average, as much more constricted individuals. They lead much more impov-

---

[4] Although there was a statistically significant difference in the median intelligence quotient for the two groups (101 for the addicts, versus 108 for the controls), there was great overlap between the two groups (the range was 82 to 133 for the addicts and 88 to 127 for the controls). The two groups were not materially different with respect to IQ. Even so, other obtained differences were systematically checked for the possibility that they might be attributable to the difference in IQ; in no instance was this the case.

[5] This test consists of ten plates, each a reproduction of an ink blot originally formed by dropping some ink on a page and folding the paper. Three of the blots were formed entirely from colored inks; two used red ink in addition to black. The subject is asked about each blot, presented in a standard sequence: "What might this be?" The subject's responses are coded according to various criteria, and scores are derived by counting the number of responses of each type and by computing various percentages or ratios. Apart from standard intelligence tests, the Rorschach is probably the most widely used test in clinical psychological practice. One way of understanding this test is to view it as a microcosm, behavior in which is coordinated with styles of behavior in the ordinary macrocosm. The subject may give an unlimited number of responses to each blot. These responses are classified according to the portion of the blot involved (e.g., the entire blot, some part of the blot, and, if the latter, the kind of part or the white space); the determinants or formal properties of the blot that determine the response (e.g., the shape and spatial differentiation of the portion of the blot involved, the color, the shading, and what is commonly taken as a "projection" by the subject—the injection of movement into the perception of human or humanlike figures); and the content or subject matter (e.g., human being, part of a human being, animal, animal detail). Some responses are classified as "popular" (i.e., commonly given) and some as "original" (i.e., rarely given). Responses may be classified in accordance with how well the percepts fit the portion of the blot involved. Other kinds of data are available for analysis, e.g., the time it takes to give the first response to a blot, the failure to give any response to a particular blot, certain aspects of the sequence of responses, and so on. The coding-and-scoring scheme used in the present study was that of Samuel J. Beck, *Rorschach's Test,* "I. Basic Processes" (New York: Grune and Stratton, 1954).

[6] This is a device introduced by Jernigan to study the effects of "stress" on the functioning of the individual. Cf. A. J. Jernigan, "A Rorschach Study of Normal and Psychotic Subjects in a Situation of Stress" (doctoral dissertation, University of Kentucky, 1951).

erished lives, inwardly and outwardly, than their immediate situations require of them.

It is possible that living in a chronically multidimensionally impoverished environment leads in some simple and direct manner to a constriction of the life space. It may well be that one needs to learn to take advantage of such stimuli and other opportunities as exist and that an impoverished environment, with its meager offerings, does not facilitate such learning. On the other hand, it is also possible that the constriction of the life space represents a defensive maneuver. Seeking to take advantage of the apparent offerings also invites disappointment. One may learn that the beckonings of opportunity all too often turn out to be empty invitations. One may, consequently, stop responding to such invitations as a technique of protecting oneself from disappointment and frustration. Observation of addicts—like the fact mentioned earlier concerning the capacity of many of them for some degree of creative expression so long as they receive specific encouragement, with subsequent relapse—suggests that we are dealing, to a considerable degree, with defensive constriction.

From the standpoint of ego development, we would speculate that serious, gross disturbances in the early life of the child must have occurred in order for him to have adopted a constricted pattern of responsiveness. Indeed, constriction is highly protective, in the same sense and with the same liabilities as a life spent in a windowless, cork-lined, air-conditioned room.

2. *Synthesis.* The term "synthesis," used in reference to ego functioning, refers to a complex of activities which have to do with the organizing of that perceived and with the coordination of conflicting needs. Although the ego usually functions silently and to a large measure subconsciously (we use the term "subconscious" to include both the "preconscious" and "unconscious" of ordinary psychoanalytic usage), it is concerned with questions which can be formulated in terms of conscious intellectual activity—e.g., Is such a course worthwhile for my future welfare? What will happen if I do this? How will I feel about it later? Judgment, reality-testing, delaying, accepting frustration, and moderating between alternatives are all involved in the synthesis of experience. In a broad sense, synthesizing entails a social-temporal orientation; we might say that the adolescent opiate addicts are disoriented in this context.

They give up school and jobs readily (in the great majority of cases, prior to drug involvement). They do not recognize that their inner demand for status implies meeting the situational requirements for achievement, e.g., sustained effort. Thus, Zimmering et al.[7] described the addicts they had observed as "unable to apply themselves to intellectual tasks"; Fort[8] emphasized the important role which "inability to form realistic goal orientations" played in the addicts' maladjustment. Inability to synthesize is one of the important factors in the early drug use and addiction of our patients. Almost every one of the addicts we studied had observed the socially degrading consequences of opiate use in his community either before his initial use of drugs or early in the course of his nonaddictive use. He learned that regular use of opiates creates dependence and tolerance; that sale, purchase, or possession of narcotic drugs is illegal; and that people are often arrested and jailed for these reasons. Despite "knowing" this very well, he was unable to make use of the knowledge. He believed that "it can't happen to me." In short, he did not utilize restraint.

Situations which are unpleasant, painful, or anxiety-provoking make special demands on the synthetic function of the ego. In a painful situation, the least difficult and most immediately effective behavior is to withdraw or to strike out angrily and directly against the source of displeasure. However, this is often not adaptive in terms of future plans and roles. For instance, adolescent addicts, in the presence of what they regard as insult, criticism, or harshness, leave the field. Thus, they quit jobs because the boss speaks harshly to them, rather than trying to determine the basis of the criticism and modifying their behavior accordingly. Early in the course of addiction, they typically suffer mild withdrawal symptoms. Though they know by then that each day of prolonging their physiological dependence makes the inevitable reckoning the more painful, they nonetheless take another shot to avoid present pain.

Clinic No. 1[9] has also observed this phenomenon. The staff comments on the addict's low frustration tolerance and his readiness for collapse and retreat into passivity. Zimmering et al.[10] have also described the reaction to frustration of the adolescent opiate addicts; they state that their

[7] P. Zimmering, J. Toolan, R. Safrin, and S. B. Wortis, "Heroin Addiction in Adolescent Boys," Journal of Nervous and Mental Disorders, 114 (1951), 19–34.
[8] J. P. Fort, "Heroin Addiction among Young Men," Psychiatry, 17 (1954), 25.
[9] Walter A. Adams, Annual Report on the Activity of Medical and Counseling Clinic of Provident Hospital and Training School (Springfield: Illinois Department of Public Health, 1954).
[10] Zimmering et al., op. cit., p. 29.

reaction to frustration typically consists of "withdrawal, inhibition and passive dependent strivings." There are a small number of adolescent opiate addicts who respond to unpleasant or displeasing orders, in the army for instance, with aggressive acting out—striking noncommissioned officers or going AWOL. Whether they respond actively or passively, in either case, from the standpoint of synthesizing, their behavior is malapropos.

We have already referred to the finding by Gerard and Kornetsky that, when asked to produce additional responses to the Rorschach ink blots, addicts are not only typically less able than controls to rally to the demand for additional output, but they also tend to show marked deterioration in performance under the stress of such a demand. Their reality-testing becomes less efficient, and their emotional participation and perception becomes "regressive."

The major difficulties experienced by adolescents (conflicts over autonomy, genitality, and particularly identity),[11] are normally dealt with gradually, progressively, and repetitively. Relationships are established, skills acquired and improved, roles clarified in innumerable settings. Through such a developmental flow of experiences, the anxiety associated with the adolescent's insecurities is distributed into, so to say, manageable bundles, and stressful situations (typically those which accentuate or bring more problems of autonomy, genitality, and identity into awareness) are kept within the bounds of an ever-increasing competence to deal with them. The adolescent addict, however, sidesteps such growth by at first simply avoiding the situations in which he can gradually acquire competence or by passively going along with the whims and decisions of others and eventually by substituting the anxiety-reducing "normative" influence of the opiate drugs. This evasion of maturation is probably the most dangerous and seductive aspect of opiate use.[12] From the viewpoint of ego function, maturation in adolescence is dependent on ability to stay within the context of the

[11] Cf. E. Erikson, *Childhood and Society* (New York: Norton, 1950).

[12] This statement, however, needs to be qualified in the light of the finding by Schiff, referred to in Chapter VII, that the onset of drug use in adolescence helps to preserve the addict from confronting his failure to make an effective transition to maturity. In other words, the addict would probably fail to mature properly in any case. The danger lies in the fact that the "helpfulness" of the drug in maintaining the level of self-esteem in the face of failure deprives the addict of the motivation to benefit from efforts to help him improve his condition. In the absence of such efforts, he is, at least in this respect and for some period of his adult life, "better off."

unfamiliar and the difficult. This calls for all those aspects of the synthetic function of the ego which we have discussed, tolerance of frustration, consideration of and recognition of the consequences of behavior in its social-temporal context, and maintenance of reality-testing under stress.

3. *Purposeful action.* The adolescent addicts display a disturbance of action. When, despite the limitations imposed by their constricted life patterns and the deficiencies of their synthetic capacities, they do embark on a realistic or (hopefully) potentially gratifying course of action, they are inhibited, slowed down, or halted. To use a term of Redl, the "power function" of their ego is defective; they have "weak egos." They have great difficulty in starting, stopping, or changing course midstream. To take a physical analogy, they suffer from inertia. They may, therefore, appear passive, fatalistic, "lazy," dependent, or negativistic. One of the clinically significant areas in which this action disturbance is important is in entering a hospital for detoxification; among even the best "motivated" addicts, this commonly takes place long after he has perceived the hopelessness of his current course and come to the conclusion that he must get help. This delay is often misperceived by the community or family or even by the addict himself as malignant, stubborn, and purposefully dilatory. In our view, it is ego weakness, not immorality. The addict commonly seeks an outside authority to incarcerate him or bring him back to the hospital because he knows he cannot get himself there even though he actually wants it for himself.

Since the influence of the ego is most evident in the organization and daily conduct of one's life, it is germane at this point to review findings reported in earlier chapters that show how differently the nondelinquent and non-drug-using peers of adolescent opiate addicts in high-drug-use areas structure their lives. The social personality of the nondeviant youth—the goals, values, content, and activities which are consciously experienced and openly manifested—is quite different from the adolescent opiate addicts'. From responses to a structured interview, we can construct a picture of the social personality of the nondelinquent, nonaddicted youth which statistically differentiates him from his addict peers. The concepts in the following paragraph should be prefaced in the reader's mind by the phrase, "In contrast to the adolescent addict, ..."

The nonaddicted, nondelinquent youth in high-drug-use areas does not feel himself to be playing the role of a grownup—a man—until he has passed some culturally defined transition point, e.g., graduating from high school or getting a job; nor does he feel that responsibilities are forced on him; nor is he nagged by his parents about his future and vocational plans. He has definite plans for his short-range future. In difficult situations, he goes to his father, teacher, or priest for advice and support. Though he knows many youths who have been in jail, reformatory, or on probation, few of these are intimate friends. He has stable, intimate friendships which he entered on the basis of association in school or purposeful selection and not simply because they happened to grow up together in the same neighborhood. He divorces himself, with considerable affect, from antisocial behavior and antisocial groups—if necessary, at the cost of loneliness. He does not spend much of his leisure time at movies, hanging around candy stores, "goofing off," going to parties or dances, or gambling at cards or pool. He spends more time in active sports. His friends are not greatly concerned about wanting to have a car, expensive clothes, and much pocket money. He has more acquaintance with boys who are concerned with current events, books, art and such things than with those concerned with going places and seeing things.

When he was about sixteen years old, he wanted, but felt he could not get, a different way of life for himself—in contrast to the addicts and delinquents, who wanted but could not get enough fine clothing. Highest on his list of values are workmanship, job security, and health—in contrast to his addict peers, who rank refinement, freedom, and comfort as their highest values. He selects his ideal in terms of personal qualities (e.g., courage and kindness), rather than in those of possessions (e.g., wealth and skills). He does not feel isolated and without support in a malicious and untrustworthy personal environment. He actively explores the limited opportunities his community offers him for leisure activities, both in and out of school. He uses public libraries or book clubs and devotes relatively little time to the reading of comic books.

B. Narcissism

In psychoanalytic thought, the term "narcissism" is applied in a number of contexts. First, there is what is sometimes described as "primary narcissism," a failure in the inner awareness and acceptance of the separateness or differentiation between self and object world: the "self" is unbounded, and the individual is hence never aware of himself as such.

In the newborn child, some degree of primary narcissism is assumed to be a normal state of affairs; in the first phase of his life, the child only gradually develops an awareness of his separateness from those who care for him. Under good conditions, he learns slowly and not too painfully that he is indeed quite separate; that he cannot make unlimited demands on their care, attention, or interest; that they have only a limited capacity to give to him; but that they are respect-worthy and lovable persons nonetheless. His earliest attachments to others are rooted in this lack of differentiation even as he begins to realize that he is, in fact, not unbounded. The others who serve him are extensions and parts of himself, in much the same sense that an older person perceives that the parts of his body are parts of himself. He seemingly has but to wish or cry out, and these extensions do what is necessary to relieve distress. Again, these extensions function in much the same way that an older person grasps a desired object; *he,* not merely *his hand,* grasps the object. Since he is not aware of external objects as such, he cannot attribute pleasure and pain, gratification and frustration to others as causal agents; affective states are conditions of being and can only be perceived reflexively. Being is wonderful, or being is hateful.

As the self becomes more bounded, more-or-less sharply demarcated from the not-self, a discriminated object in a world of discriminable objects, the infant enters a second phase of his existence, a phase of what may be described as "secondary narcissism."[13] His attachments to other persons are appropriately modified. From extensions, they become instrumentalities. The failure to make an effective transition to this type of relationship—i.e., to acceptance of separateness and to the formation of relationships with other persons who are consistently seen as different and separate—leaves him subject to certain maladaptive consequences. He never quite succeeds in perceiving others in terms of their objective properties. When they fail him, the ensuing rage is not focused simply on the frustrating object; it is, at least in part, directed at the primordial undifferentiated self, at the fact of existence. When they satisfy his needs, there is a correspondingly unbalanced and unfocused elevation of mood which embraces the inadequately perceived others in its glow, but which also cannot achieve recognition of the qualities of others that

[13] Cf. Otto Fenichel, *The Psychoanalytic Theory of Neurosis* (New York: Norton, 1950), p. 84: " . . . children frequently are in love with themselves [secondary narcissism] . . . capable of distinguishing objects and of loving objects as long as the objects procure satisfaction."

have made the desirable outcome possible or which can give due credit for services rendered. By the same token, such a person can never get to see himself in anything approaching an objective perspective. One consequence of this is that he cannot make any realistic appraisal of his own qualities and, therefore, cannot effectively deploy his resources toward the attainment of his ends.

The successful negotiation of the second stage of person–object relationships is itself normally superseded by a third stage, one in which others are no longer merely instrumentalities of one's own purposes, but beings with needs and rights of their own.[14] In part, this development is simply an emergence of the long view, a realization that, in the long run, others will not play their roles in the satisfaction of one's needs if one does not play his own roles in the satisfaction of theirs. In part, this development is a consequence of the extension of one's own need system so that one cannot be entirely happy when confronted with the unhappiness and frustration of others or feel entirely secure when others are threatened.

In a sense, the third stage represents a return to the first, in that the self, augmented by identifications with others, is again not confined to one's own person. It is a return, however, with a difference. Identification with others does not obliterate the self–other distinction, a distinction that makes possible a wholesome and realistic regard for one's own capabilities and accomplishments, along with a realistic assessment of the qualities of others and regard for their achievements. The fact that one's need system requires the support, gratification, and happiness of others only gives point to the distinction, albeit an interdependent distinction, of self and other. It is only in this stage that mature love is possible, but mature love is accompanied by an enhanced sense of one's personal existence, not by its obliteration. It is also only in this stage that one finds true self-respect, self-respect that can withstand the confrontation of one's deficiencies and accept defects that would be too costly to correct, self-respect in which the sense of personal worth is rooted in a realistic assessment of one's resources rather than in a comparison of himself with impossible ideals or, alternatively, too-low standards.

Although normal in the growing child, the failure to negotiate the

---

14 *Loc. cit.* "This [self-love], however, is certainly not yet love. One can speak of love only when consideration of the object goes so far that one's own satisfaction is impossible without satisfying the object, too."

third stage as one matures leaves a variety of psychopathic and neurotic types, just as the failure to negotiate the second leaves a variety of psychotic types and severe character disturbances.

It must not be supposed that the normal transition from the first through the third stage is a smooth one. One may progress much more rapidly and further in this development in one's relations to some people than in one's relations to others. Typically, for instance, the maturation of personal relationships is most difficult with respect to one's mother. Moreover, progress in this development does not preclude regressive movements of more-or-less brief or prolonged duration, so that one reverts to forms of object relations characteristic of earlier developmental stages, either in one's relations to particular persons or in general. Finally, the true level of progress may be more or less effectively concealed by a verbal façade; people talk the third stage even when they do not live it.

The adolescent addict has typically progressed well into the second stage, but has not outgrown and easily regresses to, the first. Although his involvement with the outside world, in the sense of establishing sympathetic and empathic relationships with peers and adults, is meager, one figure does occupy a prominent place in his psychic life—his mother. He has little love for her, in the sense of warm, sympathetic, responsible concern for the welfare of another human being. In part, this is a relationship with another person which features the gratification of many infantile impulses. In part, and in a more basic sense, it is a relationship with an undifferentiated portion of himself, with the hated, feared, and loved mother from whom he has not yet fully distinguished himself and who is still a part of himself or of whom he himself still remains a part.

1. *Deficiency in healthy self-regard.* Although it is questionable that the global concept "self-esteem" has exactly the same connotation for all clinical observers, there is no doubt that students of the addiction problem find this term useful in communicating to other clinicians about their patients. Fenichel's statement—"More important than any erogenous pleasure in drug elation . . . is the extraordinary elevation in self-esteem"[15]—emphasizes the significant role which low self-esteem plays in the motivation of drug addiction. Zimmering *et al.* explicitly described the young heroin addicts (or users) they studied as burdened by feelings of weakness, inferiority, and diminished self-esteem *even more than*

[15] Fenichel, *op. cit.,* p. 377.

the other disturbed youth on the same adolescent ward.[16] Boshes *et al.* describe their clinic patients as having "strong feelings of inadequacy, insecurity and unworthiness, sometimes manifested in overconfidence and arrogance."[17] Reference should, however, again be made to the study by Schiff, described in Chapter VII.[18]

Clinically, we have taken the concept "low self-esteem" to be relevant to individuals who have feelings of inferiority or inadequacy accompanied by intense feelings of self-denial or disapproval and who talk about this (and, for that matter, about any aspect of their life which is difficult) with great hesitancy, evasion, denial, or distortion. They are aware that they cannot communicate.

We have based our appraisal of self-esteem on:

a. The quality of the person's prior social adjustment, particularly in the context of how the person describes and evaluates his performance, accomplishments, or failures.

b. The expressed self-concept in clinical interview. It is assumed that self-esteem and defensiveness are inversely related, that acceptance of self and acceptance of others are directly related.

c. The projected self-image in response to the Rorschach, TAT, human figure drawings, and similar projective tests.

a. PRIOR SOCIAL ADJUSTMENT. The adolescent addicts we have studied had little sense of accomplishment and, indeed, had accomplished little. They had adjusted poorly prior to drug use. They had given up schooling and were involved in overt misbehavior or deviant behavior. Their work history was also unsatisfactory. If they had worked at all, their attendance and punctuality were poor. Though there were some adolescent addicts who reported these phenomena as indications of their inferiority or incapacity to deal with life, in general they usually reported these indications of their maladjustment as though they signified superiority to, and meritorious detachment from, conventional values and norms. However, when a psychotherapeutic relationship had begun to develop, even the latter often spoke of themselves in more sober and more tragic fashion. Although they confessed that their façades of ar-

16 Zimmering *et al., op. cit.*

17 Benjamin Boshes, Lee G. Sewall, and Mary Koza, paper read at the May, 1955, meeting of the American Psychiatric Association.

18 It should be recalled that the Schiff study did not include normal controls.

rogance and self-satisfaction covered considerable self-doubt and self-distrust, it was most touching, in dealing with these disturbed adolescents, to learn from them how badly they regarded themselves. Charlie, for example, who seemed the ideal example of a "cheerful psychopath," confessed after many months of treatment that he was trying—through the excitement, stimulation, and provocativeness of his misbehavior in school; his stealing; and his life as an addict—to run away from his desperately concealed feelings of worthlessness and weakness. Even as a small boy, he had believed that he behaved outrageously and sinfully toward his own family, even though in fact he was outwardly a well-behaved child.

b. DEFENSIVENESS. In clinical interviews, the adolescent addicts were extremely defensive. They strongly resisted discussion of themselves and their relationships. Despite overt and obvious evidence to the contrary, they denied emotional problems and were, in general, hostile or indifferent to treatment. Many displayed difficulties in establishing rapport, some to an almost psychotic degree. Evasion, suspicion, and hostility were common responses to the diagnostician or to the therapist who sought to intervene in their maladjustment. Conversely, they were cooperative and friendly as long as the interview "didn't count," i.e., did not imply anything about the possibility or worthwhileness of a change in their personal attitudes, orientations, or identifications. They were pleased to participate in discussions about getting drugs, the development of bebop or junkie slang, their experiences of corruption or dishonesty among politicians or law enforcement personnel.

c. THE PROJECTED SELF-IMAGE. Although indications of lowered self-esteem and a corollary dysphoria (a depressive mood and a pessimistic outlook) may be inferred from any of the projective test materials, the most explicit expression of the self-image and how it is esteemed is to be had from the Thematic Apperception Test.[19] The central characters in the TAT stories told by the adolescent opiate addicts we studied in Lexington were involved in murder, rape, strangulation, fatal cancer, rotting-away, failure, and impotence. The mood of the fantasies they created tended toward depression; their expectations were pessimistic (with occasional exceptions of bizarrely unrealistic optimism, e.g., "for

19 Like the Rorschach, the TAT is a test widely used for the assessment of personality. It consists of a series of pictures for each of which the subject makes up a story. Experience supports the view that the central characters and other features of these stories reflect various facets of the personality.

magical reasons, great success awaits me in the future"). This was covered with a façade of strength and cunning intended to impress others into seeing them as neither threatened nor weak; the world must protect itself against their predatory ability.

2. *Relatedness to others*. The normal adolescent is involved in a complex transition; his relationships are tentative, relatively loose, changeable, and not serious or "adult." He has a limited capacity for love, in the sense of establishing a warm, sympathetic understanding and responsible concern for the welfare of some valued individual.

Indeed, adolescents are not expected to love in this sense, yet they do establish relationships in which they practice the arts of love, both physical and emotional. They form "crushes" and sustain friendships which are perceived as passionate, important, and everlasting (some of which actually continue into adulthood). They choose friends purposefully as an expression and an extension of their developing self-image, identity, and goals. The adolescent opiate addicts do not form such adolescent relationships; their ability to enter close relationships of even a tentative nature is limited. Their friendships are marginal; they hang around with, but they are not actually emotionally involved with, their peers. Data substantiating this formulation come from three sources: our own personality studies, observations of other clinical observers, and personality implications of sociological studies.

All the clinical observations of young addicts accord with this formulation. Brill comments that the addicts he worked with "seem incapable of maintaining a sustained relationship."[20] Fenichel comments that addicts "never estimated object relationships very highly."[21] Zimmering *et al.* state that their object relationships are tentative and easily given up. They describe the users they studied as having no real buddies and casually accepting peer-group rejection because of their habit.[22] Adams comments that, even where the youngster experiments and uses drugs in an attempt to identify with the group, there is no real integration into it.[23] Boshes *et al.* describe them with the phrase, "shallow interpersonal relationships."[24]

Earlier chapters have reported data supporting these psychiatric

[20] Leon Brill, "Some Notes on Dynamics and Treatment in Narcotic Addiction," *Journal of Psychiatric Social Work* (1954), 67–81, p. 71.

[21] Fenichel, *op. cit.*, p. 377.

[22] Zimmering *et al.*, *op. cit.*

[23] Adams, *op. cit.*

[24] Boshes *et al.*, *op cit.*, p 8.

observations. Thus, we have learned that users have fewer intimate friends than nonusers; that the selection of friends by users is more casual than purposeful; and that, if users belong to street clubs, they tend to be marginal members. It is only to the most casual, unsystematic observer that the drug-user appears seriously, personally, "normally" involved with his peers.

One reason that nonclinical observers may perceive the adolescent addicts as capable of normal relatedness is that, like other adolescents, they do participate in group relationships. These group relationships are not, however, typical of the normal adolescent. Since the procuring, distribution, and use of drugs rests on an elaborate social structure, an ability to participate in certain kinds of peer and group activities is requisite to being a drug addict. Furthermore, the group activities of the adolescent addicts are supportive for these youths in several ways.

First, anyone is accepted in the adolescent addict group with little regard to his personal characteristics, so long as he is willing to focus his life on drug use. The activities of this group, unlike those of delinquent or nondeviant adolescent groups, are extremely limited. They do not go as a group to dances, ball games, street fights, or to the homes of their members for birthday parties or religious celebrations. They have no treasurers, presidents, or sergeants-at-arms. Their association is based only on the fact that they have a shared dominant interest—obtaining, using, and enjoying drugs. No matter how limited a particular adolescent addict may be in establishing relationships with nondeviant peers, among addicts he is welcome as long as he identifies himself as a "junkie." This has much to do with easy relapse into drug use. The path to acceptance by the nonaddict is difficult; a return to the addict group is easy.

Second, addicts of all ages participate in an isolated in-group with its special mores, traditions, and argot which encourage suspicion, deceit, and manipulativeness toward both the in-group and the world of "squares." These attitudes in the addict's social milieu lend support to his own disturbed perception of human relationships. He can conceal the discrepancy between his attitudes and expectations and those of his nondeviant peers by immersing himself in a deviant subculture. In his own estimation, he is not ill or disturbed, since he functions attitudinally like everybody else he knows.

Third, there are few barriers to membership in terms of race, religion, or nativity. Adolescent addicts are very democratic. This is a valuable feature of addiction for adolescents from deprived social groups. Interestingly, in a hospital, after they are detoxified and are no longer functioning socially as drug addicts, the "normal" group prejudices of these youths rapidly return.

3. *Persistence of a narcissistic relationship with the mother.* A prominent feature of the family situation of the adolescent opiate addict which has been noted in our own and other clinical studies is the peculiarly close relationship between the addict and his mother. It is not a closeness of warmth or mutual regard so much as it is a clinging and feeling of being bound together.

Zimmering *et al.,* Fort, and Adams have commented on this in slightly differing terms. Zimmering *et al.* note that there is a very close identification with the mother.[25] In the same report, however, they state that addicts plead to be sent where there are no drugs, whereas other boys in trouble resist giving up even the shred of a parent. In our experience, though they plead to be taken away from home, they are extremely uncomfortable as soon as this wish is granted. It is difficult to capture the force of this binding mutual attraction in words. For example, after months or years of increasing addiction, penury, delinquency, and stress, a patient gets himself to a hospital. As soon as the withdrawal experience is over—or at least the overt, painful aspects of it— he is eager to return home; he is needed there; he "belongs" there; his mother cannot manage without him; he wants to make up to her all the harm and pain he has caused her through his drug use. He may add, as an afterthought, "and, besides, I am cured now." The following case material illustrates these formulations.

Jay was aware that there was something peculiar about his relationship with his mother. He knew something troubled him when he was at home with her. He was preoccupied with this phenomenon and knew that it interfered with his life, work, and studies. He knew that his mother and grandmother fought possessively for him, and this (which had led to an earlier suicide attempt, in the setting of which he began his heroin use) was something which he feared would recur if he were to return to live with his mother in New York City. He wanted, therefore, to live with his father in California. He wrote this to his mother three weeks before he left the United States Public Health Service Hospital in Lexington, telling her that he was going to live in California. However,

[25] Zimmering *et al., op. cit.*

he reneged on this plan, deciding that he would return to New York after all to live with his mother *despite his better judgment.*

He arrived in New York at his mother's apartment without informing her that he had changed his plans. He found her living with her boyfriend with no room for him and went to live with his grandmother. He requested advice from one of the writers. Jay was referred to the Community Service Society. One of their psychiatric social workers attempted to lead him toward educational opportunities, ego-acceptable employment, and living quarters separate from his family. Despite wishing for these things, Jay sabotaged their plans. He found a night job doing unskilled kitchen work, which, he correctly observed, was below his intelligence and dignity. He continued to reside with his grandmother, who promised him financial support and educational opportunities *if he stayed away from his mother.* However, he could not do this. Within a month after his return from Lexington, his mother and her boyfriend broke off their relationship. Jay returned to her apartment; became bored, upset, and unhappy; and then returned to using drugs. It is of interest that Jay worked and stayed out of trouble while living with his grandmother despite her vituperation and emasculating criticism; return to drug use was associated with his return to his mother.

Willie, after leaving Riverside Hospital, recognized that he was better off in Washington, D.C., where he had lived with an older cousin, than he would be at home with his mother. He remained in Washington for four months, staying out of trouble, working regularly. On Mother's Day, he impulsively returned to New York City; that evening, he resumed drug use.

Harry was sent by a court in New York City to Miami to live with his aunt and uncle. There he worked steadily for almost a year and established positive, satisfying relationships with peers and with his relatives. However, he felt more and more strongly that *there was something missing from his life.* For this reason, he returned to New York City to be with his mother. He recalled that, as he stepped off the airplane, he felt that he had made a terrible mistake in returning but that he could not change his plans. Almost immediately, he resumed drug use.

In each of the three cases cited above, these patients were able to describe their mothers—probably correctly—as domineering persons who limited their sons' self-assertion, used them unfairly for their own emotional and physical needs, and gave them little in return. Despite this, they were blocked in the expression of hostility toward their mothers. The mothers, on their parts, consciously suffered from the difficulties of their addicted sons. They felt that they were being martyred by what their sons were doing to themselves. They felt that they were being depleted by the experience of supporting a chronologically almost-adult person who was not only dependent on them but stole from their purses and pawned their movable properties.

Walter Adams has placed considerable emphasis on this state of affairs.[26]

> . . . It is only in the subtle nuances picked up in the relationship [between the mother and her addicted son] that we find the subtle causative factors underlying the personality or character defect which begets narcotic addiction. . . . This feature of ambivalent and helpless clinging to a rewarding, yet at the same time nonrewarding home seems distinctive for the addict.[27]

The other side of this narcissistic relationship between the adolescent addict and his mother is seen in the often destructive and hostile behavior of the mother toward her addicted son. Though the mothers are unable to encourage or enhance the development of their sons toward independence or maturity, many have great difficulty in refusing things. They tend to be indulgent in material things, unable to discipline the boy, and inconsistent in their expectations and in the setting of limits. Some of the mothers are, however, repressive and nongiving even of material things. These aspects of the family structure, however important they may have been in the course of the adolescent addict's childhood and early personality development, take on a new and crucial significance in relation to efforts to intervene therapeutically in the addiction process. Though their mothers are consciously eager to see their sons improve, they fail to carry through on plans.

For example, when Jack left the hospital after a year of intramural treatment, his mother arranged for him to take a two-month vacation *before* going to work.

When Harry left the hospital for weekend home visits, plans were made with his mother, who was advised not to give him money. However, she did give him money—invariably, by a remarkable coincidence,

---

[26] Adams, *op. cit.,*

[27] It does not seem "distinctive" to us, since in our experience similar clinging also commonly occurs between schizophrenics and their mothers.

the current price of a bag of heroin ($3). Harry assured us, when we commented on this, that his mother knew nothing about the price of heroin.

Harry's mother was not unique in her skill in doing the most wrong things at the most crucial moments. Bob had been home on a visit and was due to return to the hospital at 9 A.M. The night before returning, he stayed out late with his friends; for this "reason" his mother did not want to awake him early in the morning. Instead, she let him sleep until the afternoon and then gave him "a real good meal" before suggesting that he go back to the hospital. Instead of returning to the hospital, he took the remainder of the afternoon off and used drugs. He returned to the hospital at night, when admission causes maximal difficulty for the nursing staff.

Willie returned to New York City from Washington, D.C., and to drug use for three months before his mother called the hospital to say that he had returned, even though she had undertaken to keep the hospital informed of his whereabouts. It was not until Willie had become increasingly involved with and addicted to drugs that his mother called, at this point to inquire what she should do. She said that she had been meaning to call before, but had been too busy to do so.

Such antitherapeutic behavior usually occurs in the context of an extraordinary eagerness to please, to cooperate, to improve the reputation of the hospital, and to keep their sons away from drug use. One of the most striking instances of this occurred in the case of Bert, a twenty-year-old adolescent addict, the son of a woman who played an extremely active role in an association of parents and relatives of addicts. With much therapeutic effort, plans were made for him to live away from the overprotective, emotionally indulgent atmosphere of his parental home. These plans were discussed at length with his mother, who accepted and agreed with them. However, as soon as Bert left the hospital, she gave him money for his rent (rather than sending a check directly to the Y.M.C.A. as had been planned), which Bert promptly converted into heroin, and arranged for him to take his evening meals at her apartment. This was interpreted by Bert as an expression of her wish that he remain at home with her, rather than establish himself independently.

These data suggest that the narcissistic relationship of the adolescent addict with his mother, this failure in psychic differentiation and separateness, is not to be understood as a pathology of the addict per se. It seems to us that there is a strong need on the part of the mothers to maintain their sons in a weak, dependent position for their own security. We regard the ambivalent interference with the therapeutic process by the addicts' mothers as an instance of such a need, rather than of ignorance or of spite.

C. Disturbance of Sexual Identification.

According to Erikson, establishing personal identity is *the* crucial adolescent problem.[28] Personal identity has many facets—vocational, religious, class, sexual, and so on. All these areas of identity are probably related; not knowing what and who one is in any of these areas weakens or complicates the sense of identity in the others.

The adolescent addict has a weakened sense of, and a deep-lying disturbance inhibiting the acquisition of, personal identity. Perhaps this is why the almost exclusive identification—"I am a junkie"—is so supportive. It is often observed that an exclusive, affect-laden, predominant group identity can conceal or substitute for a weak sense of personal identity; e.g., the person who identifies himself as *a* veteran, Rotarian, physician, and so on. Since the relationship in the primary family group between mother, father, and child plays such a central role in the decisive phases of personal development, it is no wonder that problems of sexual identification—orienting the self in terms of being or becoming a man like father or a woman like mother (or their surrogates)—plays such a central role in the total sense of identity. Whether the weakness of the total sense of identity of the adolescent addict is based on it or not, disturbance of sexual identification is a prominent area of pathology among these youths. It is not that they assert explicit concern over their sexual identities, but, rather, the subtleties of feeling about themselves—sometimes dimly conscious, more often repressed—give evidence of the disturbance.

Though this hypothesis—that adolescent addicts have a serious disturbance of sexual identification—is based on clinical experience and impressions which are difficult to objectify, there are substantiating behavioral correlates and attributes which we can cite. The concept, "disturbance of sexual identification," has two major components. For the first component, one inquires, "To which gender do you belong?" For the second component, one inquires, "Can you do that which belonging to this gender entails, socially as well as biologically?"

There are three types of historical or observational material, cited in our own and other reports, indicating that adolescent addicts display

[28] E. Erikson, *Childhood and Society* (New York: Norton, 1950).

disturbance in sexual identification in either or both of these components, that they are confused as to their genders and/or are unusually inept in carrying out their roles.

The first type of data does not have to do with sexuality in a limited biological sense, but rather with what can be inferred about the patient's masculine identification and potency from his performance in vocational, educational, familial, leisure, and other areas of his life. Being masculine is closely tied, in contemporary American culture, to a concept of the self as having power; strength; competence; effective and appropriate assertiveness; and to a role which involves being or becoming a responsible provider, father, and head of the household. In these terms, the addict patients we studied were obviously disturbed in their sexual identification. They were lacking in both the essential ingredients of such a masculine self-image and in the attributes that would justify it. They neither were nor showed any signs of becoming responsible providers. Their being and becoming was oriented, in large measure, in the contrary direction, toward passivity and dependence. They were concerned with getting, taking, or giving, but not with give-and-take. They were at the opposite end of that continuum in human development which culminates in mutually regulated, mutually satisfactory relationships. Indeed, they were occupied with some of the most primitive and basic problems of human development—with the predictability of gratification and the establishment of basic trust.

Their passivity and dependence is seen in a variety of social interactions with addicted and nonaddicted persons, both in the hospital and in the community. One of the most conspicuous manifestations of this in the hospital had to do with meeting "oral" needs with cigarettes, candy, and soft drinks. They spent a great deal of energy in the giving or taking game. Despite limited funds, they were continually giving the "oral" staples to each other, with hostility and resentment which they consciously experienced but communicated poorly and with feelings of depletion, and taking with extraordinary minimization of their own taking. "They are all taking from me," they complained, "and they never give to me in return." With very little assistance from the therapist, they rather easily expressed their feeling of being manipulated; but they learned to what extent they were themselves manipulating only when they were ready to move toward more mature forms of relatedness. This giving or taking is extremely ambivalent. When they succeed in a swindle, they experience guilt, though rarely shame. When they are taken care of, they sow discontent and doubt in the relationship; after they reap its dissolution, they bitterly accuse themselves of stupidity and misbehavior. They recurrently seek a person to love who will take care of them, no matter how irresponsibly or provocatively they themselves may behave.

Sam, for example, entered into a close relationship with a girl his own age a few weeks after he had been discharged from a city prison in which he had had a thirty-day detoxification. While this relationship was developing, he was casually and irregularly using heroin. When his girl friend discovered this, she told him that he must give up drug use if he wanted to continue the relationship. They arranged in a dramatic fashion (not uncommon for adolescents) that they would separate for a week, during which he would maintain abstinence. After a week of complete abstinence, one hour before their planned meeting, Sam obtained heroin and arrived "stoned" (acutely intoxicated) at their rendezvous. Since she did not want to be involved with him as an addict, this provocation ended their relationship. Sam was bewildered by her behavior; if she really loved him, as she claimed, how could she leave him?

On the other hand, adolescent addicts repeatedly allow themselves to be swindled of money, drugs, or the women they are keeping (or, more accurately, who are keeping them). They "trust" inappropriately, that is, they trust that they will be exempt from a generalization which they offer with acerbity—"You can't trust a junkie." In brief, they repeatedly and, one suspects, compulsively re-enact a drama of getting and losing.

The second type of data indicating a disturbance in sexual identification and role behavior has to do with their explicitly sexual behavior and relationships. These data indicate that adolescent addicts exhibit conspicuous disturbances in their sexual behavior and relationships, which may be categorized as follows:

1. Concern over sexual inadequacy;
2. Deprecation of or expressed disinterest in sexuality;
3. Homosexual relationships and/or concern over homosexual attack;
4. Preference for cunnilinction over genital intercourse.

Apart from these symptomatic disturbances, we noted that they did not experience distress when their sexual drives were curtailed or their

capacity for climax blunted or eliminated by heroin. Indeed, the casual-
ness with which they gave up orgastic potency is one evidence of their
psychosexual pathology; it is plausible to assume that one gives up or
accepts impairment in an area of function only when that area has
little or negative value. The following case material illustrates some of
the explicitly sexual manifestations of the disturbance of sexual identification we have observed in adolescent addicts.

Joe began using heroin at the age of eighteen, while living in Chicago.
He was introduced to heroin by boys four or five years older, whom he
idealized as "men . . . who knew life." He originally hesitated to use
heroin. Indeed, he had known people who had died from overdoses.
With the encouragement of his friends, who assured him that no harm
would come to him and that it would be a delightful experience, he
began to use heroin irregularly, at most once daily. This pattern of
heroin use was continued for seven to eight months. Although he stated
that he experienced "relaxation and tiredness . . . which was very
pleasant," he was particularly impressed by the regularity with which he
experienced nausea; in fact, each time he used heroin, he would get "a
miserable feeling, so sick to the stomach." From the beginning of his
addiction history, he took heroin intravenously. Without being able to
clarify the basis of this decision (further than to state that he did not
like it any more), he decided to give up heroin use. He was able to do
this without difficulty. This illustrates, incidentally, that use of heroin,
even when it is taken intravenously, not infrequently, over a period of
many months, does not *ipso facto* lead to addictive use of the drug.

Joe remained abstinent for eight months. In this period he left Chicago and returned to Jackson, Miss., his birthplace, where he courted
his prospective wife. During his courtship, he was jealous and suspicious
of Lucy. Although he went out on occasion with other girls, he threatened, with roughness and profanity, to hurt her if she went out with
other boys. After a six-month courtship in which they went out together socially at least three or four times a week, they married. At
this point, there was a remarkable change in their relationship. Joe no
longer wished to go out socially at all, but he almost insisted that Lucy
go out without him, with anybody she wished and without his supervision, control, or concern. He became aware all at once of his ambivalent feelings over the marriage. He felt he should not have married her. Although he had experienced sexual intercourse not infrequently since puberty (at age ten) he became distressed by the in-

timacy of marital life. He was ashamed of his body; he did not wish his wife to see him while he was taking a bath, dressing, or undressing. He thought that it is a blow to a man's pride to be seen naked by a woman. Other data pointing to the severity of his problem of sexual identification and role[29] indicated that the marriage was more than he could cope with. His sexual interest in his wife disappeared. He was becoming more isolated and withdrawn.

About one month after his marriage, he experienced an *urge* to use heroin. At this time, in contrast to the situation when he was first introduced to heroin, he was not solicited by his peers, but rather spent the day almost frantically trying to "make a connection." Finally, in the evening, when he was about ready to give up and go home, he at last found somebody who would sell him heroin. From that time until he came to Lexington (four months later) in 1952 as a voluntary patient, he used heroin daily, increasing his dosage to three or four shots a day, for which he spent about $20 daily.

Joe's marriage was probably a last-ditch stand against his latent homosexuality and complex dependence on his mother. When this attempt to reassure himself of his masculinity by becoming a married man failed, he became an addict and, to support his addiction, a thief.

Carl, a twenty-year-old youth from Harlem, presented himself as a mature, responsible, hard-working young man from a good, cohesive family; as socially active; and as readily accepted by his peers, both male and female. He had had several moderately prolonged relationships with nondelinquent girls of his age in which sexual relationships developed out of and were accompaniments to warm mutual regard. He was engaged to marry a good girl who had been graduated from high school and was at that time working in a bank. His marriage date was postponed as a result of his addiction, which he imputed plausibly and nondefensively to deleterious neighborhood influences.

Carl could not, however, sustain this picture of himself. Despite strong resistance—for maintaining such a façade was extremely impor-

[29] Data suggesting latent homosexuality included repetitive formation of tense friendships of short duration with older men in which the predominant theme of their interactions was discussion of the older man's sexual prowess, to which Joe listened with rapt attention.

Data suggesting a wish for sexual closeness with his mother included: "She looks too young to be my mother." "I'm crazy about her." "She treats me like a baby instead of like a man." Joe felt neglected when his mother encouraged him to independence, yet resentful when she did things for him.

tant to him—almost every aspect of this façade crumbled beneath his anxiety. He began to indicate by the fourth or fifth interview that his sexuality was not what he wished it to be. In fact, he dreaded return to the community and the risk of readdiction explicitly for this reason.

Carl had, in fact, been extremely shy with girls since puberty. When he went out with a girl he was afraid even to put his arm around her; he was unable to speak easily or casually with her. When he was twelve, his pathologically jealous and socially withdrawn father separated from his mother. When Carl was fifteen, he was sent to North Carolina to get him away from the bad neighborhood influences which interfered with his schooling. Here, living with a maternal aunt, Carl developed greater ease and confidence in relating to girls. He became a "big flier," "an operator." When he was sixteen, his father died, and Carl returned to New York to help support his mother. His comfort with girls disappeared with his homecoming. However, when he began to use heroin regularly (though not as yet addictively) at eighteen, he found that his shyness melted away. He became verbally and sexually uninhibited with girls; in his own words, he became "a terrible man." Carl liked being "a terrible man." He met his fiancée after he began using heroin regularly.

In retrospect, he became concerned over his ability to sustain the relationship without the use of heroin. He observed that, when he was going with her and was unable to get a "shot," he lost interest in her. This led to more regular and finally to addictive use of the drug. While in a New York City prison, he fantasied a reunion with his girl friend in which they would hug and kiss, freely and warmly expressing their affection. However, when he left The Tombs, he not only felt unable to kiss her spontaneously, but also, when she asked that he kiss her, refused to do so. After Carl returned to heroin use, he regained the jovial, relaxed, and easy-going "persona" through which he could express affection and participate, albeit rarely, in sexual intercourse.

Carl feared that this sequence—inhibition, taking on the heroin persona, readdiction—would recur after he left Lexington. Despite this, and characteristically for adolescent opiate addicts, he refused therapy because he hoped that his "will power" would keep him away from heroin while he developed new facilities to cope with his emotional problems. Carl married a few weeks after he left Lexington; after a few weeks of marriage, he was readdicted.

Carl's case illustrates a fairly common phenomenon among adolescent addicts—inhibition of sexual activity alleviated through heroin use. This is a consequence of the fact that heroin may diminish anxiety associated with sexuality more than it inhibits the sexual functioning per se. Parenthetically, this illustrates how complex the relationship is between activity, including sexual activity, and opiate use. Opiates depress activity, generally speaking, but also, as we shall elaborate in Chapter IX, inhibit anxiety. Consequently, the net effect of a particular dose of heroin may be to facilitate activity, when this activity had been markedly hampered by anxiety or by obsessive-compulsive symptoms related to controlling anxiety. Indeed, addicts sometimes report getting "drive" from opiates. This paradox stems from the multiple psychic effects of the opiates. The case study of RR[30] described how work inhibition was alleviated in the course of his heroin addiction, until the problems of being an addict in our society again hampered work even more than the heroin facilitated it by alleviating the obsessive-compulsive symptoms.

Mark, a twenty-year-old pimp from New York City, established parasitic, exploitative relationships with women. In his estimation, however, his women were never to be trusted. Mark had been in institutions since age sixteen in consequence of his addictive use of heroin. In the hospital where he was being treated by one of the writers, he was recurrently involved in fights with other boys because of implications that he was not enough of a man. He said that this happened to him in his earlier intramural treatment, too. Although, to the best of our knowledge, Mark has never engaged in homosexual relationships, he was extremely touchy about homosexuality and was consequently an easy target for other patients who found that they could get a rise out of him with such epithets as "intellectual faggot." Even so, Mark kept his fingernails polished with clear lacquer, was excessively vain about his hair and clothing, and spoke in a rather affected manner. At the same time, a major conscious concern was that he be helped to appear as a "real man." He solicited vitamin prescriptions in the hope that pills would help him to burgeon.

Two things are noteworthy about Mark's fighting. First, he did not look like a fighter, a "tough," or a trouble-maker. In fact, he had a reputation for pleasantness and exceedingly good manners. He presented himself to his therapist as a passive, weak victim of his mother's and sister's influence, to which he was compelled to submit. Apart from

[30] Donald L. Gerard and Conan Kornetsky, "Adolescent Opiate Addiction: A Case Study," *Psychiatric Quarterly*, 28 (1954), 367–380.

his fighting, he was a very good boy, a model patient. Second, Mark won all his fights. Despite concern over his body, he was muscular, tall, wiry, and as skillful as a boxer. After winning a fight, Mark suffered fears of revenge. He perceived his opponent (whom he would fight before an audience large enough to spread the news of his exploit to the total patient population) as a sneaky, treacherous, and unfair person who would get him "on the street" and would probably put a knife in his back. Thus, win or lose, Mark felt attacked and probably provoked attacks by other men. As he saw them, they were all out to stick their hard, penetrating weapons into his unprotected soft spots.

Mark's case illustrates a common phenomenon among adolescent addicts. On one side is the big man who exploits women; on the other is the little boy preoccupied with thoughts of the insufficient masculinity of his body, the insufficient recognition of his masculinity by his peers, and the fear (wish) that he be hurt and attacked (sexually invaded) by other men.

The third type of data indicating disturbance in sexual identification and role has to do with the persona of the addict, his façade, the trappings he displays to the world outside. These somewhat theatrical phrases are especially apt since adolescent addicts are so often like actors. Their roles are fluid, changing, so little an expression of a hard core or perhaps so different from the true core of themselves. To use Erikson's terms, they suffer from "role diffusion" in an almost explicit sense of that phrase.

A recurrent phenomenon observed by one of the writers, when he conducted diagnostic conferences at Riverside Hospital, was the frequency of flagrant discrepancies between the life history of the patient as reconstructed, respectively, by the psychiatric social worker, the psychiatrist, and the clinical psychologist from one or two interviews with the patient. These discrepancies related not only to the distant aspects of the patient's experiences but also to those immediate events which led to his hospitalization. At times, this led to bitter discussion within the staff. Whose life history was the most accurate?

The most evident source of confusion probably lay in the fact that each of the observers felt that he had established such "good rapport" with the patient that the latter could not possibly have been telling lies to him, that perhaps he had misstated his situation to the other interviewers. Not only were there discrepancies in the life-history data collected by these observers, but there were also hotly argued discrepancies in descriptions of what the patient "was like." A psychiatric social worker described patient Z as soft, passive, and helpless. The psychiatrist perceived him as ingratiating, manipulative, and cool. The clinical psychologist perceived him as aggressive, cunning, and deceitful. In view of the fact that these were not recurrent descriptions utilized by these observers, that the social worker, for instance, might perceive patient Y in the same terms that the clinical psychologist perceived patient X, it seems most likely that these youths present various aspects of themselves to various observers in a bewilderingly luxurious variety of roles. This role-playing is largely unconscious. The roles are evoked by the differing situations and by the differing object of the relationship. This phenomenon is sometimes alluded to as influenceability or as an extraordinarily well functioning "radar system"—a lack of inner-directedness.

Despite their role diffusion, there are certain aspects of the personae of adolescent addicts which are recurrently described in the literature and noted in our own observations, ways of expressing themselves to the world which are, despite the fluidity and changeability of their role-playing, fairly consistent and which point to the weakness of masculine identification.

They are soft-spoken, well-mannered, and graceful. They present themselves not as toughs, but as gentlemen. As a group, they are good-looking youngsters, often handsome, rarely ugly. They tend to be well-built and roundly muscled, to have symmetrical faces. These impressions were confirmed by our contacts with control subjects, who as a rule were not nearly so handsome, graceful, or "gentlemanly."

An extraordinarily high proportion of adolescent addicts can be seen as "pretty boys." They would not appear out of place in a musical comedy chorus. They are vain of their appearance. They spend much time preening. They are preoccupied with clothing, which they wish to be of the finest materials and the latest styles. They spend much time before their mirrors experimenting with their hair, moustaches, and goatees.

None of these preoccupations are alien to adolescent boys; the difference is of degree and not of kind. The degree to which adolescent addicts exhibit these traits and activities suggests the usual traits and activities of adolescent girls. Adolescent addicts do not look, behave, or deport themselves as adolescent boys usually do; they do not try to appear manly, rugged, vigorous, energetic, rough-and-ready.

These observations suggest that they have strong feminine identifications, a conclusion to which Zimmering *et al.*,[31] Fort,[32] and the Chicago clinics[33] independently subscribe. A variety of data are offered by those authors illustrating feminine tendencies, interests, occupational goals, and the like.

There are occasional exceptions. Some adolescent addicts are persistently and actively occupied with proving that they really are manly. They behave in an aggressive, hostile, argumentative manner. They are afraid to express or receive warm or sympathetic feelings. They are afraid that they will be found out, that someone will "get the wrong idea" about them. They approach the interviewer with the attitude that he is trying to "bug" them, and they will not give him a chance to do so. They tell with pride how they viciously assaulted a homosexual who accosted them, as though to say: "See how little I would want anything like this for myself, I practically killed him for thinking that. . . ."

They try to impress the observer with their independence and bravery, with their ability to function well in the most difficult circumstances. They know better than any middle-class professional person what life *really is*. They boast of their exploits with women, crime, and narcotics to prove what strong men they are. In one of Shakespeare's telling observations, they do protest too much; the psychologically trained observer cannot help but see through to the problems of masculine identification beneath the veneer of masculinity.

Though only the minority of adolescent addicts are actively occupied with proving their masculinity, almost all are at least episodically involved with the same issue. As a group, they respond with extreme sensitivity to remarks which might challenge their identification as men. They can be led into a variety of delinquent behaviors through teasing; not appearing "chicken" or "square" is crucial to them. Even though their manner, appearance, and concerns so clearly suggest feminine identification, or perhaps consistent with the fact that this is so, they are often involved in defensive, compensatory behavior intended to assert, guarantee, and define their manhood. Most evident among these

[31] *Op. Cit.*

[32] J. P. Fort, "The Psychodynamics of Drug Addiction and Group Psychotherapy," *The International Journal of Group Psychotherapy*, V (April 1955), 150–156.

[33] "Drug Addiction among Young Persons in Chicago," A report of a study conducted by the Illinois Institute for Juvenile Research and the Chicago Area Project (October 1953.)

are their institutional misbehavior and disciplinary problems. When the hospital staff attempts to impose controls which would be accepted, though not enjoyed, by most adolescents, adolescent addicts perceive this as a threat to their masculinity, so that they are regularly involved in such problems as truancy, keeping late hours, refusing to get up in time for breakfast, and refusing to turn the lights out at some curfew hour. They will let nobody tell them how to conduct themselves, for to do so implies that they are not man enough to know for themselves.

STATISTICAL FOOTNOTES

[a] Some relevant statistics, medians given in the order addict–control: R:20, 25; F + per cent: 80, 73; F per cent: 80, 71; M: 1, 2; Sum C: 1.5, 2.5. These group differences are all significant, by the Mann-Whitney U test, at .05.

[b] Percentages producing fewer than ten new responses: 50, 17. Percentages making regressive use of color (CF or C >FC): 89, 31. Median decrease in F + per cent as compared to initial administration: 11.5, 3.

IX

Personality and Addiction: A Dynamic Perspective

Although the opiate addiction of the adolescents we have studied grew out of a long history of maladjustment in which those structural aspects of the personality discussed above were significant, neither maladjustment nor personality structure per se is sufficient to account for their becoming addicted. Two other sets of determinants are involved.

First, from an epidemiological standpoint, the social climate, attitudes, values, stresses, and gratifications current in his community and, of course, the availability of drugs significantly affect the likelihood that any particular youth with the personality characteristics described will experiment with drug use.

Second, from a psychiatric standpoint, the likelihood that he will become an addictive user of opiate drugs is most significantly affected by his experiences with drug use in the context of his current situation as this has been structured by his entire experience. This hypothesis, which we will attempt to illustrate in the following pages, may be formulated more clearly as follows: assuming that other conditions are favorable, *the probability of addiction is greater if the person experiences changes in his situation in connection with his use of opiate drugs which may be described as adaptive, functional, or ego-syntonic and* which he describes in terms which tell us that he regards the use of opiates as extremely worthwhile despite, or perhaps especially because of, the inconveniences and difficulties of being an addict in our society. We may think of these functional or adaptive changes in terms of forces operating at four levels within the individual: at the level of conscious experience; at the level of certain defenses; at the level of unconscious process; and at the level of psychophysiological reaction.

At the Level of Conscious Experience

Closest to the surface, to the threshold of awareness and to communication, are certain common adaptive aspects of drug use. Though these are, in a sense, known to the users, they are not readily communicated by them because of problems of rapport, shame at confessing personal inadequacies, and their lack of experience in communicating subtle feelings and emotions. As they enter therapeutic relationships, they become more capable of formulating and communicating these phenomena.

One of the most striking of the phenomena is symptom relief. Heroin and morphine are efficient tranquilizing, or ataractic, drugs (at least they unquestionably are so for those individuals who become addicted). Overt symptoms of anxiety, obsessive thinking, and early delusional formations are modified or eliminated. Many individuals feel tense and restless before they begin to use opiates. When they use them they feel comfortable, relaxed, and peaceful. Apart from our own experience, some striking instances of symptom relief have been given by Wikler[1] and Lindesmith.[2]

An especially important and common instance of relief from symptoms is that opiate drugs are often helpful in quelling the anxiety and strain which addicts experience in a variety of interpersonal situations. Many feel shy, withdrawn, unacceptable, or socially inhibited. With opiates, they are able to participate more comfortably in the ordinary run of adolescent activities, e.g., dancing, dating, going out with the gang, or even in fighting. This is not to say that these are common activities of addicts, but that, when addicts do participate in them, they

[1] Abraham Wikler, *Opiate Addiction,* "Psychological and Neurophysiological Aspects in Relation to Clinical Problems" (Springfield, Ill.: Charles C Thomas, 1953).

[2] A. R. Lindesmith, *Opiate Addiction* (Bloomington, Ind.: Principia Press, 1947).

do so more effectively and with less malaise with the help of opiates than they would otherwise. This aspect of opiate use is analogous to the social use of alcohol. Paradoxically, this leads many young addicts into situations which they might otherwise avoid, but which, once entered, develop more-or-less inexorably into complex situations with which they cannot cope even with the help of drugs. Opiates can calm anticipatory anxiety, and they may sustain inadequate individuals through the trials of relatively superficial personal association, but the drugs cannot substitute for the basically adequate ego structure these individuals lack.

Many nonaddictive users of heroin may also take the drug for its helpful functions, just as many nonaddictive users of alcohol take an occasional "social drink." We speculate that the individuals who are helped to deal with difficult situations for which they have adequate resources (i.e., the drug is helpful in easing the situation, but is not essential for an adequate performance) do not become addictive users. Those who are helped to enter relatively enduring and demanding situations for which they lack adequate resources respond with in-creased anxiety as the situations develop and, hence, with a need for further ataraxia. Thus, they are led to the recurrent use of the drug, until they eventually learn to substitute the ataraxia for whatever they can get from coping with difficult situations.

Another important, consciously experienced, phenomenon is the intoxication experience itself, which the addict refers to as "being high." This experience is appreciated and enjoyed by the addict and by regular users, but by only a minority of experimental "normal" subjects. It is not, however, in any true sense, a euphoria—a feeling of stimula-tion, happiness, excitement.

The point at issue may perhaps be clarified by reference to two contrasting ideals of fulfillment: paradise and nirvana. Paradise repre-sents an ideal situation in which all desires are easily satisfied. If one is hungry, one has but to reach out, and the means of satisfying hunger are at hand. Nirvana, by contrast, represents an ideal of fulfillment through absence of desire, and desire is itself viewed as an inherently frustrated state that cannot be compensated for through the pleasure of its gratification.

At least to the normal Western mind,[3] however, the prospect of end-

[3] That the issue may well transcend cultural differentiation is indicated by various experiments on rats described by Leon Festinger. In one experiment,

less fulfillment through an absence of desire is not a particularly attractive one. Normal men, for instance, do not look forward with great eagerness to the attainment of a maturational level in which they will find themselves beyond sexual desire; and, having attained an age characterized by a marked diminution of sexual desire, they do not typically look on this aspect of their attainment as an asset. Nor does the average person look forward to the day when he will be able to satisfy the nutritive needs of his body (and even to anticipate hunger) with a pill. The nirvana-like end state of gratification may be valued and enjoyed, but the pleasure is in the activity that goes into making the end state possible; the end state is itself, at least in part, enjoyable only in the security of the belief that it is not the final end, but that it will give way to remounting desire.

Human beings have devoted great ingenuity and planning to the development of means for intensifying desire and achieving an optimal protraction of the period of activity and of the investment and distribution of effort in achieving the end state.[4] Moreover, in the very vision

---

for instance, it was established that hungry rats develop a preference for a box in which they are delayed on their way to food. "The Psychological Effects of Insufficient Rewards," *American Psychologist,* 16 (1961), 1–11.

It may also be noted that the same culture which produced the concept of nirvana also produced the most elaborate techniques for the continuance of sexual intercourse with the postponement of orgasm. If the absence of desire is the desideratum, then, short of eliminating desire altogether, the optimum condition should be to get rid of it with the utmost dispatch. The issue here is, however, complicated by one of the *mastery* of desire through its disciplined expression; the completely disciplined control of the expression of desire may be viewed as a more effective step in the direction of the *conquest* of desire than the attempt to suppress it. Closely related is the notion that pleasure itself is a snare and a delusion, not because it is sinful, but because its experience makes more difficult the passage to a state beyond desire. Hence, a major aspect of the disciplined expression of desire is the systematic cultivation of a sense of affective detachment from one's participation, an attitude remarkably akin to the high value placed by those of our youth who are attracted to narcotics on the capacity to remain "cool." In the latter terms, the most admirable performance, whether in sex, music, dancing, or whatever, is that of the virtuoso who displays no feeling whatsoever in the course of the performance. We may only be displaying our own culturocentrism when we express the suspicion that such a philosophy is attractive only to people who have been impelled by desire and tantalized by the vision of gratification, only to meet with frustration and disappointment.

[4] A great deal of confusion is generated by the failure to distinguish the pleasure of the activity leading to the end state from the pleasantness (to coin a verbal distinction, "pleasure" here signifying a turbulent, stirred-up, zestful

of paradise itself there was implanted an image of the unattainable; it is as if the creators of the myth could not tolerate the vision of the total satisfiability of all wants, some degree of frustration being necessary to the very ideal of fulfillment. And it was when they tore away this restriction that Adam and Eve lost their paradise, or perhaps they gained a deeper wisdom—that human beings do not belong in paradise, that their destiny can be achieved only through toil and pain. Adam and Eve could satisfy their wants in the Garden of Eden, but the satisfaction left little to enjoy.

At any rate, the addict's enjoyment of the "high" is not the enjoyment of a stirred-up, zestful state. It is not the enjoyment of intensified sensory input and orgastic excitement, not even on a hallucinatory or fantasied level. De Quincey and others to the contrary notwithstanding, it is not an enjoyment of enhanced creative experience or rich fantasies. It is, in fact, not an enjoyment of anything positive at all, and that it should be thought of as a "high" stands as mute testimony to the utter destitution of the life of the addict with respect to the achievement of positive pleasures and of its repletion with frustration and unresolvable

---

enjoyment; "pleasantness," a serene, calm, passive enjoyment) of the end state. Even Freud, who was well aware of the significance of foreplay in sexual activity in building up the tension of desire and presumably also of the uneven crescendo of activity leading to the climax, failed to take account of this in his theoretical formulations and landed in serious theoretical difficulties as a result. Thus, in his characterization of an instinctual drive, Freud distinguished a source (a bodily state which leads to a continuous input of excitation), an object (with which it is necessary to interact in order to achieve the aim), and an aim (the elimination of the excitation). He identified the achievement of the aim with pleasure and so formulated the pleasure principle, a formulation that would in strict logic imply that aim-inhibited activity cannot be pleasurable—a conclusion inconsistent with other aspects of the theoretical system. At any rate, he recognized that he was in trouble when he realized that he had formulated the pleasure and nirvana (a basic striving to eliminate excitation) principles in identical terms. Since he must have known that the two principles referred to basically different aspects of behavior, he did not take the logical step of concluding that there was only one principle at work, but instead accepted the weak conclusion that there must be some qualitative difference in the fate of the energies involved in the two principles. Cf. Freud, "The Economic Problem in Masochism," *Collected Papers* (New York: Basic Books, 1959), II, 255–268.

It will be noted that Freud's basic characterization of an instinctual drive took no note whatever of the nature of the interaction with the object and, hence, of the potentially pleasurable (and sought) aspects of this interaction. In other contexts, however, he distinguished two kinds of pleasure in sexual activity. Thus, in his *Three Essays on the Theory of Sexuality* (New York: Basic Books, 1962) he wrote that the erogenous zones "are all used to provide a certain amount of

tension. It is, in the main, an enjoyment of a nirvana-like state unpreceded and unenriched by the pleasure of getting there. It is an enjoyment of negatives. Awareness of tension and distress is markedly reduced. Contact with reality diminishes. Ideational and fantasy activity are decreased, often blotting out a disquieting and disturbing fantasy life that is characteristic of the unintoxicated state. Some addicts do manage unelaborated and unimaginative fantasies of wealth and status or masochistic fantasies of self-recrimination and the intention to reform. Addicts feel "out of this world" and content, as if all of their needs have been taken care of. Here, in "the junkie paradise," they experience what Wikler has described as a diminution of their "primary drives," of hunger, thirst, awareness of pain, and sexual tension. Their bodies are satisfied and sated.

There is a remarkable rhapsodic description of thumb-sucking by a grown girl (quoted by Freud in his *Three Essays on the Theory of Sexuality* [New York: Basic Books, 1962], p. 47), which could just as well illustrate the opiate high.

---

pleasure by *being stimulated* in the way appropriate to them. This pleasure then leads to an increase in tension which in its turn is responsible for producing the necessary motor energy for the conclusion of the sexual act. The penultimate stage of that act is once again the appropriate *stimulation* of an erotogenic zone . . . by the appropriate object . . . ; and from *the pleasure yielded by this excitation* the motor energy is obtained . . . , which brings about the discharge of the sexual substances. This last pleasure is the highest in intensity. . . . It is wholly a pleasure of satisfaction and with it the tension of the libido is for the time being extinguished. . . . This distinction between the one kind of pleasure due to the *excitation* of erotogenic zones and the other kind due to the discharge of the sexual substances deserves . . . a difference in nomenclature. The former may be suitably described as 'fore-pleasure' in contrast to the 'end-pleasure . . .' " (pp. 76 ff.; italics added). It is likely that Freud somehow failed to distinguish in the "end-pleasure" the pleasure of the orgasm per se (a highly stirred-up state) and the pleasantness of the aftermath (the state of reduced tension), else it is difficult to see how he identified the pleasure principle with the reduction of tension. In any case, he did not think that the "end-pleasure" was available prior to puberty, which would imply that the prepubescent individual could not be governed by the pleasure principle, an obvious internal contradiction. Similarly, his notion that perversions arise from an excess of fore-pleasure with a resultant rejection of the "normal sexual aim"—i.e., the "end-pleasure"—would imply that sexual perverts are not governed by the pleasure principle.

In other major (and typically more rigorously formulated) psychological systems, one also finds difficulties that may be traced to the failure to make the distinction. Cf. Isidor Chein, "The Image of Man," *Journal of Social Issues,* XVIII (1962), 1–35, to be published in expanded form by Basic Books.

It is impossible to describe what a lovely feeling goes through your whole body when you suck; you are right away from this world. You are absolutely satisfied, and happy beyond desire. It is a wonderful feeling; you long for nothing but peace—uninterrupted peace. It is just unspeakably lovely: you feel no pain and no sorrow, and ah! you are carried into another world.

The adolescent addict does not usually like to talk about the experience of the high, other than to commend it. First, it is difficult for him to find words to describe the experience. Second, he is ashamed, embarrassed, and secretive about it. In fact, some adolescent addicts attempt to deprecate the experience in the postwithdrawal phase of their addiction; they say that being high on heroin is nothing, marijuana is better, that they would be crazy to go back to an experience which gives them so little and costs them so much. Third, but this is more common among older and more experienced addicts, they often have a superior attitude to the nonaddict based on the idea that they possess a secret, magical, self-administrable source of pleasure which, in their estimation, is better than anything the nonaddict can have. The high is too good; verbalization at best degrades it. "If you want to know what the high is, take heroin and learn for yourself."

At the Level of Certain Defenses

The general function of a psychic defense is to avoid anxiety. This may be accomplished by a subtle reordering of experience or by an alteration in the perception or in the manifestations of inner impulses or outer events (projection, denial, reaction formation, etc.). The phenomena we have alluded to above (symptom relief, social facilitation, and the experience of the high) are to a large measure expressions of the opiate's capacity to inhibit or blunt the perception of inner anxiety and outer strain. In this sense, the drug itself is a diffuse pharmacological defense. However, there is another sense in which opiate addiction is integrated into the psychological defenses of the adolescent addict. The general structure of this integration is a mélange of projection, rationalization, and denial. The fact that he is an addict, despite the personal and social implications of opiate addiction in our society, allays the anxiety he would experience if he were to face, express, or act out certain impulses and wishes. He displaces the responsibility for his behavior onto an auxiliary, executant ego about which, in effect, he can say: "Not I, but the drug in me does these things. I am not responsible; it is the monkey on my back."

That this is not conscious duplicity is attested by the genuine horror and anxiety with which some of these "released" impulses and wishes are recalled in the postwithdrawal phases of addiction. Of course, we do not wish to imply that the opiates per se are "releasers," in some physiological sense, of repressed wishes or impulses of a specifically aggressive or sexual nature. As one of the authors has pointed out in a comparison of alcohol intoxication and opiate addiction,[5] the opiate addict to a large measure "acts out" in the process of sustaining his addiction, and usually not in the course of acute intoxication with the drug nor necessarily in the actual physiological distress of the abstinence syndrome. It is sufficient for him to identify himself as *being an addict* to reap the benefit of this auxiliary ego.

The wishes and impulses expressed through this auxiliary ego are highly individualized. In the course of the addiction, the unspeakable is spoken, and that which should never be done is done. This does not occur in diffuse, patternless, or random misbehavior, but with remarkable precision of aim and aptness to the life situations and relationships with important persons in the lives of the addicts. They do not, of course, recognize the intentions of their behavior, however obvious these intentions may be to us. It requires months of work before a patient can accept the integration of his behavior with ideas or feelings he fears to perceive or communicate. Although there is no limit to the variety of such integrations, there are a few general classes which occur frequently.

In the course of addiction, the addict may begin to express hostility toward parental figures—whom he regards as emasculating or controlling—through theft from the parental home; overt anger (becoming "evil and nasty"); or through the spiteful, wasteful, or destructive use of parental furnishings, money, decorations, or clothing. Even his general delinquency and the use of narcotics itself may contain a strong component vector aimed at his parents. By becoming an addict, he can disappoint or frustrate those parents whose hopes or ambitions for their son are of the highest. Similarly, he may utilize his addiction for the expression of passive-dependent wishes, e.g., by giving up or avoiding employment; begging for money and gifts; soliciting loans

[5] Donald L. Gerard, "Intoxication and Addiction," *Quarterly Journal of Studies on Alcohol,* 16 (1955), 681–699.

without attempt to repay them; and withdrawing from activities, interests, and relationships outside his parental home.

The mother of an addict may want to take a lover or a new husband. This is not infrequent in the lives of the male adolescent addicts we have studied. Even though he regards his mother critically, he is likely to be extremely attached to, dependent on, and overidentified with her. Thus, he experiences his mother's intentions as a threat; he fears that he will lose her love and concern to this rival. His behavior in the course of his addiction then focuses on the rival. It is the rival's suits which are stolen and pawned; it just happens that the addict comes home "high" when his mother is entertaining this friend. In short, he persuades the rival through his behavior in sustaining his addiction that gaining a liaison with his mother is likely to be more trouble than it is worth.

The addict uses his addiction to express or act out repressed impulses and needs. From the standpoint of the discharge of psychic energy, this is probably pleasurable; in terms of eventual consequences, it can be disastrous. In terms of secondary reactions of guilt, such behavior can provoke tension and distress during abstinence which are alleviated, unfortunately too readily, by further indulgence in opiates.

At the Level of Unconscious Process

It is important to clarify the role of unconscious symbolism in addiction. Dreams, neurotic symptoms, wit, and the psychopathology of everyday life are enriched or burdened by their unconscious meanings. Similarly, many aspects of the addiction experience and process are linked with and emotionally colored by wishes, drives, and bodily experiences pertinent to the addict's early development and relationships. With exceptions, these tend to be communicated or expressed symbolically in the dreams and in the art work of the patients and in their responses to projective test material. For instance, dreams have the manifest content of a needle, fat, long, sticking into my body; being snowed under a mound of heroin; drinking heroin or being attacked by a monster with a huge syringe.

The exceptions, perhaps as important as the regularities, are those patients who tell us quite directly[6] that the syringe and needle ("the

[6] Obviously, in a strict sense of the term "unconscious," such directly communicated meanings are not unconscious. The term is, however, also used in an extended sense to include that which is typically unconscious in the normal person

works," as they are called in the argot) are like a breast; when he is high, he feels that he is together with his mother, long ago, warm, comfortable, happy, at peace; when he injects the opiate solution, he mixes the solution with his blood and bounces the blood-opiate mixture back and forth from syringe to vein, and, as he does this, he has fantasies about intercourse.

By and large, those patients who directly associate their addiction experiences with these oral concepts have the most clinically evident ego disturbances; they suffer from anxiety verging on panic or are overtly psychotic. They are least able to repress or otherwise defend themselves against the perception of such ideas and images, and they are thus able to directly verbalize what may only be inferred from the symbolic communications of the others.

It is difficult to ignore the fact that unconscious symbolism of this sort occurs in addiction. The question is, "What role does it play in the genesis of addiction?" Addiction is a complex psychosocial behavior. Obviously, no one takes drugs for the first time with such ideas in mind as that the syringe is a breast or that, through taking opiates, he may regain a state of early infantile unity with his mother. No one becomes an addict simply because he is laden with unconscious oral fantasies and cravings for breasts, sustenance, or warmth. Rather, as he becomes an addict, the techniques and circumstances of drug use readily lend themselves as vehicles of expression for these facets of his unconscious mental processes. Though these unconscious symbolizations are less weighty in the motivations for becoming an addict than are the forces of conscious experience, especially the high, or the forces of the integration of the addiction in the psychic defenses, they probably do contribute importantly to the *appetite* for drug use in the same sense that spices, with their volatile oils and esters, may contribute to the appetite for otherwise prosaic foods. However, as the addiction progresses and the addict becomes increasingly involved with his addiction and correspondingly less involved in any attempt to deal with the world and current relationships, ever-larger portions of his psychic life are given over to this primitive level of gratification.

---

under normal circumstances. We have elected to go along with such usage which is likely to have a familiar ring to most readers rather than enter into a discussion of such concepts as "primary" and "secondary" process and their relation to the concepts conscious–preconscious–unconscious, on the one hand, and to id–ego–superego, on the other.

At the Level of Psychophysiological Reaction

The concepts "craving," "dependence," and "tolerance" are usually found in textbooks of pharmacology in the section dealing with the opiate drugs. Our discussion here will emphasize the more psychological aspects of these psychophysiological forces.

CRAVING

"Craving" is, of course, merely a word. In common speech or in jest, we may say that we "crave" sweets or tobacco or love. We have no psychological lien on the term, no proprietary right to restrict its meaning to a particular reference. However, it is a useful rubric, in terms of which we may discuss certain attitudes and orientations. In the sense in which we wish to develop it, craving is a pathological phenomenon which entails recurrent states of liking, wanting, and seeking an entity or object but which differs from normal wanting, liking, and seeking in several important respects.

First, craving implies an abnormal intensity of desire.

Second, craving implies an abnormal intensification of the reaction to the failure to fulfill the desire. When a normal person cannot get what he wants, he may be sad and unhappy; one criterion of normality is that he seeks legitimate means to satisfy the desire, finds appropriate substitute gratifications, or waits until gratification becomes possible. But when a craving is not satisfied, there are intense emotional reactions of anger, rage, sulking, withdrawal, sullen resentment, or action aimed at getting that which is desired without regard to the consequences.

Third, craving implies an abnormal limitation in the modifiability of the desire (e.g., giving it up, lessening its intensity, accepting a substitute) as a result of experiences which emphasize the costs or the consequences of the satisfaction sought.

The development of craving for opiate drugs is an extremely important element in the addiction process. Addicts themselves distinguish varying degrees of craving for opiates. The intensity of craving is only partly related to the history of dependence on opiates. There are addicts who experience craving, in the defined sense, after very little experience with opiates, though in general the intensity of the craving is related to the duration of and the quantity of experience with opiates. We know that craving is not merely a consequence of the ability of the opiate to relieve organic distress. Postoperative and post-traumatic patients rarely become addicted to opiates. Alcoholics, whose general personality structure is remarkably similar to those of opiate addicts,[7] readily become addicted to opiates,[8] whether they receive opiates in the medical treatment of their alcoholism or illicitly. We know that the use of opiates is a necessary but not a sufficient condition of the development of craving. There are individuals who use heroin for the acute intoxication experience, for the alleviation of organic discomfort, or for the relief of anxiety without the development of craving. We know that craving is not inherent in the reactions to the opiate drugs.

It is extremely difficult to measure craving. We could attempt to measure the sacrifices an addict would accept to pay for a dose of opiates at a particular point in the history of his addiction (or in a particular cycle of addiction). However, such a measure would entail a rational, consistent weighing of price against commodity value (a phenomenon which occurs rarely enough in the purchase of socially approved commodities, e.g., automobiles); that is, it would assume the very kinds of ego activity which are foreign to craving. Complicating the issue, craving is not a constant in the individual. We have often noted sudden fluctuations in the extent of craving, either increasing or decreasing. Craving is not an isolated or automatic psychophysiological process. Nor is it highly correlated with degree of physiological dependence; indeed, it can occur in the truly addicted individual even when he has been completely relieved of physiological dependence on the drug. As the case histories we have cited indicate, the urge for opiate use occurs in complex interpersonal contexts, although they are often difficult to elucidate. Addicts have a considerable defensive stake in maintaining the anonymity and impersonality of their motivations, just as do persons with neurotic character problems who prefer to interpret their behavior as the most reasonable or only possible reactions to their circumstances or, as may be more fashionable today, in terms of psychogenetically formulated rationalizations.

Further complicating the issue is the distinction we have already drawn, especially in Chapter II, between craving and involvement. That is, some people find rewards in the use of narcotics, for the sake of which they suffer serious penalties, but which have nothing to do with

[7] Donald L. Gerard, "Intoxication and Addiction," *op. cit.*

[8] Michael J. Pescor, "A Statistical Analysis of the Clinical Records of Hospitalized Drug Addicts," *U. S. Public Health Report Supplement* No. 143 (1943).

the psychophysiological effects of the drug. Involvement with the drug and the drug-using subculture gives them a sense of a personal identity, a place in society, a commitment, personal associations based on a seemingly common purpose, a feeling of belonging to an in-group, a vocation and an avocation, and a means of filling the void in an otherwise empty life. Such people, too, may feel that they crave the drug; but this is not craving in the sense in which we are using the term. Craving is not a response to emptiness, but a characteristic mode of coping with even minor stresses of anxiety, frustration, and pain by an intense desire to revert to an intrauterine-like state of apparent self-sufficiency—a state that the drug can induce. In a sense, it is the direct opposite of involvement, although both craving and involvement may be found in the same individual. Involvement with narcotics is an expression of a need for a sense of being alive; craving is an expression of a need to withdraw from any semblance of active life.

Why do addicts develop a craving for opiate drugs? We have no final answer to this question. First, craving is conditional on valued personal experiences with the drugs. No one craves an experience that is wholly distasteful. The positive evaluation of the intoxication experience depends on the psychophysiological reactions to the drug; the situation in which the drug is used, which influences the evaluation of the intoxication experience; and the extent of experience with the drug as a source of satisfaction and as a means for the resolution of tension and distress.

Second, craving is an expression of the preferred modes of gratification adopted by the individual and, as such, is dependent on the individual's attitudes toward objects or sources of satisfaction independently of and preceding experience with opiate drugs. Whether an individual can or is likely to develop craving depends on the degree to which craving fits into his preferred modes of gratification and on the readiness with which (and the circumstances under which) he relapses into preference for modes of gratification into which craving fits. These are matters which are best viewed in the context of the psychosexual development of the individual.

We regard the strength of an individual's craving for opiates as a resultant of two groups of forces—those which have to do with personal experiences in relation to opiate drugs and those which have to do with the shaping of the individual's preferred modes of gratification. Consequently, we would expect to, and do, observe marked individual differences in the strength of craving. We would not expect these differences to be simple, nor would we expect simple relationships between intensity of craving and any one factor—the duration of opiate use, for instance. We would expect to observe individuals who sustain themselves for prolonged periods of their lives with small doses of opiates and others whose entire lives rapidly become dedicated to the intake of large quantities of these drugs.

THE PSYCHOPHYSIOLOGICAL REACTION TO OPIATE DRUGS

Opiate intoxication is *not* an inherently delightful state;[9] neither, for that matter, is any kind or degree of intoxication. The pleasures of alcoholic beverages must be learned; they are learned in a context of beliefs and usages which support, modify, and interpret the individual's psychopharmacological reactions. Becker's study of marijuana use[10] documents the role of other users in support, modification, and interpretation of the effects of marijuana as a force in marijuana use in our culture. But it does not follow that the psychopharmacological effects of the opiates or their enjoyment are *merely* conditional on beliefs and usages. Indeed, it has been found that a minority of naïve subjects who are given opiates experimentally regard the effects as pleasant or desirable and that, by and large, this minority consists of the psychologically most disturbed of the subjects. Similarly, we believe that the prospective adolescent addict is to be found among the seriously disturbed adolescent population in those areas where drug use is endemic and among the even more seriously disturbed in those areas where it is not endemic, and we have found that, unlike naïve experimental subjects, the majority of prospective addicts enjoyed the effect of opiates from the beginning. This supports the hypothesis that psychological deviancy is a conditioning phenomenon for the liking of opiates. However, this need not be necessarily or entirely so.

There are a few apparently normal persons we have known who did enjoy their first experiences with experimental doses of opiates without apparent serious psychiatric illness. These, however, have not been naïve subjects; they knew that they were going to receive morphine, and they expected that the morphine would in some way influence their

[9] L. Lasagna, J. M. von Felsinger, and H. K. Beecher. "Drug-induced Mood Changes in Man," *Journal of the American Medical Association*, 157, (1955), 1006, 1113.

[10] H. S. Becker, "Becoming a Marijuana User," *American Journal of Sociology*, 59 (1953), 235–242.

mood or ideational state. One colleague compared the experience with a day in a Turkish bath; he liked it, but had no inclination to repeat the experience. In short, it is possible that a "normal" subject would regard his first opiate intoxication as pleasant, but it is unlikely that he would begin to crave on the basis of this experience. It should also be remembered (from chapters VI and VIII) that a substantial minority of regular users initially found the effects unpleasant. On the assumption that some of these were truly addicted, it follows that unpleasant effects on first experience are not incompatible with later addictive use.

What is enticing about the effects of opiates for those disturbed persons who do become addicts? Or, to put it differently, what are the relevant effects of the opiates on the emotional lives of these persons?

A major effect of opiates is that they reduce the awareness of sources of distress and increase the sense of detachment from or otherwise diminish the unpleasantness of the experience that would be associated with distress in less clouded states of consciousness. The pain threshold (i.e., the intensity of stimulation needed to produce pain), for example, is raised and the anxiety associated with pain is diminished so that normally painful stimulation becomes tolerable. Drive—hunger and sexual tension, for instance—is also reduced, so that there is relief from the discomforts of drive states which are blocked from normal channels of relief and from anxiety that may be associated with the unreduced drives. Opiates thus, in one way or another, give relief from distress. It is almost axiomatic that this relief-giving psychopharmacological property of opiates is a major factor in the development of craving. Conversely, a chronic need for such relief—whether because of an abnormally frequent recurrence of distress or because of an inability to tolerate relatively minor distress or to cope with sources of distress in more adaptive ways—is a necessary condition of the development of craving. Parenthetically, this is also a factor in the behavior of addicts who postpone their dose of opiates until they begin to have withdrawal symptoms; they do this to maximize the experience of relief.

Since the intensity of distress is a determinant of the quantity of relief (as impact is determined by the height from which an object falls), we would expect the degree of positive evaluation of opiate intoxication to be highly correlated with the initial level of distress. This is supported by the previously cited work of Lasagna et al. However, detailed research is still to be done. Moreover, although it is certain that opiates can influence anxiety and other distressing states, there may be important constitutional differences in responsiveness to these drugs and in the potential for relief from distress which they might afford.

There are psychopharmacological phenomena associated with intoxication with opiates apart from the "relief experience." To what extent these enter into the positive evaluation of the drug and the development of craving, it is difficult to say. For example, there is a feeling of "impact" in the stomach following intravenous injection of morphine or heroin which is characterized in addicts' terminology as "a bang." The addict may also enjoy sensations of bodily warmth, of tingling like "pins and needles," and pleasant eroticized scratching and itching. Some addicts talk of these visceral experiences as an aesthete or a gourmet talks of the objects of his special interest. However, since these visceral experiences occur at the threshold of the opiate intoxication experience and since they are most intense and evident in one particular means of opiate intoxication, particularly with the intravenous use of opiate drugs, we believe that they are of secondary importance in the development of craving.

Though it is partly feasible to discuss the psychopharmacological reaction to opiates apart from the situation in which they are used, in the reality of the addiction process this never occurs. In fact, at least in our society and in the social context in which we have studied addiction among adolescents, the life situation plays an important role in the positive evaluation of the intoxication experience.

SITUATION AND THE POSITIVE EVALUATION
OF OPIATE INTOXICATION

Many adolescent addicts we have studied were able to tell us quite explicitly that they began their opiate use in a life situation rife with anxiety, tension, or disappointment and asserted that they experienced relief from these states in their initial intoxication. We know that the condition we have described for the development of craving—a high level of distress—is a common, probably a regular, phenomenon in the early addiction history of adolescent addicts. Since there are marked difficulties of communication with adolescent addicts, we do not learn easily about the level of emotional distress as a factor in the early establishment of a positive evaluation of the intoxication experience.

The situation is seemingly complicated by the fact that the relief experience may not occur in their initial opiate intoxication. The dosage may be inappropriate, e.g., too small to effect relief or so far above the individual's tolerance level that the appreciation of the distress-relief phenomenon may be blunted by the quick onset of coma or extreme somnolence. Moreover, these emotional states may not be consciously perceived or recognized. The adolescent addict may only recall or recognize, in the course of a therapeutic investigation, that he was highly perturbed by aspects of his life situation at the time when he began to use opiates. Then, too, the situation at the initial use of opiates need not be exceptionally anxious, tense, or depressive, even though, in fact, the prevalent level of malfunction of the novice is higher than of his peers who do not use opiates. Indeed, as has already been indicated, there may be long periods of opiate use without the development of craving. Many cases can be cited of individuals who liked the effect of opiates from the beginning, but did not develop craving until a psychosexual crisis occurred. With the need for relief from anxiety verging on panic, their craving began.

Rado has hypothesized that a "tense depression" was the unique or special emotional state which was relieved by opiate intoxication.[11] In our experience, this has not been so; i.e., it is not the unique or particular emotional state in the prelude to addiction. Acute anxiety, bewilderment, incipient panic, increasing despair, and unhappiness born of a sequence of failures and disappointments are other common emotional states preceding addiction in the adolescent addicts we studied. There is another type of emotional state in the *Anlage* of addiction which is important, not so much for its frequency as for its bearing on the life situation; this is a state of longing, a distressing condition of unfulfillment pervasive of all the experience which is alleviated by opiate intoxication and may be conducive to craving.

There are some indications in the literature that something like craving may develop passively in experimental animals.[12] However, this obscures rather than clarifies the issue. Craving as clinically observed, unquestionably develops in persons who liked and wanted opiates prior to any indications of pharmacological dependence on these drugs; craving much more typically leads to the pattern of use which establishes dependence than vice versa.

There are two other phenomena in the total situation of the person

[11] S. Rado, "Psychoanalysis of Pharmacothymia," *Psychoanalytic Quarterly*, 21 (1933), 1–23.

[12] S. D. S. Spragg, "Morphine Addiction in Chimpanzees," *Comparative Psychology Monograph*, 15 (1940).

who becomes an addict which influence the positive evaluation of opiate intoxication. One is the fact that the current disturbed emotional state we have discussed above is an outstanding feature in a total situation which is grossly unsatisfactory. The "preaddict," if we may use this term, has been notoriously unsuccessful in his educational, occupational, sexual, or familial life. For those few exceptions who were able to manage without conspicuous failures in one or several of these areas, there are quite evident anxieties or psychiatric symptoms which contaminated, blunted, or negated whatever else was satisfactory in their lives. Since, by and large, they have not found satisfaction or achievement elsewhere in their lives, the opiate intoxication experience stands out with particular clarity and vividness; with opiate intoxication, they felt good as they had not felt good before and as they had not felt good with other sources of intoxication, e.g., marijuana or alcohol.

For a person who is not accustomed to the wine of success, any good feeling he creates for himself not only makes him feel good about the experience itself, but also makes him feel better about himself; in short, he has an experience of increased self-esteem or can prevent a decline in self-esteem. This is, of course, not due to the opiate itself; enhanced self-esteem is not observed in medical or surgical practice after the relief of pain by morphine. In part, it results from the achievement of a status and the provision of an alibi for failure. In addicts with strong craving, however, it is in large measure a psychic consequence of achieving a state of relaxation and relief from tension or distress through one's own activities, not through a physician's recommendation or prescription, but through an esoteric, illegal, and dangerous nostrum. We can observe an analogous phenomenon in people who win the Irish Sweepstakes; win on dice, cards, horses, or numbers; or even in persons who park in no-parking zones without getting a traffic ticket. They feel that their luck is running good; they feel important, worthwhile, and interesting; they feel a sense of pride and accomplishment. Such an illusory achievement is an important psychic phenomenon, particularly important when it stands out by contrast with the remainder of a person's life.

There is a telling Yiddish anecdote about two cockroaches who were swept out of a garbage heap in a barn. One fell onto a pile of horse manure; the other fell onto the bare ground. The one who fell in the horse manure became fat and glossy. The one who fell on the bare ground became thin and bedraggled. One day they met in the barnyard. The thin one was astonished by the appearance of his old companion and asked him, "Yankel, what is this? You are so fat and wealthy, and I am so skinny and poor." "My good fellow," Yankel replied, "my fortune is the inevitable consequence of superior industriousness, intelligently applied." The moral is that good fortune can be experienced as (belated) recognition of one's intrinsic worth. When self-esteem is meager, any satisfying experience may be a source of enhanced self-esteem, as well as of pleasure, and the means through which this experience is attained is cherished.

The other factor which conditions the positive evaluation of the opiate intoxication experience is of a social-psychological nature; it may be characterized as "looking for kicks." This phenomenon is related to widespread attitudes among contemporary adolescents, and particularly among those belonging to deprived urban groups. It is also related to the readiness for craving which we will discuss later in this chapter.

The search for kicks is a polar extreme of a valuable human and particularly adolescent phenomenon, that is, the search for new experience. Normally, the search for new experience leads to the broadening of one's intellectual and sensory horizons and to the pleasures of working at challenging and difficult situations and tasks which, despite anxiety and strain, are capped with some degree of mastery or even with nondisgraceful failure. In what strike us as the happiest lives, this is a never-ending process. In other instances, the outcome is not so fortunate. At one extreme, there is a total blunting of this complex drive; these are persons who live a life of stultifying routine. Indeed, some clever adolescents regard adult life as dull and unperceptive because they recognize that the tempo and intensity of this drive is lowered by increasing responsibilities. The search for kicks is, on the surface, at the other pole. It expresses a conscious search for new experience of a special kind; what is sought is fun, excitement, novelty, and new sensations, as though the experience of novelty per se were substituted for the confrontation and mastery of ever-new and challenging situations. The never-ending search for the essentially passive experience of novelty masquerades as a zest for living.

Any novel experience, legal or not, is regarded as worth trying, as an expression of joy, pride, and pleasure in living, provided that the venture is not fraught with the peril of evoking contempt or disgrace in the peer subculture. Though the opiate intoxication experience may be compared to other intoxications or to other experiences of release and relaxation, it is *sui generis*. The peculiar sequence of bodily sensations, of vascular and glandular responses, is undoubtedly a new experience, as is the partial disturbance of consciousness which accompanies this experience. In the argot of addicts: "Man, it's good, it's cool, it's gone." It is commendable as a kick in terms of the preaddict's values. Though we do not believe that the value of novelty per se is responsible for an inclination toward addictive use or toward craving, this is another force in the initial positive evaluation of the opiate's intoxication experience which encourages initial use and facilitates return to an experience which offered kicks.

There is a painful contrast between the theory of kicks and its manifestations in the lives of those adolescents who become addicts. In fact, looking for kicks is not a happy state of affairs or any kind of expression of joy in living. The kicks they seek are inseparably linked with trouble from the onset. Their kicks are usually highly mannered, group-oriented, and stereotyped. By and large, the new experiences they seek are limited to new ways of being intoxicated and new ways of affirming individuality through mannerisms of dress, hair style, speech, and gesture. Some have got their earlier kicks through gang membership and fighting; others, through the use of alcohol. Kicks, in effect, is a pleasure orientation by youngsters with an extraordinary lack of the capacity to feel happy; what they probably mean by the search for kicks is that they wish they could be happy and that they will try anything to achieve it. With opiates, they probably do not get what the word kicks seems to connote, but they do get relief, both from this complex drive and from other more simple drives, e.g., pain, sex, and hunger.

DEPENDENCE

"Dependence" means simply and literally that the addict comes to require, need, or lean on opiates for the maintenance of his normal or comfortable physiological functioning. We say that the addict becomes dependent on opiates in consequence of the regular use of these substances. The rate at which such dependence develops varies with the type of drugs and the quantity taken. For instance, he can become dependent on morphine through using the same small quantity once daily for a week. In order to become dependent on heroin in the dosages that are typically ingested, it must be taken at intervals closer to twelve hours than to twenty-four. One would, however, expect individual variability in this respect.

Dependence is not a conscious process, though its corollary, the acute abstinence syndrome, may be consciously experienced. When opiate drugs are taken with sufficient regularity, they insinuate themselves into the physiological processes (enzyme systems) of the central nervous system so that they become essential elements of its milieu. When this regular intake of opiate drugs is abruptly discontinued, a characteristic disturbance occurs; the intensity of this disturbance is a function of the duration of the regular use and the amount of drugs which are regularly ingested. Dependence is *not* related to psychological needs or motives; decerebrate dogs and newborn infants of addicted mothers can have an acute abstinence syndrome. Dependence is a biological process which entails the maintenance of a certain level of opiate drugs to maintain apparently normal bodily function, and, in this sense, the biological dependence on the opiates can be a force in the addiction process; without the opiate, the person indeed becomes physically ill.

The abstinence syndrome, however, unlike the fact of dependence, is much influenced and modified by psychosocial factors. It is true, in the novice addict, that the intensity of this self-limiting illness (nausea, goose flesh, restlessness, etc.) is far from unbearable. The intensity of these symptoms hardly justifies the illicit use of opiates to quell the symptoms, particularly since each evasion of the acute abstinence syndrome intensifies the ultimate experience of the abstinence syndrome. To the addict and the individual in the process of becoming an addict, however, even this relatively minor distress is intolerable; his inability to act in terms of long-range goals precludes consideration of the inevitable consequences of permitting the degree of dependence to build up.

In the case of the experienced addict, dependent on four or more injections of heroin a day to prevent the abstinence syndrome, abrupt withdrawal is an unquestionably severe physiological disturbance; he develops chills and fever, lacrimation, perspiration, vomiting, smooth and striated muscle cramps, diarrhea, tachycardia, insomnia, or restlessness. Despite this fact, even in an addict with signs of severe physiological disturbance at the withdrawal of opiates, the amount of distress is conditional on the setting in which the distress is experienced. Alone, it can be an almost unbearable experience. In a hospital ward, remarkably little medication often stills the distress associated with quite severe physiological disturbance, e.g., painful cramps and diarrhea. Conversely, patients with minor overt symptoms may be very demanding of medication. In this regard, Pfeffer has described the beneficial influence of group therapeutic interaction on a withdrawal ward.[13] Though dependence can be interpreted as a biological phenomenon, the patient's attitude toward the manifestations of dependence can only be understood psychosocially.

Lindesmith has placed considerable emphasis on this as the basic phenomenon in opiate addiction.[14] He has presented case material in support of the thesis that accepting the fact that one is "hooked" and that one must continue to rely on opiates in order to ensure freedom from withdrawal symptoms is central to identifying oneself as an addict. In part, he is correct; among adolescent addicts, the self-identification as addicts—i.e., as persons who require opiates for comfortable functioning—is an important phenomenon in their developing addiction, even though they may, in fact, at that time not yet be demonstrably dependent on opiates. The idea, "I need to have opiates," is certainly influenced by the phenomenon of dependence, but, indeed, is poorly correlated with the intensity of this biological phenomenon. An addict may experience some of the phenomena of withdrawal after a year of enforced abstinence as he enters a situation in which opiates may be obtained. By the same token, the diagnosis of withdrawal symptoms as evidence of true dependence is not a simple matter.

There is another aspect to the withdrawal syndrome; it is not merely the bane of addiction to opiates, but also its badge. Many addicts discuss their own and others' withdrawal experiences with heavy humor and boastful exaggeration, not unlike children who compete in describing the rigors of their measles or draftees who boast about the meanness of their noncommissioned officers in basic training. We are not suggesting that they regard the withdrawal experience as pleasurable, but rather that its occurrence and severity become integrated in their self-images as a valid, interesting, and necessary aspect of themselves. Though the nonaddict may regard the withdrawal experience as a terrible deterrent to addiction, the addict develops the same attitude toward dependence on opiates as the organization man does toward the "rat race" of business life in large corporations.

There is a minority of addicts who choose to endure withdrawal symptoms without medical help. They appear silent and sullen in the face of the severest symptoms. With persistence and interest, we can

[13] A. Z. Pfeffer, personal communication.
[14] A. R. Lindesmith, *op. cit.*

learn that they rationalize it as the most effective method of "kicking the habit" and, more fundamentally, that they are enacting a drama of sin and penance; they deserve to suffer for the misdeeds of their addiction, and through suffering they achieve catharsis. Generally speaking, these are the oldest and most experienced addicts, who are among the quickest to relapse after leaving a hospital, since they feel that suffering has undone their misbehavior and that they are free to sin again.

TOLERANCE

Tolerance is a concomitant of dependence. It occurs at a much slower rate than dependence; the body becomes dependent on a certain level of drug taken at a certain frequency much more readily than it acquires tolerance to that level. "Tolerance" refers to the fact that the body adapts—to varying degrees and at differing rates by the several organ systems of the body—to certain of the effects of the drug. The addict can, for instance, take quantities of opiates which would produce coma or death from respiratory inhibition in the nonaddict. Most germane to our discussion, tolerance is developed to the subtle emotional effects of the opiate which the addict craves. Though the addict can satisfy his need for normal bodily function without increasing his dosage, he must gradually raise his intake if he wishes to satisfy his craving. In the vernacular, he "can keep normal but can't get high." He no longer experiences a change of state. He is "tranquilized" so long as he can avoid withdrawal symptoms; but he gets no kicks, and he cannot "go on the nod," that is, he can no longer experience intensified relaxation and inwardness.

Interestingly, keeping normal even without getting high can for a short period be a valued experience for the addict who experiences craving. This depends on what is essentially a form or aspect of gratification through involvement. The addict holds off taking opiates as long as possible, so that he can experience the beginning of the abstinence syndrome; at this point, when he takes his usual or available dose, he experiences relief from a self-imposed physical distress. The rhythm of distress and relief, distress and relief again, becomes valued in itself. However, if his life situation is particularly difficult at this point in his addiction, he will not be satisfied with keeping normal; he will strive to get high again by increasing his dosage either in frequency or in quantity. Indeed, in general, when an addict reaches a point in a cycle of addiction where he cannot do more than keep normal either for economic reasons (the high cost and the poor quality of illicit drugs) or because he has become negatively adapted to the subtle emotional effects of the drugs, he usually "seeks a free period"[15]— withdrawal from the drug, acute abstinence, and at least a few weeks of detoxification—to be able to recapture the most valued experience of being high at a far lower level of dosage. Such patterns (postponement of drug-taking to enhance the effects, seeking a "free period," and discontent with dosage levels sufficient to merely ward off the abstinence syndrome), incidentally, may well provide diagnostic criteria of craving.

To review, the psychophysiological framework of opiate addiction may be generalized as follows: Insofar as psychophysiological factors play a role in addiction, the primary force in initiating and intensifying a cycle of addiction is craving. Dependence is a sustaining force, both physiologically and psychologically—relevant, but clearly secondary. Tolerance is a psychophysiological phenomenon which forces either increasing dosage or a free period, i.e., a period of abstinence to recapture certain of the satisfactions of opiate intoxication. Dependence is, of course, also relevant in the noncraving types of addiction, but is again secondary in importance to the underlying motivations in the development of the addiction. It may, however, play a major role in affecting the likelihood of getting into trouble. The development of tolerance is relatively unimportant in the involvement-without-craving type of addiction; in the noncraving, noninvolvement type, it plays a role in those searching for "kicks."

[15] S. Rado, *op. cit.*

X

The Family of the Addict

Considering its subject, this chapter should have been in an earlier section of the book, among the chapters on the environment in which drug use flourishes. To be sure, we are here, as in the immediately preceding chapters, dealing with a special group of drug-users, those who graduate from initial experimentation and more-or-less frequent use of narcotics to the ranks of the addicts. We are here still concerned with the characteristics of those who go on from use, not merely to the development of dependency, but to a craving for narcotics even when freed from the physiological dependence on them. In chapters VIII and IX, we described the characteristic personalities found in these cases, the kinds of people who, given the experience of narcotics, go on to become addicted. In this and the following chapter, however, we are again concerned with the environment. Personalities do not develop in a vacuum; they emerge from the interactions of individuals with their environments, particularly with the social aspects of these environments and, more particularly, with the significant others of the early family environments. The story of addiction would, therefore, not be fully told if we were to end it with a description of what we take to be the addiction-prone personality; we want to know something about how such personalities are bred.

No scientific inquiry ever leads to the end of the path. Suppose, for instance, that we were to succeed in determining the characteristics of environments that produce particular varieties of personality. We could then take the position that the full story would not have been told until we learned something about how these environments came to be, and so on *ad infinitum*. The end of such an inquiry is the probably unattainable end of science—the point at which all possible questions are answered—and no individual or group of individuals can be expected to pursue it. By the same token, then, why not stop at the point of having identified the characteristic personality of the addict and leave it to other studies to find out how such personalities are generated?

For that matter, such studies would not have to start from scratch. A good deal is already known about how personalities are formed; and, given a personality description, there is a fair likelihood that one can do a creditable job of reconstructing the kind of environment that must have produced such a personality. As a matter of fact, this was our first step in the investigation we are about to describe. We asked ourselves: What kind of early home environment must the typical addict have had? Then we set out to find out whether our imaginative reconstruction of this environment was correct.

From this point of view, the present investigation is a study of the validity of current personality theory, rather than per se an investigation of the role of the family in drug addiction. For us to undertake the latter kind of investigation on its own terms, we would have had to confront the enormous complexities of family structure and function[1] and to look for characteristic differences between the family situations of individuals who become addicted and those who do not. An inquiry of this scope did not seem to us to be indicated and was, in any case, far beyond our resources.

There was, however, a compelling reason for checking the accuracy

[1] Taking account, for instance, of variations that exist in the kinds of family status held by persons in the intimate family (i.e., sometimes including some and sometimes all of the following: grandparents, parents, stepparents, siblings, in-laws, near and remote relatives and their marriage partners and children, boarders and other household intimates, etc.); of the varying functions, privileges, obligations, role deviations, role accomplishments, and role personalizations of those who hold these family status positions; of the varying extensions of behavior governed by norms relevant to these family statuses; of the interactions of these persons in and out of these roles; of the varying positions of the families as a whole in the community; of the intrusions of extrafamilial affairs and relationships in the functioning of the family unit; of the changes over time, and so on.

of our imaginative reconstruction of the early family situations of addicts, and, for our immediate purpose, this had nothing to do with a desire to check the validity of the theorizing that underlay the reconstruction.

We did not seriously question that addicts have the kind of personality that psychiatric and clinical-psychological investigation revealed. What was open to question was whether such a personality is to be counted among the factors that lead to addiction or whether it is a consequence of addiction and the kind of life that addicts are compelled to lead. In other words, does the given personality pattern actually precede the addiction or does it emerge only afterward? Is it not conceivable, for instance, that everyone has these characteristics to some degree and that the life of the addict strengthens them while weakening and submerging compensatory and contradictory characteristics? The obvious answer is to study addicts before they become addicted or, better, to choose individuals with what is thought to be addiction-prone personalities and others with a variety of other personality patterns, expose them all to heroin, and see which ones become addicted. Needless to say, the second approach was not possible at the age levels with which we were concerned,[2] and the first approach offers its own problems.

If we were in no position, however, to study large numbers of boys, determine which ones had presumably addiction-prone personalities, and then wait to see whether the eventual addicts came from this group, we could still approach the issue indirectly. If we could show that addicts came from backgrounds likely to produce such personalities, then the supposition that the personality patterns preceded and developed independently of the addiction would be greatly strengthened. If we failed in such a demonstration, then our misgivings would be

[2] Such a study might conceivably be carried out on individuals serving life sentences in penitentiaries. Other approaches involving less extreme measures are also possible, as in the study of the relation between reactions to test administration of drugs and personality dynamics. Cf., for instance, L. Lasagna, J. M. von Felsinger, and H. K. Beecher, "Drug-Induced Mood Changes in Man," *Journal of the American Medical Association,* 157 (1955), 1006, 1113. The bearing of the latter line of investigation is, however, of limited evidential value because initial reactions are not always trustworthy guides to reactions after some experience with a drug. We have already noted that some of the boys who went on to more-or-less habitual use of heroin experienced initially unfavorable reactions. Many a tobacco-smoker will recall that his early experiences with smoking were similarly unpleasant.

intensified, although there would still remain the possiblity that our theorizing as to the early environment was at fault.

This was the reasoning that led to the present investigation, and it explains the placement of the present chapter. It is only incidentally an inquiry into environments, although the findings are of interest in their own right; it is intended primarily as a check on the hypothesis of an addiction-prone personality.

The very concept of addiction-proneness implies that the addiction-prone personality is not peculiar to addicts. The assumption is that, given this personality type, an individual who is sufficiently exposed to experiences of taking narcotics is especially likely to become addicted. The same individual obviously could not become addicted if he were never exposed. The logic of the situation, then, calls for a comparison of individuals who have a good deal of experience with narcotics but do not become addicted with individuals who have and do.

The psychiatric and clinical-psychological studies of the personalities of addicts have not been based on such comparisons. In this respect, we have not done any better. There is, of course, the logical problem of deciding whether a nonaddicted user is really *not* addicted or merely *not yet* addicted. The fact of long-continued nonaddictive use would be presumptive evidence in favor of the first of these alternatives or, at least, that such individuals are not so addiction-prone as others who have fallen along the way. Such long-continued nonaddictive users would, therefore, constitute a reasonable comparison group. Unfortunately, although we were able to establish the existence of such individuals,[3] this was done in a study of a very limited number of boys, so that the absolute number of such cases that we could readily locate was too small to meet the requirements of such a study. Moreover, the conditions of locating these cases would have made it difficult to use them in the kind of study we were contemplating.

It should, therefore, be clear that the present investigation had a limited objective. It was designed to check the possibility that the characteristic personality picture found in addicts may be a consequent rather than an antecedent of addiction. It will be seen that our conclusion with respect to this possibility is in the negative; we conclude that conditions favorable to the development of such personalities are found in the early lives of addicts. It will also be seen that such con-

[3] See above, the report of the study of drug use in street gangs, chapters VI and VII.

ditions were not found in a control group, matched with our addicts on a variety of characteristics but having no history of drug use or delinquency. It will remain uncertain, however, whether we would or would not have found similar conditions in the lives of users who do not become addicted. Consequently, it remains only hypothetical that these personality characteristics account for the transformation of users into addicts; there remains a distinct possibility that we are still dealing with factors conducive to use rather than with factors conducive to addiction, given use.[4]

Finally, before going on to the report of the investigation, we should point out that the nature of the present inquiry limits us to those aspects of the early family environment concerning which we could reasonably hope to get relevant and dependable information from a limited number of interviews with family members. Consequently, we can only hope to deal with relatively gross aspects of the personality picture developed in chapters VIII and IX.

Translation of Personality Characteristics into Hypothetical Early Environments

On the basis of studies and clinical reports of the personality of the addict, we may say that the potential male addict suffers from (1) a weak ego structure, (2) defective superego functioning, and (3) inadequate masculine identification. In addition, the typical young addict's attitude usually involves (4) a lack of realistic orientation toward the future and (5) a distrust of major social institutions.

From a psychological perspective, these may be considered personal predispositions to becoming an addict; but they may also be considered as a consequence of accepting the role of an addict, with the sanctions this entails in our society. In part, this study of the family is a further testing of the "susceptibility" alternative in terms of the following logic: (1) We assume that personal characteristics are significantly influenced by experiences in the family milieu where one undergoes his earliest,

---

[4] It should also be noted that it is possible that such early family environments may be quite characteristic of delinquents (including non-drug-using delinquents) in the urban areas from which our addicts come. Some of the personality characterizations dealt with in this chapter have been applied to delinquents, and it may well be that the others are, as well. Cf., for instance, I. Kaufman, "Three Basic Sources for Pre-delinquent Character," *Nervous Child*, 11 (1955), 12–15.

closest, and most sustained relationships. (2) If the personal characteristics of the addict are not consequences of being an addict, but are rather personal predisposing conditions to becoming an addict, then the family environment of juvenile addicts must be such that it enhances, nourishes, and stimulates the five personal characteristics listed above. (3) If the evidence indicates that the milieu, relationships, and experiences of the addict differed from that of his peers who did not become addicts, we not only will obtain support for the "susceptibility" hypothesis, but we will have another link in our understanding of why certain youths in high-drug-use areas are especially likely to become addicts.

The hypotheses of this study may be summarized now as follows: The family background of the male adolescent opiate addict is such that it interferes with the development of a well-functioning ego and superego and with his sense of identification as a male. Furthermore, his family background discourages the formation of realistic attitudes and orientations toward the future and trustful attitudes toward major social institutions.

RELEVANT FAMILY EXPERIENCES

Before the start of the actual field work, it was necessary to define each of the five personal characteristics in the light of psychoanalytic and psychological theory and research. The next step, for each defined concept, was to draw up a list of family background factors that one would expect to be conducive to the development of the personality characteristic in question. The logic involved and the steps of this procedure are given in some detail for the first hypothesis in the text of this chapter. For the remaining hypotheses, much of the relevant material is relegated to Appendix L.

Hypothesis I. The family background of the addict is conducive to the development of a weak ego structure.

Definition: A person with a well-functioning ego should be able to assess reality correctly, be reasonably inner-directed, be able to accept pain and frustration without excessive behavior disruption or personality disintegration, have an accepting attitude toward himself, have a sense of competence, and possess a meaningful sense of identity.

This definition, however, is not a sufficient basis for a categorical listing of relevant aspects of the family background to be investigated. The following statements, therefore, serve as a bridge between the definition, couched in psychological terms, and the situation, couched in experiential terms, which we regard as conditions that would interfere with the development of a well-functioning ego. The rationale for considering certain family experiences as conducive to weak ego functioning may be summarized as follows:

(1) The experience of being accepted by others and being worthy of their love is needed for self-acceptance. Hence, hostility on the part of the mother interferes with the development of self-acceptance by the child. Institutional or foster home experience also tends to diminish experiences of being accepted by others.

(2) The receiving of overwhelming love, affection, and indulgence impairs the ability to defer gratification in light of the requirements of reality. This situation also tends to magnify Oedipal conflicts, thus interfering with their adequate resolution.

(3) Overanxious parental reactions and concern with illness interfere with the development of the ability to withstand pain and discomfort. They also hamper the development of a sense of competence by facilitating a view of the world as filled with overwhelming dangers which cannot be coped with.

(4) Marked social or cultural disparities among parental and with peer identification models interfere with the development of a clear-cut sense of identity and group membership.

(5) Lack of warmth between parents makes for affective imbalance; the people whom I love and whose love I want do not love each other. This tends to impair the development of self-acceptance.

(6) Unrealistic concern about the dangers of life or unusual limitations of normal childhood experiences interfere with the development of an ability to correctly assess reality, to cope with real problems, and to feel competent.

(7) Frustration by others may be interpreted as lack of love and lack of being lovable, thus interfering with the development of a feeling of self-acceptance. Overindulgence impairs correct assessment of reality and the ability to withstand pain and frustration.

(8) Unusual limitations on the experiences of the child lead to the development of a sense of incompetence later in life when the boy is confronted with others of his own age who have developed competence and sophistication as a result of their more varied experiences.

(9) Parental expectations that are markedly higher or lower than the ability of the child may lead to an unrealistic sense of competence or to feelings of incompetence.

With this rationale[5] as a background, we can turn to our list of specific factors in the family background which we regard as interfering with the development of a well-functioning ego. The numbers after each of the items in the list in Table X-1 refer to the numbered sentence or paragraph of the rationale to which they are related.

It cannot be expected that any one of these experiences alone necessarily impedes the development of a well-functioning ego. We did assume, however, that if *many* of these features were present in the family background, ego functioning would probably be impaired. We further assumed that the impairment of ego functioning depends on the cumulative impact of a large number of such experiences and that the variety of such experiences and their persistence over time may be taken as indicators of the degree to which a home provides many such experiences. It was therefore predicted that more of these kinds of experience would be found in the background of addicts than nonaddicts. Accordingly, an index was developed to measure the extent of such experiences in the background of each boy to be studied.[6]

It is important to emphasize that the index does not and is not intended to measure the subject's adequacy of ego functioning. In fact, it does not measure any attribute of a person at all. What such an index does purport to measure is an aspect of the family environment as it impinged on the boy. The meaning of a high score on this index is that the family environment of the subject was such that, in the light of current formulations of personality development, one would expect impairment in ego functioning. Such a background is presumed to be

[5] A similar format is followed for the remaining indexes, i.e., a definition, a set of bridging statements which offer a rationale, and a list of negative or harmful family background factors based on the definition and the rationale from which the index itself is composed. The hypothesis and definition, along with sufficient discussion to clarify what is at issue, is given in the text. The bridging statements and components of the indexes are found in Appendix L.

[6] The number of listed impairing experiences or situations in the boy's history which were checked as applicable for the case was divided by the total number of listed items on which we had information. This ratio, expressed as a percentage, was treated as the index score. Scores were computed in the same manner on all five indexes. It will be noted that, in some cases, an item of impairing family experience is listed twice if it occurred during more than one period of the boy's life. Such experience would be given double weight in the index—one credit for each period in which it occurred.

TABLE X-1   *Component Items of Index I: Factors*
Conducive to Weak Ego Functioning

	RATIONALE
EARLY CHILDHOOD	
Any mother figure passionate or hostile to the boy	1, 2
One or more marked social or cultural disparities between parent figures	4
One or more marked social or cultural disparities between family and neighborhood	4
LATE CHILDHOOD	
Any mother figure passionate or hostile to the boy	1, 2
One or more marked social or cultural disparities between parent figures	4
One or more marked social or cultural disparities between family and neighborhood	4
LATE CHILDHOOD AND EARLY ADOLESCENCE	
Mother figure had unrealistically high or low aspirations for the boy	9
Father figure had unrealistically high or low aspirations for the boy	9
LATE ADOLESCENCE AND PRESENT	
Mother figure had unrealistically high or low aspirations for the boy	9
Father figure had unrealistically high or low aspirations for the boy	9
PERIOD NOT SPECIFIED	
Inappropriate handling of boy's illnesses	3, 6
Lack of warmth or overtly discordant relationship between parents	5
Boy was overindulged, frustrated in his wishes, or both	7
Prolongation of maternal functions	6, 8
Mother figure had overprotective attitudes	6, 8
Mother figure limited contacts with other children of boy's own age	6, 8
Mother figure prevented boy from experiencing the normal mishaps of childhood	6, 8
Socialization with other children was delayed	6
Boy was institutionalized or in a foster home at any time during childhood	1

conducive to weak ego development. A high score, therefore, indicates that the potential of the family background for adequate ego development is judged to be poor. What the index accomplishes is a comparison of the family backgrounds of addicts and controls in terms of their judged potential for adequate ego development as measured by this index. Details as to how the information that enters the index was gathered is presented later in this chapter.

It will be noted that we have not confined the components of the indexes to the earliest formative years and even permit some extension into the present. This would seem to contradict the basic purpose of the inquiry. We have assumed, however, some constancy in the developmental environment. Thus, a later negative environmental feature would lead us to give less weight to evidence that the same feature was positive in earlier years. Similarly, we would give most weight to a feature which is consistently negative at several life stages. The index automatically provides such adjustments for items which occur at several periods. For the nonrecurrent items, we have assumed that the rating may reasonably be taken as indicative of a persistent pattern.

A similar logic was employed for each of the other hypotheses related to the effect of the family environment. Each personality characteristic or attitude was first defined and conceptualized. Then, with the aid of a rationale for selecting relevant family experiences, a list of items was prepared to form an index of the potential harmful effects on the personality feature under consideration. For each of the remaining hypotheses, the item list and rationale can be found in Appendix L.

Hypothesis II: The family background of the addict tends to make for defective superego functioning.

Definition: By "adequate superego functioning," we mean that a person more-or-less unconsciously screens all possibilities of behavior that offer themselves to him from the viewpoint of culturally approved standards of legitimacy and obligation which he has taken over as his own and generalized from the examples set by his parents and from his experiences of the demands and prohibitions that they express.

The incorporation of these standards depends on processes independent of the standards at which the individual may arrive on the basis of his experiences of the long- or short-range consequences of particular kinds of behavior in particular kinds of situations. The social significance of the superego inheres precisely in the facts that it provides for individual standards of behavior not dependent on a person's limited experience and that their application is not dependent on the limited egocentric perspective of their situationally adaptive value to him.

At the same time, however, there does exist a second set of standards, oriented to the gratification of personal desires, but tempered by foresight with respect to the probable consequences of particular gratifications and, hence, calling for self-imposed restraint with respect to some gratifications and acceptance of some unpleasant experiences for the sake of a long-range, maximum gratification.[7]

The existence of two independently derived sets of standards generates the possibility of conflicting standards. The possibility of such conflict implies that a normal person must also have available the possibility of resolving and minimizing such conflicts. This, in turn, implies some specifications for each set of standards. On the one hand, with regard to the experientially based standards, the individual has to learn that his incorporated standards are relevant to the adaptive conse-

[7] It should be evident that the experientially based set of standards involves the ego system. Foresight, for instance, calls for the assessment of reality; and restraint and the acceptance of unpleasant experiences, even though (and perhaps especially because) self-imposed, call for the tolerance of frustration and pain. In popular expositions of psychoanalytic theory, the superego is commonly identified with conscience and the moral side of man's nature. Actually, when considered from the present point of view, the ego is fully as moral as the superego, although the two systems represent differing kinds of morality, one empirically based and pragmatic, the other transmitted and absolute. Some [cf. E. B. Holt, *The Freudian Wish and Its Place in Ethics* (New York: Henry Holt & Co., 1915), and I. Chein, "Towards a Science of Morality," *Journal of Social Psychology,* 25 (1947), 235–238] argue that the former potentially represents, in principle, a higher form of morality, provided that the range of probable consequences of actions is wide enough and the weighting of these consequences sagacious enough. The social need of the superego type of morality rests, on the one hand, on the fact that the capacity of individuals to profit from experience and the range of individual experience—even when vicariously augmented—are limited and, on the other hand, on the social necessity for a reasonably consistent set of standards even though the latter cannot be rigorously justified in experiential, pragmatic terms. The two approaches to morality and the two kinds of standards of behavior commonly interact in the evolution of the transmitted (codified and informal) morality, even though the defenders of the latter insist on no compromise. The ongoing change in the transmitted social morality is obvious in the continuous growth and amendment of formal legal codes, but it also occurs in more subtle ways (both in law and in religioethical systems) through changing interpretation of the standards under the pressure of empirical-moral considerations in the changing human situation. At the social-institutional level, there are individuals who, by variously determined status positions, act as arbiters of such change. There are, of course, no comparable arbiters within a person.

simply as a person who happens to be a legal resident and citizen of the country, but as a member of the total community) or as a member of a religious or ethnic group if he has not yet succeeded in making himself comfortable in his masculine identity.

Moreover, whatever the consequences of the degree of success in establishing a secure masculine identity, the most serious consequences occur at the threshold of maturity, with the burgeoning of sexual impulse and of a social premium on phallic prowess, the pressures toward commitment to an occupational line, the need to commit oneself to a wife, and the responsibilities of raising a family. The effectiveness of one's commitment to the masculine identity can hardly be said to be the only determinant of how well one copes with so complex a confrontation, but it is surely a major factor. We have already dealt with a number of indications that the teen-ager who turns to narcotics is especially vulnerable in this confrontation. The most important result of success or failure in establishing a commitment to the masculine identity comes many years later, as one approaches and crosses the threshold to maturity.[8]

Our assumption is that the major factors determining masculine identity are associated with the child's relationship to his father (or to some other male who stands in the relationship to him of father to child).[9] Specifically, this implies that the father figure is himself an adequate representative of socially acceptable patterns of masculinity, at least within the range of the child's perception of him, and that the child identify himself with his father. It is, of course, not within the

[8] If one can imagine a society in which there were utterly no normative correlates of gender beyond the requirement that at least some males and females fulfill the biological reproductive role and with no special rewards or penalties attached to the latter, the issue of sexual identity would be meaningless. At the opposite extreme, if the differentiation of the sexual roles were so perfectly structured as to leave the individual with utterly no degree of freedom, the issue would be equally meaningless. Actually, it is doubtful if any human society has approximated either extreme. We suspect, however, that the issue is most acute in a society such as our own, which simultaneously attaches enormous significance to the differentiation of the sexes (pervasive of almost every area of life) and provides many degrees of freedom with an associated breakdown in traditional lines of differentiation and which does not provide an institutionalized status for a "third" sex. On these matters, cf. Margaret Mead, "Sex and Temperament," in *From the South Seas* (New York: Morrow, 1939) and Mathilde and Matthias Vaerting, *The Dominant Sex* (New York: George H. Doran Co., 1923).

[9] Hence, in the following, we speak of the "father figure." Similarly, with respect to the mother, we speak of the "mother figure," meaning, thereby, that it is not necessarily the biological mother who is involved.

scope of the present study to measure the degree of identification
the father. We can, however, attempt to recapture the availabili
conditions favorable to such identification. An appropriate index of
relevant family experiences was constructed.

Hypothesis IV: The family background of the addict tends to impair
the development of a realistic level of aspiration
with respect to long-range goals.

Definition: By "level of aspiration with respect to long-range goals,"
we mean that the person has ambitions which are plausibly related to
potential and existing opportunities with the desire and ability to defer
gratification in the service of long-range goals. The corresponding index,
therefore, lists features of family experience that could be expected to
impair the development of this outlook.

Hypothesis V: The family experiences of the addict tend to encourage a distrust of major social institutions.

Definition: By "distrust of major social institutions," we mean an
outlook deviating markedly from the one described in the following
sentences. Normally, we take for granted that the governmental agencies
which protect our lives, property, and rights and that the educational,
religious, and charitable organizations which are concerned with our
welfare and personal development have a core of humanitarian concern,
honesty, and trustworthiness. This does not prohibit us from regarding
particular instances of such institutions with disapproval, anger, or
cynicism. But, despite such instances, we accept the institution as a
valid and potentially useful social arrangement. We generally trust persons who embody these institutions until they betray this trust; should
they deceive us, we criticize them as individuals, though we maintain
much of our regard for the institution per se.

We attempted to reconstruct the kind of home situation that would
be conducive to an attitude of distrust and developed a corresponding
index.

Method of the Study

Access to the families of our sample of addict subjects was obtained
through the cooperation of Riverside Hospital, which was most helpful
in this as in the other studies reported in this volume.

The control group was selected from a list of boys graduating in a
four-year period from two parochial and three junior high schools in

high-drug-rate neighborhoods.[10] These names were screened by reference to the Social Service Exchange and on the basis of information supplied by social agencies and schools in order to eliminate families in which any of the youngsters had a court record or were known as habitual delinquents, chronic truants, or narcotics-users. Letters were sent to the eligible families requesting cooperation in a study of how young men grow up in their neighborhood.

Of those available for interview, we matched the addicts and controls for age. Neighborhood influences were comparable because almost all boys in each group were selected from high-drug-use areas. Similarly, in order to make the two groups comparable as to ethnic cultural patterns, we tried to select ten native white, ten Negro, and ten Puerto Rican families for each group. The fact that the families were also found to be equivalent in occupational status of the chief wage-earners and in the educational achievement of the mother adds to the comparability of the samples (see Table X–2). It should be noted, however, that the control families were to some extent self-selected in that they were willing to cooperate in the study; it is possible that families willing to cooperate are "better" than other families in the same areas which produce neither addicts nor delinquents. The families of the addict cases, of course, also had to be willing to cooperate in order to be usable, but they were inherently under greater pressure to do so. On the other hand, however, the greatest difficulty in recruiting control families for the study was that we could not trace them so many years after the date of the last known address; if anything, one would expect the bias here to go in the opposite direction, that is, for the "better" families to be the more likely to move away. In any case, what most convinces us that we were not grossly misled in taking the results of this study seriously were the magnitude and pervasiveness of the differences that, as we shall see, appeared between the two sets of families. One would have to do much discounting, indeed, to wipe out these differences.

The interviewing of the families was conducted by twelve advanced students of social work from the New York School of Social Work and from the School of Social Service of New York University. Prior to the interviewing, a guide was constructed which focused on the areas of

[10] Most of the thirty control cases were families of the fifty control boys previously interviewed in the study of personal background of drug-users, delinquents, and controls, as reported in chapters V and VI. All the families not previously used were obtained from the basic list used in the original study. The present study was, however, carried out two years later.

TABLE X-2   *Matched or Comparable Factors in
Family Background of Addict and
Control Samples*

HEALTH-AREA DRUG RATE OF HOME ADDRESS*	ADDICTS (30)	CONTROLS (29)
30 or higher	9	21
29.9 or lower	20	7
Queens (rate not known)	1	1
ETHNIC GROUP		
Negro	10	11
White	10	9
Puerto Rican	10	9
AGE OF BOY AT TIME OF INTERVIEW		
20–23	12	15
15–19	18	14
EDUCATION OF MOTHER		
Some high school or higher	13	11
Grade school only	14	17
Not ascertainable	3	1
OCCUPATION OF CHIEF WAGE-EARNER		
White collar	7	3
Skilled or semiskilled labor	12	20
Unskilled or indigent	11	6

* Note that, as a group, the controls were selected from areas of higher drug rate than the addicts in this sample. Control cases, therefore, were potentially exposed to more juvenile drug use in their neighborhoods than were the addicts in this sample. Similarly, most of the other differences, such as they are, are in the direction indicating greater resistance to environmental pressures among the controls. Thus, being somewhat older, on the average, they have resisted these pressures longer.

family experience relevant to our indexes. The topical headings of the interview guide were: physical characteristics of the neighborhood and the house, household and family composition, health history of the family, the present and early adolescent life situation of the subject, childhood training and socialization, relationships within the family, and relationships between the family and the "outside world."

Group training and discussion sessions were held to ensure that interviews covered each of the aspects of family life in which we were interested. Two to four case-work interviews were conducted with the parents and other important figures in the lives of the patients and control subjects. For each case, detailed process recordings and an evaluative case summary were obtained.

After completing the interviews for a family, the interviewer also filled out a check-list questionnaire. This questionnaire was designed so that it would be possible to compute index scores of family experiences predicted for each of the personality and attitude characteristics. As a precaution, the interviewers were not informed of the predictions and theoretical rationale until all data had been collected. Further checks on the possibility of biased results are described in Appendix M.

Results and Discussion

Each of the five major hypotheses about the addicts' family experiences was strongly supported by the data (see Figure X-1 and Table X-3).[a] In contrast to our control cases, the addicts were reared in a family milieu which, in terms of our psychological theorizing, we would regard as contributing to the development of weak ego functioning, defective superego, inadequate masculine identification, lack of realistic levels of aspiration with respect to long-range goals, and a distrust of major social institutions. Moreover, each of the hypotheses was supported within each ethnic group separately—native whites, Negroes, and Puerto Ricans.

In addition to the hypothesis that addict backgrounds would include more experiences making for defective superego functioning, two subsidiary predictions were made in relation to the superego. Two kinds of environmental force were postulated, one making for inadequate internalization of socially accepted standards, the other making for an overly severe and punitive type of superego functioning.

We had expected, perhaps naïvely, both types of experience to be found more frequently in the background of addicts than of controls, one type for some cases, the other type for other cases.

The analysis indicates that there was a clear-cut difference between our two groups only with respect to the environmental factors that would favor weak superego functioning. There was no difference at all between the groups on our measure of forces making for strong and severe superego functioning (see Table X-3).[11] But, although almost all addicts came from backgrounds conducive to the poor internalization of socially acceptable norms, about half *also* experienced other family influences that would nevertheless tend to make them subject

[11] As in the case of the findings related to the major indexes, these findings also obtained when the results were separately analyzed for each of the three ethnic groups.

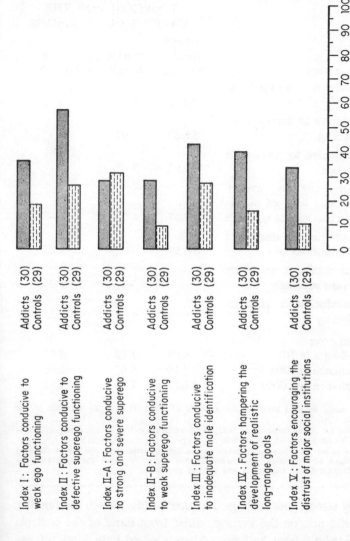

Index I : Factors conducive to
weak ego functioning   Addicts (30)
Controls (29)

Index II : Factors conducive to
defective superego functioning   Addicts (30)
Controls (29)

Index II-A : Factors conducive
to strong and severe superego   Addicts (30)
Controls (29)

Index II-B : Factors conducive
to weak superego functioning   Addicts (30)
Controls (29)

Index III : Factors conducive
to inadequate male identification   Addicts (30)
Controls (29)

Index IV : Factors hampering the
development of realistic
long-range goals   Addicts (30)
Controls (29)

Index V : Factors encouraging the
distrust of major social institutions   Addicts (30)
Controls (29)

Index score

0   10   20   30   40   50   60   70   80   90   100

All differences are statistically reliable at the .005 level of confidence or better, with the exception of Index II-A, where there is no reliable difference in mean scores.

Fig. X-1. Mean Index Scores for Addicts and Controls

TABLE X-3   *Summary Analyses of Variance* of
Scores on the Indexes*

*Comparisons of differences between addict and control family
backgrounds and among the three ethnic groups**

	F-RATIOS† FOR THE VARIOUS COMPARISONS		
INDEXES	ADDICT VERSUS CONTROL	ETHNIC GROUP	A × E INTERACTION‡
I: Factors conducive to weak ego functioning	20.07	1.70	—
II: Factors conducive to defective superego functioning	58.20	1.02	—
III: Factors conducive to inadequate male identification	8.93	3.02	—
IV: Factors hampering the development of a realistic level of aspiration with respect to long-range goals	39.05	4.53	—
V: Factors encouraging the distrust of major social institutions	26.56	—	1.17
II-A: Factors conducive to an overly strong and severe superego	—	—	2.06
II-B: Factors conducive to weak superego functioning	42.74	2.05	—
F-RATIOS NEEDED FOR:			
P = .05 (1 chance in 20)	4.03	3.18	3.18
P = .01 (1 chance in 100)	7.16	5.05	5.05
P = .001 (1 chance in 1,000)	12.19	7.93	7.93

* Table X-4 gives more detailed data on the analysis of index II-B as an example of the statistical treatment.

† For a brief explanation of the meaning of analysis of variance and of F-ratios, see Appendix M. The dash indicates an F-ratio of one or less.

‡ That is, the degree to which differences between the addict and control groups are of differing magnitudes in the three ethnic groups (or, conversely, the degree to which the differences between the ethnic groups differ in the addict and control groups).

to unreasonably strong guilt feelings. In other words, though the families of the addicts did not, on the average, differ from those of the controls in the latter respect, about half the addicts showed both kinds of environmental impairment. This finding is consistent with the assumption that the environmental forces making for strong inhibitions in the acting out of socially disapproved impulses are quite independent of those

TABLE X-4   *Analysis of Variance of Scores on*
Index II-B: Factors Conducive to
Weak Superego Functioning*

A comparison of differences between addict and control family
backgrounds and among the three ethnic groups

MEAN INDEX SCORE

ETHNIC GROUP	ADDICTS	CONTROLS
Negro (Ns = 10, 11)	35.90	12.90
White (Ns = 10, 9)	25.10	6.28
Puerto Ricans (Ns = 10, 9)	31.92	8.73
TOTAL (Ns = 30, 29)	30.97	9.24

SOURCE OF VARIATION	SUM OF SQUARES	d.f.	MEAN SQUARE	F	p
Addict versus control	7,065.24	1	7,065.24	42.74	<.001
Ethnic group	678.28	2	339.14	2.05	n.s.
A × E interaction	72.26	2	36.13	—	n.s.
Residual	8,761.06	53	165.30		
		58			

* In order to overcome the problem of unequal numbers of cases in the various subgroups, this analysis of variance (as well as all others presented in this chapter) was performed in accordance with the approximation procedure recommended by G. W. Snedecor, *Statistical Methods* (5th ed.; Ames: Iowa State College Press, 1956), p. 385.

making for strong guilt feelings. It is, of course, also possible that we were simply not able to tap those features of the environment conducive to such a severe superego. The relevant environmental vectors are to be found in the pre-Oedipal precursors of the superego, and the factors involved may well be too subtle to be detected by the method we used.

SOME COMMON FEATURES IN THE FAMILY EXPERIENCES OF ADDICTS

The over-all results of the analysis of our indexes gives strong support to the view that family experiences play an important role in the etiology of addiction.

We shall now inspect our data from a somewhat more detailed perspective, emphasizing some experiences with respect to which there are statistically significant differences between the addict and control groups. Table X-5 gives the percentages of addicts and controls who had certain family experiences as indicated by the check-list questionnaire.

LE X-5   *Selected Single Items on Which Addict*
and Control Family Backgrounds
Were Highly Contrasted

The following items differentiate addicts from controls at the .05 level of confidence or better. The number of cases varies from item to item, since some questions were not applicable to all families. There were also some cases where information on a particular item was not ascertainable, but where the question would have been relevant. The total number of cases on which relevant information was available is indicated in parentheses for addicts and controls respectively. Mainland's tables were used to evaluate the significance of differences. Cf. Donald Mainland, Lee Herrera, and Marion I. Sutcliffe, *Tables for Use with Binomial Samples* (New York: Department of Medical Statistics, New York University College of Medicine, 1956).

ITEM	ADDICTS	CONTROLS
	PERCENTAGES	
1. Boy experienced an extremely weak father–son relationship (30, 29)	80	45
2. For a significant part of early childhood, boy did not have a father figure in his life (29, 29)	48	17
3. Some father figure was cool or hostile to boy (23, 24)	52	13
4. Father had unrealistically low aspirations for the boy (late childhood and early adolescence) (16, 22)	44	0
5. Some father figure was an immoral model (early childhood) (26, 24)	23	0
6. Marked impulse orientation in father figure (23, 23)	26	0
7. Father had unstable work history during boy's early childhood (28, 28)	43	14
8. Father was unrealistically pessimistic or felt that life is a gamble (17, 19)	47	11
9. Lack of warmth or overtly discordant relations between parents (30, 29)	97	41
10. Mother figure was more important parent in boy's life during late childhood period (30, 29)	73	45
11. Some mother figure cool or hostile to boy (early childhood) (30, 28)	23	0
12. Some mother figure cool or hostile to boy (late childhood) (30, 29)	37	3
13. Boy experienced extremely weak mother–son relationship (30, 29)	40	7

14. Mother did not trust authority figures (29, 29)	38	10
15. Mother had unrealistically low aspirations for boy (late childhood and early adolescence) (29, 28)	31	0
16. Mother was unrealistically pessimistic or felt that life is a gamble (29, 29)	31	7
17. No clear pattern of parental roles in formation of disciplinary policy (adolescence) (30, 29)	23	0
18. Parental standards for boy were vague or inconsistent (early childhood) (29, 28)	55	4
19. Parental standards for boy were vague or inconsistent (adolescence) (30, 29)	63	3
20. Boy was overindulged, frustrated in his wishes, or both (30, 29)	70	10

Some of the most striking contrasts in the experiences of our addicts and controls occurred in the relationship of the boy to the father or father figure. There was no father figure at all in the homes of about one-half the addict cases for some significant period. When he was present, the father was usually emotionally distant or hostile in his attitudes toward the boy. Furthermore, when present, the father figures often presented immoral models through their own deviant activity with respect to criminality, infidelity, alcoholism, and the like. And, though only a minority of the addicts had a father figure judged to be primarily concerned with day-to-day gratification of appetites and desires and given to quick and uninhibited discharge of energy (i.e., "impulse-oriented," in the terminology of Table X-5), this was true for none of the father figures of the control subjects. As one would expect from this pattern, the father figures of the addicts often had unstable work histories. They had pessimistic and fatalistic attitudes toward their own future, and, similarly, they often held unrealistically low aspirations for their sons' careers.

In terms of the quantity of interaction between father and son, there was not much contact between them. This was because the father had little to do with his son or was openly hostile toward him or because there was no relationship at all owing to the absence of a father figure from the home.

In almost all the addict families (97 per cent), there was a disturbed relationship between the parents, as evidenced by separation, divorce, open hostility, or lack of warmth and mutual interest. In these conditions, the mother usually became the most important parent figure in the life of the youngster. But, whatever the vicissitudes of the relationship between the boy and his mother, one theme was almost invariably the same—the absence of a warm relationship with a father figure with whom the boy could identify.

The families of the addicts did not provide a setting which would facilitate the acceptance of discipline or the development of personal behavioral controls. The standards of conduct offered by the parents were usually vague or inconsistent; the addicts had characteristically (more than 70 per cent) been overindulged, overfrustrated, or experienced vacillation between overindulgence and overfrustration. For about one-fourth of the addicts, though for none of the controls, there was evidence of the absence of a clear pattern of parental roles in the formulation or execution of disciplinary policy.

When we attempt to describe the special relationship between the addict and his mother, there is little evidence of an atypical or unusual relationship between them. There are relevant items which distinguish the addict and control groups at statistically significant levels, but even the largest of the differences involves a minority of the addicts. Thus, there is a substantial group of mothers of addicts which differs from the mothers of the control subjects, but it also differs from the rest of the mothers of the addicts. These mothers had an emotionally distant or hostile relationship with their sons; they markedly distrusted the representatives of major social institutions; they had unrealistically low aspirations for their sons; and they were themselves unrealistically pessimistic or felt that life was, at best, a gamble. Like the typical fathers of the addicts, they also had weak relationships with their sons.

What about the other mothers of the addicts? There is reason to believe that the mothers of the addicts were much more involved in the development of their sons' addiction than indicated by the categories included in the indexes. Clinical observation of the present-day interactions between the addict and his mother point to an early, sustained disturbance in the mother–son relationship related to the addict's current maladaptive patterns.[12] However, a review of the detailed process recordings of the addict-family interviews strongly suggests that the

[12] We are not making a statement about clinical observations of the relations of addicts in general to their mothers, but about observations of the addicts dealt with in this chapter and their mothers.

relationship between the addict and his mother is complex and individualized. The following chapter, which is qualitatively oriented rather than statistical, presents a number of case studies in which we may perceive more clearly the nature and importance of the addict's relationship to his mother.

STATISTICAL FOOTNOTES

a Because the indexes are not perfectly independent of one another, we should note the possibility that the verification or contradiction of one hypothesis may not be completely independent of the verification or contradiction of another. That this possibility is not overly serious is suggested by the following considerations.

We may count the total number of bits of information utilized in the computation of any two indexes, and we may similarly count the number of bits common to both indexes; the ratio of the second count to the first gives us the percentage of overlap. The worst case (i.e., the greatest amount of overlap) is found for indexes IV and V, where the percentage of overlap is 21.4, a degree of overlap that would, in itself, give rise to a correlation between the two indexes of about .46. To this extent, the fates of the corresponding hypotheses are not independent. The percentage of overlap between indexes I and IV is 15.4, involving a correlation of about .39, and between indexes I and V the overlap is 8.0, involving a correlation of about .30.

The intrinsic correlation (we hesitate to call it spurious because, after all, effects in real life often are correlated) between Index IV and indexes I and V taken together (i.e., the multiple correlation) is of the order of .53. In other words, there is a fair likelihood that, if both hypotheses I and V are verified, Hypothesis IV will be carried along with them.

Similarly, the percentages of overlap between indexes I and II and between II and III are both 11.7, involving correlations of about .35; and that between I and III is 4.5, with a corresponding correlation of .21. The intrinsic multiple correlation of Index II with I and III taken jointly is about .45.

The percentages of overlap for the pairs of indexes not yet mentioned (i.e., II and IV, II and V, III and IV, and III and V) are, in each case, zero.

XI

Family Backgrounds of Selected Addict and Control Cases

The following case summaries offer a somewhat closer view of the contrasting family environments of addicts and controls than can be given by numerical indexes.[1]

The addict cases to be presented here are not the "worst" that could have been selected from the thirty available. In fact, on the basis of the indexes alone, the family background of one of these boys (James McGill) was one of the most atypical of the addict group. These histories were chosen primarily because the psychiatrist member of our team had first-hand knowledge of the boys and their families; he could, therefore, supplement and more accurately interpret the information obtained by the interviewers. The three control cases are two arbitrarily selected ones markedly typical of their group in terms of their scores on each of the indexes, whereas the third (actually the first, in order of presentation) is one of the least typical in this respect.[2]

[1] In order to protect the anonymity of the respondents, all names in cases have been changed; details which might help identify the subjects have been altered in inessential respects or omitted.

[2] In planning the study, we assumed that there would be substantial numbers of atypical cases among both the addict and control groups and hoped to be able to glean some useful insights from an intensive study of these cases. Actually, there were few, if any, cases that could be described as markedly atypical. This is indicated in the following table:

CASE 44: RICHARD STONE, ADDICT

Richard Stone is a Negro adolescent addict. He was reared as the only child in a home with two women and no men, except for the first years of his life. At the time of this study, he had been using drugs for two and a half years and was a patient in Riverside Hospital at the time that his mother and grandmother were interviewed.

Prior to his birth, the relationship between his parents was amicable, predicated on his mother's superior attitude and condescending tolerance for his father, whom she regarded as "just a boy" who was shy and inexperienced with people. They lived with her mother throughout their marriage. Both parents worked, and, after Richard was born, Mrs. Jones, the maternal grandmother, was responsible for most of his care. The circumstances following his birth are unclear. On the one hand, we were told that he was breast-fed for the first two months of his life; on the other, it was stated that his mother spent six postnatal

	Number of Cases in Each Group on the "Wrong" Side of the Median of the Contrasting Group on . . .						
	NONE OF THE INDEXES	ONE INDEX	TWO INDEXES	THREE INDEXES	FOUR INDEXES	ALL FIVE INDEXES	TOTAL
Addicts (at or below the control median)	20	7	2	1	0	0	30
Controls (at or above the addict median)	18	8	2	1	0	0	29
TOTAL	38	15	4	2	0	0	59

Thus, even with so lenient a criterion of "marked" deviance (lenient, that is, in terms of a predetermined criterion in selecting deviant cases from two groups that are being compared), almost two-thirds of the cases were not markedly deviant from their respective groups on *any* of the indexes, and only two cases were markedly deviant on as many as three indexes. Robert S. Lee, "The Family Experiences of Male Juvenile Heroin Addicts and Controls" (doctoral dissertation, New York University, 1957), has reviewed the data on the three most deviant addict and the three most deviant control cases (i.e., on the six cases markedly atypical of their respective groups on two or three indexes), only to find that, if anything, the indexes did not do justice to the marked contrasts between the two sets of families. A similar conclusion seemed to be indicated in his contrast of the records of the three most typical addict and the three most typical control families. Incidentally, the addict who was atypical on three indexes, it turns out, may have achieved this position of pre-eminence because of insufficient evidence —that is, there was an exceptionally small number of items relevant to the indexes on which we had enough information for scoring purposes; the computed indexes may, therefore, be quite misleading. It would, however, be surprising, indeed, if larger samples would not turn up more markedly deviant cases, especially among the controls.

months in a hospital because she was so weak after his birth. Though this may have been a postpartum psychosis, we could not establish this from available records. It is clear, in any case, that, early in his infancy, Richard's care passed into the hands of his maternal grandmother, Mrs. Jones.

In his early childhood, both his parents continued to work, while his grandmother, who was the superintendent of the building in which they lived, took care of him. He learned to call his mother "Sister" and his grandmother "Mother." What he called his father is not indicated, but it is reported that the extent of his father's interest in him was limited to inquiring once daily about the state of his health. His father never picked him up, never took him anywhere, never concerned himself with Richard's discipline. His mother gladly relinquished his care to his grandmother, who described his childhood as uneventful. Richard was completely toilet-trained by eighteen months. "He was always a very obedient child. He was not a fighter. When any child started up with him, he would run away and say that he is sick; he won't fight." He had "rickets of the bones," recurrent fevers, and a spot on his lungs. He was hospitalized for half-year periods at ages four, six, ten, and fourteen years. His illness first expressed itself symptomatically as a sudden inability to walk when he was four years old, which led his mother to believe that Richard suffered from polio.

Richard wanted to be an affectionate child, but Mrs. Stone regarded "all that kissing and hugging as foolishness" for which she had no time. From his mother's willingness to give his care over to her mother; from her minimal retrospective concern for or recall of his development; from her attitudes toward his efforts to express affection; and from evidence in the interview of her contemptuous identification of her son with her husband, from whom she separated when Richard was six, it seems reasonably certain that the prevalent attitude Richard experienced from his mother was one of unqualified rejection. There was no apparent area in which she felt enduring, affectionate regard for him.

The relationship with his grandmother was quite different. It was extremely close—too close. Mrs. Jones's attitude was: "You must never drive a child away from you; you should draw him to you instead." She expressed the belief that a child *wants* you to drive him away, but, if you do this, then the "bad things from the street" will be instilled in him. Even in her own estimation, however, she spoiled Richard. He could get whatever he wanted from her because she was afraid that otherwise he might take it from someone else. She never permitted Richard to run around by himself, and she took him with her wherever she went. Richard shared her bed until he was fifteen years old. (It may be symptomatic of her feelings that, as she told about sharing the same bed with her grandson, Mrs. Jones placed her hand inside her blouse, grasping her breast.) Again and again, she stressed how extremely close they were.

She taught him his arithmetic with clothespins and discussed religion and life with him every evening for many hours. Her ambition was that he should become a minister. Though they would discuss almost anything, Mrs. Jones never talked with him about what she called "common life," that is, sexuality. In her opinion: "If you teach life to a child, he has no cause to stay away from it. Children know too much, anyhow. When their mothers are pregnant, they know about it months in advance and say: 'Are you going to have a baby? I hope it will be a boy.' " She told her children that Santa Claus brings the babies. Religion and the reading of the Bible played an enormous role in the grandmother's life. There were many crosses, religious pictures and calendars, and quotations from the Scriptures hanging on the walls of the apartment. Mrs. Jones also looked back to the time when she was a house servant in a white Southern family, where everything was clean and nice, as the best time of her life. She believes that man should earn his bread by the sweat of his brow, as it says in the Bible, and that people in the city are bad because they want to live in ease and comfort.

It seems clear that Richard's early childhood situation was pathological. Continuously perceptible parental rejection and neglect vied with the grandmother's overprotectiveness and overindulgence. Attitudes of sexual prudishness contrasted with seductive intimacy. Hypermoralistic religiosity was coupled with yielding to the slightest of whims. The illusion of omnipotence generated by overindulgence was shatteringly denied by the impotence in evoking any positive response from affectionate overtures to the mother and by the grandmother's smothering of any gesture toward independence or socializing with peers. It was a situation in which conflicts over aggressivity and passivity must have been sharp. It was one in which invitation to feminine identification must have been strong and in which there was no appropriate model for masculine identification. Although it is unlikely that his illness at age four came about for psychological reasons, it is not at all unlikely that such a motor inhibition must have had serious psychological consequences, concretizing unconscious anticipation of bodily harm as a penalty for sexual interest and fantasies which must have been repeatedly stimulated by the nightly physical proximity and by hugging and kissing in bed with his grandmother.

In 1941, when Richard was five years old, his father was drafted into the Army. When he returned from service three years later, he behaved in a completely changed manner. Instead of being the docile and submissive husband who worked and brought home his pay check, he began to drink heavily. He ran around with other women. In Mrs. Stone's words, his father thought he was "a real big shot," who never bathed and who would not work. Indeed, he did not even live with his wife, but stayed mostly at the home of his aunt, who had reared him. After six weeks of intermittent contact, during which he resided with his wife and son in periods of sobriety, he finally left for good when his wife refused to give him money. She said that she was tired of supporting him with nothing in return for herself. Since then, Mr. Stone has worked irregularly, has apparently been supported by various women, and it is very likely that he earns his living as a procurer. Mrs. Stone believes that all men are this way, or at least that every man she has ever known is this way. She describes her husband as a man who never liked to be with friends, did not talk much, but liked the best clothes and had big ideas. She believes that her son is like his father. In fact, she says that they look like twins.

We get some further picture of Richard as a young boy from the statements of both his mother and grandmother. He was always a good boy, the nicest and kindest boy in the neighborhood, and always quiet. He preferred to play with younger children. He was afraid of being whipped and was consequently extremely docile.

His mother now believes that Richard has the same need for drugs as his father has for drinking. Richard used to be a quiet and good boy, the best boy in the neighborhood, but now "he stays around with garbage," with "the bums on the block." He started his foolishness when he was in junior high school when he met some very wild boys. His mother compares this change in Richard to the change that occurred in the father when he was in the Army. "After he met some bad boys, he was crazy. He never stayed home; he always wanted to go out somewhere drinking. He thought he was a big shot; he would talk a lot about all the big shots he drank with, some of his Army buddies."

Throughout the interviews, both the mother and grandmother made much of their veneration of cleanliness. For example, the grandmother wished that the neighborhood would be torn down and replaced by projects, because then at least there would be cleanliness, which would be good for the people. But, in marked contrast to their expressed concern for cleanliness, our interviewer was impressed by the extreme clutter, darkness, and pervasive stench in the apartment. All the rooms were in a mess, the beds unmade, the dishes unwashed, the religious symbols in scattered disarray, the rooms extremely poorly illuminated. The important point is not that the apartment was so poorly cared for, but rather the extraordinary discrepancy between these expressed interests and tastes of the two women who are the major figures in Richard's life and the way in which they actually live. Whether this expresses a pervasive attitude of passivity and helplessness, intense ambivalent attitudes wtih regard to cleanliness, or both, we can only conjecture. In either case, any such marked discrepancy between expressed values and actual style of living must be a bewildering and harmful experience for a developing child.

CASE 58: JAMES MCGILL, ADDICT

McGill is an Irish-American drug addict. He and his family differ strikingly from Richard Stone and his family. He has always lived in private housing developments with his parents and, as they came along, with four younger brothers. His father does not drink excessively, as did Richard's father; nor is he unstably employed; nor manifestly uninterested in James's life and development; nor, in the gross terms of our indexes, did he offer an unseemly model with whom James might identify. Again in the gross measures of our indexes, James had far fewer pathological experiences and relationships than had most of the addicts in the group. In at least the superficial aspects of his life experience and relationships, it would seem that he has been favored by fate and fortune.

James's father is a civil servant. His mother did not work during the course of James's childhood. About a year before these interviews, after James was already thoroughly addicted, she became a hostess at one of a chain of dignified ladies' tea shops in New York City.

Certain circumstances associated with James's birth were somewhat unusual. He was born after his mother had had a number of miscarriages, and, in the three years following his birth, there were several additional miscarriages. Thereafter, she conceived and bore four more sons. As a young child, James was apparently healthy. He seemed to adapt well to the regime of his parents. At one year, toilet training was begun; by eighteen months, he was dry and clean. At age three, he had an appendectomy; at thirteen, he had asthma. During some period of his childhood, he was said to have been markedly overweight. Until he was fourteen or fifteen, he bit his nails to the quick.[3] From any one of the manifestations of obesity, asthma, and nail-biting, one might infer that James had difficulty, in Erikson's phrase, in negotiating the oral phase of psychosexual development; from their conjunction, the conclusion seems virtually inescapable. We do not, however, have any data that might pinpoint the precise nature or the source of the difficulty.

It is impossible to specify the period during which James suffered from obesity. In one interview, his father stated that the period of James's obesity extended from the time he was six until he was nine years old. In another, his mother said that James became overweight after his appendectomy, that is, after age three. In a third interview, his father rationalized those of James's social difficulties which occurred when he was nine to twelve as due to obesity.

Though both his mother and father spoke a great deal when they were interviewed, there was a remarkable emptiness of communication about James's development and a vagueness about his relationships and reactions. Everything "was at the usual time"; but, for emphasis, Mrs. McGill added: "He wasn't at all advanced." At the age of two, he had the one overt temper tantrum of his life; this was while he was with his father, who walked away from James as though he had no connection with him. This, by the way, was described as singularly effective and commendable behavior by both Mr. and Mrs. McGill; indeed, they both were pleased to regard their child-rearing with composure, if not with self-satisfaction.

The vagueness about James's obesity was not the only area of vagueness. Though there is a considerable range of ages between her sons, Mrs. McGill seemed quite unable to sort them out in terms of their special behavior, characteristics, or problems. She seemed insensitive to them individually, except, significantly, with regard to issues

[3] Both Richard Stone and James McGill have unusual health histories. This is a coincidence and is not a regular or predictable feature in the background of the adolescent addict.

of obedience. Even here, however, they did not seem to stand out sharply from one another in her mind. During James's adolescence, he stretched the limits to the point of quarrels with his father. For instance, Mr. McGill made quite a fuss over the fact that Larry, the second son (who, incidentally, was given somewhat more freedom than was James), would be home by 9:30 on a summer's evening, whereas James did not get home until 10:00.

At present, there are four boys in the house, which is spotless and quiet, even though the boys were home while the interviews were going on. They are trained to go to their rooms, come when called, and are always dressed neatly—or more than neatly. They are expected and accustomed to wait, even when waiting is clearly not necessary. For example, when the doorbell rings, Mrs. McGill does not answer it. Though she may be sitting only a few paces from the door, she lets whoever has rung wait and does not get up to open the door until the bell has rung two or three times. On one occasion, a year prior to these interviews, James returned late in the evening and rang the bell; his parents decided to wait until he rang again. He did not; instead, he spent the night in the streets. There is little sense of warmth or interpersonal activity in the household; instead, there is an atmosphere of extremely efficient and disciplined interaction.

Mrs. McGill does not like to lose her composure. Her life is stiff and controlled; she is not given to affectionate or easy interaction, nor is she able to express anger or annoyance with ease. In fact, on the few occasions in her life that she could recall in which she had expressed anger or annoyance, she felt tense and self-reproachful as a consequence. She is very concerned with proper deportment, manners, and cleanliness. The house seemed to be spotless, yet, when our interviewer commented on this, Mrs. McGill responded: "Oh, there's lots of dirt still here, if you only know where to look for it." She is extremely concerned with social status. She strives for increasing status, but with measured tread; it is not seemly to seek too much too fast. She glosses over or lies about those facts in her life which might lower her status. For example, she is extremely evasive and ashamed of the fact that, during one phase of their married life, her husband worked as a waiter; he did not always have a white-collar job, and, even after he obtained one, he continued to work as a waiter on a part-time basis. Her younger children had not been told that James was in the hospital. She maintained the fiction that his work required a peculiar schedule so that he was never home on weekends, did not come home during the evenings until after his brothers—aged fifteen, ten, eight, and six—were asleep, and left before they awoke. None of the neighbors or their families were supposed to know that James was in a hospital.

Her relationship with James and, for that matter, with her husband and the other children, is and has been superficial and without warmth. The entire family attends Mass every Sunday—religiously, one might say, but not with any depth of religious feeling. Toilet-training was accomplished, manners practiced and attained. Until James was seven, he expressed appreciation by hugging and kissing, but, when he "grew away from this," Mrs. McGill was not at all regretful. Since James had begun to stay out late, become a truant, and taken to drugs, Mrs. Mc-Gill had felt "terribly ashamed," but in none of the interviews did she express anxiety, intense concern, or unhappiness for James's sake.

Some indication of her difficulties in the expression of aggression and anger is discernible in her relationship to her husband. She adheres closely to his opinions and strictures, even when these run contrary to her own views. But she constantly expresses fear for her husband's health and has threatened James and the other children with his high blood pressure: "What if your father, with his high blood pressure, fell down some stairs? Then where would you be?" She encourages him to take over household tasks (she has never washed a diaper in her life—Mr. McGill did—and this before the era of the automatic washing machine), but she will not let him clean the windows for fear he might fall out—a fear behind which one may suspect a lurking wish, since he has never fainted nor experienced dizzy spells or disturbances of equilibrium which might justify such apprehensions.

James's relationship with his father is quite a different matter and indeed rather unusual in the background of the adolescent addicts. Throughout early childhood, James hung on to his *father's* apron strings. Mr. McGill took care of much of the cooking, cleaning, and child care, although Mrs. McGill was not working nor burdened with many children. Furthermore, whatever demonstrative affection James received, he probably got from his father. This all occurred in a lower-middle-class, prewar setting in which such behavior was conspicuous, if not indecorous, and in which there was none of the ideological emphasis on "sharing" responsibility for child-rearing and household work.

Also somewhat unexpected were Mr. McGill's theories of child-rearing. He himself had "been brought up with all kinds of fears" and did not want his children to be brought up this way. He did not want his

children to be afraid of the policeman and the dentist (as he himself
had been?) and took measures to prevent them, e.g., by providing opportunities for acquaintance and play with policemen and dentists.

From age four until eight or nine, James was inseparable from his
father. Each day when his father returned from work (his job permitted him to get home about 3 in the afternoon), James would be his
companion in a walk to the river. The babble of childish enthusiasm
and adult response which makes the walking together of fathers and
sons a valid and touching human interplay was absent from their walks;
they walked in solemn silence. Where did their relationship come alive?
Only in anger. Though Mr. McGill was consciously concerned with
raising fearless children, James learned to listen with fear and resentment to his father's temper tantrums. By the time he was eight years
old, it became evident that James was neither extraordinarily intellectually gifted nor impelled toward a life of learning for any other such
reason as parental cultural achievements or interests. His school work
was, at best, average. For this, Mr. McGill would scream at James, insult him, and urge him to exert greater efforts in his studies. James's
response to these explosions over his school work was to conform outwardly to his father's demands. He did sit at his desk with his books
from 7 to 9 in the evening, but he did not really study.

Both Mr. and Mrs. McGill were proud of the fact that James never
fought back when his father scolded him. However unreasonable or
uncontrolled Mr. McGill might be, Mrs. McGill supported him. On
one of the few occasions that James came to her in tears after one of
his father's tirades, she told him that his father behaved this way only
for James's own good, that, if his father did not care for him and did
not care about what happened to him, he would not talk to him this
way. James was regularly confronted with his own shortcomings and
expected to regard his father as always reasonable and always fair.

The overt emphasis on conformity and suppression of feeling is
sufficiently clear. Nevertheless, there is some reason to suspect that
Mr. McGill warmly accepted the fact that James did not *really* conform.
For example, granted that a person may be stirred to intense anger by
evidence of one's child's shortcomings, one would hardly expect that
this anger would be completely appeased by the most superficial conformity; yet that was typical. As soon as it became evident that James
was going through the motions of study, the tirade ended—until the
occasion for the next one arose.

There are many episodes in James's recent life where delinquent or

respectfully to her, she slapped his face. She knew that he behaved this way only because he was taking "that stuff" at the time and that he would never talk back to her otherwise. (We agree.) Despite (because of?) the extraordinary and enforced closeness of Mrs. Cordova with her children, her present relationships with her children are meager. She is disappointed in all of them. The only one to whom she is close is her daughter.

Although she has lived many years in this country, Mrs. Cordova does not read English at all. This is extraordinary for several reasons. First, she is already literate in Spanish. Second, she speaks and understands English well. Third, all five of her children were educated in American school systems. Fourth, we have already noted her concern that her children should escape what she regarded as the stigma of being identified as Spanish.

She belongs to no churches, nor has she any knowledge of community house or neighborhood activities. Since she seems intelligent and observant and is ambitious, this is another indication of her self-isolating behavior. In this regard, we were impressed by her growing suspiciousness of our interviewer. Mrs. Cordova persistently doubted her integrity. She suspected that the interviewer, despite her credentials, was actually ferreting out information about Dominick and his life to make a newspaper story. Indeed, the last exchange between Mrs. Cordova and the interviewer was a request that the latter write down her name so that Mrs. Cordova could check on her again through the hospital.

To this point, we can observe some of the general characteristics of the familial situation in which Dominick was reared. He was brought up by a repressive, domineering, inflexible mother who isolated herself and her children from the dangers—and, incidentally, from the opportunities for growth—afforded by her environment. We note—as we did in Richard's case and as seems to be the usual state of affairs in the family background of adolescent opiate addicts—the small role played by an adult male figure in Dominick's life.

But probably the most important facts about Dominick's early experience have to do with his succession to the only girl in the family. Unlike his older brothers, who were equally regarded—or, in a more profound sense, disregarded—by their mother, Dominick's early childhood must have been full of evidence that his mother preferred another. His sister, Cora, who was three years older than he, was Mrs. Cordova's pleasure, hope, and pride. When Cora was born, Mrs. Cordova found the one object she could really pamper, indulge, and, in a sense, love. Dominick was another unwanted male child who could only interfere with her devoted attention to her daughter. This was so evident that Mrs. Cordova had to excuse herself frequently and rationalize her preferential behavior toward Cora by asserting that girls inherently need more than boys. Parenthetically, Mrs. Cordova was, herself, the oldest girl in a sizable family, but, rather than being the preferred and favored child, she was body servant and maid-of-all-work to the others in the family.

Though Mrs. Cordova and her children were supported by the Department of Welfare, somehow she found the means of having Cora trained to become a ballet dancer. Now that the sons are scattered around New York City, Mrs. Cordova and Cora, now married, occupy separate apartments in the same building. Cora gave up her career as a dancer (unlike her ballet classmates, who now are dancing throughout the country) and has earned her living as a typist in a bank. Mrs. Cordova is disappointed by Cora's abandonment of a career as a dancer, but Cora is still the apple of her mother's eye. Mrs. Cordova went out of her way to introduce Cora to our interviewer and tried to arrange for the interview to take place in her daughter's apartment rather than in her own.

When Dominick was fifteen, Mrs. Cordova tried to have him committed to a state school for wayward minors. Since his misbehavior was limited to truancy without other delinquency, the judge refused to commit Dominick and instead scolded the mother. In Mrs. Cordova's present contacts with Dominick, she has told him, as she tells us, that, if he were to return to his old habits (not holding a job steadily, hanging around with drug-users, and so on), she would have nothing more to do with him. Dominick's mother is quite capable of carrying out her threat to have nothing more to do with him. When she cuts someone out of her life, she cuts completely and thoroughly. When she separated from her husband, she moved out of the apartment in which she had reared her children, so that there would be no stimulus to remember that there had ever been a father in the home. She is emotionally so withdrawn from her husband that she will not even complain, criticize, or be angry with him. She asserts, with no special feeling, that he was a fine man and that "he had a good reputation."

CASE 17: JOHN CRAWFORD, CONTROL

The Crawford family lives in a predominantly Negro slum area in lower Harlem. The household is overcrowded. In addition to Mrs. Crawford and John, her oldest child, there are a grandmother, an aunt, John's two sisters, and a foster child.

Mrs. Crawford and her husband separated when John was eight. According to Mrs. Crawford, her husband had an unstable work history, did not provide adequate financial support for the family, and, in fact, was rarely home. According to her: "He was always out of the house, drinking and running around." For a while after the separation, she was kept busy running to the Family Court in repeated efforts to get Mr. Crawford to pay for the support of the children. Eventually, the family had to seek assistance from the Department of Welfare. After the separation, John continued to see his father occasionally until about a year before our interviews.

According to his mother, John was never any trouble to her. He was always a quiet boy and a good student. He was quite precocious. She says that he not only walked by himself by the time he was eighteen months old, but that he already could count at that age. As early as five, John began to contribute to the support of the family by turning in what he could earn by shining shoes. Although he later began college, he dropped out in order to support the family. John now "works for a big company, and he got the job by passing a test."

In fact, John is the man of the house in other ways, as well. For instance, Mrs. Crawford says that John sometimes loses his temper when disciplining his youngest sister and may slap her. "You've got to have a father in the house. So I let John take over. I never interfere when John disciplines Margaret. I can't do it all myself, and it's good to have someone to rely on." This is not simply a recent development, for Mrs. Crawford has apparently always pushed him toward the assumption of responsibility.

The relationship between John and his mother is a close one. Although she struck our interviewer as a rather aloof person in the course of the several contacts with her, Mrs. Crawford has warm, motherly feelings toward John and takes great pride in his accomplishments. In return, John discusses things with her and confides in her. At the time of the interviews, John had been "going steady" for about a year and a half, but our interviewer thought that she detected a note of relief in Mrs. Crawford's assessment of the relationship as not yet having "reached the serious stage." Mrs. Crawford does, however, have apparently realistic plans for her own future. She has a skill that can be developed as a basis for earning her livelihood when her most pressing homemaking responsibilities diminish.

Academic achievement on the part of the children is very important to Mrs. Crawford, and she has particularly pressed John in that direction. She sees herself as both culturally and morally superior to her neighbors, with whom she does not socialize. She hates Harlem and would like to live elsewhere. She feels that her values differ from those of the others who live nearby, and she speaks with contempt of the women on the block for their lack of interest in the activities of their children. She feels that the children are permitted to stay out too late and that the mothers are generally irresponsible in not knowing where their children are. At the time of the interviews, Mrs. Crawford was especially concerned about her youngest daughter, Margaret, and made a special point about not liking to see her come home late, "because there are dope-pushers and alcoholics on the stairs of this building." She was also concerned about the sexual immorality prevalent in the neighborhood. "The mothers around here don't seem to care about their girls. That's why you see them going to school in the winter and walking baby buggies in the spring." That she recognizes that there are limits to the protection a mother can provide and that a child who yields to the pressures of a bad environment is still entitled to parental support is indicated when she adds: "I hope nothing like that will happen to Margaret, but, if anything did, I would stand by her."

We do not know much about the quality of John's relationships to the other members of the household or about their relationships to one another.

There are obviously features of John's home environment that, taken by themselves, cannot be regarded as wholesome—most notably, a father whose irresponsibility, incompetence, and profligacy set a bad example and the total absence of any adult male in the household during the latter part of his childhood and adolescent years. The pressures of economic adversity and toward the premature assumption of familial responsibilities are not normally favorable circumstances, either. There were, however, also compensatory features in his situation, in part determined by his own precocity. Most notably on the favorable side of the balance was his warm and close relationship with his mother, who, despite the fact that she may have pressured him too much for comfort, nevertheless respected his integrity as an individual and accepted and nurtured his sense of masculine initiative and competence in a household where it could easily have been crushed. John's home did not provide an appropriate model of manliness with which he could identify, but his mother, perhaps because of her own dependency needs, nevertheless found the means of showing him the way. She did not find in him a sexual object on which to play out the repressed themes of her own unfulfilled sexuality. Perhaps these needs were not very strong, perhaps they were otherwise satisfied, perhaps they were effectively repressed— we do not know; but she did find in him, and helped him to discover, a man. Moreover, in her own person, she offered him a model of one who does not passively accept defeat, but who continues to strive in adversity; and she demanded of him, somehow without overwhelming him in the process, that he live up to the model.

CASE 30: LOUIS HORA, CONTROL

Like John Crawford, Louis Hora is a product of a broken marriage. He lives with his mother, stepfather, brother, and half-brother in a spotless, attractively furnished, and well-equipped apartment in a dirty apartment house in a run-down Manhattan neighborhood.

Louis' father has returned to Puerto Rico, but Louis still keeps in constant contact with him and his paternal relatives by mail. He writes to his father for guidance and consults him on every important move that he contemplates. Mr. Hora has always urged Louis to aim at a higher occupation than that of a factory hand, and the letters from the relatives are full of admonitions to work hard, not to play too much, and not to waste his time.

According to Louis' mother, Mr. Hora had been very strict with the boy and, indeed, she describes his entire family (to whom she laughingly refers as "a bunch of old goats") as extremely pious, moralistic, strait-laced, and industrious. Mrs. Hora describes herself as having shared fully in this disciplinary approach, and, between her and her first husband, the boy was watched over constantly and given little opportunity to get into trouble. At any sign of misbehavior, a "look" was sufficient to institute control.

Despite Mrs. Hora's self-characterization as a full partner in setting a stern disciplinary regimen for Louis, the interviewer who had an opportunity to observe mother and son together described their relationship as a warm one enriched with humor and mutual tolerance. During one of the interviews in which Louis acted as interpreter for his mother, who speaks little English, Mrs. Hora enumerated a list of illnesses from which her present husband suffers, and the two of them were greatly amused at the length of the list. They spoke of the stepfather with a sort of amused fondness, as though he were a rather pleasant addition to the household, rather than the head of it. In another context, the mother referred to the fact that Louis may bring friends into the house for parties and added that, if there is too much noise, she goes out.

The point is not that Louis' mother exaggerates her standards or that she is indecisive in applying them to her children; far from it. She clearly gives the impression of being a strong and purposeful individual and that it is she who takes the lead in making family decisions. But she keeps things in a good-humored perspective and makes allowances for the needs of the other members of her family even if these involve some inconvenience. This is why she is rather contemptuous of Mr. Hora's family. It is not that she deprecates their standards, but their rigidity and their failure to discriminate between essentials and nonessentials.

Louis' stepfather, Mr. Domingo, is described by the interviewer as a warm, friendly, rather emotional man in his fifties. He formerly owned a small retail establishment, but a series of illnesses had forced him to retire. He seems to be quite fond of Louis, whom he has known since the latter was nine years old. According to him, Louis has never been in any trouble, and, if there was any issue of discipline, all that was needed was to talk to him, although "sometimes he talked back. You know, the way a kid does."

Louis himself is described as a boy content to stay around the house most of the time. He never wanted to play with older boys who might lead him into trouble. He has belonged to the Boy Scouts for many years and also to a number of other organizations.

In line with his father's admonitions, Louis has always wanted to enter some profession and, for some years, has aspired to become a physician. This was, however, considered beyond the family means, and they did not believe that he would be able to win a scholarship. Recently, therefore, be settled upon optometry (a decision that was facilitated by the fact that Mr. Hora himself was, at that point, also preparing to become an optometrist in Puerto Rico), and he has just re-

of the control cases: divorce is not necessarily disastrous to the children.

The intactness of the family is a surface manifestation; what matters, we think, is the history of personal relationships that lead up to the break and issue from it. The broken home is more likely to be one in which interpersonal relations are unwholesome, especially in the case of divorce. After all, divorce does not come out of the blue, and no one, to our knowledge, has ever explicitly suggested that divorces are made in heaven. All too often, in the case of divorce, neither parent is capable of sustaining the respect for the other's integrity and individuality that are required by an enduring intimate relationship. This incapacity is as corrosive of their relationships to their children as it is of their relationships to each other. That this is not necessarily the case is, apart from common experience, evidenced by the cases of John Crawford and Louis Hora.

Moreover, the case of John Crawford stands witness to the fact that there can be compensatory adjustments for even the total absence of an adult male model in the family. Indeed, in its own way, the case of Louis Hora makes a similar point; for, although the gentleness and emotive spontaneity of his stepfather must have had some attenuating effect on the model set by the reputed inflexibility of his actual father, Louis still, in the main, cast his ego ideal in terms of the latter.

On the other hand, the case of James McGill serves as a reminder that an intact family may provide a far from ideal developmental environment, and this in a home not marked by an unusual degree of friction between the parents. Obviously, there are marriages that do not —for religious, social, economic, and even psychological, sadomasochistic reasons—end in divorce, even though relations between the parents are as marked by vicious cycles of mutual irresponsibility, reciprocal frustration, clashing values, and incompatible purposes as are many marriages that do. The marriage of the McGills does not meet these specifications; there was a conscious effort on the part of at least Mr. McGill to establish a wholesome relationship with his son and to foster his psychological growth. Again one is pointed toward the subtleties of personal relationships rather than toward the grossly observable and easily describable aspects.

There is another rather striking aspect of the cases we have reviewed, one far removed from the issues of divorce and broken homes, that also points in the same direction. Running through five of the cases

—all three of the addicts and two of the three controls—is a major concern with cleanliness and order. To be sure, this concern was most ineffectively implemented in the home of one of the addicts. We are not, however, directing attention to the actual degree of cleanliness, but to the spirit of the concern. In the homes of the controls, cleanliness and neatness were simply means of facilitating a good home life—people do not exist to be clean; cleanliness is simply a means of helping them to live better. In the homes of the addicts, cleanliness seemed to have become an end in itself, divorced from the welfare and happiness of the people who had to live with it. In the Stone home, it was not even something that people bring about by themselves; it was a state of grace that descends upon them through the providence of others. James McGill was constantly hamstrung by his mother's obsession with cleanliness and order and with the necessity for suppressing human feelings. Dominick Cordova had to learn to "play" with his three brothers and one sister in one room which never became disordered, and the one point of pride his mother could find in her son was that he could do housework like a woman.

Whether it involved cleanliness or countless other issues, this was a recurrent difference in the lives of addicts and controls. The spontaneity, flexibility, and warmth of the human relationships was paramount in the homes of the controls; the essential ignoring of the human being, whether through the application of inflexible rules of child-rearing, home care, and conduct or through outright rejection or withdrawal was paramount in the homes of addicts. The addict fairly typically grows up in a home where he is an *object* to be manipulated and controlled, to be ignored except when he gets in the way of the grownups, or to serve as a target for poorly repressed impulses. The control typically grows up in a home where he is another *person,* to be responded to with the give and take that his *person*ality implies, with respect for and adaptation to his needs and with appreciation for what he, as an individual, has to offer. The difference even emerges in the manifestations of religion in the family life. In the one case, it is formalistic, ritualistic, empty of genuine feeling, essentially manipulative or conciliatory of supernatural powers for the advancement of one's own ends; in the second, however prominent actual ritual may be, it makes for a sense of oneness and lends grace to the home.

These qualitative subtleties are so important that one may wonder that our indexes, based as they were on quite unsubtle matters, should have so effectively differentiated between the two groups. That the two groups did come out so differently with respect to the indexes is testimony, therefore, not merely to the grossly different patterns of familial experience, but to the fact that the subtle differences tend to go along with the gross ones. To take but one example: Relative to a boy's developing a clear sense of masculine identity, there is some likelihood that there will be adequate compensatory adjustment for the absence of a father figure during a significant portion of the boy's childhood; there is also some likelihood that, despite a father's presence throughout his son's childhood, other factors will interfere with the emergence of a clear sense of masculine identity. The first likelihood is apparently substantially less than the second; therefore, the absence of a father figure may be taken as predictive, albeit not perfectly so, that the boy will grow up confused with respect to his masculine identity. It was on the basis of such reasoning that we expected the ingredients of our indexes to work. Though we readily grant that we may have proceeded on false premises for some of the items included in the indexes, we cannot think of any compelling reason why the indexes should have discriminated the two groups other than that our reasoning was, in general, correct.[4]

The conclusion seems inescapable: the addicts grew up in, and were at least in part shaped by, homes that were far less wholesome than those in which the controls were nurtured. The differences extend from the gross indicators of family pathology utilized in the indexes to the subtler features of personal relationships that are correlated with the gross indicators.

[4] We deal with an alternative explanation, interviewer bias, in Appendix M, where we have described the data that led us to reject this possibility. We have conscientiously tried to think of other alternatives and have felt compelled to dismiss those that have occurred to us. For instance, the use of an interview technique to explore the past is always fraught with the danger that the present may color the past. For instance, the parents of addicts may unwittingly darken the past histories of their wayward sons, whereas the parents of the controls—boys who have avoided serious trouble—may have brightened the histories of their sons. This possibility is not only precluded by the nature of the items we have included in the indexes, but, as illustrated by the six cases described in this chapter, is also precluded by the fact that the past differences are consistent with the observable present. Contrariwise, the contrast between the warmth and relaxation of the control homes and the coldness and tension of the addict homes may be a consequence of having had to deal with well-adjusted, as against maladjusted, children. That such effects are real, it seems to us, is hardly debatable; but then it is also hardly likely that the differences are of recent origin or that parents have been reacting over the years to their well-adjusted or maladjusted children, while the children have been pursuing their own inner growth potentials, uninfluenced by their relations to their parents.

XII

The Female Addict

What about girls who become addicted to drugs? We have already explained in Chapter II our reasons for concentrating on males. This was not, however, to gainsay the desirability of knowing whether similar or different factors are responsible for female involvement than for that of males. The present chapter reports on two small studies of young female addicts.

A word may be in order on the issue of the smaller proportion of female involvement. About all that we can say with any degree of assurance is that the issue is probably not a simple one. It is known that the much higher incidence of the use of opiates among males is paralleled by similarly marked disproportions in the incidence of alcoholism, juvenile delinquency, and crime. These differences cannot be easily explained by the greater psychological stability of the female constitution or the more effective sheltering of the female from psychological stress. Women, for instance, take up as many mental hospital beds as do males, and the relative number of females in outpatient and private psychiatric or psychotherapeutic treatment is, if anything, even higher.

That females, as such, do not have a lesser diathesis toward drugs is indicated by the fact that, prior to the Harrison Act, the incidence of narcotics use by females equaled and probably exceeded that among males.[1] The simple hypothesis sometimes appealed to in explaining the sex differential in delinquency and crime—namely, that females are more apt to be protected from the social consequences of their actions—seems clearly inappropriate in relation to drug use. The incontinent use

[1] Cf. Alan S. Meyer, *Social and Psychological Factors in Opiate Addiction: A Review of Findings together with an Annotated Bibliography* (New York: Bureau of Applied Social Research, Columbia University, 1952), p. 38.

of drugs is not easily concealed. Moreover, one effect of such protection would be to increase the proportion of females in hospitals and decrease the proportion in jails and reformatories. If anything, this differential runs the other way. As reported in Chapter II, slightly more than one in five known cases of drug use were female, both in the below-sixteen and in the sixteen-through-twenty age ranges. This may be compared to an average of one in eight in new admissions to Riverside Hospital.

Perhaps the major plausible, relatively simple hypothesis remaining is that females are less likely than males to express their tensions in ways that are detectably and flagrantly violative of prevailing social codes. It may be noted that such a sex differential would have been operative with respect to the use of narcotics to a much lesser degree, if at all, prior to the Harrison Act than subsequent to its passage. Not only was the medically nonprescriptive use of narcotics not illegal, but females could readily obtain narcotics in the context of an acceptable social alibi: narcotics were major ingredients of proprietary medications for the then eminently respectable and vaguely designated array of disturbances that masqueraded under the title of "female complaints." One contemporary effect of greater female conventionality would be, of course, to inhibit girls in experimentation with drugs and thus contribute to the lower incidence of their involvement. Another less direct effect contributing to the same end would be that their lesser involvement in delinquency would also decrease the likelihood of their coming into contact with the drug-using subculture. This would, of course, also obtain with any sex differential in the incidence of delinquency, regardless of how the delinquency came about.

Another possibly relevant consideration in the explanation of the lower incidence of narcotics involvement among girls is that females have available to them another technique of "acting out" which may subserve many of the same needs served by narcotics (albeit in a dramatically different fashion) and which is not available to males, namely, the out-of-wedlock pregnancy. To be sure, there must be some male involved in every pregnancy, but the drama is enacted largely in the life of the female. It is not clear, however, if this is a relevant factor, why the sex ratio of drug involvement should be the same (or somewhat lower) for cases under sixteen as for cases in the sixteen-through-twenty age range.

The general questions we have attempted to answer about female adolescent opiate addicts in this study are the following: (1) What is the nature of the addiction process for female adolescent addicts? (2)

What are their personal characteristics, relationships, and psycho-pathology? (3) What is their social background—the structural and dynamic characteristics of their families? (4) What role does addiction play in their lives?

Where it was feasible and relevant, we have contrasted the character-istics of the female patients with the male patients (based on our own comparable studies) in order to cast light on the final question, namely: (5) Whether and how the process, characteristics, background, and function of opiate addiction of female adolescents differ from those of male adolescent addicts.

The Sample

Twenty female patients were selected for clinical study. These were serial first admissions who came to Riverside Hospital through the Screening Clinic operated by the hospital in conjunction with the Nar-cotics Term Court of the New York City Magistrates' Court system. Of these twenty patients, eleven were Negro, three were of Puerto Rican or other Spanish-speaking Caribbean origins, five were of white ethnic groups, and one patient had a Puerto Rican mother and an American Negro father. At the time of admission they ranged in age from seven-teen through twenty years, with a median age of eighteen and one-half. Except for two cases missed during the vacation of the psychiatrist who interviewed these patients, these were all the female patients admitted between September, 1955, and November, 1956.

In the thirteen months required to obtain this sample of twenty pa-tients, there were twenty-two first-admission female patients and 225 male patients, a ratio of one to ten. Serial first admissions were selected rather than a block of patients resident in the hospital during a shorter period, partly in order to study patients who were not overinterviewed (and interview-wise), but mainly in order to study patients comparable in their hospitalization experience and treatment. Furthermore, by studying patients serially, there were never more than a few patients in clinical investigation at a time, a factor which would maximize the pa-tient's individuality in the eyes of the investigator. All these patients were under the care of the same psychiatric team in the hospital. The data to be reported take into account relevant observations by the psychiatric social worker, psychologist, nurse, occupational therapist, and school personnel who constituted the team; but, in the main, they were assembled by one of the writers (who was the psychiatrist in charge of the hospital team) in the course of from two to twenty interviews (with a median of six interviews) with each of the patients.

In order to study the family background of the female adolescent addict, we took for our sample the families of twenty-two female patients who were resident in Riverside Hospital between November, 1955, and March, 1956, who had a parent or parents who could be interviewed at home by specially trained second-year social work students. All these families had had some (usually little) contact with psychiatric social workers in the hospital. None had been previously visited in their homes. Although we would have preferred to have made home visits to all the families of the patients we studied clinically, our social work investigators had to do all their interviewing between the limiting dates, since some of the data they obtained were to be used by them in a group master's thesis project at the New York University School of Social Work.[2] However, ten of the patients in the family study were also in the clinical study.

The Clinical Study

Beginning with the response to her hospitalization and to the interview, a picture of the life history, relationships, and psychopathology was constructed for each of the patients. Though we did not use any formal questionnaire, we planned to elucidate the following matters through the interviews: (1) experience with opiate and nonopiate drugs and with drug-users; (2) personal adjustment, including school and work experiences, pattern of interpersonal relationships, goals, expectations, and interests; (3) family structure, background, goals, achievements, and status characteristics; (4) interview behavior, e.g., general behavior, appearance, rapport, productivity, affect, style, intellectual functioning, and memory; (5) emotional response of the interviewer to the subject, and vice versa; and (6) medical psychiatric history, emphasizing symptoms related to psychiatric disorders.

The Family Study

Six second-year social work students participated in group training sessions in which the questionnaire which we had developed for our earlier study of male adolescent addicts was discussed, modified, and elabo-

2 At that time, part of the NYU Graduate School of Public Administration and Social Service.

rated on by the group to meet the needs of describing the familial experiences of female adolescent addicts. In the course of these sessions, as in the corresponding training sessions of the earlier study, the special research needs of thoroughness and objectivity were discussed in a variety of contexts, and the all-too-common social worker's fear and misconception of research instruments and questionnaires were worked through.

Each of the families was interviewed at home, two to four times. A process recording of the interview was written immediately after each interview; a case summary (which followed a topical outline) was also written, and a check-list questionnaire was filled out after the interviewing was completed. The process recording, the topically organized case report, and the questionnaire were reviewed and edited for internal consistency and completeness in a final discussion of each family.

Findings of the Clinical Study

THE ADDICTION SYNDROME

Seventeen of the twenty patients were addicted to heroin, in some instances supplemented by morphine or methadone, prior to this hospitalization and displayed unquestionable symptoms of a withdrawal syndrome on hospitalization. One patient had a history of addiction, but came to the hospital without current dependency. Two had no history of addiction, but were using drugs regularly and increasingly—up to five times weekly—in the month prior to hospitalization. Nine of the patients had had previous medical treatment for addiction or had found themselves in the clutches of the law. Eleven had not experienced any external interruption in their use of drugs until the present situation led to hospitalization.

Eleven of the patients came to the hospital following an arrest for possession of heroin and/or other charges, e.g., prostitution or theft. Three were brought to the hospital by their families. Six initiated the hospitalization themselves. Of these six, two came to the hospital because of a change in their external circumstances which interfered with their ability to get heroin; they had depended on a male addict-pusher to support their habit, and, when he was arrested, they found that they could not manage. Another sought hospitalization because she could not "get high" any more; she needed and wanted a "free period." A fourth came to the hospital because her increasing habit could not be supported through her legitimate earnings as a dietitian's assistant in a hospital; though she wanted to turn to prostitution, she could not make herself do so. A fifth came for reasons known only to herself, although it seems likely that she sought hospitalization because of some practical difficulties associated with addiction rather than dissatisfaction with heroin use per se. The sixth came to the hospital because she felt that heroin use was hurting her and her baby.

Thus, the major factor leading to hospitalization was clearly in the situation and not in the patient. In a minority of cases, the mounting difficulties of supporting a habit in our society may lead to voluntary hospitalization, but only after other courses are attempted. The rarest of reasons for hospitalization of the female adolescent addict is that she regards her heroin addiction as harmful.

These data are consistent with a general impression that the typical young female addict who is hospitalized in connection with her drug-use problem has already experienced prolonged and regular use of heroin or other opiates. The hope that either male or female adolescents who become hospitalized in connection with drug use are involved only superficially or transiently with opiate drugs is not often supported by our observations.

First use of opiate drugs among the twenty female patients took place at a median age of sixteen; the range was from fourteen to nineteen years. For the majority, heroin was their first source of intoxication. Only nine had previously used any other intoxicant drug. Two regarded themselves as alcoholics before they began to use heroin; another three had used alcoholic beverages for intoxication, but did not like to do so, because they felt that they "lost control" when intoxicated. Only seven of the twenty patients had ever tried marijuana. Two gave it up because they did not experience any satisfaction from this drug; two gave it up because they regarded the giggling and silliness of the marijuana intoxication as alien to their ideal of being able to stay "cool" and "adult"; two gave it up because they became anxious when they began to feel that people were staring at or talking about them during the state of marijuana intoxication; one gave it up for both of the two last-named reasons; and one gave it up because she was frightened by disturbances in spatial perception.

What is the function of opiates in their lives? This question must be answered at several levels, as we pointed out in Chapter IX. The generalizations we offer there for male adolescent opiate addicts are equally applicable to the female adolescent addict—they take opiates because of certain highly estimated, consciously experienced effects of the drug; as a defensive reorganization of their lives; for deep, unconscious "symbolic" needs; and for the complex psychophysiological processes of tolerance and dependence. In the simplest of terms, they feel better when they use drugs than when they abstain.

We were interested in the setting of the onset of drug use. Since addiction is preponderantly a problem of young men, we were inclined to expect that the setting of initial use would typically be that of some man introducing heroin to an adolescent girl. Our data indicate, to the contrary, that only a minority (six cases) received their first heroin from a male user. The most typical setting (thirteen cases) of initial use was with one or more other female users. One took her first dose while she was alone. Slightly more than half received their first heroin from a person in their own age range (eleven cases); the rest (nine cases), from an older person. None purchased their first heroin. It was, in the main, given to them, ostensibly with some reluctance, by a donor who was already an experienced user, though not necessarily an addict; two, however, stole their first heroin, one from her addict-pusher brother, the other from an addict-pusher girl friend.

As the frequency of their use of heroin increased, there was a shift from predominant use with other female users to predominant use with male users or with a mixed group in which male users were much in the majority. In short, the companions of onset were not the companions of regular use, though the companions of onset were usually persons who "made some difference" in their lives.

The life situation at the time of onset is difficult to clarify. The ostensible motivation for first use was "curiosity." All the patients knew that heroin is illicit, habit-forming, and possibly lethal (through an overdose), and they believed that heroin use is debilitating. However, they were also aware of its reputation as "a good way to get high," that is, they expected relaxing and comforting effects. Their first use clearly did not express ignorance, but rather disregard for what they knew about the long-range probabilities of harm and trouble in the quest for immediate pleasure. Only occasional patients were consciously motivated by forces other than curiosity. Two were aware of nervousness, anxiety, or unhappiness. They felt that heroin would make them feel better, and it did. Though three others were chronically depressed, their conscious motivation for heroin use was "curiosity," rather than relief. None of the patients first used heroin in response to a severe and distressing situation except when such a situation—death of a baby (in one case), loss of a boy friend (in two cases), or bitter quarrel with a father (in one case)—occurred in the setting of prolonged and pervasive maladjustment.

Thirteen of the patients recalled quite clearly how they responded to their first use of heroin. Ten got what they wanted—e.g., being high and liking it—on their first use. Three did not enjoy their first experience, but returned for more in the hope that they would learn to like it, and, of course, they all did. Seven patients were too vague or evasive in the reconstruction of their early heroin use for us to judge how they responded to their first experience.

In the course of their continued use, they had to spend increasing amounts of money to maintain themselves without withdrawal distress and with continuing satisfaction. They usually supported their habit in the course of their addiction by several means (in order of descending frequency): by living with an addict-pusher (nine cases); by abusing the confidence of friends or relatives (eight cases); by working (seven cases); by prostitution (six cases); through a relative who was an addict-pusher (two cases); through theft (two cases); and, in one case, by gifts of drugs from friends who were users.

PERSONAL CHARACTERISTICS, RELATIONSHIPS,
   AND PSYCHOPATHOLOGY

Slightly fewer than half the patients (eight cases) approached the interview in a compliant and cooperative attitude. They were quite willing to talk about themselves and their life situations. Though they were skeptical and negativistic about the likelihood that anything could be done to help them in their difficult situations, they were grateful for the asylum and support of the hospital. They hoped to reorganize themselves in the course of the hospitalization in order to cope better with their lives than they had in the course of their drug use.

About half the patients (nine cases) approached the interviewers in an angry, demanding, and complaining attitude. Though they answered questions about themselves, they did so in a flippant and resentful manner. They insisted that they had been deceived in their expectations of the hospital and by the statements made to them about how they would be treated. They regarded hospitalization beyond detoxification as an unwarranted and unnecessary intrusion into their lives, which they con-

sidered quite under control and manageable, despite quite extensive
evidence to the contrary.

The remaining patients showed gross disturbances of communication.
It was quite difficult to obtain information about them and their life
situations. Two were quite willing to remain in the hospital. The third
shared the indignant attitude of the second of the above groups.

Though the patients in the first group were compliant and cooperative,
they could not be regarded as well-motivated psychiatric patients. No
clinician would mistake their superficial compliance and cooperativeness
for a genuine wish to explore their current and past relationships and
feelings. None, despite their cooperative attitudes, could be regarded as
having insight into the fact that their lives prior to drug use were troubled
nor into the fact that they had some role in creating these difficulties. In
brief, none of the patients had the inclination or the modicum of insight
necessary for voluntary involvement in psychotherapy. We do not mean
to imply that these patients were unable to participate in psychotherapy,
but rather that their lack of insight and their conscious attitudes with
regard to need for treatment made the initiation of treatment difficult
and slow. It is possible, with patience and persistence, in a controlled
environment, where conscious attitudes and fears about treatment can
be worked through, to get these patients into therapeutically more prom-
ising relationships and communication.

The utilization of hospital facilities by the female adolescent addict,
as by the male adolescent addict, is typically characterized by meager
participation in or utilization of hospital resources, whether educational,
recreational, or psychotherapeutic. They do participate in sadistic hazing
of new patients, in sexual affairs, and in inciting fights over them by the
male patients. They do not take work assignments seriously. They have
a high incidence of physical complaints without demonstrable physical
pathology. Unlike the males, who generally try not to attract attention
from the hospital staff, the female *gets* herself noticed. Perhaps this reflects a characteristic difference between men and women in our culture. Whatever the basis of the difference, female adolescent addicts are
unquestionably far more demanding of the time and energy of the staff
than are male patients.

From our interviews, we learned that the relationships and social
adjustment of our patients prior to their drug use were conspicuously
troubled and stormy. Of the nineteen patients who had had any school
experience in this country, only three had a scholastic career devoid of

extensive truancy, learning difficulties, or notable misbehavior with teachers and with fellow students. Two of these three left school because of out-of-wedlock pregnancy. What their school career would have been without this interruption (by the fourth term of high school) is a moot question. The third was graduated from high school without incident, but managed to insulate herself from the educational process. In a less enlightened period, she would have been dismissed from school as a poor student. Since she attended fairly regularly, stayed out of fights, and behaved politely, she was awarded her high school diploma.

Of the twenty patients, six could be regarded as having made some positive vocational adjustment. Two of these were employed by their families in undemanding and protective circumstances. One was a barmaid in her father's saloon; the other did domestic work in her grandmother's boarding house. Four of the twenty patients unquestionably made a good vocational adjustment, prior to and continuing into their heroin addiction, working steadily with a sense of purpose and satisfaction. The remaining fourteen were either never employed or worked for short periods at many jobs with long intervals of unemployment.

Only six of the twenty patients had no conspicuous behavior difficulties at home. Of these, two were remarkably overindulged children whose whims were law. Neither was able to get along in school; one made a good vocational adjustment in a situation in which she was the petted and praised youngest worker, a situation quite analogous to her family situation in which she was the petted and praised baby sister of five brothers. The other four who manifestly caused no distress at home did so by adopting a passive-submissive attitude to mothers who were hostile, demanding, and critical. The remaining fourteen were recurrently in trouble with their parents, with whom they were disobedient, demanding, and disagreeable.

Eleven of the twenty patients acquired an out-of-wedlock child or pregnancy preceding their addictive drug use. Another two avoided this outcome by chance; they were sexually promiscuous and neither took nor demanded any contraceptive measures.

Eight of the patients had been seriously maladjusted in the areas of family life, school, and work; eight were notably disturbed in two of the three areas; three patients in one of the three; and only one (discounting an out-of-wedlock pregnancy and a consequent disastrously unsatisfactory marriage) could be described as showing no abnormal disturbance in any of the three areas. Even the last and most favorable

of these patients could hardly have been expected to make a satisfactory
life adjustment if she had not become involved with narcotics; her comparatively "good" adjustment was achieved through an evasive, guarded,
and controlled participation in school, work, and family rather than as
an expression of adequate, intact ego functions.

From our interviews, the patients' histories, and the psychological
testing, it seemed clear to us that the female addicts, like their male
counterparts, were seriously maladjusted adolescents prior to addiction.
Like any other set of psychiatric patients, the female addicts could be
described in the terms of any standard psychiatric nomenclature. However, we believe that it would be more useful to classify and describe
them *sui generis,* in terms of the personal living situations and relationships, as well as in terms of their formal psychopathological manifestations. Although we have reworked our phenomenological typology several times since we first struggled with the general description and
diagnosis of adolescent addicts, the formulation we offer here for the
female adolescent addict remains a slight variant of the schema in our
report on male adolescent addicts. This schema is not intended as an
exhaustive typology. It is intended as a compromise between the bare
diagnostic terms of the current nomenclature and the at-least-several-
hundred-word summary of the ego functions, symptoms, defenses, and
relationships which we would need to properly and uniquely describe
each of the patients.

Overt Schizophrenia. These patients were not hallucinating or psychotically disturbed. However, they displayed inappropriate affect, labile
emotionality, serious thinking disorders, and delusions of reference and
grandeur. Rather than being quietly withdrawn, they were too much
in everyone's attention through making trouble, but in their relations
with the staff and with other patients they were empty of feeling and
relatedness. Three patients of our sample were in this category. All three
had been regarded as queer, bizarre, and unreachable since childhood.
One had been hospitalized prior to drug use and diagnosed as schizo-
phrenic, hebephrenic type.

Borderline Schizophrenia. These patients were struggling against a
disorganizing and disruptive process in which they experienced extreme
anxiety related to feelings of inadequacy and low self-esteem. Paranoid
trends and early thinking disturbances were noted. Though moralistic
and struggling toward conventional goals in work, family living, marriage, and education, they found themselves unable to carry out the

required roles and relationships. Suppression of resentment and hostility toward their mothers was one of the most pressingly and poignantly conscious issues in their lives; they regarded their mothers as depriving, critical, and dominating, yet they clung to them as potential sources of love and support. In short, their relationships with their mothers were intensely ambivalent. These observations are incorporated in the diagnostic description not because they were subtle or inferentially "dynamic factors," but because they were acute concerns with which they were struggling. They were depressive, anxious, or guilt-ridden. Five of the twenty patients could be placed in this category.

Inadequate Personalities. These patients showed a paucity of interests and goals and an impoverishment of thinking and emotional expression. They were neither "good" delinquents nor "good" schizophrenics. They were successful in establishing role systems in which people responded to them almost as though they were just "not there." Although other cases of this type are encountered, which justifies noting it, only one in our sample could be so classified.

Complex Character Disorders. These patients can be described in general as follows: they regard their difficulties and symptoms as ego-syntonic. Their neuroses, to use the collective term, are alloplastic rather than autoplastic. They perceive their difficulties as imposed on them by fate, chance, or by an unfavorable environment. There are three major types within this category, types which differ by the degree to which particular relationships and recurrent experiences occurred in them. The types are not exclusive; the salient features which define them can often be perceived more subtly or less extremely in the others.

The Sadomasochistic Type. The key themes in the lives of five of the patients was a struggle between efforts to control aggression, on the one hand, and sadomasochistic involvement, on the other. Every so often they would be overcome by anger and resentment, only to suffer consequent anxiety and pangs of self-reproach, which, in turn, were alleviated by brief periods of penitence. From childhood into the period of their sexual affairs, they were continually involved in relationships in which they were beaten, mistreated, and picked on. They were accident-prone and seemed to invite teasing and provocation. The pattern of teasing and abuse was already evident in their early childhood relationships with one or both parents.

The Angry, Aggressive Type. Four of the patients were openly aggressive, stubborn, negativistic, and quarrelsome. They were going to take nothing from anyone, ostensibly in affirmation of their independence. This independent attitude, carried out to the point of a caricature, was a defensive denial of their wish for passivity and dependence. Their anger and hatred was the rule, placidity or satisfaction, the exception. Unlike the sadomasochistic type, they experienced no anxiety or self-reproach for their anger or their troublesome behavior. They could project, rationalize, and justify their rage; their worlds were out of joint, not they.

The "Cool" Psychopath. Two of the patients were cool, glib, smooth, clever, manipulative, apparently free of anxiety, and facile at rationalization. They looked at the experience of hospitalization with calm superiority and on the other patients as crude roughnecks. They had no need or wish to modify their behavior on the basis of their experience, since they regarded their experiences, however deplorable they might seem to the rest of the world, as wonderful, interesting, and remarkable.

It may be appropriate to note (see Table XII–1) the similarity in the distribution of diagnoses for the female addicts of this sample and the sample of male addicts reported previously.

TABLE XII-1   *Diagnosis of Male and Female*
Adolescent Opiate Addicts

	FEMALE		MALE	
	N	PERCENTAGE	N	PERCENTAGE
Overt schizophrenia	3	15	6	19
Borderline schizophrenia	5	25	8	25
Inadequate personality	1	5	4	12
Character disorder	11	55	14	44

The only notable difference in frequency (which, however, is not statistically significant) is in the category of character disorder. However, the differences in the qualitative aspects in this area are quite striking. Thus, the subtypes we used to describe the male adolescent addict in the general category of the character disorder were "pseudopsychopathic delinquent" and "oral character." Both these subtypes defined their lives in terms of aggression and hostility experienced as pleasurable or as justified reaction to mistreatment or frustration. For the female adolescent addict, these themes were absent. The angry, aggressive type did not wear the façade of "joy in battle" of the pseudopsychopathic delinquent, even though some of their outward behavior was quite similar. The oral male addicts whose rage and anxiety in response to frustration was episodic—as was the anger and resentment of the sadomasochistic type of female addict—did not experience anxiety and self-reproach following their episodes. In short, the *Gestalten* of the character disorders of the male and female adolescent addict were quite different.

Findings of the Family Study

The families of the female addicts, like those of the male addicts, seemed heterogeneous, both in structure and in the relationships between the teen-aged daughters (who became opiate addicts) and the important figures in their lives. Like the male addicts, their families were of the types which clinical experience suggests are productive of serious difficulties in living. Their parents were rarely as responsible for their children's—or their own—welfare; or as warm, objective, and encouraging of their personal development; or as steady and reasonable in disciplinary practices; or as free from psychopathology as we would like any families to be. In staff diagnostic conferences, the impression we garnered from the presentations of family backgrounds, as seen by the hospital psychiatric social workers, was, at best, that there were some positive features in some families, but that these were far outweighed by grossly pathogenic features and, at worst, that there was a congeries of pathogenic features without any apparent countering salutary influences.

Turning from general clinical experiences and impressions of the family background of the female addict, we can construct a picture of her typical family background out of the explicit categories of our own investigation. For simplicity in reporting, we shall describe those aspects of familial relationships or experiences which we regard as pathogenic and which occurred in 50 per cent or more of the cases as "usual" and those which occurred in 70 per cent as "typical"; an unqualified generalization is to be taken as "typical."

The relationships between the parents of the female adolescent addicts were typically discordant. Their fathers were usually absent from the parental home for prolonged periods in our subjects' childhoods; typically, at least one parent figure was absent from the home for a prolonged period in early or later childhood. In early childhood, their mothers were usually the dominant figures (i.e., clearly dominant—

father minimally involved in handling money, administering authority, making decisions); in later childhood, this was typically the case. Similarly, the mothers were typically the important parental figures (the one the patient went to for advice, affection, or disciplinary statements). They were the ones who made and enforced disciplinary policy, which typically took the form of physical punishment, threat of reformatory or police, cruel and sadistic ridicule, locking up the child, taking away various privileges, humiliation, withdrawal of food, or threat of these, rather than offering or withdrawing love.

Our subjects typically did not receive warm, affectionate treatment from their parents. The relationships between our subjects and their parents fell at the extreme of our scales. They were usually denied gratifications or spoiled (overindulged) or overindulged at some times and harshly frustrated at others. Parental expectations for their behavior and for their future were typically vague or rigid. Their ties with their mothers or fathers were typically either weak or intense. The mothers were usually insecure women, concealing their conflicts and insecurities behind a façade of efficiency, responsibility, and excessive mothering; they were usually religious and prone to preaching; they were opinionated, judgmental, rigid, authoritarian, and dictatorial; and they were punitive or indifferent in regard to their daughters' sexual functions and development. The fathers were usually "immoral figures," practicing infidelity, pimping, homosexuality, crime, alcoholism, or drug use. In almost half the instances, they could be described as weak, immature, quiet, and passive in their family roles. They were usually impulsive, concerned with immediate gratification, improvident, and unrestrained in their discharge of hostility. Both the mothers and fathers were usually distrustful or manipulative of authority figures. Neither the mothers nor the fathers made use of community resources for recreation or for cultural enhancement.

In summary, the clinical impression that the female adolescent addict has developed her difficulties in relationships and her psychopathology through immersion in a malignant familial environment is amply documented by the family study data.

In viewing the data on the family backgrounds of the female addicts, there are two points to be considered. First, though the unmentioned categories of family characteristics were not frequent, they might well have occurred with greater frequency in the family backgrounds of female addicts than in those of other adolescent girls in the same communities. Since we did not have a control group of nonaddicted, non-delinquent girls, we cannot answer this question. For example, six (more than one-fourth) of our patients had at some time lived in foster homes or institutions. Though this can hardly be said to be characteristic of female addicts, it may have nonetheless occurred more frequently in the lives of this group than in those of such appropriate controls.

Second, we were concerned with the difference in background of male and female adolescent addicts. As pointed out previously (chapters VIII and X), the male adolescent addict can be described in terms of three general aspects of personality structure and two patterns of attitudes and values. These are: weak ego function, defective superego function, inadequate masculine identification, lack of middle-class orientation, and distrust of major social institutions. Working definitions were written for each of these five personal characteristics. A list of family background factors which psychiatric and psychoanalytic literature and relevant research suggest are plausibly related or conducive to the development of such personal characteristics was drawn up. Our working assumption was that, the more frequently such factors occurred, the greater would be the likelihood of these characteristics in the individual; none of the factors in themselves need lead to these personal characteristics, but an accumulation of such factors would. An index score for each male addict and control subject was obtained for each of the five characteristics by taking the ratio of the number of factors categorically described (experiences or situations) which occurred in any individual to the total number of factors listed. Our hypothesis was that the index scores would be higher in the family background of the male adolescent addict than in the background of the male control subject. The data indicated that the male addict developed in a milieu which afforded far more of these factors for each of the five personal characteristics.[3]

Excluding as irrelevant the index of factors leading to inadequate masculine identification, we compared the families of male and female adolescent addicts.[4] There were no significant differences in factors

[3] This paragraph in effect summarizes Chapter X; the reader is referred to that chapter if he wishes to refresh himself on the details of methodology, analysis of data, and interpretation of results.

[4] Since the female sample was preponderantly Negro, our comparison of the family background of male and female addicts is restricted, of necessity, to a comparison of the family backgrounds of ten male and eighteen female Negro adolescent addicts.

leading to weak ego function or defective superego function. However, the family backgrounds of the female addicts had fewer of those factors leading to lack of realistic middle-class orientation (Index IV) and distrust of major social institutions (Index V).[a] These index differences between male and female addicts were based on a few items which were much more common among the male than among the female patients. These were not items which significantly differentiated the male addicts from the male controls, and it may be that we are dealing here with a general sex difference in the subcultures from which our cases came. Moreover, it is quite possible that unrealistic aspirations on the parts of the parents and distrust of social institutions are not so forcefully communicated to the female child as to the male or that, if they are, they do not have the same impact on their psychosocial development. Thus, if a girl accepts marriage as the major goal of personal fulfillment, the consequences of frustration ensuing from unrealistic parental aspirations may be less pervasive of the significant areas of her life than they would be of her brother's. By the same token, it is likely that we did not look for realism of expectations in the relevant life areas (and, for that matter, it would be much more difficult to do so), i.e., in those areas of specifically feminine roles. Similarly, attitudes of cynicism and distrust toward the larger society may have much less consequence for a girl than for a boy if she remains closer to the intimate environment. Such considerations would lead one to expect that the variables represented by indexes IV and V do not play much of a role in the genesis of female addiction and hence that the families of female addicts are not, on the average, markedly deviant in these respects.

There were only three items which, individually, significantly differentiated the families of the male and female addicts. It was more often the case with the male addicts than with the female that their mothers had unrealistically high or unrealistically low aspirations for them in their early childhood; that their mothers had unrealistically high or unrealistically low aspirations for them in later childhood; and that their fathers had unrealistically high or unrealistically low aspirations for them in their early childhood.

Comparative data on the family situations of male and female addicts are given in tables XII-2, XII-3, XII-4, and XII-5. Although we give the parallel figures for the total male and female samples in these tables in addition to those for the Negro subsamples, it should be apparent that, because our female sample is composed mainly of Negroes, the only dependable comparisons are those between the Negro subsamples.

With respect to socioeconomic conditions, the family situations of male and female Negro addicts are essentially similar. It may be recalled from Chapter V that the Negro male addicts are the most deprived among the male addicts; the female Negro addicts match them in degree of deprivation. This is evident when we consider the conditions of housing, family income, and regularity of employment of the family breadwinner. On the composite measure of socioeconomic status, however, the females seem to be at a greater disadvantage.

TABLE XII-2   *Socioeconomic Status of the Male and Female Adolescent Opiate Addicts*

	ALL PATIENTS		NEGRO PATIENTS ALONE	
	MALE	FEMALE	MALE	FEMALE
HOUSING				
Satisfactory	16 (55%)	9 (43%)	3 (33%)	6 (35%)
Marginal	8 (28%)	7 (33%)	4 (44%)	7 (41%)
Unsatisfactory	5 (17%)	5 (24%)	2 (22%)	4 (24%)
Data not available	1	1	1	1
INCOME				
Adequate	18 (64%)	8 (36%)	4 (44%)	7 (38%)
Marginal	7 (25%)	8 (36%)	4 (44%)	6 (33%)
On welfare	3 (11%)	6 (27%)	1 (11%)	5 (28%)
Data not available	2		1	
EMPLOYMENT OF BREADWINNER				
Regular	20 (66%)	12 (55%)	6 (60%)	10 (56%)
Irregular	7 (23%)	3 (14%)	4 (40%)	2 (11%)
Unemployed	3 (10%)	7 (32%)	0	6 (33%)

The family integration of the male and female addicts does not differ. However, when we look at the family integration controlling for ethnic background, we note that Negro female addicts tended to come from better integrated families than did the male addicts, a finding consistent with that reported above with regard to our fourth index in the extended-family–background study, i.e., female addicts came from families with more realistic middle-class orientation than did male addicts.

Family deviance with respect to health problems and social maladaptation was no more frequent among the female than the male samples, for the total sample or for any ethnic group, except that the parents of the Negro female addicts more frequently had alcoholism problems (50 per cent) than did the parents of Negro male addicts (30 per cent)—a difference which, however, in view of the small sample sizes, is not statistically significant and which is offset by small differences favoring the males in other categories of deviance.

Finally, it may be of interest to note the neighborhood distribution of the female addict. The patients and the families we studied lived in those areas of the city where opiate use was most prevalent. In fact,

TABLE XII-3   *A Composite Measure of Socio-economic Status of Present Parental Home*

	ALL PATIENTS		NEGRO PATIENTS ALONE	
	MALE	FEMALE	MALE	FEMALE
Optimal (housing satisfactory, income adequate, regular employment)	13 (43%)	4 (18%)	2 (20%)	3 (17%)
Fair (one step lower than optimal in one of the three areas, e.g., housing marginal, optimal in the other two)	5 (17%)	4 (18%)	3 (30%)	4 (22%)
Poor (one step lower than optimal in two of the three areas, optimal in the third)	2 (7%)	3 (14%)	1 (10%)	2 (11%)
Very poor (other than above)*	10 (33%)	11 (50%)	4 (40%)	9 (50%)

* The cases with missing data noted in Table XII-2 clearly belong in this category regardless of the status of the missing items.

this generalization is accurate for all female patients ever admitted to Riverside Hospital. Like the male adolescent opiate addicts, they came from those areas of the city which are least suitable for living—areas of inadequate housing, of the highest population density, of maximum unemployment, and of familial disorganization. Though they resided in these settings, their families were no worse off on the whole than other families in the same communities. The heterogeneity in the social char-

TABLE XII-4   *Family Integration of Male and
Female Adolescent Opiate Addicts*

	ALL PATIENTS		NEGRO PATIENTS ALONE	
	MALE	FEMALE	MALE	FEMALE
Optimal (parents together in an apparently stable relationship)	14 (47%)	9 (41%)	2 (20%)	8 (44%)
Fair (parents separated but living, both parents available to patient)	3 (10%)	2 (9%)	2 (20%)	2 (11%)
Poor (only one parent available)	13 (43%)	11 (50%)	6 (60%)	8 (44%)

acteristics of their families again suggests that personally experienced poverty or low status were neither necessary nor outstanding factors in their addiction, though the prevalence of poverty and low-status families in the community could not but unfavorably affect their development and relationships. We remind the reader that, though the "ecological" pattern of adolescent opiate addiction is not related in a simple way to the vulnerability of any individual to becoming an addict, it is unquestionably related to the prevalence of the problem.

In summary, we have found that female adolescent opiate addicts had serious difficulties in their lives prior to becoming addicts or beginning to use drugs—difficulties expressed in disturbed relationships and behavior in school, at work, and with their families. They began to use drugs in the context of serious maladjustment, into which they had limited insight. They were most often introduced to heroin by their female peers, who were ostensibly reluctant to involve them in opiate use; they were not introduced to heroin by older men seeking to "enslave" them. The prevalent conscious motive for their initial use was "curiosity." They were not naïve as to the personal or legal consequences of opiate addiction in our society. They supported their habits through a variety of means, of which the most common were living with a male addict-pusher and taking advantage of the confidence of friends or relatives.

Hospitalization was initiated through external forces, usually through

TABLE XII-5   *Health Problems and Social Mal-*
               adaptation in the Present Family
               Situation

	ALL PATIENTS		NEGRO PATIENTS ALONE	
	MALE	FEMALE	MALE	FEMALE
Optimal (none)	14 (47%)	9 (41%)	3 (30%)	7 (39%)
Less than optimal (any of the following: mental illness, physical illness, alcoholism, drug addiction, criminality)	16 (53%)	13 (59%)	7 (70%)	11 (61%)

being arrested. Once in the hospital, they usually began to demand their
release or accepted a stay in the hospital in a passive-dependent attitude. They had no insight as to their need for psychotherapy and only
minimally accepted their need for further education, vocational training,
or placement. Their behavior in the hospital as a group was conspicuously, rather than quietly, nonconforming.

They lived in neighborhoods that we found to be high-drug-use areas
for teen-aged boys. Their families resembled the families of the male
adolescent addicts, in terms both of their life-long family situations and
their current familial environments, the notable exceptions being that
indexes of unrealistic aspirations for the children and distrust of major
social institutions were found to be lower for the families of the girl
than of the boy addicts. There is thus reason to believe that the female
adolescent opiate addict developed her difficulties in social adaptation
and her psychopathology through immersion—or at least while immersed—in a malignant familial environment.

STATISTICAL FOOTNOTE

a These differences are significant at the .05 level. We must point out that
such small samples as we worked with here can verify only the grossest differences. There may be more points of difference than these data indicate.

PART
2

WHAT TO DO?

XIII

Some Matters of Perspective (I)

Given a society without unlimited resources, the amount of money and effort that can be invested in an attempt to cope with a problem depends on how grave it is in comparison to other problems which also demand money and effort. As a first approximation of the justifiable investment, we might allocate the available resources proportionately to the assessment of the gravity of the problems, subject, of course, to the qualification that no problem will be assigned a larger share of the resources than is necessary to cope with it.

It is likely that the resources thus allocated to some problems will be less than adequate. We must then confront the question of whether the returns to be expected from an inadequate investment justify any investment at all. That is, the returns are not necessarily proportionate to the size of an investment, and the expected returns from an inadequate one may be so disproportionately small, either in absolute terms or in relation to the magnitude of the desired effect, that a sound, businesslike approach would compel us to concede failure in advance. We may, of course, hope that the problem will, in time, solve itself, as many problems do; but, in any case, we would delete such problems from our list and either reallocate the available resources to the remaining problems or simply reduce the over-all expenditure.

Let us, for the sake of argument, assume that drug addiction poses such a problem. The per-patient cost of running a hospital facility for teen-aged addicts such as Riverside Hospital is extremely high (especially if we were to include the cost of the special school which is part of the total operation), and the percentage of patients who are "cured" (i.e., who will not relapse) on discharge is extremely small.[1] To a hard-headed businessman, such a state of affairs represents a compelling argument that society must be prepared to live with the problem and to permit the addicts to die with it, without any wastage of society's precious resources.

Such economics are simple. The issue, however, is not quite so simple. There are returns from an investment other than the direct payoff. If the purpose is firm enough, there is the pleasure of tilting at windmills, the excitement of mobilizing one's puny resources against the challenge of seemingly hopeless odds. There is the sure knowledge that the record of human progress is, in large measure, a history of setbacks to the apparently impossible. There is the sense of vitality that comes with the tightening of belts to make available greater resources in the service of dedicated purpose; resources do not come in fixed quantities, but in proportion to the intensity of the will that deploys them. There is the uplift that comes, even in defeat, from the assurance that one has striven nobly and given of one's utmost in the service of a cause one believes in, even though one may have judged the initial entrance to the lists to have been foolhardy.

Conversely, there is the sheer debilitating consequence of a society's readiness to bow to its vision of the dreadful inevitable or to shape its every will according to the decisions of carefully computed coefficients

---

[1] Cf. M. A. Alksne, R. E. Trussel, J. Ellinson, and S. Patrick, "A Follow-up Study of Treated Adolescent Narcotics Users" (Columbia University School of Public Health and Administrative Medicine, 1959). In an earlier study of our own, we had found that twenty-nine of thirty selected patients on whom we followed up after discharge were back on drugs within six months, and the thirtieth had entered the army during this interval, so that we were unable to keep track of him. Actually, such evaluation is hardly to be taken as conclusive, even in its own terms. Some psychiatric experience suggests that patients become more amenable to psychotherapy after several discharges. No critical study of this has, however, been done. It is also known that some addicts (and this is also true of alcoholics) apparently spontaneously stop using drugs at some time during their maturity (the alcoholics somewhat later than the opiate addicts). Again, no critical study has been done of the selective factors involved in these remissions, and it is not known whether early hospitalization experience, with or without efforts at psychotherapy, increases, decreases, or leaves unaffected the likelihood of later remission. That is, the payoff on hospitalization may not be detectable until long after discharge.

of risk.[2] Surely, a society that dares not defy the impossible and that sets numerical values to the lives and essential dignities of human beings is, at least, sick, if not positively moribund. No viable society dares, save under extraordinary circumstances, to set dollars-and-cents or number-of-man-hours values on the lives and dignities of identifiable sectors of its population. Lives may only be balanced against more lives, the dignities of the few against the dignities of the many and even this kind of balancing may only be countenanced in the context of explicit, time-tested governing values and within the limitations of full regard for due process.

Not even the most calloused budget-balancer or meeter-of-payrolls, placed in a position of high public trust, dares abandon human beings to their misery in undissimulated dollars-and-cents terms. If he does make a decision that is, in effect, one of abandonment, the human consequences of this decision are entirely evaded (that is, one talks about anything but the people involved; e.g., "The trampled park grass is a blight on our city"); rationalized in high-sounding terms (e.g., "They will, in the long run, develop greater maturity, responsibility, and happiness if they are compelled to work out their problems by themselves"); justified as proper punitive measures (e.g., "The mother with one illegitimate child may be forgiven her transgression and must be helped; but, if the offense is repeated, she has to be taught to mend her ways");

---

[2] The coefficient of risk may be described as the ratio of the product of the net worth of an outcome and the probability of achieving it to the product of the net cost of an alternative outcome and the probability of the latter. Thus, if one stands to win $100 and sets the worth of the pleasure of the play and of winning at $50, the net worth of success is $150. Similarly, if one must invest $10 to stand a chance of winning the $100 and he sets the pleasure of the play at $5 and the negative worth of the frustration of losing at $15, the net cost of failure is $10 + 15 − 5 = $20. If, now, the probability of winning is 1 in 5 and the probability of losing is 4 in 5, the coefficient of risk is

$$(150 \times 1/5) / (20 \times 4/5) = 30/16.$$

Since the ratio is greater than one, the game is worthwhile and, if the calculation has not taken all of the pleasure out of the game, one should join the play if he is fortunate enough to encounter such opportunities. Both the concept and the illustration have been oversimplified, inasmuch as provision has only been made for two discrete, mutually disjunctive, and collectively exhaustive alternatives. The reasoning employed can, however, be adapted to much more difficult decision situations. For instance, if there are many discrete alternative outcomes, the coefficient can be defined as the ratio of the sum of the worth-probability products for each favorable outcome to the sum of the corresponding products for each unfavorable outcome.

or supported by some combination of such maneuvers (as, in the last instance, resolutely ignoring the question of what happens to the innocent second or third out-of-wedlock child).

In practice, the degree of investment in a problem of society will be determined by a more-or-less (mostly less) scientific weighting of each need in the total array of competing social needs (the weights being determined, on the one hand, by some kind of scaling of the intensities of the needs and an estimate of the probable effectiveness of the uncommitted resources that can be brought to bear and, on the other hand, by the evocation of the sense of challenge and the arousal of the social conscience). The process is, in essence, a rational one, involving as it does a balancing of competing considerations; but the outcome is not necessarily the most valid.

The scaling of the intensity of competing needs is typically a matter of the number and location of voices raised, of who can shout the loudest (and get the maximum amplification for his voice through the media of communication) and into the most strategically located ears, rather than one of careful diagnosis. The assessment of the probability of success typically rests only on crude impressions gained in the course of experience, and there often is no directly relevant experience on which to base estimates of the probable effectiveness of alternatives of action.

And, alas, the spirit of high adventure that is ready to take on all comers in a challenging-enough cause and the social conscience that can enlist such a spirit are all-too-readily lulled by superficial activities that are known to be ineffective, but that generate the illusion that society is trying to meet its obligations and that the social conscience is functioning. Or the spirit of high adventure and the social conscience are all-too-readily aborted by the failure to recognize genuine suffering, by the mistaking of some reactions to suffering as wickedness, and by high-sounding formulas that seem to be compelling as long as one does not come into proximity with the areas of suffering. The fortunate can live at peace with themselves, secure in the fiction that that which needs to be done is being done, perhaps even being done to excess.

The problem of drug addiction is a case in point. The gravity of the problem has, to our minds, been grossly misassessed, not so much in terms of the investment in it as in terms of the gains which the investment is calculated to achieve. Judging from the deployment of efforts, from policies adopted, from the emphases and conclusions of legislative commissions of inquiry, from statements made by responsible individuals in testimony before such commissions of inquiry and in the public media of information, the major goal is to *suppress* the problem, rather than to deal with its causes.

Take one trifling illustration. A highly knowledgeable physician in this field, when asked about the possibility of rehabilitating addicts while maintaining them on drugs, responded that it was his responsibility as a physician "to cure people, not to keep them sick." Knowing something of the background of this man, it is difficult for us to believe that he meant what he said; we must rather assume that he was carried away by the atmosphere of the inquiry. Certainly, no physician would express a similar attitude with regard to diabetic patients, who must be maintained on insulin or on one or another of the recently developed substitutes. Nor would any physician refuse to prescribe a prosthetic device for a physically disabled patient on the ground that such a device maintains the patient with his disability and is in no way calculated to cure him. We are not at the moment concerned with the issue of whether addicts can or should be rehabilitated while maintaining them on drugs; we are concerned with the ease with which knowledgeable and sensible people yield to the forces of unreason in the context of the drug-addiction problem.

It is as though opiate addiction were per se so horrible and menacing an evil that one hardly dares entertain any thought but that of eradicating it by whatever means come to hand. Yet opiate addiction is, in itself, neither so horrible nor so menacing. In Chapter XIV, we shall develop the thesis that by far the most horrible consequences, personally and socially, are directly traceable to its *de facto* illegality,[3] and we shall note, in passing, that the incontinent use of opiates is far less dangerous, both personally and socially, than that of alcohol, a drug the use of which has also been the object of a now-largely-abandoned repressive approach. We are not, of course, saying that drug addiction is a good thing, and we do regard its occurrence as a social problem.

The most rational roots of the image of opiate addiction as a menace are the beliefs that it is a virulently contagious disease and that it is a major cause of crime. Let us first consider the issue of crime. There can be no question but that large proportions of metropolitan-origin

[3] It will be recalled that it is the possession of the drug which is illegal, not its use.

jail and prison populations are or have been drug-users; many of these are certainly addicts, although no estimate can be made at this time of how many would meet some specified criterion of drug addiction narrower in scope than "having a history of drug use." Assume the worst, that all who have been called "addicts" actually are addicts in the worst sense of the term. Would this prove that addiction is a major cause of crime? Not at all.

To begin with, for the present purpose, we cannot count those who are in prisons or jails for direct violation of the narcotics laws. The question at issue is not whether violations of these laws occur, but whether those who violate these laws also commit other kinds of crime. Of those left, we must still discount those who would be in prison or jail even if they were not addicts, including those whose history of addiction is related to their inclination to violate the law rather than vice versa. Of those left after this second subtraction, we must again discount those who would not have committed other crimes and who would not have been led into a life of crime if they had had legal access to narcotics under controlled conditions. How many addicts are then left whose addiction may plausibly be interpreted as a significant causal contributor to their crimes? We do not know. It may, however, be recalled that in Chapter III we showed that, for the period 1949–1952, there was no increase in crimes committed by boys in their later teens in neighborhoods of increasing drug use in Manhattan, although the areas of highest drug use did show a change in the relative incidences of various types of crime.

In brief, we know of no good reason to believe that the use of narcotics per se increases the absolute volume of crime. Its relationship to crime is complex, but not of a kind that justifies panic or the invocation of the rule of "clear and present danger."

Is addiction a virulently contagious disease? All of the evidence that we have and that we have reviewed in Part One indicates that it is not. The spread of drug use is associated with human misery, not with any intrinsic contagiousness. To be sure, where misery is widespread and narcotics are freely available, addiction may be said in a sense to be contagious, that is, to individuals whose resistance is extremely low. Even so, there was only one census tract (a few square blocks) in New York City where as many as 10 per cent of the late-teen-aged boys became involved, in one way or another, with narcotics in the course of a four-year period.[4] Ninety per cent of the boys did not become noticeably involved with narcotics in the four-year period. Even if we were to interpret all of the cases in the tract as due to contagion, the degree of contagion is obviously limited.

Does this constitute a threat of a contagion that threatens to engulf society? Additional perspective may be provided by statistics from an earlier period. In 1915, the most responsible estimate[5] sets the total number of addicts in the United States at somewhat less than 215,000. This was the year that the Harrison Act went into effect and some years before any serious efforts at enforcement had begun. Up to this time, with the minor exception of smoking opium, opiates could be obtained without prescription at any apothecary's shop. Opiates in significant dosages were common ingredients of widely used proprietary medications. Many physicians prescribed opiates as readily and as lavishly as contemporary physicians prescribe recently developed tranquilizers and other "wonder drugs." If ever the availability of narcotics could threaten a plague, this was the period; and alarmists were numbering addicts in the millions. Against this background, 215,000 addicts does not sound quite so bad as it otherwise might.

Moreover, even this figure must have been based on a fairly loose usage of the term "addicts." The same study reports that, by 1922, a year or two after fairly vigorous efforts at enforcement of the Harrison Act had begun, the number of addicts had declined to about 110,000. In other words, even if one were to make the obviously unreasonable and far-fetched assumption that, for some mysterious reason, there was not a single new case in this entire period in all of the United States, almost half the addicts of 1915 had died or were cured in less than ten years. The figure is simply not credible of addicts with full-blown

[4] This was a tract with an exceptionally small over-all number of boys in the age range under study. Because of the small denominator, a slightly higher or lower detection rate than usual would markedly affect the drug rate. Since this is an extremely deviant high-rate tract, it is likely that the high drug rate is in part due to an unusually high detection rate. Assuming that failures in detection are unlikely in the most seriously involved cases, it is not unlikely that an unusually high detection rate means that an exceptionally high proportion of less seriously involved cases were caught. In other words, the extremely high drug rate in the census tract referred to above may well exaggerate the true situation.

[5] Lawrence Kolb and A. G. Du Mez, "The Prevalence and Trend of Drug Addiction in the United States and Factors Influencing It," *Public Health Reports,* 39 (1924), 1179–1204.

cravings. It is to be noted, moreover, that at no time subsequent to the passage of the Harrison Act or to the beginnings of its vigorous enforcement was there any evidence of an epidemic of serious withdrawal sickness (and, probably because of the customary dosage levels, the withdrawal syndromes of that period were typically far more severe than they are today), of hordes of desperate addicts descending on beleaguered physicians and pharmacists, of a tremendous upsurge of illegal entry into pharmacies and physicians' offices, or of vast numbers of "dope fiends" turning to fanatical criminal efforts to satisfy their suddenly illicit cravings.

No, drug addiction is not so grave a menace that we can hardly entertain any thought but that of exterminating it. Not, that is, unless we were to anticipate an enormous expansion in human misery and a sense of hopelessness at being able to do anything about the misery; with respect to such a prospect, alarm about the possible spread of drug addiction would seem to be misdirected.

Let us, however, for the sake of argument, assume that the only conceivable approach to the problem of drug addiction is the suppression of traffic in narcotics. On this assumption, is it a good business practice to make the effort? Or would it be sounder to direct the resources that would be utilized in such an effort into efforts to ameliorate other social ills or even not to mobilize the resources at all so that we may achieve the general benefits of a somewhat lessened tax burden?

The issue thus raised is one of the probable effectiveness of measures that may be taken to suppress the traffic in narcotics. Highly relevant here is the economic law of supply and demand. Given large numbers of addicts, we start with a fairly high level of demand. The effectiveness of law enforcement measures lowers the supply. The selling price, and hence the potential level of profit that accompanies the successful evasion or corruption of law enforcement efforts, rises. To the unprincipled traffickers in narcotics, this counterbalances the increased risk and justifies an increased countermobilization effort to evade and corrupt the law enforcement efforts and to increase the market by expanding the number of addicts. The investment in law enforcement then rises, the counterinvestment goes up, and the vicious cycle rolls merrily along. There are, of course, ups and downs along the way—the ups being hailed by those who believe in the law enforcement approach as evidence of the effectiveness of the approach and the downs as evidence of the need for increased effort.

The suppression approach is, of course, not simply one of increasing the number of police officers devoted to catching offenders. It also includes a demand for increasing police powers (which always carries with it increased infringement of the guaranteed constitutional liberties) and increasingly severe penalties (with special emphasis on the death penalty, the exaction of which is not only conventionally considered the supreme deterrent, but is also so much more economical than long prison terms).

It is, however, only a tribute to the integrity of our courts that judges, confronted by the misery involved in individual cases, become extremely reluctant to impose the most severe available penalties and that, the more severe the minimum penalties and the more dictatorial the police powers, the more the judges lean over backward in imposing the traditional burden of proof on the prosecuting attorneys. In other words, the more severe these measures, the more difficult it becomes to obtain convictions. Yet it may be taken as axiomatic that the effectiveness of the punitive aspects of law enforcement depends on three factors: the severity of the punishment, its immediacy, and its certainty. If an increase in one of these factors is offset by a decrease in another, then where are we?

There is another aspect of the law enforcement approach to narcotics which tends to be self-defeating. The structure of the illegal narcotics business is that of a pyramid, or a series of interlocking pyramids resting on the same base. At the bottom of this structure and constituting the vast majority of individuals involved in the business are the addict-pushers. These are usually people impelled to narcotics by their own uncontrollable cravings who would otherwise be unable to support their habit. Consider an enforcement unit which has to justify its existence in the results it can show. Going after higher levels of the narcotics business pyramid, to say nothing of the apex or apexes, is a long, hazardous, and at best uncertain affair. To be sure, a monthly raid or so, netting a large supply of more-or-less pure heroin (measured in ounces or pounds, but impressively valued on the illegal market in thousands or even millions of dollars) and a half-dozen or so culprits is assured of its half-column or so in the daily press (but, save when there is a paucity of other news, there is no assurance of a mention in radio or television newscasts). Even so, an annual record of a few score convictions can hardly be impressive when violators of the law are numbered in the thousands.

By contrast, the addict-pusher is a sure bet. All that is needed is to keep an eye on him once he has been released from serving his sentence and, sooner or later, usually sooner, he will be caught selling or at least in possession. This poor wretch does not command the services of high-priced legal talent, and the case is quickly processed through the courts with a minimum of waste of police time. The result is an impressively large record of arrests and convictions for the individual officer and for the enforcement unit as a whole. Inevitably, a large share of the activities of the enforcement unit goes into this kind of revolving-door enterprise—a revolving door for the police as well as for the addict. It is our impression that being caught in a revolving door is not an effective way of going somewhere.

The latest development in the approach that takes as its central goal the suppression of the evil is that of compulsory therapy. The idea is to sentence addicts to indefinite terms of psychotherapy in prisons-turned-hospitals, discharge being contingent on a certificate of cure. Judges, it is expected, should not be reluctant to hand out such sentences, since they are for the benefit of the prisoner-turned-patient. Hardly any thought is given to the question of where the needed therapeutic personnel are to be recruited. Even less thought is given to the question of whether psychotherapy is something that can be administered by force. Or to the question of whether even the willing addict patient can benefit from continuous psychotherapy uninterrupted by bouts with the responsibilities and temptations of freedom. Or to the implications of releasing the cured patient to the very conditions in which he succumbed in the first place. Or, for that matter, to the meaning of "cure."

It may be inferred that we do not believe that this method of dealing with the problem has great likelihood of achieving even its own professed goals. No one seems to have yet thought of the possibilities of setting aside sizable territories—separate ones for males and females, of course—bounded by concrete walls and surrounded by shark-infested moats. Anyone suspected of illegal involvement with narcotics could be dropped into such a territory by parachute, as could all of the necessities and comforts of living, including large supplies of tranquilizers (other than heroin, of course) and anaphrodisiacs. Medical care could be provided easily through the physician and nurse addicts. These areas could be patrolled by automated radar and target-finding missile bases to prevent the intrusion of unauthorized aircraft. We could then be certain that there would be no possible spread of contagion from within the pale. Who knows but that such a humane procedure might even work, and it might incidentally contribute to the solution of such other social problems as the population explosion. It might even prove comparatively inexpensive and eventually recommend itself for application to sex deviants, multiple offenders, and witches.

Pending the adoption of such a procedure, however, the suppression approach is not good business. But what of the challenge of the problem, the do-or-die attitude, and the social conscience? Great challenge does not emanate from fear, nor do great causes emerge from panic; people who are seen as being led into trouble by their own weak characters and wicked choices do not enlist the social conscience. To be sure, one of the great dangers of addiction is commonly taken to be contagiousness, and it is necessary to protect the good citizens from this menace; but somehow those who do become infected do so of their own volition and because of their willingness to enter into a compact with evil.

We may have exaggerated somewhat. There are people who see the core of human misery at the root of the problem and more who see the misery associated with addiction. There are, consequently, scattered and woefully inadequate efforts to provide help. More and more voices are saying that basically the problem is not one for the police and the criminal courts to solve, that it is only compounded by existing law, and that it is likely to be only more confounded by current proposals to strengthen the law toward the goal of suppression. Few indeed, however, even among these are ready to face the issue of whether drug addiction is itself the ultimate evil. In any case, the great body of aroused public opinion and the bulk of public effort to do something about the problem seems to have foundered in a morass of irrationality. Our reservations are no less with regard to voluntary self-commitment for a prescribed minimum period, an idea that is commonly included in compulsory therapy plans. The considerations involved are exactly the same as those raised in the preceding paragraph, on therapy.

That the basic concern of compulsory therapy plans is suppressive rather than therapeutic and that ideologies of suppression and of therapy do not easily mix is most evident in the qualifications that are generally introduced as to which addicts are to be eligible for compulsory therapy as an alternative to jail sentences. Apart from the restriction that addiction cannot relieve an individual from responsibility for

major crimes, the qualifications generally have the effect of making
the most seriously affected cases ineligible. Thus, there is generally a
limit set on the number of times a patient may avail himself of the
therapeutic alternative, and a self-committed addict who seeks discharge
before his time is up renders himself ineligible forever. It is as if one
were to declare that an easily cured patient is sick, but a hard-to-cure
patient is a scoundrel. A parallel instance would be to rule that a
chronic ulcer patient is eligible for hospitalization only twice (and only
once if he has left the hospital prematurely the first time) and thereafter must seek his own remedies.

XIV

Some Matters of Perspective (II)

In this chapter, we want to set the record straight on a variety of relevant historical, medical, cultural, psychiatric, and pharmacological matters.

What Is a Drug?

"Drug" is not a scientific term. It has its origin, the dictionary tells us, in a misconception. It is derived from the Low German *droge vate,* which means literally dry casks or goods stored dry, and the contemporary meaning developed from a linguistic error; the adjective *droge,* which described the state of the contents, that is, that they were dry, was wrongly taken to be a designation of the contents themselves.

In Goodman and Gilman's textbook of pharmacology,[1] the term is defined as "any chemical agent which affects live protoplasm." The authors comment that "few substances would escape inclusion by this definition," but they attempt no further definition. By intent and implication, they use the word for all the substances used by clinical physicians in the treatment of disease or by researchers in the investigation of disease or the physiology of organisms, whether human, mammalian, or whatever.

Despite the fact that physicians prescribe "drugs," which we com-

[1] L. Goodman and A. Gilman, *The Pharmacological Basis of Therapeutics* (New York: Macmillan, 1941).

monly purchase with toothpaste or household supplies at a "drug-store" from a reputable individual, a graduate pharmacist (Ph.G.) whom we call a "druggist," the predominant associations of the word "drug" emphasize negative, dangerous, or undesirable effects, as "under the influence of drugs" or "he was drugged." Indeed, we have gone along with the popular misuse of the term by using "drug use" and "drug addict" to refer to the subjects of our investigation.

We note the assiduous avoidance of the word "drug" for the great variety of products purchased openly in drug stores, e.g., vitamin pills, analgesics, hormonal preparations, and certain antibiotics, which are sold without prescription and without the name, "drug." In short, what the physician or pharmacologist would term a drug, the layman calls a medicine or remedy, or he evades the issue entirely by identifying his drugs by a common or general pharmaceutical name, e.g., aspirin, vitamin, or hormone.

The only exception that clearly and regularly occurs is in the term "wonder drug," which was used first for the sulfonamides, later for the mold substances (penicillin, Aureomycin, streptomycin, etc.) used in the treatment of bacterial infections, and more recently for the steroid substances (cortisone and other adrenal hormones) used in the treatment of a variety of diseases of the connective tissues (collagen diseases). It is notable that "drug" is acceptable and common where the use of the substance is novel or "wonderful."

We also note that the term "drug-user" is generally pejorative. When an elderly person with chronic pain (e.g., from an inoperable tumor) uses morphine, Demerol, or codeine, he is not regarded as a drug-user; nor are those who regularly use alcohol, coffee, tea, tobacco, insulin, or vitamin-mineral preparations or the person who makes use of the "wonder drugs." The term "drug-user" is applied only to those using substances which are regarded negatively and critically. Furthermore, these negative and critical evaluations are not apparently based on the nature of the chemical agent or on its effects per se.

With so undisciplined a word, it may be well to recall Owen Meredith's warning:[2]

> Words, however, are things; and the man who accords
> To his language the license to outrage his soul,
> Is controll'd by the words he disdains to control.

[2] Owen Meredith, *Lucile,* Part I, Canto II, Stanza 10.

Social Attitudes toward the Use of Chemical Agents

It is easy to lose perspective when we consider the opiate and cannabis drugs as though they had always been negatively sanctioned or as though they were inherently dangerous, even poisonous, substances. In fact, these drugs have not always been regarded this way; on the other hand, not only alcohol but even coffee and tobacco have been proscribed as harmful and undesirable substances. Indeed, there are some remarkable historical and cultural differences in the acceptability and use of both coffee and tobacco which indicate how sanctions on drug use are related to the putative effects of the drug or to the meanings of the substance for the community (in the sociological sense of this word).

We take our coffee for granted, as though it had always been regarded as a desirable substance, fitting and proper for use by adolescent and adult males and females, at breakfast and coffee break, in coffee houses, and after dinner. Coffee is regarded as a wholesome dietary substance for which a great variety of cooking utensils, serving dishes, and tables are designed and widely advertised. This is so even though persons report dependency on coffee ("I don't feel really right until I have my morning cup of coffee"), psychic craving (there are individuals who regularly drink ten or more cups of coffee daily), and adverse physiological effects ranging from diarrhea to insomnia (for which a large industry assiduously removes the caffeine while retaining the flavor—remember Mr. Coffee Nerves).

The first recorded use of coffee was by the Arabian physician Avicenna about 1000 A.D. Most likely, its use by Near Eastern peoples long precedes this date. There is a legend that the leader of a Mohammedan cloister learned from his herdsmen that goats became frisky and wakeful after eating the beans of a certain plant; he prepared a drink from these beans in order to keep himself and his dervishes awake when they had to conduct prayers throughout the entire night. However, by the sixteenth century, there were religious controversies over coffee in the Moslem world. Some physicians declared it harmful; others vociferously defended it as salutary. Among religious leaders, it was regarded as an intoxicant analogous to alcohol and therefore forbidden any devout Moslem. Indeed, if a man requested his wife to serve him coffee, it was regarded as legal basis for a divorce.

In Europe, by the end of the eighteenth century, coffee was widely accepted, though only after a long history of opposition to its use. In

in this hole; then the miscreant was ridden about on an ass to be publicly mocked. In Russia, Peter the Great abolished the death penalty for smoking (which had been supplemented by the appropriation, by the state, of the property of persons in the tobacco business). At the same time, he sold to the English for 15,000 pounds sterling the privilege of exporting tobacco to Russia.

King James I of England attributed many of the evils of mankind to tobacco. However, like the enlightened Peter, he learned that his disapproval of tobacco could have its most effective public expression by taxing it. This was an excellent source of revenue. A similar moral can be drawn from our own history; since we repealed the Eighteenth Amendment, we have taxed liquor heavily.[5]

Turning from history to sociology, we note that the attitudes toward the use of any drug—or, in fact, of any dietary entity—range from prescription to proscription; that these attitudes are related to differences in the social structure, e.g., to age group, sex, and social role; and that the attitudes are integrated with certain social functions, e.g., rituals, medical or therapeutic settings, and certain informal group interactions.

Many groups in contemporary America insist that all members, including children, have at least a sip of wine or brandy on festive or religious occasions. Jews drink in this fashion at Passover, on Sabbath eve, and the high holidays. Catholics and some Protestant sects sip wine at Communion. Most ethnic groups in this country encourage alcohol-drinking among all participating adults at weddings, religious confirmations, and similar family feasts. Many groups virtually prescribe alcohol-drinking at some social gatherings, e.g., the cocktail party and the wake. The use of table wine or beer is proscribed in this country for most children at least up to adolescence, though in France (where there probably is a serious alcoholism problem)[6] and in Italy (where there probably is not) children take table wine from early childhood.[7]

In the United States and many European countries, drunkenness is regarded as a vice or weakness. The ideal is to drink as much or more than the next person without becoming visibly intoxicated; the goal is

[5] The preceding historical and ethnological details are also from Lewin, *op. cit.*, pp. 305–335.

[6] G. Mouchot, "Letter from France," in R. G. McCarthy, ed., *Drinking and Intoxication* (Glencoe, Ill.: The Free Press, 1959).

[7] G. Lolli, *Social Drinking* (Cleveland and New York: World Publishing Co., 1960).

to "hold" your liquor. This is in remarkable contrast to the majority of primitive peoples, who take alcoholic beverages to become as drunk as they can as quickly as possible.[8]

Sanctions and Science

Our survey indicated that there have been extreme sanctions against the use of certain substances which are now in common usage. These sanctions are hardly justified by the inherent or unconditional harmfulness of the substance. Demonstrable harmfulness is, at best, a supplementary basis for legal sanctions; if invoked at all, it is as secondary argument. There is no need to invoke moral sanctions against the public sale of arsenic and strychnine. They are identified as toxic substances, and measures are taken to prevent their misuse and to make publicly available means for coping with and preventing their accidental, malicious, or careless use. On the other hand, some demonstrably harmful drugs are used freely.

Alcohol is a dangerous substance. Used excessively—no rarity in our civilization—it is a pathogenic factor in the etiology of cirrhosis of the liver, industrial absenteeism and accidents, traffic fatalities, and diseases of the central and peripheral nervous systems. There is a growing body of evidence that tobacco, and particularly cigarette-smoking, is pathogenic in or a contributor to the etiology of certain cardiovascular and neoplastic diseases and good evidence that it is a harmful substance for persons with peripheral vascular disease. However, it is unlikely that either alcohol (again) or tobacco (ever) will be prohibited or federally controlled in this country. Many patent medicines, vitamins, hormones (in so-called beauty preparations), cathartics, analgesics, stimulants, sedatives, and the like are not difficult to obtain without prescription by a physician. Since most of the bodily troubles of mankind, the aches and pains, insomnia, indigestion, skin discomforts, menstrual pains, constipation, and so on are not usually based on demonstrable organic disease, not much harm is done by the substances per se. However, harmful temporizing with malignant tumors, endocrine disturbances, chronic infections, and serious emotional disturbances through legally permissive self-diagnosis and self-medication has had dangerous consequences.

[8] Donald Horton, "The Functions of Alcohol in Primitive Societies," in *Alcohol, Science, and Society* (New Haven: Quarterly Journal of Studies on Alcohol, 1957).

The permissive use of certain drugs known to have harmful effects, like the sanctions against the use of other drugs, is not based on objective scientific grounds, other than that the substance is not very harmful in itself as it is "intended" to be or is customarily used. Conversely, we are quite aware of the fact that positive steps benefiting the health and welfare of the public are hindered by antiscientific considerations, e.g., the current social issues of fluoridation of public water supplies, establishment of medically sound commitment procedures to state hospitals, reasonable divorce laws, and the like.

In review, the basis for sanctions is predominantly attitudinal-moral; when culture and custom support the use of a substance, considerations of this substance's harmfulness are remarkably ineffective. When culture and custom proscribe the use of a substance, arguments based on scientific evidence are far from effective.

Drugs Have Many Functions and Effects

The textbooks of pharmacology make elaborate distinctions between classes of drugs in accordance with their major uses or pharmacological characteristics. A vast number of drugs intended for other purposes may nevertheless be used in one way or another for psychic satisfaction, for the relief of tension or distress, or for other more limited medical function. For example, carbon tetrachloride is used in the treatment of certain types of intestinal worm; it is also a dangerous source of intoxication, dangerous because of its effects on the kidneys and liver. Although penicillin has no direct effect on the central nervous system, the anxiety associated with pneumonia is alleviated as the bacterial infection is controlled. Some cathartics act primarily by irritant stimulation of the colon; fecal evacuation per se is a form of pleasure which is not (yet) widely advertised in uneuphemistic terms, but we know that for some individuals the function of the bowels is related to both pleasure and conflict. The widespread use of cathartic medicines for children is largely based on the psychic needs of parents and only to a trifling extent on the child's "defective" bowel function. In one way or another, a drug may attain psychological meanings and effects entirely unrelated to its explicit or intended use. Patients may, for instance, demand antibiotics for minor virus infections for which they are not indicated.

On the other hand, there are drugs which are used for their effects on mood, ideation, affect, feeling, anxiety, pain, or tension. These drugs may be used in distressing organic diseases which affect the psychic organization; e.g., in acute coronary thrombosis, morphine is used to combat the pain and anxiety (not infrequently bordering on panic) associated with the illness. In other circumstances, these drugs are used outside the context of distressing organic disease for the effects of the drug on the psychic organization itself. Since the pharmacology of these drugs is so varied, it is difficult to categorize them with any of the conventional pharmaceutical names. We suggest that this growing class of drugs (alcohol, the xanthines, cannabis, mescaline, cocaine, amphetamine, the barbiturates, Thorazine, Serpasil, lysergic acid, and so forth) be called "psychic modifiers."

They are of particular pharmacological and psychiatric interest because their effects as psychic modifiers are neither consistent nor universal, whereas their effects in the laboratory on limited tissues or organs may be quite specific and consistent. Morphine has quite consistent effects on smooth muscle in the gastrointestinal tract, on pupillary contraction, and on respiration. Nicotine is an autonomic blocking agent and also blocks the neuromuscular junction of skeletal muscle, having a curare-like action which may lead to respiratory failure. Alcohol is an irritant to the gastric mucosa and a depressant of the central nervous system, probably impeding the transmission of impulses across the synapses of the brain cells, particularly of the cortex.[9] However, when we observe the response of the whole person to such commonly used psychic modifiers as cannabis, alcohol, and the opiates, we note that there are remarkable individual and cultural differences in the responses to these substances. The next two sections report some of the cultural and experimental psychopharmacological data relevant to this point.

Cultural Setting and Drug Effects

Two of the most common and widely used psychic modifiers are cannabis and alcohol. The cannabis drugs are prepared from the flowering tops, leaves, seeds, and stems of the hemp plant, *cannabis sativa*. This may be made into cigarettes (sometimes mixed with tobacco), eaten as a confection prepared with honey, or drunk as a watery or alcoholic solution. Names for various preparations from this plant are legion. It is best known in the United States as marijuana or by a number of

[9] Actually, the neuropharmacology of alcohol is far more complex, but the details are not relevant here.

slang terms. Descriptions of the effects of the cannabis drugs are quite varied, owing in part to the concentration of the active principle in different specimens of the plant and different degrees of extraction of the active principle in accordance with the method of preparation and in part to the effects of the drugs with which it may be taken, e.g., alcohol. The varied means for fermentation and distillation of sugar, starch, grains, or fruits are the basic means of preparation of ethyl alcohol, are well known, and need not be discussed here.

In India, an infusion of the stems and the leaves of the hemp plant (bhang) is used by Brahmans, who, according to Carstairs,[10] find a "modicum of bhang to be helpful . . . in their practice of devoting some minutes or hours every day to sitting in a state of abstraction and prayer." Among the Brahman priesthood, large quantities of bhang may be taken to facilitate entering devotional trances. Although they appear drunk—their coordination and gait are grossly impaired, and their orientation in time and place is disturbed—they regard themselves, when under the influence of bhang, as empty of all worldly distractions, concerned only with God. The god Shiva is cited by them as a bhang drinker and as a paragon of the contemplative life. The use of bhang is consecrated to achievement of their contemplative and ascetic ideal, to the practice of severe and prolonged austerity, to the withdrawal of their attention from the distractions of the sensible world. The holy man attempts to go beyond the minutes or hours of abstraction and prayer of the lay Brahman to the point where he exists for hours in an oblivious, inward state.

The Tunisian cannabis-users smoke a preparation called *takrouri;* they smoke it in a quiet room, scented and decorated with flowers and with erotic prints calculated to stimulate vivid ideas and images appropriate to their anticipation of paradise. Though the themes of intoxication differ from those of the Brahmans, like the Brahman, the Tunisian Muslim uses cannabis in the context of his religious beliefs.

Carstairs cites a number of sources and his own experiences to suggest that cannabis leads to feelings of detachment, extreme introspection, loss of volition, and a dreamlike impression of heightened reality. As he describes the cannabis drugs, they are a means to attain renunciation of the active life. He contrasts this to the effects of and the motives for using alcohol, which he describes as a means of releasing sexual and

[10]G. M. Carstairs, "Daru and Bhang: Cultural Factors in the Choice of Intoxicates," *Quarterly Journal of Studies on Alcohol,* 15 (1954), 220–237.

aggressive impulses, of proving or asserting in an exaggerated manner the individual's competence to deal with the problems, fears, and anxieties of life in the tangible outer world. We learn from him that the Brahmans revile *daru,* a potent distilled alcoholic beverage. The Brahman regards the use of alcoholic beverages as "foul, polluting, carnal and destructive to the spark of Godhead which every man carries within him." Carstairs quotes one informant: "The result of eating meat and drinking liquor is that you get filled with passion, rage—and then what happens? The spirit of God flies out from you."

Most North African users of cannabis also use alcohol. In short, there is no pharmacological basis for not mixing these drugs. In the United States, the cannabis user, like his Indian counterpart, typically does not use alcohol, although he does not "revile" alcoholic beverages. That is to say, he uses alcohol if he cannot get cannabis (marijuana). However, when we contrast his cannabis use (in the form of marijuana cigarettes) to the Indian use of bhang, we note that the goals of use, the behavioral effects, the themes of meaning and interpretation, the social behavior, and the setting are all remarkably different. First, marijuana is most often used in a social setting, in a group of users who mutually enjoy the effects of the drug. Second, the intent is to heighten enjoyment of outer experiences, e.g., conversation, listening to or performing music, dancing, joking. Unlike the Brahman priest, whose vocabulary during his intoxication is limited to repeating one of the names of his God, the marijuana devotee laughs, giggles, eats without restraint, tells jokes, participates in sexual relationships, and takes pleasure in the company of both men and women, especially if they are also using marijuana. Third, the effects are interpreted by a marijuana-user as analogous to those of alcohol. He prefers marijuana because the effects are more rapid and "neater"; there is no hangover and no debilitating physical consequences of chronic use.[11]

Thus, the use of cannabis in our society is to attain an experience which, far from renouncing the active life in favor of a contemplative, ascetic ideal, affirms the pleasures of sex, music, food, laughter, and human companionship. Among contemporary American students of drugs and their effects in our society, cannabis is likened to the effects of alcohol,[12] in contrast to the European and Oriental sources cited by

[11] H. S. Becker, "Becoming a Marijuana User," *American Journal of Sociology,* 59 (1953), 235–242.
[12] *Loc. cit.*

Carstairs, which suggest or state that the effects of cannabis and alcohol are almost antithetical.

Wikler has pointed out how carefully one must define the experimental conditions in which the "pharmacologic effects" of a drug are observed.[13] We must add to his remarks the caveat: the cultural setting in which a drug is used is a significant determinant of the effects of the drug as a psychic modifier.

Similar data indicating gross cultural differences in the goals of use, behavioral effects, and themes of meaning and interpretation of alcohol have been reported by Bunzel[14] and Horton.[15] Bunzel described two Central American cultures, both of which used alcoholic beverages in feast-day rituals and to varying degrees in their personal lives. Among the Chichicastanango, feast-day drinking leads to fighting, quarreling, and sexual license—violation of the central norms of their domestic life in which the repressed anger associated with their rigidly patriarchal, patrilineal, and repressive social order gains some outlet, only to be followed by guilt and depression in their subsequent sobriety. Among the Chamula, drinking is part of the everyday life of almost the entire community. From the youngest child to the oldest woman, drinking of *aguardiente*—a potent distilled beverage—is the rule. Drinking is an essential part of their daily social interactions, and drinking to intoxication is the norm. Unlike the Chichicastanango, it is usual for the Chamula to wake up the morning after one of the stupendous drinking bouts a little weak and shaky, but otherwise well and cheerful, ready to laugh at the absurdities of the previous day. There are no complaints of headache or dizziness, no guilt, and no noticeable repression.

Horton has pointed out a remarkable uniformity in the drinking behavior of primitive peoples. In general, they drink to get drunk as quickly as possible, with no emphasis on the taste of the beverage or on the subtle appreciation of mild changes in mood or thinking, e.g., philosophical reflections on man, on his nature, or on the relaxed conviviality which enters so strongly into our own rationalizations for drink. This is remarkably in contrast with the rich variety of group responses to alcoholic beverages among our civilized contemporaries.

We are familiar with social types and groups whose use of alcohol is for social facilitation or ritual; consider the wine-taster or the con-

[13] A. Wikler, *Opiate Addiction* (Springfield, Ill.: Thomas, 1953).

[14] R. Bunzel, "The Role of Alcoholism in Two Central American Cultures," *Psychiatry*, 3 (1940), 361–387.

[15] Horton, *op. cit.*

noisseur of brandy, Scotch whisky, or beer. We are also familiar with such groups as Horton's primitives which drink to excess for the loss of restraints and the acting out of sexual or aggressive impulses with the support of their coparticipants. We are also familiar with the problem drinker whose drinking may be consciously motivated by a wish for social facilitation or group-supported "unrestraint," but who recurrently leaves these motives far behind as he progresses to a degree of intoxication which permits neither social facilitation nor group-structured activities, restrained or unrestrained.

In short, the use of alcohol, however consistently it may act as a depressant (inhibitor) of synaptic transmission, elicits behavior and leads to the expression of motives which are inherent in the user and/or in the social setting of use, and not in the alcohol itself. Even in a single social setting, the cosmopolitan cocktail party, there are remarkably individual reactions to alcoholic beverages, which are not only observed, but actively discussed by the participants. There is the person who becomes sleepy after a few drinks; the melancholy Slavic soul whose grandparents immigrated to this country from Russia sixty years before but who still must become moody or depressed to advertise his heritage; there is the cocktail party lecher, politician, and Indian wrestler; there are those who stop drinking at a point where they anticipate they might misbehave and those who continue to drink to the point where others may be obliged to intervene to stop them from misbehaving. What is remarkable—or commonplace, depending on one's perspective—is the fact that there are also extraordinary differences in response to the opiate drugs.

Individual Responses to Drugs

Though we have no formal anthropological study of the opiate drugs in various cultures, we have another and even more relevant source of data. In the past few years, a number of systematic laboratory studies comparing the effects of some psychic modifiers have been made which indicate that there are remarkable individual differences in reactions to the psychic modifiers in the laboratory and that these differences are related to the personality structure, level of anxiety, type and adequacy of ego controls, and to the presence and type of psychiatric pathology.[16]

The majority of normal subjects, young men ranging in age from

[16] L. Lasagna, J. M. von Felsinger, and H. K. Beecher, "Drug-induced Mood Changes in Man," *Journal of the American Medical Association*, 157 (1955), 1113.

twenty-one to twenty-seven, in controlled studies of response to drugs, reported displeasure or experienced no effects on their moods from initial injection of heroin or morphine. Pleasure was experienced by only the minority of nonaddicts; the typical response was indifference or actual dislike. Those subjects who received second injections of morphine or heroin had essentially the same reactions as they did to their first. There is no evidence that repeating the experience enhances the acceptability or liking of these drugs. Lowering the dosage to levels well below those of clinical practice (i.e., for the relief of pain) increased the proportion of subjects who experienced no effect on their moods. There is no evidence that the use of these drugs in such subclinical dosages enhances the acceptability or liking of the drugs.

Hospitalized men and women, ranging in age from forty-five to eighty-seven, chronically ill with malignant disease or neurological disorder, described their responses to the injections of drugs. Only one-third felt happy (or "happier") after injections of heroin or morphine. Since the same proportion felt happy (or "happier") after the injection of a placebo, there is no evidence that the opiates are inherently euphoriant even for individuals suffering from pain or the distress of chronic illness. Indeed, the use of morphine for relief of pain is rarely followed by euphoria; only three of 150 postoperative patients studied in Beecher's laboratory had genuine euphoria following morphine, although a larger minority felt "pleased" for relief of their pain.

Only about half the sample of hospitalized postaddicts (a term used in the Lexington laboratory to describe subjects in the research wards at Lexington who had been addicted to opiate drugs) reported a pleasurable response to heroin, whereas almost all of such subjects reported pleasant reactions to morphine. Thus, even for postaddicts, morphine is preferred to heroin; heroin's reputation as a superior "euphoriant" is hardly supported by these data. Only those "normal subjects" whose reactions to psychic modifiers differ from those of the majority of their peers (atypical reactors) are likely to regard the sedative effects of morphine or heroin as valuable, desirable, or attractive.

These data indicate that opiates are not inherently attractive, euphoric, or stimulant substances. The danger of addiction to opiates resides in the person, not in the drug.

Despite these findings, the opiate drugs are commonly regarded as seductive substances which should be kept away from the unsuspecting and the innocent, who otherwise, it is feared, would become addicted.

An elaborate system of social controls and sanctions has been constructed for their protection; to what extent these controls and sanctions are effective or useful, to what extent they introduce corollary social problems of equal or greater moment than addiction to opiates, are complex and important questions.

Sanctions and the "Dangerous" Drugs

The League of Nations, the United Nations, and state and federal bodies governing the distribution and use of certain drugs have never found or utilized an adequate, encompassing definition or designation of the drugs they seek to control. Although perfection of definition is hardly a necessary basis for sanctions, whatever definitions have been written have not been applied. The term "addicting" is used largely out of tradition; drugs which are clearly not addicting in the sense of inducing physical dependency—e.g., cannabis and cocaine—are included in their lists. Drugs which are demonstrably dependency-inducing and/or dangerous, with serious withdrawal syndromes—e.g., barbiturates and alcohol—are not. The various regulating bodies have generally fallen back on the term "dangerous" and have specified each drug they regard as such, rather than depending on any general formula, theory, or pharmacological reasoning. But, however accurately the sanctions against the use of certain drugs reflect their inherent "dangerousness," it is clear that these sanctions, once they are imposed, contribute to the danger of any use of the drug outside prescribed settings.

Since the opiates are legally regarded as dangerous drugs, their use is proscribed outside medical settings for the treatment of illness or of the withdrawal syndrome of addicts. In this country, opiates may not be prescribed for the maintenance of addiction, according to the Bureau of Narcotics of the Treasury Department and according to most, though not all, interpretations of the pertinent laws by the Supreme Court.[17] This has far-reaching consequences for the illicit user of opiates.

Since opiates cannot be purchased legally, the addict is forced to purchase an uncontrolled product of dangerously variable concentration and often containing poisonous adulterants. He does not receive in-

[17] William L. Prosser, ed., "The Narcotic Problem," *UCLA Law Review*, 4 (1954). Rufus King, "Narcotic Drug Laws and Enforcement Problems," *Law and Contemporary Problems*, 22 (1957), 113–131.

struction in the hygiene of self-administration and, even if he knows better, is typically compelled to take the drug under circumstances that do not favor sensible precautions. He literally stakes his life every time he takes a dose; death, both of the quick and relatively slow varieties, is tragically common.

If he has previously had access to a private physician, the physician is, more often than not, too terrorized to treat him, even for ailments other than his addiction—a terror of police persecution, not of any direct menace in the behavior of the addict—and shunts him off to the relatively impersonal, understaffed, overcrowded, and underequipped public clinic. Abuses by some physicians have created a condition in which every physician who treats an addict is, in the eyes of the narcotics agents, guilty until proven innocent, and he has some reason to expect continuous harassment once he comes under their scrutiny. In the light of the right of every physician to select his own patients so long as other sources of treatment are available, the Hippocratic oath readily functions, when it comes to addicts, on a sharply sliding scale.

Because the possession of narcotics is illegal, the addict is necessarily in violation of the law. The effect of the illegality is, however, far more extensive. The unconscionably high black market prices place the drug far beyond his capacity for legitimate income. Normal employment becomes meaningless to him. Inevitably, he is driven to the unlawful activities that promise him the income he needs to maintain his habit. If he has had any law-abiding associates, these must be sacrificed to the all-absorbing preoccupation with maintaining his contacts and his standing with his illegal sources of supply. Willy nilly, he becomes a cog in an international criminal business. Sooner or later, he falls into the toils of the law and becomes a marked man. He has stepped onto the merry-go-round which carries him in and out of hospitals, in and out of jails, from degradation to degradation, increasingly enmeshed in the company of the scum of the earth, with nothing to look forward to but the ever-more-blessed relief of narcotized oblivion.

Let us not exaggerate. We are not suggesting that the typical addict would lead a sane, respectable, productive, and responsible life if the drug were legitimately accessible or, for that matter, if he had never had access to the drug in the first place. Our point is that whatever chance he may have had to make something of his life, whatever modicum of human dignity it may have been possible for him to extract from it, virtually disappear once he has become an addict. This is not because of any intrinsic effect of enslavement to the drug, but because he is enslaved to a drug the possession of which and traffic in which is subject to vigorous persecution. By far the worse consequences of addiction are associated with its illegality.

At the same time, the illegality contributes to the reputation of opiates as esoteric, euphoriant substances and lends them the aura of forbidden fruit. The use of opiates in this unsanctioned setting makes it disruptive to the user and to the community. However, the sanctions on opiates were not established with these consequences in mind. They were intended to control the use of the drugs. Why? This is difficult to understand without appreciating the historical context in which this prohibition or limitation of the use of opiate drugs took place.

The Historical Context and Sanctions on Opiates

There are three historic phenomena of particular relevance. First, the temperance movement itself, with its particular but not exclusive emphasis on alcoholic beverages; second, the international conferences intended to cope with the problem of the use of opiates in the Orient; third, the need to protect the public against the patent medicines whose active ingredients were predominantly unlabeled, unidentified opiate drugs.

The prohibition or temperance movement regarded all intoxicants as harmful on moral as well as on medical-social grounds. Though it did not succeed in maintaining prohibition of alcoholic beverages for more than two decades, there evidently was enough popular support for the ideals and opinions of the movement to pass an amendment to the Constitution. The logic and assumptions of this movement have been summarized by Warner in a panel discussion on the temperance movement.[18] From his remarks, we have abstracted three major assumptions of the temperance movement.

First, any substance which is liable to rob a man of his senses and render him foolish, irascible, uncontrollable, or dangerous is unsafe. Second, alcohol offers neither a natural nor a healthy way to achieve happiness or reduce unhappiness; the natural means for achievement are through work, play, socialization, and so forth. Third, the gratifications afforded the moderate user of alcohol are outweighed by the dangers

[18] H. S. Warner, "Philosophy of the Temperance Movement," in *Alcohol, Science, and Society* (New Haven: Quarterly Journal of Studies on Alcohol, 1957).

to society of immoderate use and the fact that, with alcohol available, there will always be incontinent users.

The legality of prohibition of alcoholic beverages (for other than medical, sacramental, mechanical, or scientific purposes) was supported by the Supreme Court, which accepted the "demoralizing effect of drunkenness upon society." The justices agreed that:

> The state has the right to subject those members of society who indulge in the use of such liquors without injury to themselves to deprivation of access to liquor, in order to remove temptation from those whom its use would demoralize. . . . When liquors are taken in excess the injuries are [not] confined to the party offending. . . . The injuries it is true first fall upon him in his health, which the habit undermines, in his morals, which it weakens, and in the self-abasement which it creates. But, as it leads to neglect of business and waste of property and general demoralization, it affects those who are immediately connected with and dependent upon him.[19]

In 1914, the House of Representatives passed the Hobson Amendment, which "proposed to prohibit merely [sic] the sale, manufacture for sale, and transportation for sale of intoxicating liquors." However, it did not receive the required two-thirds vote for passage to the Senate for ratification prior to being voted on in the states in order to become an amendment to the Constitution.

The assumptions of the temperance movement vis-à-vis alcohol and the legal opinions of the Supreme Court are equally applicable as arguments against the use of opiate drugs. Indeed, the same Congress which passed the Hobson Amendment passed the Harrison Act. It is an interesting historical anomaly that the Hobson Amendment could not pass into law without an amendment to the Constitution, whereas the Harrison Act was effectual as a prohibition of opiates solely on the basis of a tax measure and interpretations of rulings of the Treasury Department. In retrospect, it is quite unlikely that there would have been much difficulty in passing an amendment to prohibit or limit the use of opiate drugs, and it is equally unlikely that such an amendement would have been counteramended, as the Eighteenth Amendment was by the Twenty-first.

[19] Quoted in E. B. Dunford, "Moral Aspects of Prohibition," in *Alcohol, Science, and Society* (New Haven: Quarterly Journal of Studies on Alcohol, 1957).

The widespread use of opium by the Chinese, to the economic advantage of the British, and to a lesser degree the American, shipping industries, was regarded not only as immoral, but also as a basis or a strong supporting factor of the lack of material progress and political growth of the Chinese people. Although there are no data of number or percentage of Chinese who used opiates in an addictive manner (in the sense of daily use with development of dependence and tolerance), probably very many did use opium. To what extent this was a consequence of the lack of opportunity for material welfare and personal development and to what extent a cause of these conditions is difficult to say. But, however little the cost of the opiates per dose, any money not utilized for capital development, the development of industry, the improvement of agriculture, and the improvement of the public health drains money from the public welfare of an impoverished population. For a poor country, the widespread use of opiates is an ill-afforded luxury which may not only quell the pains of hunger and soothe the anxiety and sadness of a marginal existence, but may also inhibit or depress the inclination to do something about these conditions. Karl Marx characterized religion as "the opiate of the masses," but in fact opium itself has been and, in certain undeveloped Eastern countries, still is the opiate of the masses.

On the basis of such reasoning, the British House of Commons adopted "a resolution to the effect that 'this house reaffirms its conviction that the Indo-China opium trade is undefensible, and requests the government to bring it to a close.' "[20] American missionaries in the Orient appealed to Pres. Theodore Roosevelt "that the United States take the initiative in obtaining an international agreement to control the use of opium by those governments in whose far eastern territories opium smoking was a problem."[21] In 1908, an international commission of these governments met in Shanghai to discuss the problem and recommend possible solutions. In 1911, an international conference took place in The Hague which culminated in an international legal instrument, the Hague International Opium Convention of 1912, pledging the contracting powers to "enact pharmacy laws or regulations to limit [the opiates] exclusively to medical and legitimate purposes. . . ."[22] This became the basis of our Harrison Act.

In the nineteenth century, prior to the development of medicine as a science, self-medication and self-diagnosis were commonplace. Patent

---

[20] Prosser, *op. cit.,* p. 458.
[21] *Ibid.,* p. 459.
[22] *Ibid.,* p. 459.

medicines were advertised for the cure or amelioration of almost any condition without specification of their ingredients. Most of these nostrums were used for the endemic coughs, dysenteries, and upper respiratory infections which were the consequence of poor or primitive sanitation and hygiene,[23] as well as for the more serious cardiovascular and pulmonary diseases, especially tuberculosis. Sufferers from dysmenorrhea and unspecified "female complaints," from the pains of chronic infection, poorly performed amputations, and traumatic neuritides (these last the legacy of the Civil War) were a splendid market for remedies whose effective agents were alcohol and opium, morphine, or heroin.

The user of the patent medicines was in a difficult situation. The unidentified opiates did relieve his pain or cough, but since the source of his distress was often a chronic or subacute disease process, he made daily or more frequent use of these nostrums for relief. However, when he sought to stop taking the nostrum when the symptoms abated, he developed malaise, aches and pains, and gastrointestinal and other symptoms which could be perceived as a relapse and occasion for continued medication, but which in fact were indications of early dependence on the opiates. Though there are no contemporary data on how many persons became medically addicted through the use of such patent medicines, the impression from the sources cited by Terry and Pellens is that great numbers of persons became addicted in this fashion.[24] But it is to be noted that "addiction" is here used in the sense of "dependence" and that there is no basis whatever for determining the proportion of addicts who also developed craving.

Another reason for the great number of persons who were medically addicted—not through self-medication but through the prescription of physicians—was that the opiates, and morphine in particular, were among the few widely effective drugs available to the practicing physician. There was no rational pharmacopoeia based on systematic clinical and experimental observation, and disease processes were only beginning to be understood. Symptomatic relief—and the opiates could

[23] The paper cup, screening against flies, pasteurization of milk, safe public water supplies, inspection of public markets and restaurants—commonplaces of our day—were rarities, opposed or not thought of.

[24] Charles E. Terry and Mildred Pellens, *The Opium Problem* (New York: The Committee on Drug Addiction in Collaboration with the Bureau of Social Hygiene, Inc., 1928).

grant this blessing for a variety of symptoms—was often the aim of medical care.

The situation today is quite different. Our knowledge of disease is vastly superior to that of the nineteenth-century physician. Today, the aim of most medical treatment is to affect the underlying disease or physiological process, not merely to yield relief of distressing symptoms. Furthermore, with improvements in public sanitation and water supply, improved surgical technique and asepsis, with the freer use of that true miracle drug—aspirin—and other more dramatic pharmacological developments, the medical need for opiates has diminished. Even by the early 1900's, however, the use of opiates for prolonged treatment of illness or bodily distress was not so much a consequence of the limitations of medical science as it was of the patent medicine industry, which was, from a physician's standpoint, very much in need of control.

The Attitudinal Context

By the middle of the twentieth century, along with the development of sanctions on opiate drugs, certain attitudes about the effects of opiates on personality and social behavior developed which continue to be prevalent in this country. These may be generalized simply: the use of opiates is harmful to health, morality, and public welfare.

Since social attitudes are rarely based on medical or other scientific evidence, the common notion that opiates are harmful to health is perforce vague, expressed in terms of "degeneration" or "deterioration" rather than by reference to disorders of particular organs, systems, or tissues. There is a stereotype of the opiate addict: his complexion is sallow, posture stooped, musculature weak and flaccid; he is emaciated and dirty or at least unkempt. This stereotype is justified at least in part by experience. The "down-and-out" addict who has spent his last nickel and pawned his clothing to purchase drugs—which are dreadfully expensive on the illicit market—is concerned with his appearance, nutrition, and sleep only after his need for drugs has been satisfied. But the stereotype reflects the problems of obtaining drugs rather than the effects of the drugs themselves. Those who are able to obtain drugs without the difficulties imposed by our laws appear no different when chronically addicted than when in a prolonged period of abstinence. Anecdotal reports of persons who were not recognized as drug addicts until they were in a setting where drugs could not be obtained lend credence to this statement. Most relevant, however, is the appearance of post-addicts who are readdicted in the research wards at Lexington. They appear healthy, well-nourished, clean, and respectable.

Turning from the nonspecific stereotype to the systematic study of the effects of opiates on health, we note that there are no known diseases of any tissue or organ associated with chronic addiction to opiates, as there appears to be with chronic use of alcohol, tobacco, or with chronically excessive caloric intake (the diseases associated with or intensified by obesity). This is not to say that opiates have no effects on the functions of the body. Examples of the effects are pupillary constriction, paradoxical constipation, orgastic impotence in the male, and amenorrhea and/or infertility in the female. However, none of these conditions interfere greatly with day-to-day living, nor are they permanent or total.

However, the health of drug addicts in the present social and legal context may be impaired by prolonged neglect of diet and by participation in deviant (mostly lower-class) social environments where venereal and other diseases are widespread. There are, furthermore, the special risks of being an addict in our society. For example, as we pointed out before, they may receive poisonous adulterants in their heroin. When they steal, they run the occupational risks of the criminal, for example, being shot by the police. Death by suicide or by accidental overdose of heroin is also a serious hazard. Although the suicide may come at a point in the cycle of addiction when the addict is no longer able to obtain sufficient drugs to experience the psychic effects he craves, in our experience with adolescent addicts, suicide occurred early in a cycle of readdiction after discharge from a hospital, at a point when the addict was remorseful and depressed by his failure to remain abstinent and by his intensified awareness of the difficulties of being an addict in our society.

The putative effects of opiates on morality are based largely on the characteristics of those social groups who notoriously used opium (or other intoxicant drugs). In part, this is a legacy of the opening of the Far West and particularly of California, where many of the men without families who gambled, sought gold mines, or swindled their fellows adopted the smoking of opium from the Chinese.[25] As a group, these men separated themselves from the conventional morality and standards of the Eastern United States. They valued neither their own nor their

[25] Alva Johnston, *The Legendary Mizners* (New York: Farrar, Straus, 1953).

neighbors' lives highly; they sought whatever excitement and novel experience they regarded as worthwhile or interesting. Since they used opiates, it was simple to identify their values—which included the use of opiates and especially smoking opium—with the effects of the drug itself.

On the other hand, there is the divergent tradition that opiate use leads to submission to an unrewarding life. This is based primarily on observation of the materially depressed Chinese laborers (in China and the United States) who did, in fact, utilize opium in their need to adjust to a way of life in which personal upward mobility or even marriage and a family was often impossible.

Though the exuberant search for new experience and submission to fate are antithetical, popular attitudes about the effects of opiates on behavior have synthesized these disparate notions into the concept that opiate use is harmful to morality. The fact is that the cart was simply placed before the horse. It is true that persons who dissociate themselves from the norms and values of their fellows may, in a search for new experience, use opiates. It is true that the opiates have been used by materially depressed populations. The point is that the use of opiates is one way to fulfill these needs; it does not initiate them.

There are three aspects to the notion that opiate use is harmful to the public welfare. The first is that opiate use releases or stimulates violent and antisocial impulses. Opiate intoxication is not clearly differentiated attitudinally, as it is in fact, from intoxication with alcoholic beverages. Consequently, the opiate addict is thought to become aggressive and sexually stimulated when he is under the influence of opiates. There is, for instance, a passage in Briffault's novel, *Europa*, in which a sexual orgy is aggressively initiated by a protagonist after he gives himself an injection of heroin. A generation or more of American readers and movie-goers acquired their image of the addict from Sax Rohmer's, *The Mysterious Dr. Fu Manchu*.

In fact, however, the effect of the opiates is remarkably unlike this. Though the addict does not necessarily object to company or to participating in sexual play or intercourse, he usually prefers to be by himself, quietly withdrawn from any social interaction. If disturbed, he may become irritable and short-tempered. "Don't bother me," rather than, "I'll bother you," is the motif of his behavior. The behavior of the opiate addict after an injection of morphine or heroin is remarkably unlike that of the usual social drinkers (or problem drinkers) in our society, who so often become boisterous, aggressive, or troublesome after a few drinks. With regard to effects on sexuality, the effect of the opiates is to diminish, if not do away with, sexual appetite. The addict "loses his nature." He may participate in sexual play, but with retarded ejaculation or orgastic impotence. The woman addict is almost always frigid or uninterested in sex after receiving opiates.

The second aspect of this image is that use of opiates seriously undermines the person's interest or ability to work. But, in fact, the relationship between opiate addiction and work is quite complex. The number of professionally successful persons who were or are addicted to opiates is an indication that there is no necessary relationship between opiate use and an unproductive life. There are also a number of addicts who, indeed, never worked, if they could help it, before they used drugs and who continue not to work, if they can possibly avoid it, after they become addicted. There are a number of such marginal deviants as race-track characters, gamblers, hustlers, and confidence men of various persuasions who become addicts and continue to support their addiction through these vocations.

There are many addicts we studied who continued at their jobs, with sufficient industry and deportment to satisfy their employers. If, however, they were unable to satisfy their self-induced need for drugs before going to work, they might be too restless and irritable (early symptoms of the withdrawal syndrome) to work or be late or absent from work because of many hours spent "making a connection." If addicts lose their jobs, it is because they could not regularly obtain drugs, not because the opiates made their work unsatisfactory to their employers. In our experience, there are also a number of addicts who are able to work better when receiving drugs than when abstinent. Such a person is often preoccupied with obsessive doubts which inhibit him in the simplest tasks; when he uses opiates, he gets "drive," his obsessive doubts are suppressed, and he is able to make decisions and act.[26]

The work habits of the few carefully observed patients who were re-addicted in the research wards at the United States Public Health Service Hospital in Lexington, were not sufficiently different from those of the other, abstinent patients to provoke comment. These patients may have worked at a slower pace than some of their peers, but their efficiency and attentiveness were not otherwise impaired.

[26] We are not suggesting that opiates generally improve motor performance. These addicts were individuals unable to function because of anxiety, tension, ambivalence, or other disturbances.

In brief, there is no simple or single effect of opiates on work and productivity. Instead, a variety of behaviors vis-à-vis work may occur when a person is regularly using opiates. Whatever behavior we observe in a particular addict resulted not merely from the opiates, but rather as a consequence of interactions between his needs and motives for addiction, his personality structure, and the neurophysiological effects of the drugs.

The third aspect of this image is that the use of opiates leads to crime. We have already dealt with this issue at some length. There is no evidence that opiate use produces such temporary abeyance of judgment as would lead to violence or destructiveness. We have been told that at one time such claims were made by attorneys who pleaded temporary insanity caused by intoxication with opiates in defense of their clients. In fact, the opiates sedate rather than stimulate, pacify anger and resentment rather than encourage these sentiments. In periods of addiction, when the person needs to make connections to purchase drugs or steals money for this purpose, he has no heart for gratuitous aggression; he is seriously devoted to the most efficient and least conspicuous means of achieving these goals. Though he will disregard the property rights of other persons, he has no interest in hurting them.

In summary, the attitude that opiate use per se is harmful to health, morality, and the public welfare finds no support in any evidence known to us. There is evidence that persons already participating in a life whose values and goals are regarded as harmful to morality and to the public welfare will probably continue in such a life after they become addicts. However, there is considerable evidence that there are unanticipated consequences of the attempt to proscribe opiate use which are, in fact, harmful both to the addict and to the common good.

Opiate Use outside the Historical and Attitudinal Context

AN EXERCISE IN "WHAT IF?"

What predictions and general observations are to be made about opiates if they are regarded neutrally, solely in terms of their pharmacological and behavioral effects and in terms of the social interactions and behavior of users?

First, we would have to note that opiate use is hazardous. Overdose leads to respiratory inhibition, coma, or death. Since the quantity of opiates sufficient to produce such respiratory failure is considerably greater than dosages used for the treatment of pain or for other psychic effects, it would be appropriate to recommend that they always be carefully labeled and compounded in such a fashion—e.g., in varisized and -colored capsules—as to avoid accidental misuse. This is particularly important for heroin, which is readily mixed with milk sugar and other vehicles. Furthermore, people should be informed of proper techniques for the sterilization and use of their injection apparatus to avoid abscesses and other infections of the skin and veins and to avoid contagion with malaria, hepatitis, or other diseases.

Second, we would note that there are a number of disturbances of bodily function associated with the opiates; for example, pupillary constriction may interfere with vision under conditions of poor illumination. Constipation, amenorrhea, and sexual apathy may also occur.

Third, we would note that the regular use of opiates leads to physiological dependence and tolerance. This dependence and tolerance develops according to the frequency of dosage, the quantity of opiates used, and the characteristics of particular drugs, e.g., the dependence on Demerol or codeine is less marked than on morphine or heroin. In order to satisfy the dependence and also to obtain psychic effects, the dosage will probably be gradually raised to a point far beyond initial levels of use. Theoretically, a level of physiological dependence and tolerance may be reached for which no quantity of opiates would suffice except to forestall symptoms of withdrawal. Practically, the addict usually continues for long periods at a particular dosage. In order to achieve a lower level of dependence and tolerance, a brief period of abstinence is necessary. Since there is an unpleasant withdrawal syndrome during this period of acute abstinence, he may seek medical assistance. This pattern is likely to persist for many years. There are no systematic data indicating how often the pattern is spontaneously given up. It may, however, be recalled from our discussion in Chapter II of the Federal Narcotics Bureau file of drug-users that more than 9 per cent of drug-users whose names were first listed during 1955 and who were not known to have used drugs in the following five years were individuals who had a history of drug use extending from ten to fifty-one years prior to 1955.[27] On the other hand, there are many cases of life-long habituation.

We must also note that the addict does not find the dependence or habituation so burdensome as one might anticipate. Indeed, because of the gratification it affords him, he finds it far less burdensome than does

[27] Charles Winick, "Maturing out of Narcotic Addiction," *Bulletin on Narcotics*, 14 (1962), 1–7.

the diabetic, who may also have a lifelong dependence on a drug. Nonetheless, it should be made explicit that the regular use of opiates may place the person in a prolonged dependence on drugs and on the apparatus for injecting the drugs which may limit his travels or occupation, since unavailability of opiates would subject him to quite disagreeable and, in rare circumstances, dangerous symptoms.

Fourth, we would note that some people find the occasional use of opiates a welcome form of intoxication. The major overt effect on their behavior and mood is relaxation and somnolence. Most people, however, do not value this experience highly. Though they may feel relaxed, they do not experience those subtle effects on their mood and ideation which the few characterize as a special sense of well-being. Others may find that this occasional intoxication facilitates their social behavior, just as many welcome occasional intoxication with alcoholic beverages, especially when their social behavior has been severely inhibited by anxiety, feelings of inadequacy, or of "not belonging." However, acute intoxication with opiates is quite unlike acute intoxication with alcohol.

There is a general sequence of events which commonly occurs when a sober person begins to drink alcoholic beverages. These events are expressions of the degree to which the person has lost control over his speech, emotional expression, and motor behavior. The rate at which this effect takes place is related to the quantity of alcohol ingested, to the rapidity of absorption, and to the body weight of the drinker. With the first few "social" drinks, the individual's judgment and inhibitions are affected. He talks and otherwise participates more freely in social interaction. In the early stages of intoxication, his cultural expectations of the effects of alcoholic beverages on behavior or mood may lead to the expression of such effects long before sufficient alcohol is ingested and absorbed to "account" for these effects neurophysiologically. As intake continues and the blood-alcohol level rises, motor coordination becomes poorer. The drinker's insight into his level of coordination may also become poorer, so that he may endanger himself and others by driving a car, attempting feats of strength or skill, and so forth. As drinking continues, motor incoordination is accentuated, and social behavior deviates even more from the individual's usual roles and norms. Finally, with continued drinking, stumbling, slovenliness, loss of bladder control, anesthesia, stupor, and even coma ensue.

Acute intoxication with opiates is very different. In part, but not entirely, the effects differ for the novice and for the habituated user. The common sequence of events after administration of a dose of opiates is as follows: (1) There is a transitory nausea which may, particularly in the novice, be followed by effortless and emotionally nondistressing vomiting. (2) There is a period of maximal appreciation of the subtle effects of the drug. Some of these are: body sensations, for example, a feeling of impact in the stomach, bodily warmth, "pins and needles," and itching sensations of a rather pleasant and eroticized nature; a feeling of lethargy, somnolence, relaxation, and relief from tension or anxiety; and the experience of the "high." This experience, as reconstructed from the reports of addicts and some normal subjects, is one of comfortable detachment from and lack of involvement in current experiences. The person feels "out of this world," all his demands have been fulfilled, everything is taken care of. Perhaps the most instructive of a variety of phrases used by addicts to describe this experience is "being in the junkie's paradise." (3) Following the period of maximal appreciation of the effects of the drug, there is a gradual return to a "normal" state. The user returns to his normal activities but continues to maintain, although to a lessened degree, the comfort, detachment, and loss of tension which he had experienced most intensely in the first hour or two after taking the drug. Depending for its rate of onset on the degree of physiological dependence, in the next few hours there develop feelings of discomfort comparable at first to normal hunger, but mounting in intensity until relieved by a new dose or until the appearance of the full-scale withdrawal reaction.

Chronic intoxication with opiates is quite unlike chronic intoxication with barbiturates or alcohol; the latter drugs progressively interfere with the person's coordination, intellectual functioning, and judgment. With chronic opiate intoxication, disturbances in coordination, intellectual functioning, and judgment are strikingly associated with withdrawal from opiates rather than with the intoxication per se. The alcoholic may be said to suffer in his intoxication; the opiate addict suffers in his abstinence. The alcoholic pays the piper through the disabilities of his intoxication; the opiate addict pays through the disabilities of abstinence.

Fifth, what about the effect on social behavior? It is likely that addicts would be treated with disdain or lowered respect whether or not their behavior were conspicuous or deviant. According to various religious elements in our culture, comfort and pleasure are regarded as the just rewards of effort and achievement; it is not quite moral to be happy or at ease without earning it through struggle and work. On the other hand, among the rebellious, individualistic, and antiauthoritarian elements in our culture, it is not fitting to be quietly and inconspicuously intoxicated. The drinking boasts of the pioneer and the frontiersman are not merely expressions of alcoholic exuberance; they express significant and normative cultural themes. Speaking generally, we esteem both moral discipline and immoral rebellion; speaking equally generally, opiate intoxication quietly thumbs its nose at both of these, quietly sidesteps the virtues and excesses of both.

However, discipline and rebellion do not exhaust the variety of possible patterns of living in our multifaceted culture. There is still some room for the person who holds his peace and lives inconspicuously with minimal striving for personal possessions or even personal expression. Such a person is often regarded as weak, ill, or deviant; however, he may also be regarded as harmless. Partly in reaction to their rejection by the majority for being culturally out-of-step, it is likely that many addicts would dissociate themselves from the mainstream of American life. It is probable that they would continue to participate in work and in certain limited social interactions without full involvement or without lending much credence or support to the dominant ethos.

Sixth, we cannot assume that people with criminal or other deviant associations and behavior will not use opiate drugs; however, their behavior in the course of acute or chronic intoxication with opiates should not be excused or explained by the drugs themselves.

This exercise in "what if" may be summarized briefly. It seems possible to have a society in which opiate addiction is not prohibited by law without disastrous effects on the social structure. We are not, at this point, recommending such a change in our social arrangements, but merely pointing out that prima facie it does not seem intrinsically evil or unmanageable. All novel social arrangements probably have undesirable and unintended consequences, and we are at this point intensely aware of the unintended consequences of the Harrison Act. Whether other social arrangements for the addicted person and the use of opiates could be made more wisely and effectively is a moot question to which we shall return.

Why Is Opiate Addiction a Social Problem?

Having reviewed some of the historical, sociological, cultural, pharmacological, and personal phenomena of opiate addiction, we can now turn to the central problem of this chapter, namely, why should we be concerned with opiate addiction, as social scientists, physicians, or as citizens? There seem to be two groups of reasons for concern. The first is because opiate addiction and use is occurring in a historical and attitudinal context which makes its use a social problem.

Whether or not we regard the assumptions, traditions, and historical currents as a sufficient and logical basis for our current proscriptive legislation, these proscriptive laws and supporting sanctions do nonetheless exist. Whether we approve of these laws or not, they have consequences which make opiate addiction a major hazard to the person who becomes an addict and a burden to the community in which opiate addiction or use is endemic. Thus, a person who obtains drugs outside authorized medical settings is perforce participating in a criminal transaction. Through such transactions, he helps support local and international criminal organizations; he lends support to what we surmise to be the interlocking directorates of extralegal big business. Indirectly, he supports a variety of antisocial organizations and activities. He incurs the possibility of arrest and a jail sentence. Through regular use, he incurs the possibility of addiction and the need for the daily use of a cheap substance at an exorbitant price. Since the drugs he buys illegally are neither carefully compounded nor honestly sold, he runs the risk of not even getting his money's worth or of purchasing inert or poisonous adulterants. If the person who uses opiates illegally wants to obtain a period free from drugs, he is not likely to find sympathetic and objective medical care without stigma unless he happens to be extremely wealthy. His stature in the community is threatened. For the community, extralegal use of opiates calls for the utilization of public money and social energy for special police, courts, and hospitals.

The second group of reasons has to do with the individual apart from the legal context and its consequences. We now know that the person who becomes addicted to drugs or who uses drugs regularly and persistently for the alleviation of tension, anxiety, or for more subtle reasons of which he may not be aware is seeking help which he has not been able to find elsewhere in his life. He is not easily motivated to use drugs. Like schizophrenia, drug use is "a way of life."

We have reason to believe that, even if there were no sanctions against opiate use, we would regard or would learn to regard the people who become addicts as seriously disturbed in their relationships with themselves, with their families, and in the complexities of their relationships with what is loosely called "reality." Conversely, had there never been a possibility for adolescent opiate addicts to obtain drugs, we have reason to believe that, by virtue of their functioning prior to and apart from their first use of opiates, their lives would have entered other maladaptive paths, ranging from serious behavior disturbances to neurotic character disorders to psychoses. We would have to be concerned under either of these conditions (i.e., whether opiates were freely available or absolutely unobtainable) with the person for whom opiate addiction represents a valid potential. In short, we have reason to be concerned with opiate addiction because of its human significance as an indicator of trouble within the individual and, because of the endemic nature of opiate addiction, as an indicator of trouble within many individuals in our society.

There is a related basis for regarding opiate use as harmful to the individual. This reason is based on some of the ethical assumptions of psychoanalytic theory and of much medical practice, to say nothing of the ethical imperatives of a democratic society. We assume that a major therapeutic goal is to help every person achieve the fullest development of his capacities to love, to work, to play, and to conduct himself as a reasonably responsible member of society. We regard anxiety as a significant value in human development and growth, as a stimulus calling for adaptive responses. These responses are not merely means for coping with present sources of anxiety, but rather the nucleus around which a further development and enrichment of the person may occur.

From this standpoint, every neurotic symptom is a hindrance to the fruition of the person. Similarly, every substance (such as the tranquilizer drugs) which, through its pharmacological nature, can alleviate anxiety may impede the development of the person's own resources. We do not mean to be uncompromising, moralistic, or rigid. Such substances or such symptoms may be valuable and necessary alternatives to states of anxiety beyond the defensive and constructive powers of a person's ego. But there is the possibility that escape by pharmacological means may not be the best available route; the possibility exists not only that the person might find socially less incommoding means, but also that the search might in itself strengthen his self-esteem and his capacity to bear what may have been perceived as an unbearable anxiety.

For a person whose contact with the world is painful in consequence of, for example, a weakened capacity to mediate between his impulses and the situational possibilities for gratifying them, the potential of the opiates to relieve anxiety may be extremely seductive. In this sense, by camouflaging anxiety beneath the haze of an altered state of consciousness, opiates may harm the person in his development. By offering immediate relief from tension or anxiety, the opiates make him less willing to participate in the difficult processes of growth.

We must, however, take note of the fact that society's concern for the problem of opiate addiction is not based on this kind of concern for the welfare or development of the addict. Indeed, were it not for the legal situation, the addict would probably be regarded as far less of a nuisance than a person with a drinking problem or one who is chronically unemployable or dependent. As an individual human being, the addict deserves no more or less of the benevolent concern of the community than the person who has other, e.g., neurotic, difficulties in living. The authors have come to regard addiction, viewed outside the legal context, as another complex expression of human suffering and human attempts to cope with it and as another manifestation of widespread need for therapeutic and preventive efforts. We must also note, however, that taking away this inferior mode of adaptation on the high-sounding excuse that it is good for the person while doing nothing to help him find and remove the obstacles to a superior form of adaptation is the sheerest hypocrisy and a refined form of cruelty.

THE PROBLEM OF ADOLESCENT ADDICTION

To this point in this chapter, we have not attempted to demarcate adolescent from adult opiate addiction. When we began our research, it was in a context of beliefs which sought to differentiate the "innocent" adolescent user from the "vicious" adult addict. A tentative early report by competent psychiatrists[28]—erroneously, we believe—fostered this belief by stating that the adolescent did not have an addiction problem. This was based on two special facts. First, the investigators had at that time limited clinical experience with adolescent drug-users (and probably even less with adult drug-users). Second, the hospital population they studied was limited to boys who had not reached their sixteenth birthday. Thus, they reported on a limited segment of what we would regard as the adolescent period (from puberty to legal

[28] P. Zimmering et al., "Heroin Addiction in Adolescent Boys," *Journal of Nervous and Mental Diseases,* 114 (1951), 19–34.

majority) and, as we were later to learn, on that range of the adolescent years which largely precede those in which opiates are first used by adolescents who later become addicts.

There were, however, more enduring sources for these beliefs. It was shocking to the public understanding and attitudes about opiate addiction to think that any adolescent, any child, would endanger his life by the use of such nefarious substances as heroin without having been somehow seduced or deceived by a vicious adult into using them. In this "age of the child," it is painful to accept the fact that many adolescents are already active bearers of the traits and attitudes which would be regarded in their adult counterparts with intense disapproval. Redl and Wineman have pointed out that the programs of support for youths who are delinquent (who act against or outside social norms) sow the seeds of their future disappointment and discouragement by unrealistic and exaggerated sympathy for the delinquent as a victim.[29] Victim he often is, but in the sense that a monstrous neonate is the victim of an unfavorable prenatal environment; he has been transformed in the course of his victimization and cannot be restored to normalcy by procedures that ignore what he has become.

In this regard, it is quite unlikely that any significant support for special hospitals or for research into the problems of adolescent opiate addiction would have been available if the adolescent opiate-user had not been seen as vastly different from the adult opiate-user. Yet this is a belief which seems impossible to substantiate by our research or experience. The adolescent addict is not typically seduced by vicious adults; he does have an addiction problem; he is an active bearer of the traits and attitudes of the adult addict. In fact, statistical studies in the 1920's and 1930's had already pointed out that the majority of adult addicts began their addiction in their adolescence or in early adulthood.[30] Thus, we cannot regard the problem of adolescent opiate addiction as inherently separate from the addiction problem in general.

Our justification for studying adolescent opiate addiction per se is —at least a posteriori—not that we regarded adolescent addiction as different from the adult addiction problem, but rather that the public

[29] Fritz Redl and David Wineman, *Children Who Hate* (Glencoe, Ill.: The Free Press, 1951).

[30] Alan S. Meyer, *Social and Psychological Factors in Opiate Addiction: A Review of Findings together with an Annotated Bibliography* (New York: Bureau of Applied Social Research, Columbia University, 1952), pp. 60–64.

concern and action on behalf of the adolescent addict permitted us to identify and study adolescent addicts more readily than adult addicts. Second, because of his age, the adolescent addict is still more closely connected to the community and familial setting in which his addiction began. In this sense, we can study adolescent opiate addiction, if not *in statu nascendi,* at least in closer physical and temporal relationship to the onset and early development of addiction. Though our study has focused on the adolescent addict, we believe that our findings are relevant for the majority of the addict population.

XV

Treatment, Prevention, and Control of Addiction

It is perhaps axiomatic that, if there were no access to narcotics for a sufficiently long period, there would be no narcotics addicts. It is not equally obvious that efforts to suppress uncontrolled traffic in narcotics offer an effective means of significantly reducing, to say nothing of eliminating, narcotics addiction. Opiates are not exempt from the law of supply and demand. The very effectiveness of efforts to suppress the traffic creates a situation in which prices rise if there is no corresponding decrease in demand. From a business viewpoint, all that this means is that an increase in risk is balanced by an increase in potential profit. If the businessman is not adept in the mathematics of risk and is, moreover, inclined to gamble (as is likely to be the case for someone engaged in the narcotics traffic), he may even be willing to operate under quite unfavorable conditions of risk relative to the possibilities of profit if the potential returns seem to be great enough. In other words, the effectiveness of police activity may simply have the consequence of increasing the efforts to outsmart or to corrupt the police, the volume of business fluctuating around some stabilization point. Thus, it is not enough that police activity be moderately successful in catching and convicting violators of the narcotics laws; it must offer the promise of being almost perfectly successful for a long period before we can take it seriously as a measure of control.

Price is, of course, not unrelated to demand. In a normal commodity market, an artificial or natural shortage of a particular nonvital commodity may drive its price to a level at which its purchase entails the frustration of other economic and psychological wants (for instance, in addition to other desired commodities, a desire to maintain a safe margin of savings and desires not to look like a fool or like one who cannot control his own avidity). As such a point, varying from person to person, is approached, the individual's desire to purchase the commodity declines. As the price goes up, the number of potential purchasers who decide that purchase is not worth their while increases, and the market demand decreases. If the supply does not correspondingly diminish and if the retired potential purchasers cannot be replaced by more avid ones or persuaded that they have underestimated the value of the commodity, the price comes down.

Why should the same considerations not apply to narcotics? That is, why would it not be enough to have the effectiveness of enforcement carried to such a point that the price could no longer rise and still find a market sufficient to justify the risk? An increment of effectiveness beyond such a point, no matter how small, could not then be matched by a price rise balancing the risk. Marginal entrepreneurs would drop out, decreasing the number of lawbreakers whom the police must outwit and thereby permitting the police to increase their effectiveness. Soon, no narcotics traffic. A beautiful vision, indeed!

The fact of the matter is that illegal narcotics are not in a normal commodity market. The customers have long since established themselves as individuals virtually immune to competing considerations, so vital does this commodity seem to them; and the market price of heroin is already far beyond the level that the majority of customers can afford, to say nothing of the perils to the consumer-purchaser of dealing in the market. The higher the price, the more desperate the stratagems to which these consumers will resort, and these often include efforts to convert others to the likes of themselves. In other words, they turn to fund-raising crime to manage the costs, and they become a potent force in spreading the market.

It seems a rare month, indeed, when newspaper-readers are not treated to accounts of the smashing of a major narcotics ring. We cannot but admire the persistence, the ingenuity, and the devotion to duty of the narcotics officers who score these triumphs. Nor can we persuade ourselves to believe that these victories make much difference in control of the traffic. The more successful the police, the greater the inducement to new rings. In fact, we find it quite easy to believe that, if the police were to desist entirely, the narcotics traffickers themselves would carry on for them. The illegal narcotics traffic cannot afford free competition, and, considering the unprincipled characters involved, it seems likely that, if there were signs of competition's developing, they would start assassinating one another—as even now they seem to do from time to time. The police, of course, carry on the job of reducing competition in the business in a socially more acceptable way.

We are not questioning the integrity of the enforcement officers. Nor do we have any reason to doubt that they do the job that has been laid out for them as well as it can possibly be done with the resources at their command. We do not doubt that, given additional resources, they could do this job even better. We are not saying that they do not have a most important, proper function in narcotics control. We are saying that the job laid out for them makes no sense and that this is not their fault, although it is quite understandable that a person who has been assigned to a senseless job should try to convince himself and everyone else that his job is of the utmost significance. That the enforcement officers believe in what they are doing and that they should be inclined to view any critic as an enemy of society is perhaps a credit to their high morale, but it can hardly be taken as compelling evidence that they are right. The important point is that, barring an enormous increase in the resources at their command for a long period (and this would entail great sacrifices with respect to far more pressing social needs), they cannot possibly have much impact on the volume of the illegal narcotics traffic if there is not, independently, a great reduction in demand.

There is an obvious expedient for reducing the demand—if not the demand for narcotics per se, then at least the demand on the illegal market—and that is to make a better quality of narcotics, and far more cheaply, available to addicts on a legal market. There are many advocates, the present writers included, of one variant or another of such a plan; and the numbers seem to be increasing. No one, of course, advocates putting narcotics on the open shelves of supermarkets. The basic idea is to make it completely discretionary with the medical profession whether to prescribe opiate drugs to addicts for reasons having to do only with the patient's addiction.

Whenever there is a strong push for a major change in social policy, one may anticipate a powerful mobilization of effort in the opposite direction. The issue of the discretionary prescription of narcotics is no exception. Unfortunately, the issue has been confounded and confused by arguments about the so-called English system. The simple facts seem to be that British physicians do have the discretion of administering narcotics (including heroin) to addicts and that, despite allegations to the contrary, they do in fact exercise this discretion. It is, moreover, generally agreed that the total number of addicts in England is extremely small—a maximum of perhaps five hundred cases—and there is every reason to believe that the method of counting addicts inflates the figures in England, just as it does in the United States. Considering the small number of English addicts, it is understandable why some Americans who go to England to study the system seem to find it impossible to locate English physicians who have patients to whom they continue to prescribe narcotics. And there are other reasons why the British are inclined to deny the existence of an English system that is, in practice, in any way different from the American system,[1] especially to physicians from the United States whose initial skepticism may carry an aura of hostility to the system.

Apart from disputations as to whether the English system actually exists, the big argument settles down to the question of the relevance of the English experience to the United States. The pro's attribute the small numbers of English addicts to the existence of the system; the anti's argue that England is entirely different from the United States. The facts are with the anti's. Not only are there major differences in culture, tradition, population composition, and social organization, but the sheer numerical difference may be a materially relevant fact. Moreover, English addicts are geographically dispersed, rarely in contact with one another, and probably predominantly middle-class. And there is no tie-in between the illegal sale of narcotics and large-scale

[1] See Edwin M. Schur, *Narcotic Addiction in Britain and America* (Bloomington: Indiana University Press, 1962). Apart from the light that he throws on the reluctance to talk about the English system, we may take as a crude index of the difficulty in locating physicians with addict patients the fact that, according to Schur, the *thirteen* physicians whom he interviewed had contact with virtually all known English addicts.

criminal syndicates (the latter being the sequela of another noble American experiment in suppression).

The relevance of the British experience is consequently, at best, highly debatable apart from the purely negative conclusion that it has not produced a situation comparable to that which exists in the United States; but it is also quite trivial in terms of the effect on the illegal traffic of introducing low-priced, high-quality narcotics in competition with the illegal product. It is time, we think, to forget about England and to consider the issue on its merits vis-à-vis the United States. There are many arguments against the adoption of such a plan.

The first concerns the addicts themselves. Let us for the moment confine ourselves to the purely economic aspects. It is argued that addicts will continue to buy their supplies on the illegal market. Addicts, it is argued, are irresponsible, irrational, immoral people. They will dislike the discipline of keeping medical appointments. They will be unhappy about the quantities that physicians will prescribe for them and, if they cannot succeed in getting themselves treated by more than one physician simultaneously, will supplement their prescription on the illegal market. They will not want to run the risks of being identified as addicts (as though substantial numbers of them could now escape these risks and as though being known to the police were preferable to being known to a physician or clinic).

Suppose all this were so. Still, no one contends that *no* addicts would take advantage of the availability of narcotics via medical treatment. Or, to put the issue differently: if addicts were to take only trivial advantage of the opportunity to receive drugs legally, the present situation would not be materially altered by giving physicians total discretion as to whether to prescribe narcotics. If, on the other hand and as is far more likely, many addicts were to take advantage of the opportunity, then, even though many of the same individuals were to continue to purchase some of their supplies on the illegal market, the demand on the latter would markedly diminish—provided, of course, that there were no compensatory increase in the number of addicts making some use of the illegal market.

There are two important qualifications in the preceding sentence that call for some discussion. But let us, for the moment, assume that we can accept the first ("even though . . . on the illegal market") with equanimity and that there is no great danger of the second ("no compensatory increase . . . making some use of the illegal market"), and follow the economic implications. Under the envisioned circumstances, the more difficult it would be for an addict to obtain his supplies on the illegal market (and increasing prices represent one factor of difficulty), the greater would be his incentive to turn to the legal market; the demand pressure on the illegal market would not adjust freely to diminished supply, and a safety valve would be introduced that limited price increases. Consequently, the illegal market must lose in its flexibility to adjust to effective law enforcement activity. In this event, even the present level of effectiveness might be sufficient to make the business unprofitable, and any increase in effectiveness would make it even more likely that the business would become unprofitable.

Why talk of the possibility of increased effectiveness in the present context? On the assumption that the new policy would not increase the number of addicts, for every addict who passed into the legal channels, the number of lawbreakers must decrease; and even for those addicts who made only partial use of the legal channels, the total volume of lawbreaking must diminish. The enforcement officers would consequently have less to occupy them on the addict front and, with no increase in their resources, would be able to concentrate greater efforts on the manufacturing, importing, and wholesale end of the business.

The definition of drug use per se as a matter of occupational concern solely to the medical profession would force a basic redefinition of the proper function of the enforcement authorities. The Harrison Act and all its derivatives were aimed at preventing the indiscriminate use of narcotics. More and more local and state enforcement efforts seem to be turning to "internal possession" as a legal violation and to the development of means of establishing internal possession. That the Harrison Act took the form of a tax measure does not gainsay its fundamental intention; it attests, rather, to the fact that the fundamental intention was politically repugnant, so that it could only be expedited by devious means, and the essential dishonesty of the internal-possession construction speaks for itself. One might speculate whether dishonest means can ever be anything but self-defeating, even with regard to the noblest of intentions; this, however, is irrelevant to our present concerns.

Immediately relevant is the fact that the new policy would deny that the law has any primary business with whether people do or do not take narcotics; that is the business of medicine. This is not to say that the law has no business with narcotics. It is a proper function of the law to protect the public from adulterated drugs, from drugs that are packaged in ways that mislead consumers as to the dosage levels that they contain, and, by implication, from unprincipled manufacturers and distributors of drugs; if the most immediately affected part of the public happens to be composed of addicts, so be it. But, once the law had been freed of its preoccupation with drug *use,* it would become clear that the addict-pusher represents a relatively trivial aspect of its proper function, and it would be freed to deploy its resources in the direction that would do the most good from the viewpoint of its proper functions, namely, concentration on the manufacturing, importing, and large-scale distributing of illegal narcotics.

We have argued that, unless enforcement can be made enormously more effective than it now is, the enforcement approach to the control of the illegal traffic in narcotics must be self-defeating if there is not an independent reduction in the demand on the illegal market. We have further argued that such demand could be reduced by providing legal access to quality-controlled and much less expensive narcotics through the discretion of the medical profession. We have, finally, argued that by-products of the medical-discretionary policy would be a more tenable definition of the function of law with regard to narcotics and more effective, non-self-defeating enforcement with no increase in— but with considerable redeployment of—enforcement resources.

There is an increasing likelihood of some small-scale experimentation on the discretionary administration of narcotics in the management of addiction. It is to be noted that such small-scale experimentation could not test the large-scale economic effects we have been discussing.

Our argument, however, rests on certain assumptions which must now be examined. The most important of these is that the new policy would not result in an increased number of addicts making use of the illegal market. There are two parts to this assumption: that it would not result in an increased number of addicts and that, even if it did, the new addicts would not use the illegal market enough to maintain demand on it. Note that a mere increase in the number of addicts would not upset the force of the economic argument as long as they do not make more than trivial use of the illegal market. Since new addicts are, by the very novelty of their habit, least integrated into the addict subculture and least set in their ways of maintaining their supplies of narcotics, they should be the ones who could be most easily moved into the legal channels of supply. Hence, unless the number of new addicts greatly exceeded in number those current addicts who defect in greater or lesser degree from the illegal market, our economic argument remains valid.

Would a policy of total medical discretion, however, increase the number of addicts? Small-scale experimentation might answer such a question, but the selection of the subject population for such an experiment would have to be made on a principle diametrically contrary to the principle espoused in current proposals for small-scale experimentation. All current talk about such experiments is in terms of "carefully selected cases"—meaning cases with most favorable prognoses and those most likely to abide by the discipline of medical treatment. These are precisely the cases least likely to take an active part in the induction of new addicts. For small-scale experiments to have any bearing on the present issue, the cases selected should be the "worst" cases, not the "best."

In any event, there is not the slightest reason to suppose that the new policy would increase the number of addicts. If anything, it would tend to inhibit the induction of new cases. The logic of the expectation of an increase is simple—childishly simple: A person who takes a narcotic must have got both the idea of taking it and the supply from someone else; therefore, addiction is contagious; therefore, every addict is the narcotics analogue of a "Typhoid Mary"; therefore, anything which makes it easier for addicts to get along in the open environment is bound to bring with it an epidemic; therefore, permitting physicians to use their own discretion about prescribing narcotics for addicts is bound to increase the number of addicts.

These *non sequiturs* overlook some relevant facts, for instance: (1) that many habituated users sought the initial supply on their own; (2) that attempting to convert others is not induced by missionary zeal, but is a practical adaptation by many addicts to the problem of maintaining their own supplies under the conditions of current public policy; (3) that the addict who would impulsively or out of a desire to look like a "big shot" share his legally obtained supply of narcotics with others would, thereby, also be endangering his own supply, since no one would be offering him unlimited supplies; (4) that the pushers in high-use gangs tend to "lay off" their most vulnerable acquaintances —fellow gang members who have recently returned from hospitalization or imprisonment; (5) that one factor making the use of narcotics attractive in the delinquent subculture is precisely the fact that it is illegal; (6) that it takes much more than an occasional shot to make an addict, namely, apart from frequent repetition, a high degree of personal alienation and psychopathology; (7) that the epidemiology of addiction was self-limiting even under the completely open market prior to the Harrison Act, together with the common practice of including dependency-producing levels of narcotics in many proprietary medications; and (8) that 65 per cent or more of those listed as addicts by the Federal Bureau of Narcotics are not again heard from for at least five years as users of narcotics.

The opponent of legalization can also abuse the medical profession. He must be careful, of course, never to charge openly that physicians are unworthy of trust, since that might remind the public that it daily puts its trust in the physician in matters personally far more consequential than whether the number of addicts goes up or down. Also, he should not raise the question of what the untrustworthy physicians are likely to do that would increase the number of addicts. Appeals to unreason are often most effective if they are subtle. So, if the opponent of legalization gets into an argument about whether to give total discretion to physicians in matters of the use of narcotics, he might casually mention some of the abuses that led to court decisions which have in effect strait-jacketed the medical profession in the treatment of addicts, for instance, the case of the physician who was conducting a national mail-order business in prescriptions for narcotics. He should be careful not to mention the fact that the medical profession has developed highly effective machinery for dealing with abuses of professional ethics. Also—and this is a most effective form of argument— he should be certain to introduce a special version of the numbers game mentioned in Chapter II. He can point out that the drug-addiction rate among physicians is higher than for any other occupational subgroup in the population, and the argument will go across even more strongly if he leaves out the qualifier, "occupational." He should not raise the question of what "addict" means in this context; nor mention that the "highest" rate is still very low; nor, above all, mention that the cure rate among physician addicts is extraordinarily high—so high, in fact, that it has been remarked that the most effective form of treatment of drug addiction may well be to send all addicts to medical school. Mention of the cure rate might only raise questions as to what the word "addict" means in such a context.

There was a second assumption in our argument for giving total discretion in the use of narcotics to the medical profession. It was that we can accept with equanimity the possibility that many addicts who would take advantage of the opportunity to obtain narcotics from physicians might supplement their supplies on the illegal market. There are actually a number of assumptions concealed in this one.

One is that many addicts would not be content with maintenance doses. In fact, no true addict is content with maintenance doses because such dosage levels do not satisfy his craving; because of the effects of tolerance, they do not ease his anxiety, give him relief from tension, or provide the experience of the "high." We see no reason, however, if there are no other contraindications and if there is no better form of treatment available (not merely in principle, but in fact—and that means, among other things, that the cost of providing him more fundamental treatment would be covered), for limiting him to maintenance doses, especially if giving him his "high" would keep him off the illegal market and provide the "high" under conditions of maximum safety to him and others. In fact, we see nothing wrong, under the conditions stated, with having the physician help such an addict plan his drug-taking strategy—switching drugs from time to time, helping him with planned and optimally spaced withdrawals, mixing drugs, or whatever it takes.

In other words, it would be quite feasible to reduce the addict's inducement to resort to the illegal market to a minimum—a minimum, rather than zero, because the typical addict is not the most responsible and controlled of individuals. If he did not get along with his doctor, for instance, he might well turn to the illegal market just out of spite. Or, he might find the very acceptance of his infirmity too much to take, arousing strong masochistic needs. What should concern us most, however, is not that he would be getting more narcotics than his physician had prescribed for him, but that he would be getting them from an unreliable and dangerous source. The former may be contraindicated, but the latter is far more dangerous.

There is, thus, a far more fundamental assumption in our argument than our ability to accept with equanimity an occasional foray by an addict into the illegal market, namely, our ability to accept with equanimity the addict's taking any drugs at all, under any conditions. We are well aware that we have written some fighting words and can anticipate opposition. We think it high time, however, to call a policy of forcing the addict from degradation to degradation, and all in the name of concern with his welfare, just what it is—vicious, sanctimonious, and hypocritical, and this despite the good intentions and manifest integrity of its sponsors.

We are not suggesting that any addict automatically be given all the narcotics he wants and, in effect, abandoned to his addiction. We are not even suggesting that every addict be continued indefinitely on at least maintenance doses. We are saying that every addict is entitled to assessment as an individual and to be offered the best available treatment in the light of his condition, his situation, and his needs. No legislator, no judge, no district attorney, no director of a narcotics bureau, no police inspector, and no narcotics agent is qualified to make such an assessment. If, as a result of such an assessment and continued experience in treating the individual addict, it should be decided that the best available treatment is to continue him on narcotics, whether on maintenance or higher doses and whether in conjunction with other treatment or not, then he is entitled to this treatment. Addicts have been known to lead productive and useful lives as long as they were free of harassment.

We have no objection to any plan that would put so momentous a decision in the hands of a medical, psychological, sociological, and social-casework review board, rather than leaving it to the individual physician, provided that such a plan were adequately financed, ensured that each case receive the full and prompt attention of the board, and that the implementation of such a plan not endanger other vital services by absorbing an excessively large proportion of competent personnel. Simply to put the matter in proper perspective, we would similarly have no objection to any realistic plan guaranteeing that no one would ever have to undergo major surgery without the consensus of a number of expert consultants.

Up to the last few paragraphs, we have put the argument entirely in economic terms. We have said that an enforcement approach to addiction, by itself, cannot work. We have pointed out that providing a legal channel for drugs, even to the point of more than maintenance doses, would relieve the demand on the illegal market, make it possible for enforcement with redefined objectives to become effective, and would not aid the spread of addiction. In the last few paragraphs, we have gone beyond the economic argument. We have argued that any human being in distress is entitled to the best that can be offered him by way of alleviating or minimizing the distress, preferably by getting to the root of the trouble, but, if necessary, by purely symptomatic treatment. In extreme cases, it may be that the best that can be offered an addict is to help him stay chronically narcotized; if so, the person is as entitled to such treatment as is a terminal cancer patient.

Let us now assert that the premise that *human beings in distress are morally entitled to the best help that can be offered them is valid regardless of the effect on the illegal narcotics traffic*. The only condition that can ever justify any action contrary to this premise is a due-process judgment, reluctantly arrived at in the light of overwhelming evidence, that the welfare of an individual must be sacrificed for the general welfare. This is basic to the democratic way of life, and it is basic to those religions which take it as given that every human being was created in the image of God. We can think of no valid reason to suspend the premise in the treatment of addiction.

We have deliberately left a hole in our argument thus far because it involves a much larger issue than whether and under what conditions an addict should have access to narcotics. Suppose that the policy we are advocating were adopted. We have argued that a normally adjusted person is not attracted to narcotics, except perhaps by way of flirtation with a novel experience, in which event he will not become addicted. There are, however, a great many people who are not normally adjusted. Many of these may perhaps now stay away from narcotics out of fear. What would happen to them if we removed the occasion for fear? Would they not discover a means of ridding themselves of their miseries and deliberately get themselves addicted? We strongly doubt that there can be many such (and, just to avoid any confusion with regard to our earlier argument, let us point out that, if there were, they would get off the illegal market as quickly as possible). We are here envisioning action in accordance with a long-range plan based on an assessment of one's problems. Addiction-prone individuals are simply not given to such action.

Suppose, however, if only for the sake of argument, that there were, in fact, many people who would pursue such a course of action. Note that we are positing that they would be doing this in order to escape from their miseries. In other words, these would be individuals who had already failed to find alternative solutions to their problems and who had not received any effective help in doing so. It follows that the posited line of action would, for them, be adaptive; they would be seeking what seemed the best available treatment for their distress. It may be that, in thus calling attention to themselves and to their problems, they could be helped to find more adequate solutions. But what if not? By the very premise we have just been discussing, what moral right would we then have to interfere? If the best that our society has to offer them is narcosis, what moral right would we have to withhold it from them? Dare we, in our arrogance, take the position that it is proper to keep these people from finding relief merely because their method of finding relief is offensive to us? Is a society which cannot or will not do anything to alleviate the miseries which are, at least subjectively, alleviated by narcotics, better off if it simply prevents the victims of these miseries from finding any relief?

Drug use breeds on certain forms of human misery. The major problem posed by narcotic addiction is not at all the problem of getting people to stay away from narcotic drugs. It is the problem of getting at the sources of such misery. Unless and until we have got to work with a will to do something effective about coping with them, we will not have begun to touch on the real problem of narcotics addiction.

In principle, we believe that it should be discretionary with the physician whether to prescribe narcotics for a given case, and we favor establishment of the principle. In practice, however, the privately practicing physician would not be within the reach of the great majority of addicts. There are other reasons, too, that indicate clinics as the best place for the treatment of addiction. And it is no ordinary medical clinic that we think of as optimal.

A clinic geared to the treatment of addiction should include a wide variety of services. Addicts could be referred to other agencies for special services, but every additional step that they have to take and every additional waiting period increases the likelihood of failure. The clinic should provide (not necessarily in one physical plant, but in close proximity), in addition to basic medical services and a withdrawal unit, psychotherapeutic opportunities, family casework, vocational counseling, a sheltered workshop,[2] and at least the beginnings of vocational re-

[2] A sheltered workshop is a subsidized manufacturing enterprise in which (1) the line workers are individuals who could not otherwise hold jobs because of physical or mental handicaps, (2) the foremen are specially trained to cope with such workers, (3) the higher-level personnel include social workers, psychologists, and psychiatrists, and (4) work inefficiency, absenteeism, chronic lateness, and the like are dealt with as adjustment problems rather than as reasons for dismissal. Some of the client-employees may never learn to manage jobs in the open market, but for most the sheltered workshop is a step toward complete rehabilitation.

training, job placement facilities, chaplains, food, financial assistance, a lounge where the addicts would be welcome to just come and relax, and a residential shelter. Such a clinic should be open on a twenty-four–hour basis, although it is not necessary that each of the services be available on such a schedule. All this would have to be provided with a minimum of stress and without the herding of patients, the long waiting periods beyond appointment hours, and the depersonalization that characterizes so many medical clinics. It calls for infinite patience and a high degree of frustration tolerance as patients backslide, break appointments, come in without appointments, and the like. This implies not merely a high professional-to-patient ratio, but a great deal of in-service training to affect the attitudes of the clinic personnel toward the patients.

Above all, what the average addict most needs as a first step in his rehabilitation is a place with the homelike qualities that he never found in his own household and the discovery that he, as an individual human being, matters and can be respected as such. At the beginning, he may need to learn that he can be accepted by authority figures completely on his own terms and to master the anxiety that such acceptance can evoke. One can be reasonably certain that he will be testing for such acceptance by attempting to provoke outright rejection. This does not mean that those who deal with him must pretend to share his values or be indifferent to his failures, but that he needs to be convinced that the manifest difference in values will not lead to a loss of acceptance or of respect for him as a fellow human being. He needs to be convinced that his being accepted is not contingent on any desire to manipulate or mold him into someone else's image. Basic acceptance of himself and trust in others is a necessary condition of his maturation. One has to remember that, though matured in years, he has not yet successfully managed the developmental hurdles of infancy (the acquisition of what Erikson has called "basic trust") and that, unlike the infant who has before him the tasks of achieving self-acceptance and trust in others, the addict is already carrying the psychic scars of his own failures and of the social world that has failed him.

It may be a long time before he is ready for such services as vocational counseling and even longer before he is ready for anything but supportive psychotherapy. His first introduction to the latter may be a simple invitation to attend group therapy, just to see what it is like; and, if he makes progress, his help may be enlisted to try to make it easier for the "weaker" newcomers to these sessions. In time, he may be rewarded with a supervised "big-brother" relationship to another addict; and his introduction to individual psychotherapy may take the form of discussion of the problems of his "little brother" and of his own problems of dealing with him. Similarly, in the sheltered workshop, there may be a progression from timid, sporadic, "observer" visits to the role of mentor to one or more others. In effect, we envision a series of progressive exercises in ego development, adapted to the individual patient in accordance with experience with him.

At the beginning, the patient might be given his shots without question and be asked to come in, or just to stick around; he might then be introduced to the discipline of hygienic self-administration. Later, he might be encouraged to introduce delays, if only to enhance his relief. In time, he might be given a supply sufficient for a day or two. In effect, the very ritual of taking narcotics may become a starting point for training in disciplined behavior. He would merely be informed that other services were available and that he could take advantage of them if he wanted to, but that this was in no way a condition of his welcome. Later, as the relationship with him developed, he might be given more positive encouragement to participate, if only as an observer, and so on. The first contacts with him, apart from such ministering to his needs as he requested, could be casual conversations with him in the lounge or in the course of the need-ministering treatment, designed merely to demonstrate that he was a person of interest to the clinic personnel.

Not every addict need be dealt with as though he were at the zero point of human development. There are, for instance, even under present conditions, addicts who are capable of and who succeed in keeping their jobs. Nor do we believe that all addicts need to be bribed with the maintenance of their addiction to avail themselves of the clinic services; many are sincerely motivated to quit, provided that they can be helped to cope with their other problems. The demands made on them by the staff and by their circumstances are not excessive; occasional backsliding does not turn them into pariahs or convince them of the hopelessness of trying; and they can be helped to keep in proper perspective the fact that the use of narcotics is not their major problem. The important point is that the clinic be able to provide many kinds and levels of service according to the assessment of individual needs. Not all the clinic services need be aimed directly at the patients or conducted on the clinic premises. A good deal of work may, for instance, be focused on the patient's immediate environment in the form of family casework and counseling with the patient's employers, to say nothing of the job of locating individuals who are willing to employ addicts and accept counsel concerning the conditions of their employment.

It is theoretically possible to divide such a variety of services among a number of social agencies instead of allocating them all to one. We believe, however, that this would be a mistake, even though it is now the common pattern for providing social welfare services. The point at issue is contained in an old vaudeville script, in the course of which a patient complains to her physician: "My head aches, my eyes are burning, there is a buzzing in my ears, my nose is stuffed, my throat is sore, my stomach feels queasy . . . and I myself also don't feel so good." The needy individual finds an agency concerned with his finances, another agency concerned with his marital problems, another concerned with his health—and in this agency there is one department concerned with his ears, nose, and throat; another with his eyes; another with his stomach; and so on. In all this welter of fractionated services, there does not seem to be anyone concerned with him as a person. The "I myself" somehow is ignored. The addict, more than most people, needs to feel that he, as a person, is of concern to others. This feeling can be most effectively conveyed within the framework of one agency through a continued relationship with one staff member who guides the addict through the various services, personally introduces him to the various staff members with whom he will be dealing, is interested in his reactions to his experiences, and makes certain that a maximum of coordination is maintained.

It must be expected that progress with most patients will be extremely slow and the setbacks numerous; there may be some with whom no progress seems possible.

We have placed the ideal treatment in a "clinic," rather than in a hospital. We do not mean to preclude the possibility of relatively brief periods of hospitalization. We do, however, regard with great skepticism current proposals of relatively long, enforced periods of hospitalization, whether by induced self-commitment (e.g., as an alternative to a jail sentence) or by court commitment. Although it has become quite fashionable, even among enforcement authorities, to declare that addiction is an illness and hence requires hospitalization, we think that this new outlook is merely a device to get addicts out of the open society. The idea is to lock the addict up. Currently, an addict can be locked up only if he is convicted of committing a crime—in some localities, including the crime of "internal possession." But, if he can be declared to be suffering from a dangerous disease that requires commitment, then he can be locked up even though there is no legally sufficient proof of the commission of a crime. This idea has the further virtues of relieving both the overcrowding of the jails and the consciences of the enforcement people, who are finally beginning to understand the essential inhumanity of the enforcement approach. If the maneuver results in the useless overcrowding of hospitals instead of jails, and if the consciences of the hospital personnel become afflicted as they come to understand their fruitless participation in a gigantic social hypocrisy, that is their problem; the pressure on the jails and on the consciences of the enforcement people will have been relieved.

The simple fact of the matter is that, short of physical measures (e.g., shock therapy, brain surgery, and, under some circumstances, drug therapy), no treatment of psychic disturbances can be successfully accomplished by force. All that force can accomplish is to heighten the dependency and the alienation of the patient, and this is a most undesirable result in the treatment of the addict, since his is a passive-dependent, alienated personality to begin with. To be sure, in the hospital environment, he may seem like a well-adjusted person, displaying no signs of craving; but this is precisely because the management of his life has been taken over, and, if he is a true addict or even another of the varieties of addicts described in Chapter II, he will shortly revert to narcotics when he returns to his normal environment. He will in no sense have been cured.

Success in overcoming the illegal traffic in narcotics and in the treatment of individual addicts will still have done nothing toward meeting the manifold social and personal problems that make so many individuals vulnerable to drug use and addiction. What is called for is a multipronged program going far beyond the direct, manifest problems of addiction to intensified family casework services and special services designed to increase the supports for and incentives to legitimate endeavor. The details of such a program are far beyond the scope of this book. The most general objectives are easily stated: to provide convincing evidence to the individual that he does not stand alone and that his fate does, in fact, matter to society and to provide him, in the fullest possible measure, with the competencies and aspirations most fitting to a human being. There are obviously strata of our society for which no special program with such an objective is needed. The stratum from which most addicts (not to mention delinquents, psychotics, and human derelicts) come is much in need of such a program.

If the ideas presented in this chapter seem visionary, then those who fall by the wayside are, by that very token, entitled to their drug-induced nirvanas. Obversely, if that seems intolerable, then we cannot afford to regard these ideas as visionary. The price of moral indignation is civic responsibility.

APPENDIXES

APPENDIX A

Calculation of Drug Rates

The Early Period

Drug rates for the forty-six–month "early period," which began on January 1, 1949, were computed on the assumption that the number of males sixteen to twenty for a given geographic area remained constant over this period— move-outs being compensated for by move-ins and boys growing out of the age group being compensated for by boys growing into it—and equaled the number reported by the 1950 census for the fifteen-to-nineteen age bracket (i.e., sixteen to twenty in 1951). Drug rates were calculated in terms of the number of drug cases per one thousand males counted by the census in this age range. A drug rate of fifty would therefore mean that, for every thousand boys between sixteen and twenty years old in 1950, fifty drug-connected cases in that age bracket at the time of discovery came to official attention during the forty-six–month period. The reader should note that this does not mean that 5 per cent of the boys living in the area at one time or another and in the designated age range for at least part of the period became drug cases during the period with which we were concerned, since each year sees additional youngsters coming into the age bracket and others growing out of it. Our base unit was a hypothetical boy living in the area and in the age bracket for the full forty-six months. Such a unit might, for example, be made up of two actual boys, one meeting the qualifications for fourteen months and the second for thirty-two months. The reported drug rates should be interpreted as *indexes* of narcotics activity which helped us compare the *relative* incidence of new cases from neighborhood to neighborhood.

A more refined method of calculating rates was also tested. It took into account the number of new cases each year and the eligible population for that year, still, however, making the necessary assumption that move-outs were balanced by move-ins. Thus, for 1951, the rate was calculated as

$$\frac{D_{1951}}{N_{1951} - (D_{1949} + D_{1950})},$$

where D_{1949}, D_{1950}, and D_{1951} are the numbers of new cases for the designated years and N_{1951} refers to the number of boys in the fifteen-to-nineteen age range at the time of the census (i.e., in the sixteen-to-twenty age range in

1951). The reason for subtracting D_{1949} and D_{1950} from N_{1951} is that these cases are no longer part of the eligible population. Similar rates were computed for each year of the period (with an adjustment for the number of cases in 1952).[1] The over-all rate was obtained by adding the yearly rate and multiplying by 1,000. After calculating rates both ways for twenty-three census tracts, it became obvious that the two methods were yielding virtually identical results (the correlation was .996), and the simpler method was adopted.

The rates were computed for a forty-six–month period. The reader who prefers to see rates on a yearly basis should multiply the cited figures by 12/46, or .26. Such an adjustment would have no effect on the comparisons made.

The Later Period

As we get further away from the year of the census, the census figures become less dependable. It was consequently necessary to prepare revised estimates of the number of males in our age bracket who resided in a given area. Since we could get data relevant to such estimates only on a health-area basis, drug rates for the later period were computed only for health areas.

THE NUMERATOR

The period of observation for the later period was thirty-six months, beginning November 1, 1952, in comparison to the forty-six–month earlier period. In order to make the rates comparable to those of the earlier period, the number of drug-involved cases in each health area was multiplied by 46/36; the resulting numbers were used as the numerators in computing drug rates. Although the numbers for the early and late periods were thus comparable, errors of measurement (i.e., enumeration errors) must be of relatively greater magnitude for the later period. It should also be remembered that we have greater confidence in the comprehensiveness of the case-finding procedures in the early period; this, too, would affect the accuracy of the rates.

THE DENOMINATOR

Three separate estimates were made of the number of males in the sixteen-to-twenty age bracket in each health area; two of these were for the base year 1954, and one for the year 1955. Drug rates were computed on the basis of each estimate. The logic of the three estimates was the same; only the data utilized were different. It was assumed that the number of males in our age bracket in a given health area would increase or decrease relative to the 1950 figures in proportion to the increase or decrease in the total population. Thus,

$$\frac{N_{1954}}{N_{1950}} = \frac{P_{1954}}{P_{1950}}, \text{ or } N_{1954} = \frac{P_{1954}}{P_{1950}} \times N_{1950},$$

[1] At the time these rates were calculated, we did not have the data on cases detected during the last two months of 1952. This also accounts for the forty-six–month period referred to in connection with the method of computing rates.

where N_{1954} is the number of males in the indicated age bracket in 1954, N_{1950} is the number of males aged twelve to sixteen in 1950 (these are, of course, the ones who were in the age range sixteen to twenty in 1954), P_{1954} is the total population in 1950, and P_{1950} the total population of the health area in 1950.

We assumed that the number of births (or, alternatively, deaths or, again alternatively, dwelling units) for a given year was directly proportional to the size of the total population. That is,

$$\frac{B_{1954}}{B_{1950}} = \frac{P_{1954}}{P_{1950}} \text{, hence, that } N_{1954} = \frac{B_{1954}}{B_{1950}} \times N_{1950},$$

where B_{1954} and B_{1950} are the number of births in a health area in, respectively, 1954 and 1950. Similarly with regard to the number of deaths and the number of occupied dwelling units. Since additional information was available in connection with the birth and death data, the actual calculations were somewhat more complicated. All these data were made available to us through the cooperation of the Department of Planning of the City of New York.

Estimate Based on Birth Data. We had or could calculate the number of births in 1954, in each health area, to white mothers who were themselves born in Puerto Rico, to nonwhite mothers from Puerto Rico, to other white mothers, and to other nonwhite mothers. This suggested the possibility of estimating the numbers of males aged sixteen to twenty in each of these four groups. For 1950, however, we did not have precisely parallel information and, consequently, had to estimate it. We did have the 1950 health-area figures for numbers of births to all white and nonwhite mothers; and we had the 1950 totals, by borough, for each of the four groups.

For each borough, we divided the number of births to white Puerto Rican mothers by the total number of white Puerto Ricans. Multiplying this ratio by the number of white Puerto Ricans in a given health area gave us an estimated number of births to white Puerto Rican mothers in that health area in 1950; and so on for each health area. For each health area, we now subtracted this estimate from the number of births to *all* white mothers, in order to get an estimate of the number of births to non-Puerto Rican white mothers. A similar procedure gave us estimates for each health area of the number of births to nonwhite Puerto Rican mothers and of the number of births to the other nonwhite mothers.

Finally, we had to estimate for the individual health areas the numbers of boys in the twelve-to-sixteen age range in each of the four groups in 1950. We computed the ratio of the number of white Puerto Rican boys in the twelve-to-sixteen group to the total number of white Puerto Ricans in the city[2] and multiplied it by the number of white Puerto Ricans in the health

[2] Actually, this also involved an estimate. The census tabulation did not give the number of white Puerto Rican boys in the twelve-to-sixteen age group; it gave the total for the ten-to-eighteen range. We estimated the number who were twelve-to-sixteen years old by halving the latter number.

area. Subtracting this estimate from the total number of white boys in this age range gave us an estimate of the number of white non-Puerto Rican boys in the desired age range. A similar procedure gave us estimates of the numbers of nonwhite Puerto Ricans and of other nonwhites in each health area.

We now had, for each of the subgroups, actual counts of the numbers of births in 1954 and parallel estimates of the number of births in 1950; and we had estimates of the number of boys in the twelve-to-sixteen bracket in 1950. We could, therefore, from the basic formula described above, estimate, for each health area, the number of boys in each of the subgroups in the sixteen-to-twenty bracket in 1954. Totaling the estimates for the four subgroups gave us our estimate of the total number of boys in the sixteen-to-twenty bracket in each health area in 1954.

Estimate Based on Death Data. We had, for each health area, the numbers of deaths among whites and nonwhites in 1954. We had parallel information for 1950. We also had, for each health area, the number of whites and the number of nonwhites in the twelve-to-sixteen age group in 1950. That is, we had all the data necessary to estimate, on the basis of the death data, the numbers of white and nonwhite boys in each health area in 1954; all that was necessary was to substitute in the basic formula. Adding the two estimates gave us the desired estimate of the total number of boys in the sixteen-to-twenty bracket in each health area in 1954.

Estimate Based on Occupied Dwelling Units. The Sanborn Map Company made a count of the number of occupied dwelling units in each health area in late 1955. We had parallel information and also the total number of boys in the twelve-to-sixteen bracket for each health area from the 1950 census. Substituting in the basic formula gave us our third estimate of the total number of boys in the sixteen-to-twenty bracket in each health area in 1954.

COMPARABILITY OF DRUG RATES

The three procedures for estimating the denominators for computing the health-area drug rates were so different from one another and the data utilized were also so different, that it became desirable to check on the consistency of the results obtained by the various methods.

In our maps of the distribution of drug rates in the early period, we had distinguished seven levels of drug rates. We accordingly classified each of the drug rates for the later period obtained by each of the estimating procedures into these seven levels. We then computed Robinson's coefficient of agreement[a] to measure the concordance among the three methods in terms of the way each method would classify an area into one of the seven class intervals used on our maps. For the 265 health areas with which we are concerned, the Robinson measure indicated that the three methods would yield virtually identical drug-rate maps. The coefficient of agreement between the system based on births and that based on deaths was .98; between the birth system and the dwelling-unit system, .99; and, finally, between the death system and the dwelling-unit system, .98.

These high degrees of agreement should not engender false optimism. Basically, they mean that estimates of the population totals obtained by the three methods should be highly consistent. It should be remembered, however, that a health-area drug rate computed by each of the methods involves the same adjusted numerator, and the denominator involves the same assumptions in the basic formula, e.g., the constancy over time of the proportion of the age cohort to the total population in each health area. In other words, there are possible sources of error common to the three procedures. On the other hand, the basic formula was applied in such differing ways in calculating the three denominators (to three subgroups separately in the birth-data method, to two in the death-data method, and to the total group in the dwelling-unit method) that the common assumptions involved in calculating the denominators would have been severely strained if they were not at least approximately correct.

Final Estimates of Later-Period Drug Rates. The later-period drug rates used in the final analysis—i.e., in the correlations with the early-period drug rates—were simple averages of the three estimates. This would tend to average out variable errors in the three estimates. It would not, of course, get rid of common errors.

STATISTICAL FOOTNOTES

[a] W. W. Robinson, "The Statistical Measure of Agreement," *American Sociological Review*, 22 (1957), 17–25. Robinson's measure of agreement is a variant of the intraclass correlation coefficient, itself a variant of the familiar Pearson product-moment correlation which we have used elsewhere. Unlike the usual product-moment correlation, the intraclass correlation is sensitive to absolute, rather than simply relative, discrepancies between two sets of scores.

APPENDIX B

Definition of Independent Variables

For the analysis of data in the epidemic and border-zone areas, the variables listed below under the lettered headings were combined into more comprehensive indexes by ranking census tracts for each component and averaging the ranks. To be so combined, components had to satisfy two criteria: (1) they had to be conceptually linked to a more inclusive concept, and (2) they had to show similar patterns of correlation in a preliminary analysis in each of the three boroughs. A number of such combined indexes that had been considered were abandoned because the components did not satisfy the second criterion. The preliminary analysis was carried out on the census tracts in the epidemic areas; correlations were computed by dichotomizing each of the variables as nearly as possible at its median value and calculating phi coefficients.[1] The original intention had been to restrict the analysis to the epidemic areas, and the comparison of the epidemic and nonepidemic areas was not carried out until later (even though it is reported earlier in Chapter III). On the basis of the latter analysis, it became apparent that, on borough-wide bases, the respective components of the inclusive indexes do not "behave" in the same way. Hence, for the epidemic-versus-nonepidemic–area comparisons, the data are reported for the individual variables.

[1] The phi coefficient is identical with the regular Pearsonian correlation as applied to dichotomous variables. See Appendix C.

NAME OF VARIABLE*	NUMERATOR (N)	DENOMINATOR (D)	INDEX
A. Index of disrupted family living arrangements			Average rank of indexes 1–7
1. Percentage of population residing in hotels or large boarding houses	Number of persons living in households	Noninstitutional population	$100 - \dfrac{100N}{D}$
2. Percentage of population not living with a relative	Number of unrelated individuals	Noninstitutional population	$\dfrac{100N}{D}$
3. Percentage of working women	Number of females in civilian labor force	Number of females aged fourteen and over	$\dfrac{100N}{D}$
4. Percentage of divorced or widowed wives	Number of still-married females	Number of females who have ever been married	$100 - \dfrac{100N}{D}$
5. Percentage of wives separated from husbands	Number of married couples	Number of still-married females	$100 - \dfrac{100N}{D}$
6. Percentage of husbands separated from wives	Number of married couples	Number of still-married men	$100 - \dfrac{100N}{D}$
7. Percentage of married couples not living in their own homes	Number of married couples without their own households	Number of married couples	$\dfrac{100N}{D}$

* The definition of drug rate is given in Appendix A.

NAME OF VARIABLE	NUMERATOR (N)	DENOMINATOR (D)	INDEX
B. Index of density of male adolescent population			Average rank of indexes 8–10
8. Average number of male adolescents per block	Number of males aged fifteen to nineteen	Number of blocks with dwelling units	N/D
9. Average number of male adolescents per adult	Number of males aged fifteen to nineteen	Number of men and women aged twenty-one and over	N/D
10. Percentage of male adolescents	Number of males aged fifteen to nineteen	Noninstitutional population	$\frac{100N}{D}$
C. Uncombined variables			
11. Percentage of unemployed men	Number of unemployed males	Number of males in civilian labor force	$\frac{100N}{D}$
12. Percentage of income units earning $2,000 or less	Number of units earning $2,000 or less in 1949	Number of units reporting income in 1949	$\frac{100N}{D}$
13. Percentage of dwelling units that are highly crowded	Number of dwelling units with more than 1.5 persons per room	Number of dwelling units reporting on persons per room	$\frac{100N}{D}$
14. Percentage of men employed in "lower" occupations	Number of male operatives and less skilled workers	Number of employed males	$\frac{100N}{D}$
15. Percentage of adults with fewer than eight years of school	Number of persons aged twenty-five and over with fewer than eight years of school	Number of persons aged twenty-five and over reporting on schooling	$\frac{100N}{D}$
16. Average number of vacant dwelling units per block	Number of vacant dwelling units	Number of blocks with dwelling units	N/D

	Variable	Numerator (N)	Denominator (D)	Formula
17.	Percentage of dwelling units without television	Number of dwelling units without television	Number of dwelling units reporting on television	$\dfrac{100N}{D}$
18.	Average number of business establishments per block	Number of business establishments	Number of blocks with dwelling units	N/D
19.	Number of local employees per resident	Number of employees in local establishments with twelve or more employees (Source: N.Y. State Dept. of Labor)	Noninstitutional population	N/D
20.	Percentage of the population that is Negro	Number of Negroes minus nonwhite Puerto Ricans	Total population	$\dfrac{100N}{D}$
21.	Percentage of the population that is of Puerto Rican origin	Number of persons classified as Puerto Rican	Total population	$\dfrac{100N}{D}$
22.	Percentage excess of females over males (twenty-one—and-over age group)	Number of females twenty-one years of age and over	Number of males twenty-one years of age and over	$\dfrac{100N}{D} - 100$
23.	Percentage excess of females over males (fifteen-to-nineteen age group)	Number of females in fifteen-to-nineteen age group	Number of males in fifteen-to-nineteen age group	$\dfrac{100N}{D} - 100$
24.	Percentage of population living at a new address	Number of persons living at a different address in the preceding year	Number of persons one year old and older	$\dfrac{100N}{D}$

APPENDIX C

Meaning of Correlation Coefficients

The correlation coefficient is a measure of the degree of association between particular scores in one variable and particular scores in another when both sets of scores are expressed in the same standard units.

Suppose, for instance, that we wanted to measure the degree of association between height and weight. Experience would tell us that, on the average, taller people are also heavier, that is, height and weight are positively associated. But there are also some tall people who weigh less than some shorter people; the association is not perfect. But how far from perfection?

Height is measured in inches, and weight in pounds. If they were expressed in the same units, the question of how close the association between the two is would be relatively simple. If the association were perfect, then every person would have exactly the same height as weight. If the association were less than perfect, then at least some persons would have heights that differ from their weights, and, the greater the average difference, the less the correspondence between height and weight. But if, as just noted, height and weight are normally expressed in different units, we can still express them in the same units and thus be able to directly compare the heights and weights of persons, as follows:

(1) We subtract from the height of each individual the average height of the entire group, and, from each weight, the average weight. The scores are now expressed in what are called "deviational" units, but they are still in terms of, respectively, inches and pounds. If the average weight is 150 pounds, a person who weighs 160 has a deviational score of plus ten pounds, and a person who weighs 145 has a deviational score of minus five pounds. (2) We now relate the deviational scores to the respective variabilities of heights and of weights. Specifically, we divide each deviational score in height by the standard deviation[1] of the heights, and each deviational score in weight is divided by the standard deviation of the weights.

[1] The standard deviation is the square root of the average of the squared deviational scores. Like the deviational scores, the standard deviation has the same dimension as the original scores. Thus, if the original scores are measured in inches, the standard deviation is measured in inches. To discuss why we take the standard deviation rather than the simple average of the deviations would

As a result of these transformations, we get two sets of scores which are directly comparable to each other. The units are no longer pounds and inches, but "standard deviations." For example, if the standard deviation of heights is 5 inches and the average height is 69 inches, then a person who is 65 inches tall has a standard score of −.80; that is, he is 8/10 of a standard deviation below the average height. If the average weight is 150 pounds, the standard deviation 10 pounds, and if the same person weighs 142 pounds, he has a standard score of −.80; that is, he is 8/10 of a standard deviation below the average weight. This means that, relative to the dispersions of heights and of weights, this person is exactly as far below the average height as he is below the average weight—a perfect correspondence, in this case. Another person might also have a standard score of −.80 in height, but a standard score of .20 in weight. This is a considerable discrepancy, as such scores go, and this person's standing with respect to weight is much higher than with respect to height.

When scores are expressed in the same units, we might, as suggested above, take the average of the differences between corresponding scores as a measure of the degree of association—the larger the average difference, the smaller the degree of association. For reasons that we cannot go into here, we take *half* the average of the *squared* differences instead of the average of the differences. Again, however, the larger this number, the smaller the degree of association. This number, it can be shown, cannot be larger than 2, and it obviously cannot be smaller than zero. It will, in fact, equal 2 when every score is of exactly the same magnitude as the score to which it is being compared, but reversed in sign, for instance, −.80 in height and +.80 in weight, +1.23 in height and −1.23 in weight, and so on. It will equal zero when all the corresponding scores are exactly alike. It will equal 1 when the standard scores in one variable are randomly associated with the scores in the other, that is, if there is absolutely no consistent trend for the standard scores in one variable to be like or different from the standard scores in the other.

In order to assign the highest possible degree of positive association (when all the differences equal zero) a value of +1.00 and the maximum possible degree of negative association (when all the corresponding scores are of the same magnitude but opposite in sign) a value of −1.00, we subtract half the average of the squared differences from 1. Perfectly random association will then have a value of zero. The result, somewhere between +1 and −1, is the coefficient of correlation.[2] The important point to remember is that the correlation coefficient does not depend on the absolute values of the original scores

---

involve us in technicalities that would take us too far afield. For present purposes, it is enough to note that the procedure involves the comparison of each deviational score to a deviation that may be said to be characteristic of the entire set of scores.

[2] This account does not parallel the familiar versions of the product-moment correlation formula, but is algebraically identical to them and offers what seems to be the simplest explanation of what is involved. No one would, of course, actually compute a correlation coefficient in the manner described, except possibly for didactic purposes.

but on the consistency of the relative standings of the cases with respect to the distributions of two variables.

As far as the degree of association goes, the sign of the correlation does not really matter. A correlation coefficient can always be reversed in sign without changing its numerical value, simply by turning one of the variables around. Thus, height and weight are positively correlated; by and large, taller people tend to be heavier and shorter people lighter. If we were to correlate *shortness* and weight, however, assigning higher scores to shorter people and lower scores to taller people, the correlation would be negative. Similarly, if we were to correlate height and *lightness,* the correlation would be negative. But if we were to correlate *shortness* and *lightness,* the correlation would again be positive.

The sign of the correlation gives the direction of the relationship, as the variables are defined. If we have reason to be interested in the direction, then the sign of the correlation becomes important. Thus, if a hypothesis calls for a positive correlation, then a negative correlation is more disconfirming of that hypothesis than would be a zero correlation. There are occasions, however, when we have no special interest in the sign other than for orientation. In Chapter IV, for instance, we report on an inquiry into families of variables,[3] and, for such a purpose, the magnitudes of the correlations are of paramount importance.[4]

[3] Such an inquiry is referred to as a cluster analysis, the idea of which is explained in Chapter IV and Appendix E. A cluster analysis was also carried out on the variables dealt with in Chapter III. We have not, however, reported this analysis, because it does not materially add to or subtract from the story we have told. The definable clusters vary somewhat from borough to borough, but this is related to a point we deal with in the chapter, viz., that some of the variables do not have consistent meanings in the three boroughs in terms of their patterns of relationships with the other variables. The point is of special significance only in relation to general studies of urban ecology and in inspiring caution with the apparent face validity of many ecological variables.

For the same reason, we have not reported the beta coefficients in the multiple correlation analysis. As might be expected, the highest betas in each borough represent all the clusters and, in Manhattan and the Bronx, some of the variables that stand off by themselves, e.g., the percentage excess of adolescent females over males. Such a scattering of betas lends emphasis to our final point in the chapter that no one group of unwholesome factors can be said to be exclusively associated with the vulnerability of neighborhoods to the use of narcotics by juveniles. The prepotency of the economic factor again shows up in the fact that, in Manhattan and Brooklyn, poverty (i.e., percentage of units with incomes of $2,000 or less) has the highest beta—twenty-five times as large as the smallest in Manhattan and twelve times as large as the smallest in Brooklyn; in the Bronx, this variable has a relative weight of twenty-six, but is exceeded by two of the more ambiguous variables (percentage of families living at a new address and number of employees per resident, the latter with a negative beta). The betas were computed only for the multiple regression equation involving all the variables but percentage of Negroes and percentage of Puerto Ricans.

[4] The signs enter also, but there is no special interest in the sign of the correlation between any pair of variables other than in determining sets of variables

Correlation between Two-Valued Variables

Many variables can be measured along dimensions that, in principle, permit an infinite number of points if the precision of measurement is great enough; it is possible, however, to compute correlations for variables that permit as few as two possible points, e.g., the answers to an item on a test which may be scored zero or 1. When both variables are of this two-valued, or dichotomous, variety, the correlation coefficient we have described above is generally referred to as the phi coefficient or as the four-point correlation. The four-point correlation, however, suffers for certain purposes from the handicap that, if the over-all distributions of the two variables are not identical in shape, it is impossible to get correlations of +1.00 or −1.00; that is, the possible range of values is restricted.[5] Hence, correlations obtained for differently distributed variables are not directly comparable.

Since, in Chapter IV, we deal with the correlations between two-valued variables, the particular device we have adopted to overcome the handicap should be explained. A many-valued variable can be rendered into a dichotomy by cutting it at some point. Thus, we can form two classes of heights, one consisting of persons who are less than, say, sixty-eight inches tall and the other of persons who are sixty-eight or more inches tall. Conversely, we can think of most dichotomies as the results of a cut in a many-valued variable. Thus, we can think of people who can give the right answer to a question as

---

that stand in a special kind of relationship to one another. Variables are freely reflected (turned over) in order to minimize the number of negative signs, a process that makes it easier to find such sets.

[5] In principle, the same limitation applies to the general case; it has less material consequence, however, as the number of distinguished points in each variable rises. If 100 people answer two items, and, say, fifty answer the first correctly and only twenty answer the second correctly, then, scoring each item zero for an incorrect and 1 for a correct answer, the average on the first item is .5 and, on the second, .2. For the first item, there are fifty people with deviational scores of +.5 and fifty with −.5; the standard deviation is .5. For the second item, there are twenty people with deviational scores of +.8, and eighty with −.2; the standard deviation is .4. Hence, for the first item, there are fifty cases with standard scores of +1, and fifty with −1. By contrast, for the second item, there are twenty with standard scores of +2, and eighty with −.5. Even if all the people who gave the right answer to the second item also answered the first item correctly, each of them would have one standard score of +1 and one of +2, and the difference obviously does not equal zero. Similarly, if all the people who got the first answer wrong also gave the wrong answer to the second, they would have standard scores of −1 and −.5, and, again the difference does not equal zero. So, even for the people with perfectly matching performances (right on both items or wrong on both items), we do not get perfectly matching standard scores; and, with one item breaking 50–50 and the other 20–80, it is impossible not to get cases without matching performances. The highest possible positive four-point correlation in this instance is .50; the most extreme negative four-point correlation possible is −.50.

knowing more about the subject of that question than people who cannot answer the question correctly. A more finely graded test would make many distinctions among the people who answer the question correctly and, similarly, among those who answer it incorrectly. Moreover, whatever the shape of the many-valued distribution of scores, the scores can always be transformed in such a way that the distribution closely approximates the normal, or bell-shaped, distribution.[6] A set of scores so treated is said to have been normalized.

If two dichotomies result from the cutting of two normal distributions, then, because of certain mathematical relationships involved, we can estimate from the joint distributions of the dichotomized variables what the correlation would have been if we had cross-tabulated the full sets of the original scores and computed the correlation therefrom. A correlation coefficient so estimated from the joint distribution of two dichotomies (i.e., on the assumption that each dichotomy represents a cut in a many-valued dimension in which the scores are normally distributed or in which the distributions have been normalized) is known as a tetrachoric correlation. The correlations among questionnaire items dealt with in Chapter IV were computed on this basis. Tetrachoric correlations have theoretical limits of +1 and −1 regardless of whether the two over-all distributions of the two-valued variables are identical.

Let us illustrate the idea of correlations among items with some hypothetical distributions. We shall consider two questionnaire items for purposes of the illustration.

G 26. Most addicts who take the cure never go back on drugs again.

True_____   False_____   I don't know_____

G 3. Heroin is probably not so bad for a person as some people say.
I agree_____   I disagree_____

We shall treat these as two-valued variables. Giving the correct answer to the first and expressing what we take to be the desirable attitude toward the second are, respectively, the high-scoring responses; failing to give the correct

[6] The normal distribution has the following distinctive properties: there is a piling-up of cases around the average; as one moves in either direction from the average, the number of cases falls off; between the average and any given point above it, there is the same number of cases as between the average and a point equally distant below it; 34 per cent of the cases are found between the average and a point one standard deviation above it, and a like proportion of cases, between the average and a point one standard deviation below it; 47.7 per cent of the cases are found between the average and a point two standard deviations away from it, 49.87 per cent of the cases between the average and a point three standard deviations away, etc. The normal distribution is a common one in nature, and it often, but not always, makes sense to assume that, if the obtained distribution is not normal, the fault is in the measuring instrument, rather than in the true distribution. In such cases, the scores are commonly normalized. The IQ's, for instance, determined by one of the most commonly used intelligence tests are based on normalized, rather than directly obtained, scores.

answer to the first and expressing the undesirable attitude toward the second are, respectively, the low-scoring responses.

Let us consider a hypothetical distribution of the responses of 100 subjects to these two items:

		Heroin not so bad		
		AGREE	DISAGREE	
		(LOW SCORE)	(HIGH SCORE)	TOTAL
Addicts are	False (high score)	5	31	36
permanently	True or don't know			
cured	(low score)	35	29	64
	TOTAL	40	60	100

Notice that about 86 per cent (31 out of 36) of those who give the correct answer to the first item disagree with the second, whereas about 55 per cent (35 out of 64) of those who do not give the correct answer to the first agree with the second. A total of sixty-six of the 100 subjects are either high-scoring or low-scoring on both items; only thirty-four score high on one but low on the other. In this instance, there is a positive correlation between giving the correct answer to the first and expressing a desirable attitude on the second. That is, there is a considerably higher probability of expressing the "right" attitude among subjects who give the correct answer than among those who do not. The calculated value of the tetrachoric correlation coefficient is approximately $+.67$.

Compare this outcome with the following hypothetical distribution:

		Heroin not so bad		
		AGREE	DISAGREE	
		(LOW SCORE)	(HIGH SCORE)	TOTAL
Addicts are	False (high score)	14	22	36
permanently	True or don't know			
cured	(low score)	26	38	64
	TOTAL	40	60	100

In this case, the probability of expressing the "right" attitude is almost exactly the same (60 per cent) among those giving the correct answer as among those who do not. Just about half are consistently high or consistently low on both; about half are high on one, but low on the other. The correlation is about zero.

And consider, finally, the following hypothetical distribution:

		Heroin not so bad		
		AGREE	DISAGREE	
		(LOW SCORE)	(HIGH SCORE)	TOTAL
Addicts are	False (high score)	35	1	36
permanently	True or don't know			
cured	(low score)	5	59	64
	TOTAL	40	60	100

In this case, 97 per cent of those giving the correct answer (35 out of 36) express the "wrong" attitude, whereas 92 per cent of those not giving the correct answer (59 out of 64) express the "right" attitude. Only six of the 100 respondents are consistently high or consistently low on both items; ninety-four are high on one, but low on the other. The correlation is negative, about —.98.

Note that, in all three illustrations, the marginals (i.e., the over-all distribution of each variable) are exactly the same. That is, 36 per cent of the total group of subjects give the correct answer to the first item, and 60 per cent express the "right" attitude. Obviously, if we were to consider only the marginal totals of the individual items, we would be neglecting fairly vital information. Note also that the over-all distribution of one variable differs from that of the other—a 36–64 break in the case of one, and a 40–60 break in the case of the other. This does not stop us from getting a tetrachoric correlation of virtually unity.

Interpreting a Correlation Coefficient

All that a correlation between two variables can tell us is that the corresponding scores tend to be associated in some way. It does not tell us why or how that correlation comes about. It may help to maintain perspective on correlation coefficients to indicate some of the ways in which substantial correlation can come about:

(1) Two variables may directly involve common components. With greater height, for instance, there are more of certain bones, flesh, and sinews; flesh, bones, and sinews, of course, contribute to weight. A high correlation between census-tract drug rates and delinquency rates would result if narcotics and other violations were committed only by socially alienated individuals and if such individuals always committed both types of offenses. It would follow that, the more socially alienated individuals in a census tract, the higher both rates would be; the socially alienated individuals would be common components of both rates.

(2) Two variables may be determined by a common cause. Assume, for instance, that poverty generates disrespect for social standards in a society that emphasizes economic success and plenty. Assume, further, that aggressive individuals with disrespect for social standards strike back in the form of criminal activity and that passive individuals with similar disrespect for social standards seek substitute, if illicit and illusory, gratification, such as that provided by drugs. Assume, finally, that each census tract is endowed with its fair share of highly aggressive and of highly passive individuals, although poverty is distributed in unequal proportions. In such a situation, there would be a high correlation between census-tract drug and delinquency rates, even though different individuals commit the two types of offense. The common cause is poverty.

(3) One variable may be in the causal sequence that leads to another. As-

sume, for instance, that illegal drugs are costly and that addicts must commit crimes to obtain the funds to buy drugs. Assume, further, that some census tracts have many more addicts than others. Such a state of affairs would lead to a high correlation between census-tract drug and delinquency rates. Drug use is a cause of delinquency. But, one may argue, delinquency existed before widespread drug use and cannot be caused by something that came after. Such an argument is commonly compelling. For instance, we note in Chapter III a high correlation between juvenile drug rate and poverty. Since the poverty rates were measured as of 1949, and since there were still very few juvenile users in 1949, it is absurd to think that juvenile drug use caused poverty—even if there were no other reasons for considering such a hypothesis untenable. The drug-rate–delinquency-rate example cannot, however, be so readily dismissed. It is conceivable that current delinquency is largely generated by drug use, i.e., that other causes of delinquency have virtually disappeared. This, for instance, is an inference (a not-logically-required inference, we must say) drawn by many from statistics that 60 per cent or more of the inmates of penal institutions are "drug addicts."

On the other hand, assume that people who are criminally inclined are attracted to narcotics precisely because they are illegal. In this event, we would also get a high correlation between drug and delinquency rates, but delinquency would be the cause of drug use. We report in Chapter V, that we found great difficulty in locating delinquents in the high-drug-rate areas who were not also drug-users. The assumption we are discussing might offer one explanation of such a finding.

(4) What may be interpreted as a special case of common components or of common cause—viz., correlated errors of measurement—may also bring about substantial correlation. Assume, for instance, that the true drug rates and delinquency rates are the same in all census tracts, but that the intensity of police activity varies markedly. This would produce a high correlation between the two obtained sets of rates, but each of the variables would actually be measuring intensity of police activity, the common component of the two measures, rather than what it purports to measure.

(5) The basis of the relationship may be complex, involving common components, common causes that tend to produce both effects independently, some reciprocal causation between the variables, and correlated errors—all operating at the same time.

(6) A real relationship, on whatever basis, between two variables may be masked by the operation of one or more additional variables. This point can be illustrated with the following hypothetical data. Assume that we have subdivided an area with 100,000 boys into 100 sections with 1,000 boys in each. Assume further that we have classified each section into the twenty-five sections with the highest poverty rates, the twenty-five sections with the next highest poverty rates, and so on. Similarly, assume that we have classified each section as one of the fifty highest in rates of change of residence or as one of the fifty lowest. Finally, assume that we have calculated drug rates, with the following results:

Quartiles of Poverty

	LOWEST	SECOND	THIRD	HIGHEST	TOTAL
High moving rate	(20)	(20)	(5)	(5)	(50)
	20	30	40	50	29
Low moving rate	(5)	(5)	(20)	(20)	(50)
	0	10	30	40	29
TOTAL NUMBER OF TRACTS	(25)	(25)	(25)	(25)	(100)
	16	24.5	32	42	29

The numbers in parentheses designate the numbers of sections in each poverty-moving category. The other numbers designate the number of drug-involved cases per thousand boys. Observe that, at each poverty level, the drug rate for the sections in the high-moving-rate category is higher than for those in the low-moving-rate category. Yet, if we were simply to examine the relationship between drug rate and rates of changing residence without reference to poverty, the high- and the low-moving-rate sections have exactly the same drug rates. The relationship between moving rate and drug rate would be obscured by the relationship between moving rate and poverty.

Apart from the sheer fact of concomitant variation, a correlation coefficient is an ambiguous datum. It can only be interpreted in the light of additional information which heightens the credibility of one of the possible alternatives and lessens the credibility of others.

In the same manner, a high correlation between two questionnaire items, A and B, may be open to a variety of interpretations. Thus:

(1) A contributes directly to the causation or generation of B, or vice versa. In the first of the preceding hypothetical examples of a correlation between two items, we portrayed the high correlation between the awareness of the great difficulty of curing drug addiction and the feeling that heroin is indeed harmful in terms that suggested that the first is the cause of the second. But we could also interpret the correlation as follows: a strong feeling that heroin is harmful may dispose one to assume that addiction is difficult to cure, and skepticism about its harmfulness may dispose one to assume that addiction is readily curable. In other words, we could interpret the correlation by assuming that the answer to the second item tends to determine the answer to the first.

(2) A may generate a chain of events which lead to B, or vice versa. Thus, learning that, once an addict, always an addict, may conceivably sensitize one to other evidence of its undesirability, evoke unconscious complexes about incurable diseases (e.g., "wages of sin"), and so on, and it may be that these processes are the factors that lead to the conclusion that heroin is harmful.

(3) A and B may have no direct influence on each other, but each may be generated by the same set, or by correlated sets, of conditions. Thus, we might explain the correlation by assuming that the cultural atmosphere disposes one to answer the two items in a consistent manner, even though the two are never brought in apposition.

(4) A may be a component of B, or vice versa; A and B may contain common aspects or elements; or, under certain conditions, A may take on the coloration of B, or vice versa. Thus, "incurability" may be one of the meanings attributed to "harmfulness," or "harmfulness" one of the meanings attributed to "incurability." Or both items may have in common the fact that they offer an opportunity to express one's acceptance or rejection of the mores of society. Or, in an environment which is not overly hostile to the use of narcotics, ignorance may tend to robe itself in the garb of tolerance.

(5) All or some combination of the foregoing bases of relationship and possibly others as well may be simultaneously true. Thus, the relationship between the response tendencies evoked by the two items may be one of a vicious or beneficent circle; for example, ignorance of the facts about curability may produce, under certain conditions, a tolerant attitude which, in turn, may create a mental block toward learning the true facts and, hence, a rejection of the sources of authority which seek to propound the true facts; this rejection, in its turn, may cause one to lean over backward to be even more tolerant, and so forth. We could then conclude that the outlook on the cure of addiction tends to be shaped by an attitudinal, rather than an informational, current in the cultural atmosphere. The alternatives selected by individuals in responding to the addiction-cure item tend to be determined by where they stand with respect to the attitudinal complex or with respect to the forces that shape this complex.

This inherent ambiguity, from the viewpoint of causality, of described relationships between variables is not limited to the case where the relationship is expressed in the form of a correlation coefficient. That is, the ambiguity is not in the coefficient, but in the fact of correlation—of concomitant variation —itself, however such correlation may be described. We made our points, for example, about the "real" relationship (in the hypothetical illustration) between rates of changing residence and drug rates and about the masking of this relationship by the relationship between moving rate and poverty rate by displaying a table; we did not compute any correlation coefficients at all. In the same table, it is easy to see the existence of a relationship between drug rates and poverty rates even if one does not express the *degree* of relationship in a number or express the *form* of the relationship in a mathematical equation.[7] Whether or not we take the latter steps, the relationships themselves are

[7] To the student of statistics, this is apt to be one of the most familiar properties of the correlation coefficient; it is the essential term in the equation of a straight line. If both variables are expressed as standard scores, this equation is

$$z_{1(2)} = r_{12}z_2,$$

where $z_{1(2)}$ designates the "expected" score in Variable 1 that corresponds to a particular standard score in Variable 2, z_2 designates standard scores in Variable 2, and r_{12} is the coefficient of correlation between the two variables. Hence, the correlation coefficient describes a relationship which has the *form* of a straight line. The "expected" score $z_{1(2)}$ that corresponds to a particular z_2 is an approximation of the actual average score on Variable 1 that is obtained by the individuals who earn that particular score on Variable 2. If we were to compute a series of such actual averages on Variable 1 for each of the scores

subject to the varieties of interpretation that we have discussed with respect to the correlation coefficient. Does poverty, for instance, lead to drug use, or is there a factor that independently produces both?

Observed relationships have to be interpreted, and the interpretation has to be based on the additional information and the variety of alternative hypotheses that can be brought to bear on the issue. The process of interpretation requires judgment, and there is no alternative to this, short of direct experimentation.[8] One type of additional information that can be brought to bear on the interpretation of a relationship is to examine it in the context of a larger set of relationships. This does not eliminate the judgmental process; it simply increases the informational base in terms of which judgments are rendered. In Chapter III, we made use of correlation data to examine the contribution that individual variables can make to a statistical accounting of drug rates, by themselves and in combination with other variables. In Chapter IV, we make use of a network of correlations in a somewhat different fashion. There is no one variable on which we wish to focus to begin with; it is the network itself that is of primary interest to us.

The Correlation of Rates

We must here face an issue that has been touched on in an earlier footnote. Rates are tricky variables in correlational analysis. The issue may perhaps be made clear by an illustration due to Jerzy Neyman.[9] Neyman correlated birth rates with the number of storks in various counties of the United States and found a substantial correlation. The greater the number of storks, the greater, on the average, the birth rate. Before one takes this finding as support for a certain theory of childbirth, however, one must note that it is a statistical artifact. Birth rate happens to be positively correlated with population size, the denominator used in computing birth rates. Storks, on the other hand, not indigenous to this country, tend to be found in zoos and menageries, which, in turn, tend to be located in highly populated areas, with the largest zoos in the most heavily populated areas. The correlation between birth rate and number of storks, it turns out, simply reflects the correlation between population size and number of storks; when a control is introduced for population size, the earlier correlation vanishes.

It should be obvious from this illustration that what has been called "spurious index correlation" is a special case of the more general proposition that

---

on Variable 2 and if these averages did not tend to fall along a straight line, the relationship would be said to be *curvilinear;* in such an event, the correlation coefficient we have described would underestimate the true degree of relationship, sometimes quite markedly so.

[8] This point is discussed in the text of Chapter III.

[9] J. Neyman, *Lectures and Conferences on Mathematical Statistics and Probability* (2nd ed.; Washington: Graduate School, U.S. Department of Agriculture, 1952).

correlation may arise between two variables as a result of their respective correlations with a third variable. The caveat expressed by many statisticians against spurious index correlation is a special case of the more general caveat against the possibility that a correlation between two variables is due to their respective associations with a—possibly unsuspected—third variable. The more general possibility does not bother us particularly. We do not correlate an index of poverty, for example, with drug rate because we suspect that poverty per se causes drug use. We know of no reason to suspect this as a possibility; quite the contrary, because illegal drugs are so terribly expensive. We carry out the correlation precisely because we suspect that poverty is associated with something that does stand in a causal relation to vulnerability to drug use. Whether that something is itself a cause or a consequence of poverty is, at the moment, of secondary importance.

We have already conceded that the most we can hope for from our analysis is a reasonable interpretation or a number of alternative reasonable interpretations, albeit interpretations based on established facts. Whether we interpret the "something" as cause, as consequence, or as incidental correlate of poverty depends on the plausibility of the hypotheses that might explain the obtained relationship between poverty and drug use. If our constructive imaginations have failed us in the interpretation of findings, we hope that some of our readers will be stimulated to come up with better interpretations or at least with alternative plausible interpretations that we may have failed to consider.

The possibility of spurious index correlation is, however, bothersome. The reason for the worry can be most readily explained by illustration. Suppose that drug rate is substantially correlated with number of adolescent boys, that percentage of income units earning $2,000 or less is substantially correlated with the number of units reporting on income, and that (as is likely to be the case, because both denominators are presumably substantially correlated with the size of the total population) the number of adolescent boys is substantially correlated with population size. Then the correlation between drug rate and this index of poverty could be, in whole or in part, the result of the respective correlations between each of the indexes and population size. This possibility, however—and it is one that is invited by the correlation of rates—is so remote from the thinking that leads us to investigate the correlation between the two indexes in the first place that we would not like to have to entertain it.

Fortunately, it turns out that the correlation between drug rate and number of adolescent boys within the groups of census tracts we are studying is just about zero. Hence, any correlation between drug rate and any of the other variables cannot have such a "spurious" basis.

We did not investigate the possibility of spurious index correlation among the other variables. The possibility is irrelevant, because we are not interested in explicating the causal contexts of the other variables.[10] Moreover, in the

10 It should be pointed out that spurious index correlation between these variables would make for a higher common factor variance than would be found if some procedure other than the computation of rates were used to control for the

case of these other variables, rates are precisely what we are interested in. Our assumption is that it is the *relative* incidence of, say, poverty that makes for a community climate hospitable to drug use.[11]

---

respective sizes of the base populations. The procedure suggested by Neyman is to partial out the population. Thus, if drug rate had been substantially correlated with male adolescent population, an alternative to drug rate would have been the number of drug-involved cases minus the number to be expected on the basis of the correlation between the number of cases and the number of adolescent boys. If there were a substantial curvilinear component in the latter correlation, the procedure would be more complicated, but the same in principle. The same procedure would, of course, be followed for all indexes involving a relative-to-the-population aspect.

[11] Our assumption is that the relative incidence of poverty is more easily discernible as a rate than through some complicated statistical inference based on the relation between number of impoverished families and another variable—population size. By placing the advantage on the side of discernibility, we think that we have increased the likelihood that the "something" linking poverty and drug rate is in the causal sequence between the two, rather than in the causal sequence leading to poverty. The alternative procedure mentioned in Note 10 would, we think, give less emphasis to the psychological aspect of poverty, as it would to the other variables.

APPENDIX D

The Questionnaire

NOTE: *The first part of the questionnaire is labeled "Form F"; the second part, "Form G." The questionnaires were administered to both boys and girls, for reasons of convenience, but only the returns from the boys were analyzed.*

FORM F **Teenage Opinion Survey**

THIS IS NOT A TEST.

DO NOT SIGN YOUR NAME.

When were you born?
Month_____ Day_____ Year_____ _____Boy
_____Girl

School_____ Class_____

Teen-age Opinion Survey

This is a public opinion poll. There are no right or wrong answers. We just want to find out what young people think about different things.

Be sure to answer *every* question. If you are not sure, make your best guess.

THIS IS NOT A TEST.

DO NOT SIGN YOUR NAME.

Here are some things people say at times. Some people agree with them. Other people do not agree.

Do you agree or disagree with these things?

If you agree, put an X in front of I AGREE. If you do not agree, put an X in front of I DO NOT AGREE.

1. I am a very lucky person.
   ____I agree
   ____I do not agree

2. I often think that parents don't want their kids to have any fun.
   ____I agree
   ____I do not agree

3. You should never be loud around the house.
   ____I agree
   ____I do not agree

4. There is not much chance that people will really do anything to make this a better world to live in.
   ____I agree
   ____I do not agree

5. I can get away with doing things other people can't.
   ____I agree
   ____I do not agree

6. Most policemen can be paid off.
   ____I agree
   ____I do not agree

7. There are many times when it's O.K. to use bad words in front of older people.
   ____I agree
   ____I do not agree

8. Even when I get into trouble, I can usually get out of it.
   ____I agree
   ____I do not agree

9. You should always treat girls nicely, even when you don't like them.
   ____I agree
   ____I do not agree

10. You're a fool if you believe what most people try to tell you.
    ____I agree
    ____I do not agree

11. I hardly ever worry about anything. Things always come out right in the end.
    ____I agree
    ____I do not agree

12. It would be better if more parents thought less about themselves and more about their kids.
    ____I agree
    ____I do not agree

13. There is nothing wrong with talking with food in your mouth.
    ____I agree
    ____I do not agree

14. I am sure that most of my friends would stand by me no matter what kind of trouble I got into.
    ____I agree
    ____I do not agree

15. Nothing can stop me once I really make up my mind to do something.
    ____I agree
    ____I do not agree

16. Even in the worst kind of trouble, a kid can always count on his parents to help.
    ____I agree
    ____I do not agree

17. Most policemen treat people of all races the same.
  ——I agree
  ——I do not agree

18. The thing to do is to live for today rather than to try to plan for tomorrow.
  ——I agree
  ——I do not agree

19. The police often pick on people for no good reason.
  ——I agree
  ——I do not agree

20. Sometimes I think people like me are hardly good for anything.
  ——I agree
  ——I do not agree

21. Everything parents want their kid to do is for the kid's own good.
  ——I agree
  ——I do not agree

22. The way things look for the future, most people would be better off if they were never born.
  ——I agree
  ——I do not agree

23. The police usually let their friends get away with things.
  ——I agree
  ——I do not agree

24. Parents are always looking for things to nag their kids about.
  ——I agree
  ——I do not agree

25. Everybody is just out for himself. Nobody really cares about anybody else.
  ——I agree
  ——I do not agree

26. Even if you can't stand some people, you should still be nice to them.
  ——I agree
  ——I do not agree

Here are some things that many people want. Many people would want all of these things, but they might want *a few* of them more than almost anything else in the world.

For example, nearly everybody wants to spend a lot of time with good and close friends. But some people want to do other things even more.

Other people, though, would rather spend a lot of time with good and close friends than do almost anything else in the world. How do YOU feel about this?

Think about each one of the following things very carefully. Is it one of the things that YOU want more than almost anything else in the world? If your answer is YES, put an X in front of YES. If your answer is NO, put an X in front of NO.

Remember, you *can't* want *everything* more than anything else in the world. So be sure that you put an X in front of YES only for those things you really want that much. For all other things, put an X in front of NO —even if you want them.

27. Do you want this much more than almost anything else in the world? **To spend a lot of time with very good and close friends.**

——yes
——no

28. Do you want this much more than almost anything else in the world? **To always be doing a lot of new and exciting things—to be on the go all the time.**

——yes
——no

29. Do you want this much more than almost anything else in the world? **To be able to get other people to do what you want.**

——yes
——no

30. Do you want this much more than almost anything else in the world? **To be very popular and have a lot of people look up to you.**

——yes
——no

31. Do you want this much more than almost anything else in the world? **To be able to take things easy and not have to work hard.**

——yes
——no

32. Do you want this much more than almost anything else in the world? **To be able to finish everything you start so well that you know it is perfect.**

——yes
——no

33. Do you want this much more than almost anything else in the world? **To be free to do what you want, and not be held back by other people.**

——yes
——no

34. Do you want this much more than almost anything else in the world? **To be able to do things for other people even if nobody ever finds out about it.**

——yes
——no

35. Do you want this much more than almost anything else in the world? **To have a job you can count on and know that you can always get along.**

——yes
——no

36. Do you want this much more than almost   _____yes
    anything else in the world? **To be able to** _____no
    keep up with the people you like and do
    what they do.

[Girls skip this]

37. Do you want this much more than almost   _____yes
    anything else in the world? **To be strong and** _____no
    manly.

38. Do you want this much more than almost   _____yes
    anything else in the world? **To enjoy life by** _____no
    having lots of thrills and taking chances.

39. Do you want this much more than almost   _____yes
    anything else in the world? **To have good**   _____no
    taste—to be a person who can enjoy good
    music, good art, and the finer things in life.

40. Do you want this much more than almost   _____yes
    anything else in world? **Never to have any** _____no
    kind of sickness or be hurt in any way.

Here are a few questions about you and your home.
DO NOT SIGN YOUR NAME.

41. Does your family speak Spanish?   _____yes
                                               _____no

42. Was your mother born in the U.S.A.?   _____yes
                                               _____no

43. Was your mother born in the South?   _____yes
                                               _____no
                                               _____I don't know

44. Was your father born in the U.S.A.?   _____yes
                                               _____no
                                               _____I don't know

45. Was your father born in the South?   _____yes
                                               _____no
                                               _____I don't know

46. Did you go to church in the last two weeks? _____yes
                                               _____no

47. Are you the youngest person who lives in   ———yes
    your apartment?   ———no

48. Are you the only person under eighteen who   ———yes
    lives in your apartment?   ———no

49. Does anyone else sleep in the same room   ———yes
    where you sleep?   ———no

50. Is your father living where you live now?   ———yes
                                                 ———no

51. Is your family better off than most families ———yes
    on your block?   ———no

FORM G   **What I Really Think about Drugs**

THIS IS NOT A TEST.

DO NOT SIGN YOUR NAME.

When were you born?
Month——— Day——— Year———   ———Boy
                                           ———Girl

School——————————————   Class——————————

What I Really Think about Drugs

We want to know what boys and girls your age think about drugs.

We are NOT trying to find out what any *one* person thinks. THIS IS NOT A TEST. We want to find out what the whole *class* really thinks.

DO NOT SIGN YOUR NAME. Nobody will know which is your paper.

Do not be afraid to show what you really think.

Answer every question. If you are not sure, just make your best guess. If you agree, put an X in front of I AGREE. If you do not agree, put an X in front of I DO NOT AGREE.

Do not leave anything out. If you are not sure, just make your best guess.

Suppose you find out that one of the boys on your block is *using* heroin. What should be done?

1. Nobody should do anything. It is his own private business.

    ——I agree
    ——I do not agree

2. Tell the school or the police about him.

    ——I agree
    ——I do not agree

Here are a few things that people have said about taking drugs. Some people agree with them. Other people do not agree. Put down what you REALLY think.

Place an X to show if you agree or do not agree with each of these statements.

Don't leave anything out—if you are not sure, just make a guess.

3. Heroin probably is not so bad for a person as some people say. They make too big a fuss about it.

    ——I agree
    ——I do not agree

4. Just taking a little heroin once in a while never really hurt anybody.

    ——I agree
    ——I do not agree

5. It's O.K. to smoke a little *marijuana* from time to time at parties.

    ——I agree
    ——I do not agree

6. Just the idea of smoking marijuana is the worst thing I can think of.

    ——I agree
    ——I do not agree

7. A person should never take heroin no matter what.

    ——I agree
    ——I do not agree

8. It's O.K. to use heroin if you feel like it, as long as you make sure that you don't get hooked.

    ——I agree
    ——I do not agree

Some people say that fellows who use heroin are different from other fellows. Other people say they are about the same. What do you think?

Even if you are not sure, make your best guess. Write an X in front of the answer you think is right. Do *not* leave anything out.

9. Who have fewer brains?

    ——fellows who use heroin
    ——fellows who do not use heroin
    ——both about the same

10. Who are more fun to be with?

    ——fellows who use heroin
    ——fellows who do not use heroin
    ——both about the same

11. Who wear better clothes?

——fellows who use heroin
——fellows who do not use heroin
——both about the same

12. Who get fewer kicks out of life?

——fellows who use heroin
——fellows who do not use heroin
——both about the same

13. Who have fewer close friends they can trust?

——fellows who use heroin
——fellows who do not use heroin
——both about the same

14. Who can get along better on their own?

——fellows who use heroin
——fellows who do not use heroin
——both about the same

15. Who are better able to take care of themselves?

——fellows who use heroin
——fellows who do not use heroin
——both about the same

Here are some things people say about drugs. Some are true. Some are false.

If you think the statement is true, put an X in front of the TRUE. If you think the statement is false, put an X in front of FALSE.

If you don't know, put an X in front of I DON'T KNOW.

Do not leave anything out. Answer every question.

16. Heroin is made from the same plant as marijuana.

——true
——false
——I don't know

17. If a person is caught with exactly a quarter ounce of heroin on him, he gets a *lot more* punishment than if he had *just a little bit* less heroin.

——true
——false
——I don't know

18. In a hospital the doctors usually don't give any drug at all. They just let the addict sweat it out.

——true
——false
——I don't know

19. Most steady users began using heroin before they were thirteen years old.

——true
——false
——I don't know

20. It is legal to buy heroin from a drugstore, but a person has to have a doctor's prescription.
———true
———false
———I don't know

21. If the police find more than one-quarter ounce of heroin in a car, the law says that just the driver is guilty.
———true
———false
———I don't know

22. Heroin can be bought for less than $1 a shot.
———true
———false
———I don't know

23. It is against the law to sell heroin or marijuana, but they can't touch a person if he gives it away.
———true
———false
———I don't know

24. All of the marijuana used here comes from other countries.
———true
———false
———I don't know

25. If a person is caught with exactly half an ounce of heroin on him, he gets a *lot more* punishment than if he had *just a little bit* less heroin.
———true
———false
———I don't know

26. Most addicts who take the cure never go back on drugs again.
———true
———false
———I don't know

27. More girls than boys use heroin.
———true
———false
———I don't know

28. If a person is caught with heroin on him but was not caught selling it, they can't jail him for more than three years.
———true
———false
———I don't know

29. A marijuana cigarette costs about as much as one shot of heroin.
———true
———false
———I don't know

30. No city hospital will take in a drug-user for treatment.
———true
———false
———I don't know

People who don't use heroin give all sorts of reasons why they don't want to try it. For example, the *main* reason why one person doesn't try it is because he does not want to become a slave to heroin.

You yourself may feel that, while this may be a *good* reason, there are still better reasons, or you may agree with him that this *is* one of the *main* reasons not to try heroin.

How do *YOU* feel about that reason?

If you think it is one of the *main* reasons not to try heroin, put an X in front of YES. If it is *not* one of the *main* reasons, put an X in front of NO.

31. **You become a slave to heroin. You become com-** ———yes
    pletely tied down to the habit. Is this one of the *main* ———no
    reasons that would keep YOU from taking heroin?

32. **You will hurt the people who are close to you.** Is this ———yes
    one of the *main* reasons that would keep YOU from ———no
    taking heroin?

33. **After awhile the kick wears off but you still have to go** ———yes
    on taking it. Is this one of the *main* reasons that would ———no
    keep YOU from taking heroin?

34. **You become a helpless tool of the people who sell** ———yes
    drugs. Is this one of the *main* reasons that would keep ———no
    YOU from taking heroin?

35. **People will look down on you.** Is this one of the *main* ———yes
    reasons that would keep YOU from taking heroin? ———no

36. **You'll be alone in the world. You won't have any real** ———yes
    friends. Is this one of the *main* reasons that would keep ———no
    YOU from taking heroin?

37. **You'll lose your chances for a good steady income.** Is ———yes
    this one of the *main* reasons that would keep YOU ———no
    from taking heroin?

38. **You will never feel safe from the police.** Is this one of ———yes
    the *main* reasons that would keep YOU from taking ———no
    heroin?

[Girls skip this]
39. **You can't be the same as most of the other fellows** ———yes
    any more—you will become too different. Is this one of ———no
    the *main* reasons that would keep YOU from taking
    heroin?

40. **You won't be able to work well or be good at sports.**   ——yes
Is this one of the *main* reasons that would keep YOU   ——no
from taking heroin?

41. **Your health will be ruined and life will be full of**   ——yes
worries and troubles. Is this one of the *main* reasons   ——no
that would keep YOU from taking heroin?

Here are a few questions about you and your home.

Make sure that you DO NOT SIGN YOUR NAME.

42. Does your family speak Spanish?   ——yes
——no

43. Are you the youngest person who lives in your apart-   ——yes
ment?   ——no

44. Are you the only person under eighteen who lives in   ——yes
your apartment?   ——no

45. Does anyone else sleep in the same room where you   ——yes
sleep?   ——no

46. Is your father living where you live now?   ——yes
——no

47. Where did you pick up *most* of what you do know
about drugs?
Check only one of these.
    A. From reading about it.   ——A
    B. From what the fellows talk about.   ——B
    C. From teachers in school.   ——C
    D. From my parents.   ——D
    E. From what I myself see going on.   ——E

48. Did you ever see anybody taking heroin?   ——yes
——no

49. About how many people do you know who use heroin?
Check only one of these.
    A. One or two people   ——A
    B. Three, four, or five people   ——B
    C. Six or more people   ——C
    D. I don't know anybody who uses heroin   ——D

50. Did you ever have a *chance* to use heroin?   ——yes
——no

APPENDIX E

Meaning of Item Clusters

The basic data of cluster analyses are correlation coefficients;[1] in the case of the cluster analysis reported in Chapter IV, these are tetrachoric correlations between items.[2]

It is obviously possible that neighborhoods differ in the ways responses to the items are correlated, and this independently of whether they differ in the distributions of responses to the items individually. That is, it is possible that certain information is more closely linked to certain attitudes in one neighborhood than in another, that the possession of one bit of information is more closely linked to the possession of another in one neighborhood than it is in a second, or that one attitude is more closely linked to another attitude in one neighborhood than in the second.

In line with this reasoning, we computed all the correlations among items, separately for each neighborhood. With seventy-two items, however, we get 2,556 correlation coefficients, and this for each of the three neighborhoods, or a grand total of 7,668 correlation coefficients. It would obviously be an impossibly tedious job to attempt to discuss all of them, to say nothing of the imposition on the reader.

We could, of course, compromise by selecting the most interesting correlations to discuss. But, not only is it not entirely clear what the criteria for "most interesting" should be, there is also a more fundamental difficulty. The ambiguities of interpreting the meaning of a response also affect the interpretation of a correlation coefficient.[3]

The recognition of the ambiguity of a correlation coefficient with respect to the relationship between the two variables should, nevertheless, not blind us to the fact that two relatively highly correlated variables are, in some sense, akin. Similarly, we may note that a low correlation between two variables

[1] See Appendix F for an explanation of why we did not make use of factor analysis. For more elaborate discussions of cluster analysis, see R. C. Tryon, "Identification of Social Areas by Cluster Analysis," *University of California Publications in Psychology*, 8 (1955), 1–100; also, more recent publications of the same author.

[2] See Appendix C for an explanation of tetrachoric correlations between items.

[3] See Appendix C for a discussion of the ambiguities involved in interpreting a correlation coefficient.

does not necessarily mean that there is no relationship between them. Thus, one item may be fundamentally akin to another, but undetected ambiguities in its wording may introduce a random element in the distribution of responses to it; the random element would, of course, lower the correlation and thereby conceal the evidence of kinship. Or the ambiguities of wording may raise an issue not systematically related to issues posed by any of the other items, but which nevertheless determines the responses of a sizable number of subjects. The effect may be to conceal the fact that the remaining subjects do respond to the item in a way that makes it akin to other items and the possibility that even the subjects who respond to the extraneous issues might have responded in the same way if the extraneous issue had been eliminated.

For instance, highly sophisticated subjects might well get lost in the issue of whether "take the cure" is intended to mean "merely go for detoxification" or "voluntarily continue over a long period in an intensive psychotherapeutic relationship," whereas the naïve subject would presumably respond to the phrase, with no special thought or verbalization of the meaning, in the sense that we intended, viz., "receive the commonly available form of treatment." In the distribution of responses to the item, we could have inextricably mingled at least four distinct groups of subjects: the naïve subjects, the sophisticates who arbitrarily decide that "take the cure" means one thing, the sophisticates who arbitrarily decide that it means another, and the sophisticates who decide that they do not know how to answer. The correlations of responses to this item with those to other items may well be of opposite sign in one group of sophisticates than it is in the others. The over-all correlations could thus be lowered by an essentially arbitrary decision on an extraneous issue.

We may sometimes be interested in tracing the precise nature of a relationship, and it is possible to design studies to do so. At other times, however, we may be interested in the mere fact of kinship without being concerned with the precise nature of the relationship. This is the case in the present study. We are concerned with the cultural climates in which drug use does or does not abound, rather than with the precise nature of the influences which bring the various aspects of a particular climate into a common one. Nor, for that matter, are we concerned with the precise degree of kinship between any two elements of a given climate; we want to get an over-all picture of the climate. For this purpose, it seems inappropriate to focus on the degrees of correlation among all or some of the *pairs* of items. What we really want to discern are the kinship groupings, the families, the *sets* of items that evoke responses that tend to hang together.

How can we establish these kinship groupings, or sets of items, from the correlation coefficients? The most obvious stratagem is to select sets of variables with relatively high average intercorrelations, but this procedure would not detect the kinships that might be concealed behind low correlations. We therefore used a more complicated procedure. Let us for the moment pursue the analogy of a family group. Not only does such a group include individuals only indirectly related to one another (e.g., the wife's mother and the husband's mother), but, in addition, even intimate kin may grow apart, so that the relationship is apparent only in certain conditions. The second of these considerations concerns us more than the first. That is, we are not particularly concerned whether the basis of relationship which puts items into the same kinship group is indirect. But we are concerned that the fact of relationship, whether direct or indirect, be more than historical; we want to be certain that the relationship is a continuing one, evident when the "parties" involved are examined in a wide variety of contexts.

To illustrate the point, let us consider the item on cure of addiction. The correlations in one of our neighborhoods between this item and all of the other items are shown graphically in the solid line in figures A-1 and A-2. Thus, this item correlates .35 with Item G 19, .12 with Item G 27, .23 with Item G 21, and so on. Such a graphic representation of the correlation of one variable with a whole series of other variables is known as a correlation profile. The broken line in Figure A-1 is the correlation profile of the item calling for agreement or disagreement with the statement: "Most policemen can be paid off." The broken line in Figure A-2 is the correlation profile of the item calling for a "yes" or "no" to the question: "Do you want this much more than almost anything else in the world: to have good taste—to be a person who can enjoy good art, good music, and the finer things of life?" Each of these items has almost exactly the same degree of correlation with the addiction-cure item—fairly low, but nevertheless definite. That is, by the test of direct correlation, there is a slight degree of kinship between the belief that addiction is usually permanently cured and the rejection of the idea of the venality of the police and the same slight degree of kinship between the belief in curability and the unwillingness to accept "refinement" as one of the greatest values in life.

But look at the two pairs of profiles. Obviously, the first two are much more alike than the second. That is, the degree of relationship, or lack of relationship, of the addiction-cure item to the numerous other items tends to be paralleled by the police-venality item, but not by the value-of-refinement item. Thus, although both of the latter items are directly related to the addiction-cure item to the same degree, the police-venality item shows similar relationships and lack of relationships, whereas the value-of-refinement item does not. In this extended sense, the members of the first pair are much more akin than are the members of the second; they function much more consistently as members of the same family.

We may also consider the issue in more sober statistical, and less metaphorical, terms. The demonstration of greater-than-zero correlation between two items implies that, knowing the response to one, we can make a better-than-chance prediction of the response to the other. With two-valued variables and greater-than-zero correlation, the predicted response to one item from a high-scoring response to the other would *always*[4] be a high-scoring response

[4] This is the strategy that would, in the long run, produce the fewest errors of prediction. To the mathematically naïve, it may seem that the predictions should be distributed in the same way as the odds go, but it can be shown that,

if the correlation is positive or a low-scoring response if the correlation is negative, and this *regardless of the size of the correlation.* Similarly, from a low-scoring response on one item, we would predict a low-scoring response on the other if the correlation is positive and a high-scoring response if the correlation is negative. If the size of the correlation does not affect the nature of the prediction, however, it does affect its precision. With a perfect correlation, we would never make errors in the prediction, and, with a zero correlation, our predictions would be no better than guesswork. The closer the correlation to one, the fewer would be the errors of our predictions; the closer the correlation to zero, the greater would be the number of errors. It follows that the size of the correlation between two items tells us the degree to which the response to one is latent (i.e., contained by statistical implication) in the response to the other. From this, it follows that two items with identical correlation profiles have an identical pattern of implication; and, the more similar the correlation profiles of two items, the more similar are the patterns of implication. Thus, the more similar the correlation profiles of two items, the greater the correspondence between the implications of the responses to these items.

Conversely, suppose that we want to predict the responses to an item from the responses to all the other items. The predictions of the scores of two items with identical correlation profiles would be identical; the precision of these predictions would also be identical. Thus, the more similar the correlation profiles of two items, the greater the correspondence of the implications for these items of the responses to the remaining items. It is in these senses that items with similar correlation profiles are akin. We may say that their latencies are alike.

The degree of kinship, in this extended sense, can be measured simply by computing the degree of correlation between the correlation profiles. We did this and then sorted the items into sets, each set consisting of items with relatively similar profiles. The items were arranged in order of the magnitude of their average tetrachoric correlations (disregarding signs) with all of the remaining items. Starting with the first item on the list, we added to it the item with the highest profile correlation[5] with it. To these two items, we added the item with the highest average profile correlation with them; to the three, the item with the highest average profile correlation with them; and so on. The only restriction was that no item could be added to the set if it had a profile correlation of less than .40 or a tetrachoric correlation of less than .20 with the items already selected. We continued in this way until there were no more items that would meet these qualifications. This gave us our first "trial set."

Eliminating the items of the first trial set, we started again with the re-

---

in the long run, this strategy would produce more errors than the strategy of *always* predicting the most probable outcome, and this even in the case when the odds are almost equal.

[5] For convenience, we refer to a correlation between two correlational profiles as a profile correlation. Profile correlations were computed on the usual Pearsonian product-moment basis, rather than as tetrachorics.

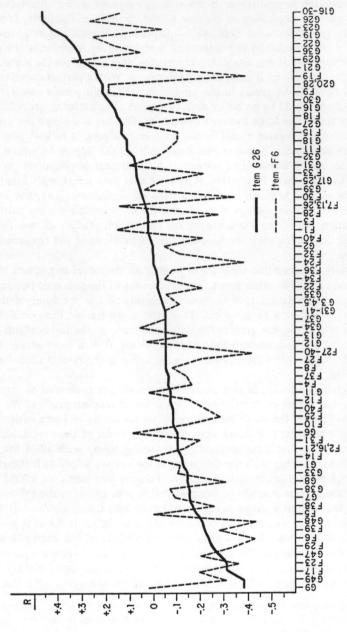

Fig. A-1. Correlation Profiles for "Addicts Are Cured" (G 26), "Police Not Bribable" (–F 6) (Lower East Side)

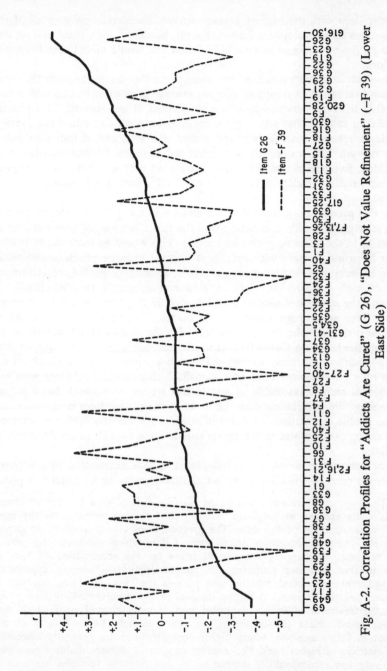

Fig. A-2. Correlation Profiles for "Addicts Are Cured" (G 26), "Does Not Value Refinement" (–F 39) (Lower East Side)

Item G 26
Item –F 39

maining item with the highest average tetrachoric correlation with all of the other items and developed a second trial set. Similarly, for a third trial set and so on until no additional sets could be found that would meet the stated qualifications.

For each item, we calculated the average profile correlation with the items of each trial set. If an item had a higher average profile correlation with a trial set other than the one in which it was included, it was moved. This process resulted in revised trial sets. Again, for each item we calculated the average profile correlation with each of the revised trial sets, and, if indicated, items were moved. The procedure was continued until no further changes were indicated. Every item was thus located in the set with which it had the highest average profile correlation (or in no set at all). Such a set we refer to as a "prime cluster."

By this procedure, it is possible for an item in one prime cluster to have as high an average profile correlation with the items in a second prime cluster as the items in the latter do with one another. This would be particularly true of items in prime clusters with very high internal average profile correlations. Thus, an item in a cluster whose items have an average profile correlation of, say, .80 with one another might have an average profile correlation of, say, .60 with the items in a second prime cluster. If the items of the latter prime cluster have an average profile correlation with one another on the order of .60, the item from the first prime cluster fits the second about as well as the items of the latter do themselves. It seems reasonable to include such an item in the second set of items, as well as in its own prime cluster. Similarly, if the items of a prime cluster have exceptionally high profile correlations with one another, it seems reasonable to add to this set an item which has a higher average profile correlation with the items in the cluster than is characteristic of the profile correlations of items in other prime clusters with one another, even though it does not fit the prime cluster quite so well as do the items of the latter.

When the set of items in a prime cluster is thus augmented by additional items, we refer to the augmented set of items simply as a cluster.[6] A prime

[6] The number of clusters and prime clusters distinguished by this procedure involves the exercise of judgment in a search for what seems to be the most sensible construction of the data. The procedures of cluster analysis do permit more rigorously parsimonious descriptions of data which are useful for certain purposes, e.g., in mapping domains of items for the construction of tests or other indexes. For our purposes, the present application seemed appropriate and sufficient. In general, whether one pursues the logic of cluster analysis or of factor analysis, it seems to us that the goal of "most parsimonious description" gives the treatment of data a deceptive aura of mathematical rigor which they do not merit unless the communalities are extremely high. This is clearly evident in factor analysis, where higher communalities are generally associated with matrices of higher rank, i.e., a larger number of distinguishable dimensions. Relatively low communalities suggest to us that relevant variables are missing from the matrix, so that the true dimensions of the data are collapsed into a space that is of lower-dimensional order; this puts things together that do not

cluster is analogous to an immediate family; a cluster, to an extended family. A given item may belong to no cluster at all, to a prime cluster only, or to a prime cluster and to one or more other clusters. An item which belongs to two or more clusters may be said to share in two or more kinship groupings.

In the neighborhood for which the data of figures A-1 and A-2 are presented, the addiction-cure and police-venality items are found in a common cluster, but they do not belong to a common prime cluster. The addiction-cure and value-of-refinement items do not even belong to a common cluster.

The items in a cluster identify a current in the cultural atmosphere of a neighborhood, a current which brings the ideas, attitudes, information, and values with which the items are concerned into common contexts of meaning. This is not to imply that particular items do not retain idiosyncratic shades of meaning for particular individuals or groups; but the statistical behaviors of the items nevertheless tell us something of the properties of the world in which these individuals live.

Since, however, an item that is added to a prime cluster fits its own prime cluster better than it does another one to which it is added, it follows that there are aspects of its character that are more salient than the aspects by virtue of which it fits the latter. Hence, the items in a prime cluster are the ones that fit best together by virtue of their most outstanding characteristics. Moreover, by the procedure we have adopted, the prime cluster is the heart of any cluster, and the additional items are introduced only because they have implications resembling those already defined by the prime cluster. It follows that the meaning of a cluster may be most evident in a scrutiny of the items in a prime cluster and that any interpretation of a cluster is apt to be aberrant if it is not consistent with the prime cluster. The augmented cluster merely furnishes additional detail to what is already latent in the prime cluster; it helps to focus and sharpen what may be perceived in the prime cluster.

---

really belong together. This introduces elements of arbitrariness into the analysis which are hidden behind the pseudoprecision of the technique. The issue is analogous to that of the number of significant digits with which data are reported; the rules of arithmetic, for instance, generally permit calculating statistics to an endless number of decimal places, but the quality of the data generally does not. Relatively crude data do not justify high-precision techniques. The cruder the data, the more we have to rely on good judgment for their analysis, rather than on mechanical rules of procedure; if the data are crude enough, they may not even justify that much.

APPENDIX F

A Note on Factor Analysis

Some statistically sophisticated readers may wonder why we did not make use of factor analysis, an alternative and much more common procedure. We must confess to some bias in this respect—not against factor analysis as a computational device, but against this form of analysis as an end in itself. The cluster analysis we have mentioned of the data in Chapter III was, for instance, carried out on the basis of a principal-axis solution, dropping the factors with negative average factor loadings, estimating revised communalities from the remaining factors, and repeating the process until the communality estimates stabilized and the excluded factors had average loadings of about zero. The distances between varied vector points in the multiple-factor space were then calculated from the final communalities and the correlations of the variables and variable clusters determined accordingly.

Our objections to factor analysis as an end in itself may be explained as follows: (1) Unless the data permit a unique simple structure solution,[1] the final selection of reference axes is arbitrary, whereas the relative positions of the variables in the multiple-factor space is always invariant with respect to a given set of data. We prefer to deal with the givens, rather than with arbitrary constructions on them. The latter can, in our view, be quite deceptive. In one instance, we cluster-analyzed a set of data from a published factor analysis which purportedly supported a series of hypotheses and found that every one of these hypotheses was flatly contradicted by the actual variable configurations. The deceptiveness of the factor analysis came from the arbitrarily chosen reference axes and the common practice of examining factor loadings for each factor separately. It is obvious, however, that variables which cluster in the multiple-factor space must have similar "factorial compositions," regardless of which reference axes are chosen—a fact which can be brought out only by examination of the pattern of factor loadings of each *variable* rather than by examination of the pattern of factor loadings for each *factor,* and this amounts to a cluster analysis.

[1] See L. L. Thurstone, *Multiple Factor Analysis* (Chicago: University of Chicago Press, 1947). The criteria for unique simple structure are apparently so rigorous that one hardly hears of the concept. If a unique simple structure solution is possible, the outcome would necessarily be virtually identical to that of a cluster analysis.

(2) The general theory of factor analysis seems to us to be the indefensible view that the *sole* source of correlation between variables is the presence of common components. To be sure, such an assumption is not mathematically necessary, since one may think in purely actuarial terms of "accountable" portions of the variance, and one may think of the factors as hypothetical variables which are more-or-less predictable from the actual variables rather than as representing that which is common to them. On this basis, however, the reason for any special interest in such hypothetical variables becomes obscure. As long as one thinks of a factor as a common component, it is clear that it may be regarded as a real variable and, if the original matrix is large enough and encompasses a judicious selection of variables, as a probably unitary, or at most limitedly divisible, one. If one abandons the common-component notion, however, why think of it as *a* variable at all? And, even if one does, the usual practice of interpreting or "naming" such a variable—i.e., speculating on what can be common in variables with high loadings and missing from variables with low loadings—becomes indefensible. We can think of no reason for assuming that correlations with such hypothetical variables (i.e., the factor loadings) should have fewer possible sources than correlations among other variables. Suppose, for instance, that the following census-tract variables turn out to have high loadings on a common factor: percentage of Negroes, poverty rates, percentage excess of females over males, and index of disrupted family life. What sense would it make to look for a common component in these variables? Or a common cause? Or a common anything else? Would it not make better sense to assume that these variables have "got together" for a complex variety of reasons?

This is not to say that there may not be circumstances when factor analysis is justified as more than a convenient tool. Thus, if there are independent grounds (e.g., a theoretical schema) that require the postulation of a particular variable, it seems to us to be entirely legitimate to test relevant data for their compatibility with such a postulate.

APPENDIX G

Reasons for Not Taking Heroin

In reviewing the two delinquency-orientation clusters and the drug-subculture cluster in High, we found that ten of the eleven items in the questionnaire which dealt with reasons for not taking heroin formed part of the drug-subculture cluster and that nine of them were included in one of the delinquency-orientation clusters; the eleventh item was, as already explained, not included in the cluster analysis. We now note that these ten items and an eleventh composite item, G 31–41 ("Agreeing to nine or more of the eleven arguments"), form prime clusters in each of the three neighborhoods. What does this clustering betoken?

One possibility is that these items tap a yes- (or no-) saying tendency in the subjects that functions independently of the content of the items. All are identical in form and call for a response of "yes" or "no." In favor of the possibility is the fact that, in all three neighborhoods, substantial proportions of the boys (35 per cent in Low, 46 per cent in Medium, and 55 per cent in High) said "yes" to nine or more of the eleven arguments. Against the possibility, however—and compellingly so in our estimation—may be cited the following facts: In the first place, the items associated with the prime clusters do not follow the same pattern. The associated clusters include two items in Low that do not call for a yes-no or agree-disagree response, one such item in Medium, and three in High. Even more to the point, each of the clusters includes items that, from the point of view of agreement, are scored in the direction opposite that of the prime cluster. There is one such item in Low, one in Medium, and eight in High. In addition, the Low cluster involves a compound item in which one of the three components has to be answered in the direction opposite that of the items in the prime cluster, although the other two are scored in the same direction. The Medium cluster also includes this compound item and another in which all three components have to be answered in the opposite direction. The High cluster includes the latter compound item.

In the second place, each of the arguments was paralleled in the questionnaire by a more general item which (except for the specific reference to heroin and a structural difference which will be noted below but which is irrelevant to the present discussion) is extremely similar to it in both form and content. The parallel items are the value items. Thus, Item G 35 ("People will look down on you") involves the value of achieving favorable recognition and is paralleled by F 30 ("To be very popular and have a lot of people look up to you"). Similarly, G 37 ("You'll lose your chances for a good steady income") is paralleled by F 35 ("To have a job you can count on and know that you can always get along"). There was also a discernible tendency to say "yes" to the value items.[1] The important point, however, is that, not only did the value items not cluster with the set of argument items, but they did not even form a single prime cluster of their own in any of the neighborhoods.[a] Moreover, the index of agreement with the arguments bore little relationship to the index of agreement with the value items. The tetrachoric correlation between the two indexes was .31 in Low, .39 in Medium, and .19 in High. The profile correlations were .21, .22, and .07.

The clustering of the argument items, then, cannot be accounted for in terms of a generalized tendency to agree or disagree. We may, therefore, look to the specific contents of the items in the augmented clusters for clues as to the character of the prime clusters.[b]

Some speculation may first be in order as to why the arguments did not divide themselves into the same kinds of differentiated clusters as did the value items. Apart from a major structural difference between the two sets of items,[2] the clustering of the arguments was affected by whether the subject

[1] In Low, 47 per cent of the boys said "yes" to nine or more of the fourteen value items, 52 per cent in Medium, and 48 per cent in High.

[2] It is to be noted that all of the arguments involved the negative of values. For obvious reasons, we could not parallel the value items with arguments *for* the use of heroin. In principle, however, we might have done so. For instance, we might have included the following: "Suppose you believed the following statements to be . true. Which of them would most influence you to try taking heroin?. . .'Taking heroin makes a person feel strong and manly.' . . . Would this be one of the things that would be most likely to lead you to try taking heroin?" On a priori grounds, we would expect that such arguments would indeed show a structure similar to that obtained with the value items. The point is that asserting a *positive* puts the content of the assertion into the foreground; in the language of Gestalt psychology, such an assertion has figural quality. The subject has to indicate whether the given figure *is also present* in his life space. The assertion of a negative, however, simply tends to leave one with no content. To say that something is or will become absent does not say anything about what will happen at the site of the void. The subject has to evaluate how much of a difference the absence of a figure will make in his life space. Absences, we would suggest, are much less finely differentiated from one another than presences.

Granted, however, that this mechanism for the lesser differentiation of the arguments is operative and contributes to the over-all effect, it seems to us that the explanation advanced in the text must be primary not only because of its prima-facie plausibility, but because it also helps to account for the neighborhood differences in the complete argument clusters.

believed them. If the subject did not believe that taking heroin would have a particular consequence, then, regardless of his attitude toward the consequence, he would reject the corresponding argument. If he had a generalized disposition to disbelieve that evil consequences flow from the use of heroin, he would tend to reject all the arguments. Contrariwise, if the subject believed that a particular consequence would ensue, then, again regardless of the relative position of the entailed value in his hierarchy of values, the corresponding argument would tend to become a major deterrent. All the values involved in the arguments tend to be of considerable, if not of equal, importance to all people. If he had a disposition to believe that many evils flow from the use of heroin, the respondent would tend to accept all the arguments, including arguments the soundness of which he could not evaluate in any realistic fashion. The general disposition to accept or reject arguments might thus be indicative of a general attitude toward the use of heroin or even more general attitudes in which the attitude toward heroin was imbedded.

In light of these considerations, it is not surprising that one of the differences between the neighborhoods was in the number of items that clustered with the prime argument clusters. There were seven additional items in Low, eleven in Medium, and eighteen in High. That is, on the assumption that the clustering of the argument items reflected more general attitudes, the latter were least pervasive in their implications in Low and most pervasive in High. Moreover, the particular items entering the augmented clusters supported the assumption, although the pattern was rather different in Medium than it was in Low and High.

In Medium, the cluster developing around the arguments included a complete prime cluster of what may be referred to as "high ideals." Specifically, the acceptance of the arguments went with F 27 ("Values intimate companionship"), F 32 ("Values workmanship and being good at sports"), F 34 ("Values being of service"), F 36 ("Values conformity and keeping up with people you like"), and F 39 ("Values refinement"). The rejection of the arguments, of course, went with the rejection of these values. In addition, accepting the arguments went with F 2, 16, and 21 ("Favorable to parents on all three items"); G 1 ("Taking heroin not a private affair"); G 2 ("Tell authorities about boy on block who uses heroin"); G 3, 4, and 5 ("Antidrugs on all three items"); G 6 ("Idea of smoking marijuana worst thing can think of"); and G 9 ("Heroin-users have fewer brains").

Although five of the eleven supplementary items also occurred in the Medium delinquency-orientation cluster[3] and three of the five in the prime cluster as well as in the general delinquency-orientation cluster, the predominance of other items and the relative independence of the prime argument cluster from the latter[c] suggest that the delinquency and argument clusters are derived from relatively independent cultural currents. The inclusion of the prime-value-item cluster in the argument cluster suggests that the latter de-

[3] In referring to these items before, the paraphrases of the items were oriented in the opposite direction. Here, we are focusing on the acceptance of the arguments and have oriented the paraphrases accordingly.

rives from a cultural current concerned with what would be described, in middle-class society, as the finer things in life.

In both Low and High, we had similar value clusters, but these did not become involved in the argument clusters. In other words, the acceptance or rejection of the arguments tended to derive from cultural currents that were independent of those affecting the acceptance or rejection of the "high-ideals" value items, and, as we shall see in a moment, the tendency to accept or reject the arguments was not independent of the delinquency-orientation and drug-subculture currents. The Low argument cluster included none of the value items, and the High included only one, F 39 ("Values refinement"). All the seven supplementary items in the Low argument cluster were also in the neighborhood delinquency-orientation cluster—three in the prime cluster and two of the latter plus one other in the general delinquency-orientation cluster. Similarly, sixteen of the seventeen supplementary items in the High argument cluster were in the neighborhood drug-subculture cluster.[4] The one item that seemed out of place was F 39 ("Values refinement").

A reasonable interpretation of the patterns is that the clustering of the argument items was influenced in Low by a generalized attitude or set of attitudes generated by contact with the cultural currents that produced the delinquent subculture and, in High, by contacts with the cultural currents that shaped the two delinquency-orientation and the drug-subculture clusters.[5]

Two other aspects of the responses to the argument items merit some attention—an apparent paradox and the comparative rank order of the arguments.

[4] Nine of the sixteen items in the general delinquency-orientation cluster were included; these nine items, of course, occurred in both the neighborhood delinquency-orientation clusters. Three other items, not in the general delinquency-orientation cluster occurred in both the neighborhood delinquency-orientation clusters. Three other items occurred in the second neighborhood delinquency-orientation cluster. In all, fifteen of the eighteen supplementary items were found in the latter cluster. Only one of the supplementary items, G 12 ("Heroin-users get fewer kicks out of life") occurred exclusively in the drug-subculture cluster, and this was one of the weakest items in the latter set, with an average profile correlation of .43 and an average tetrachoric of .11 with the items of the prime cluster. It is, therefore, something of a tossup whether to describe the supplementary items as being drawn mainly from the drug-subculture cluster, from the second delinquency-orientation cluster, or from contact with the cultural currents that established the two delinquency-orientation and the drug-subculture clusters.

[5] The full set of supplementary items in Low consisted of F 2, F 16, F 21, F 17, F 24, G 6, G 7, G 11, and G 47. In High: F 4, F 6, F 7–13–26, F 22, F 23, F 24, F 25, G 3–4–5, G 8, F 5, G 2, G 47, G 6, G 7, G 12, F 39, and G 17–25. In apparent contradiction to this interpretation, one may be struck by the relative paucity of image-of-the-heroin-user items in the clusters; three of the most relevant ones, however, were not included in the cluster analysis, for reasons already indicated. A fourth which seems directly relevant is G 13 ("Users have fewer close friends they can trust"). Logically, this seems to parallel G 36 ("Be alone, won't have real friends"). G 13, however, may be taken in the sense of an initial personal deficiency rather than as a consequence; e.g., it clusters with G 9 ("Users have fewer brains").

First, the paradox. Fifty-five per cent of the boys in High accepted eight of the ten arguments in the prime cluster, as compared to 47 per cent in Medium and 35 per cent in Low.[6] More than 25 per cent accepted all ten, as compared to 16 per cent in Medium and 14 per cent in Low. On the face of it, these percentages diminish in the wrong direction. That is, one might expect that, if anything, there would be the least acceptance of the arguments in the area of highest drug use, rather than the opposite. The same paradox appears at the low end of the scale: only 10 per cent of the boys in High rejected seven or more of the ten arguments, as compared to 12 per cent in Medium and 18 per cent in Low. Correspondingly, the average number of arguments accepted was greatest in High and smallest in Low.

The apparent paradox, however, presumably stems from our presuppositions, rather than inhering in the facts themselves. It seems reasonable to assume that, the more pervasive the illicit use of narcotics, the more pervasive is the evidence that there are many evil consequences associated with the practice. Presumably, the youngsters with whom we were dealing were not immune to the testimony of their direct or vicarious experience. Hence, it was not at all paradoxical that the youngsters in High should accept more evils as associated with heroin use, and, as already noted, the arguments were such that accepting the consequence made it difficult to reject a given argument.

Where, then, is the paradox? It is not in the tendency to accept a greater number of arguments in High, but in the fact that the higher level of acceptance was not sufficient to overcome the attractiveness to many of the youngsters of the drug-using and delinquent subcultures. This, however, places the paradox in our naïve assumptions about human nature, viz., in the assumption that agreeing that some practice is dangerous and that accepting the appreciation of the danger is a deterrent sufficient to shape one's attitudes toward the practice. Suppose, for instance, we were to ask adolescents with the habit of cigarette-smoking whether they believed that cigarettes cause cancer and found that most agreed that they probably do. Suppose, further, that we asked them whether the relationship between smoking and cancer "is one of the main reasons that would keep you from smoking" and found that most said "yes." To many people, such an outcome (which, in the opinion of the writers, is highly probable) would be incomprehensible. The point is, however, that how one responds to direct confrontation with an issue bears no necessary relationship to whether one normally and spontaneously confronts that issue and, if one does, to one's capacity to segregate that response from other relevant attitudes and practices. Moreover, one of our cigarette-smoking adolescents might well say to us: "Of course, the danger of cancer is one of the main reasons that would keep me from smoking, but who said that the danger of cancer tells the whole story?"

In this light, the concurrence of a greater readiness to agree that various

[6] We have already mentioned corresponding figures when the eleventh argument is included. They are virtually identical (55 per cent in High accepted nine of the eleven, 46 per cent in Medium, and 35 per cent in Low) because of the very high percentages of acceptance of the eleventh argument.

dire consequences of heroin use are major deterrents with an attraction to the drug-using subculture and a sharing of its attitudes does not seem so paradoxical. At the same time, we should not forget that, relative to the other youngsters in High, those who tended to share the attitudes of the drug-using subculture and, to a somewhat lesser extent, those who tended to share the pessimistic version of the delinquent subculture were the ones most likely to reject the arguments.[7]

The second additional aspect of the data on the arguments that merits attention has to do with the rank orders of the arguments in the three neighborhoods. In each neighborhood, we could determine the argument with the highest percentage of acceptance, the argument with the second highest percentage, and so on. The resulting rank orders were quite similar in the three neighborhoods[d] despite the differences in the tendency to give blanket assent to the arguments and the differences in the absolute levels of the individual arguments.

In all three neighborhoods, the most agreed-to reason for abstaining from heroin was G 41 ("Health will be ruined and life full of worries and troubles"). Other relatively strong arguments in all three neighborhoods were G 39 ("Become too different from other fellows"), G 37 ("Lose chances for good steady income"), and G 40 ("Won't be able to work well or be good at sports"). Relatively weak arguments were G 33 ("Kick wears off, but you still have to go on using") and G 35 ("People will look down on you"). The argument which showed the most marked change in rank was G 31 ("Become a slave to heroin"), which held second place in Low, third place in Medium, but ranked 8.5[e] in High. No other argument approached this degree of variation in its rank positions.[f]

To summarize, in all three neighborhoods, there was evidence of a generalized tendency to accept or reject arguments against taking heroin, over and above the specific reactions to particular arguments. This tendency seemed to be part of larger constellations of attitudes that included aspects of the delinquent and, in the case of High, drug-involved subcultures of these neighborhoods. It was not, however, a direct expression of these subcultures, since there were many aspects of the latter not associated with the argument

[7] Although we have noted that the major determinant of the acceptance of the arguments in Medium was associated with a cultural current concerned with the "finer" things in life, it is also true that those who shared the attitudes of the delinquent subculture in this neighborhood tended to be the ones most likely to reject at least some of the arguments. It may be recalled that three of the argument items were part of the delinquency-orientation cluster in Medium: G 32 ("Hurt people close to you"), G 36 ("Not have real friends") and G 39 ("Become too different"). In effect, we seem to have here a convergence of two cultural currents on these specific items: the negativistic individualism of the neighborhood's delinquent subculture, which would tend to generate an attitude that these cannot be good reasons for not doing something, on the one hand, and the concern with the finer things in life, with its high valuation of intimate companionship, doing things for others without regard to personal returns, and conformity, on the other.

cluster. Despite the generalized tendency, the arguments formed a fairly stable hierarchic order of appeal in the three neighborhoods, the threat to health and the incidence of "worries and troubles" evoking the most nearly universal assent. The deterioration of capacity to work well and to participate effectively in active sports and the fact of tolerance (diminished reaction to drugs) along with continued addiction were reasons with relatively low appeal. The danger of addiction itself constituted a relatively strong argument in Low and in Medium, but it was one of the least persuasive in High. The generalized tendency to accept arguments was strongest in High, possibly as a consequence of a counter–to–drug-using subculture generated by a more pervasive concern with issues of drug use. A point of caution worth bearing in mind is that agreeing that something is one of the most potent deterrents is not the same as accepting that something as a sufficient deterrent.

STATISTICAL FOOTNOTES

a Three of the value items were members of the same prime clusters in each of the three neighborhoods. These were: F 32 ("Values workmanship"), F 34 ("Values being of service"), and F 39 ("Values refinement"). Three others were members of the same prime clusters, but other ones than the first three. These were: F 28 ("Values constant novelty and excitement"), F 33 ("Values freedom from restraint"), and F 38 ("Values thrills and chances").

The first trio constituted a prime cluster in High; in Medium, it constituted a prime cluster together with F 27 ("Values intimate companionship") and F 36 ("Values conformity and keeping up with people you like"); in Low, the last five items, together with F 40 ("Values freedom from sickness and pain") made up a prime cluster. Acceptance of one of the arguments was part of the augmented cluster in Low, of six of the arguments in Medium, and of four in High. G 34 went with the Low and High clusters; G 33 and G 40 with the Medium and High; G 32, G 37, G 38, and G 39 with the Medium; and G 35 with the High.

With reference to the second trio of value items, it constituted a prime cluster in Medium; together with F 29 ("Values power"), F 30 ("Values being popular and looked up to"), and F 31 ("Values being able to take things easy and not having to work hard"), it made up a prime cluster in Low; and, with the last three items, F 36 ("Values conformity and keeping up with people you like"), and F 37 ("Values being strong and manly"), it made up a prime cluster in High. Note that F 36 was associated in prime clusters with the first trio in Low and Medium and with the second trio in High. F 37 was a relatively strong member of both augmented value clusters in Low and High and of the first value cluster in Medium; it did not occur at all in the augmented second cluster of the latter neighborhood. None of the argument items were associated with any of the second value clusters. Presumably, quite different aspects of the meaning of F 36 and F 37 were tapped in the various cluster contexts.

The average profile correlation of the two prime value clusters in Low was —.02, and the average tetrachoric, .02; the corresponding statistics for Medium were .20 and .13; for High, .55 and .28. Although the profile correlation in the last-named neighborhood was high enough, by our criteria, for the two prime clusters to be joined in one cluster, the between-cluster statistics may be compared to the within-cluster statistics for purposes of perspective. In High, each item of the first prime cluster had an average profile correlation with the others of .74, and the lowest average tetrachoric was .40; for the second prime cluster, the lowest average profile correlation of any item with the other was .70, and the lowest average tetrachoric was .31. Scores based on the two prime value clusters (using only the items common to the three neighborhoods in each prime cluster) correlated to the extent of .20 in Low, .14 in Medium, and .23 in High. (These are regular Pearsonian correlations, not tetrachorics.) When the effect of the tendency to agree with the value items is discounted (by a statistical technique known as partial correlation), these correlations become, respectively, —.48, —.46, and —.45. That is, basically, the two sets of values tend to be mutually contradictory.

There may be some interest in the distribution of scores on the common items of the prime value clusters. The strongest appeal of the first set was Medium, where 56 per cent of the boys said "yes" to all three items; the weakest, in Low, where 36 per cent accepted all three. One subgroup in Medium stood out, the white parochial-school boys, with 71 per cent getting the maximum score. In High, 52 per cent scored three. On the second trio, there was little variation in the scores, except for the adjustment-class boys in High. Over all, half the boys scored two or more; but, in the adjustment classes, this figure ran to 62 per cent.

b This is not a contradiction of what was said earlier concerning the importance of looking at the prime clusters before attempting to interpret the augmented clusters. In the present instance, however, we are dealing with three identical prime clusters (with the minor exception that G 2 joins the prime cluster of arguments in Medium); the only clues as to possible differential meanings of the prime clusters come from the items in the augmented clusters. Meaning is, of course, an interaction process.

c The average profile correlation in Medium between the items in the prime argument cluster and those in the prime delinquency-orientation cluster was —.33; the average tetrachoric, .02.

d The coefficient of concordance was .79. This coefficient is an index of the correspondence between several sets of rankings. A coefficient of 1.00 would mean that all the rankings were identical.

e This means that this argument was tied with another in percentage of acceptance, the two arguments being in eighth and ninth place; in such a case, the items involved in a tie are assigned the average of the ranks for which a tie exists. Note that, in the present instance, there were two items with lower percentages of acceptance (ranks 10 and 11) and seven arguments with higher percentages of agreement (ranks 1 through 7); this left ranks 8 and 9 for the two tied items, and each item got the average of 8 and 9, viz., 8.5.

f The next most discrepant ranks were for G 34 (with ranks of 7.5, 4.5, and 8.5 in Low, Medium, and High) and G 38 (with ranks of 7.5, 9, and 5).

APPENDIX H

Credibility of Contact Claims

We have, at several points in the text discussion, had occasion to refer to the statistics of items G 48 ("Seeing someone take heroin") and G 49 ("Knowing at least one heroin-user"). Thirty-nine per cent of the boys in High claimed that they had seen someone take heroin, and 45 per cent claimed that they knew one or more heroin-users. The corresponding figures in Medium were almost 25 and 33⅓ per cent, respectively, and in Low they were 13 and 17 per cent. Add to the statistics on these items those of G 50: 10 per cent of the boys in both High and Medium and 6 per cent of those in Low claimed that they had themselves had a chance to use heroin. It should be remembered that we are talking about eighth-grade boys—thirteen and fourteen years old. Are the figures credible?

Even if we were to assume that the boys responded to these items with complete honesty, there might still be special factors operating to inflate these figures. Thus, it is possible that much furtive-appearing behavior lends itself to the imaginative but incorrect interpretation that someone is taking heroin. Similarly, peculiar behavior of any sort may be interpreted as owing to the influence of dope; it may be that the interpretation, "He must have just taken . . ." is readily transformed in retrospect into, "I saw him take. . . ." Also, there is a fairly good likelihood that the boys did not distinguish any more than do adults between rumors and factual knowledge concerning a person's habits. As to the opportunity to take heroin, how fine a line can youngsters (or adults, for that matter) be expected to draw between a real offer, with the drug in physical evidence, and a suggestion made by someone who merely claims to have access?

Granted that it would be naïve to accept the positive answers to these items at face value, the neighborhood differences in percentages do constitute prima-facie evidence that drug use by older individuals does touch the lives of eighth-grade children and that, the greater the incidence, the more this tends to be generally true. The differences in percentages of positive response did correspond to known differences in incidence of drug use.

Moreover, the responses to at least G 48 and G 49[1] were internally consistent. The tetrachoric correlations between the two items were .84 in Low and .76 in both Medium and High. The profile correlations were .86 in Low, .84 in Medium, and .91 in High. The profile correlations were particularly

[1] As already explained, correlational statistics were not computed for G 50.

impressive because they indicated that not only did the boys tend to answer the two items in the same manner, but that, depending on their answers to these two items, they tended to maintain corresponding consistent patterns of response to all items in the questionnaire.

The internal evidence also indicates that, however inflated the claims of knowing heroin-users and having seen people taking heroin may be, the positive answers to these items were, in fact, associated with contact with the drug-using subculture. Apart from their correlations with each other, the highest correlation of each of the two items was with G 47, the positive answers to the contact items tending to go with the claim to have got most of one's information about drugs from the street.[a]

In this connection, one would expect a priori that "information" from teachers and parents would be primarily on moral and health aspects and that "information" from reading would be primarily newspaper accounts of the perennial wiping-out of the narcotics traffic, the sheer fact that such traffic is illegal, the association between narcotics and crime, and the occasional deaths resulting from overdosage. The information items in the questionnaires had little, if anything, to do with these varieties of information,[2] but were mainly concerned with matters that would be of some functional significance to someone attracted by drug use. We have already noted that the kinds of information sampled in the questionnaire tended to go with the two contact and the information-from-the-street items. That is, positive answers to these items bespoke contact with the drug-using subculture, if not direct acquaintance with heroin-users or the witnessing of heroin use.

There is also some internal evidence in connection with the information items that, if the figures on G 48 and G 49 were inflated, they were less so in High than in Low. Of the ten highest tetrachoric correlations with G 48 in High, five involved information items; of the ten highest with G 49, seven involved information items. In Low, on the other hand, there were no information items involved in the ten highest correlations with G 48, and five in the ten highest correlations with G 49. Thus, the relationship between claimed contact and information seemed to be more intimate and direct in High than in Low, suggesting a stronger foundation for the claims in High.

A related finding pointing in the same direction involved a compound item, G 17, 25. This item was designed to test knowledge of the difference between a misdemeanor and a felony[3] in the possession of heroin. According to the

---

[2] Some were, of course, covered in the argument and image-of-the-user items. On other possible items, we anticipated that the information would be so generally available as to produce no discrimination. On supposed health effects, we know of few effects that can be consistently attributed to the drugs themselves, rather than to the conditions of taking them—e.g., the risk of infection in unsterilized needles, the unstandardized dosages in the illicit product, the chronic anxiety of the addict over maintenance of supply, the neglect of a balanced diet, etc.—and these would be either too technical or have to be stated with too many qualifications to be usable as true-false information items.

[3] The legal terms were, of course, not used. The distinction was put in terms of the amount of punishment.

law at the time of the administration of the questionnaire, the possession of one-quarter ounce was a felony, of a smaller amount, a misdemeanor. The first of the component items correctly placed the dividing line; the second incorrectly placed it at one-half ounce. Knowledge of the point at issue would require saying "true" to the first and "false" to the second. Too few of the boys (from 10 to 15 per cent) gave both correct responses to justify the utilization of the item in the cluster analysis.

The pattern of errors is, however, of interest. Many more of the boys who gave definite responses to both items—i.e., did not say "don't know" to either —in Low than in High (60 versus 29 per cent) said "false" to both. The implication is that either one-half ounce does not sound like much or that the possession of any amount is equally against the law; in either case, the pattern does not bespeak much contact. Saying "true" to one, however, and "false" to the other—or, for that matter, saying "true" to both—does, at least, suggest an awareness of the principle that the amount of heroin in one's possession makes a difference from the viewpoint of the law and of the fact that a half-ounce is an appreciable quantity.

STATISTICAL FOOTNOTES

[a] The tetrachoric correlations of G 47 and G 48 were .58, .50, and .51 in Low, Medium, and High, respectively; for G 47 and G 49, they were .72, .48, and .57.

APPENDIX I
Some of the Indexes

Index of Family Cohesion

The family-cohesion index was constructed from answers to seven questions concerning practices of the family group in which the boy lived longest in the period between the age of ten and his critical age. Each answer was given a score of zero, 1, or 2—the higher score indicating a higher frequency or intensity of the given practice. These are the questions and scored answers:

1. How were Christmas, Thanksgiving, and other holidays celebrated?

   Celebrated elaborately   2

   Celebrated routinely   1

   Not celebrated   0

2. How did you celebrate birthdays? (If Catholic, also saints' days)

   Celebrated elaborately   2

   Celebrated routinely   1

   Not celebrated   0

Criteria for the distinction of "elaborate" and "routine" celebration were as follows: "elaborate" celebration means that, aside from the usual activities common in our society, there was a feeling of festivity, anticipation, and excitement in the family; "routine" refers to a perfunctory observance of the customs of the holiday. The interviewers were asked to probe for a description of a typical holiday or birthday and took verbatim notes on the boys' responses.

3. How often did your family have dinner together?

   Always or usually   2

   2–3 times a week   1

   Rarely or never   0

If the answer was "always or usually," the question was asked:

4. Did the family break up immediately after dinner, or did it stay together for a while afterward?

   Always or usually stayed together   2

   Occasionally stayed together   1

   Rarely or never   0

5. Did your family ever go out together—visiting, on picnics, and so on?

    Frequently (more than once a month)   2

    Occasionally   1

    Rarely or never   0

6. When one of the family was sick in bed with a fever, how did the rest of the family act toward him? Did they try to be considerate of his feelings? Did they fuss about him, if that was what he liked, and leave him alone, if he wanted to be alone, or did they just disregard him? Or did they get annoyed even though they tried to be helpful? Or were they just plain mean? How did they act?

    Very considerate or helpful but annoyed   2

    Indifferent   1

    Mean   0

7. In most families, there is some quarreling and fighting between parents and children, among brothers and sisters, or between the parents. How often were there quarrels and arguments in your family? I don't mean kid stuff, but more-or-less *serious* arguments.

    Frequently (once a week or more)   0

    Occasionally   1

    Rarely or never   2

The sum of the scores which each subject received on each item constituted the index score; the higher the score, the more cohesive the family as measured by this index. Twenty-eight per cent of all cases had an index score of 7 or less (4 to 7) and were classed as "low" on family cohesion; 37 per cent received scores of 8 to 10 (classed "medium"), and 35 per cent scored 11 to 14 ("high").

Index of Family Mobility

The number and type of changes of the family residence to the time of the boy's critical age were recorded. Each type of move was assigned a numeri-

DESCRIPTION OF MOVE	INDEX	CASES (PERCENTAGE)
Family never moved	0	15
Within one community and one section of the city, from one house to another	1	33
Within one community, from one section to another	2	26
Between one big city and another	3	7
Between small town and big city	4	12
Between rural area and big city	5	6
Insufficient information		1
		100

cal value of 1 to 5, depending on how drastic the move could be considered in the sense of entailing a more-or-less radical shift of the social scene. Thus, a move between rural area and big city was given a score of 5, and a move within one community, from one section to another, a score of 1. The mobility index consists of the highest score assigned to any of the recorded moves; its range is thus from zero to 5.

Indexes of Socioeconomic Status

Index 1: *Source of family income.* The question was: "Was your family usually self-supporting, or did they generally have to go to friends, relatives, or social agencies for financial help?" In cases in which the family did not have consistent means of income, the source which was used for the longest period of time was considered "usual." In the great majority of cases, the "usual" source of income could be determined without difficulty from social work or probation records. Eighty per cent of all subjects were self-supporting.

Index 2: *Breadwinner.* The identification was made on the basis of answers to the question: "Which person in the household contributed the greatest share of the family income?" In cases where two persons contributed an equal share or where no member of the household contributed at all, occupational data (for Index 3) were coded concerning the person who ranked highest in the following order: father, stepfather, or foster father; oldest male; mother, stepmother, or foster mother; oldest female. In 74 per cent of all cases, the father was the breadwinner.

Index 3: *Occupation of breadwinner.* After ascertaining the identity of the breadwinner, the question was asked: "What does [breadwinner] normally do for a living?" Both the type of work and the industry were ascertained. The classification of occupations was as follows for the 140 subjects on whom information was complete:

	PERCENTAGE
Day laborers	21
Semiskilled laborers	25
Skilled or stable semiskilled laborers	34
Lower white collar	11
Upper white collar	0
Professionals	1
Business-owners	8
	100

Index of Housing Facilities

The index of housing facilities was constructed on the basis of information on the number and kind of facilities in the boys' homes, including such essential facilities as sanitation and heating and such "luxury" facilities as radio, television, and telephone. To each of the "essential" facilities, a weighted score was given as follows:

FACILITY	WEIGHTED SCORE
Water	
No running water	0
Running water, no hot water	1
Running and hot water	2
Sanitation	
No toilet, no bathing facilities	0
Toilet, no bath	1
Toilet and bath	2
Refrigeration	
None	0
Icebox	1
Mechanical refrigerator	2
Steam heat	
Not available	0
Available	2
Separate kitchen	
Not available	0
Available	2

The sum of scores for each facility is the index score for each case, giving a possible range in scores from zero to 10. The actual range of index scores was from 4 to 10. In addition, each case was classified as having "all three" luxury facilities (radio, television, telephone), "two of the three," "one of the three," or "none." The final categories of "best," "good," "fair," and "poor" housing facilities combined these two classifications as follows:

HOUSING FACILITIES	RADIO, TELEPHONE, TELEVISION	INDEX SCORE	CASES (PERCENTAGE)
Poor	One of three	6–8	8
	None	4–10	
Fair	Two of three	6–8	31
	One of three	9–10	
Good	All three	8	32
	Two of three	9–10	
Best	All three	9–10	29
			100

APPENDIX J

The Logic of Statistical Inference

To the statistical laity, a sample that is not deliberately picked for the characteristics that will be studied is a "random" sample. The statistician's criteria of randomness are somewhat more complicated, and, from this point of view, the samples with which we are dealing in this study are not random ones. The point is germane because the logic of statistical inference and the mathematical formulas that are used in statistical inference are predicated on random sampling in the technical sense of the term. Such a state of affairs (i.e., non-random sampling) is not uncommon in behavioral science research (and, in fact, in all research involving human beings), and the use of inferential statistics is predicated on a fiction—that the samples involved are "quasi-random" samples of populations which are not precisely identified but which are hopefully not very different from the populations one is trying to sample. The effects of the fiction are that one cannot be certain of the sample characteristics with respect to which generalizations are relevant and, hence, that generalizations must be regarded with caution.

In the comparison of groups, in such an event, statistical inference offers, at best, a rough guide as to which differences to take seriously, i.e., as of sufficient magnitude to make it unlikely that they would arise by chance in sampling. The risk, however, that such significant differences are related to unidentified characteristics of the populations of which the comparison groups are samples, rather than to the characteristics with which one thinks one is dealing, cannot be assessed by any statistical method. The considerations of mathematical-statistical logic aside, we took the differences reported in Chapter V seriously because they were internally consistent (e.g., except when otherwise noted, they held up for each of the ethnic groups), coherent (i.e., when taken together, they told an intelligible story), and externally consistent (e.g., the differences between delinquents and nondelinquents were similar to those reported in other studies, even when drug use was held constant—a factor not considered in other studies comparing delinquents and nondelinquents). In relation to the third point (external consistency), we have repeatedly been told by people with experience with drug-users that we seem to have hit the nail on the head; and, with one exception not relevant to Chapter V (the point is discussed when it arises), no expert has ever suggested to us that we were mistaken in this.[1]

There is one point that may be troublesome to those who have not studied the logic of statistical inference. This is that differences of the same magnitude are sometimes described as statistically significant and sometimes as not. One circumstance in which this can happen is easily explained. Assuming random sampling, the larger the number of cases on which a statistic is based, the less likely it is to differ greatly from the true population figure. Hence, a difference of, say, 15 per cent between small samples is not so dependable as the same difference found between large samples.

A second circumstance is a bit more complicated. A statistic obtained by sampling a relatively homogeneous population is more dependable than one obtained by sampling a less homogeneous population; one is less likely to get a sample of atypical cases in the first instance than in the second. Hence, the dependability of a statistic depends, not only on the size of the sample, but also on the heterogeneity or variability of the population from which the sample was taken. Exactly how one takes into account the probable heterogeneity of the population is a matter too complicated to explain here. Suffice it to say, however, that this factor makes it possible to get differences of the same size between two samples which are sometimes dependable (statistically significant with a given risk of error) and, in other instances, not dependable, even though the numbers of cases involved are identical. The issue is further complicated by the number of groups being compared at the same time. We have followed the convention that, when more than two groups are being compared, no difference between any pair of groups is accepted as significant unless an over-all test indicates that there are significant differences among the groups in the set. This, too, is a matter too complicated to discuss here.

To say that a difference is not statistically significant—i.e., that it is not large enough to justify the belief that it did not arise through the process of sampling and, hence, that it is not safe to generalize the fact of the difference to the populations involved—is not to say that the populations are actually alike in terms of the comparison. The statement concerns the evidence and not the fact. "We have no evidence that the difference would hold up if the entire populations could be compared" is not to be interpreted as saying, "If the entire populations were compared, there would not be any difference." The weight of the evidence is always on the side of what is actually found, but that evidence can be quite convincing or it can be quite weak. On the other hand, to say that a difference is significant is not to say that it certainly reflects a true difference between the populations. It is in the nature of probability that the improbable can happen. "Statistically significant" means, in a convention of the behavioral sciences, that the odds are at least nineteen-to-one

[1] For a more complete and nontechnical discussion of the logic of sampling, see Isidor Chein, "An Introduction to Sampling," in C. Selltiz, M. Jahoda, M. Deutsch, and S. W. Cook, *Research Methods in Human Relations* (New York: Holt, 1959).

that the difference did not arise by chance. This leaves one chance in twenty
that it did, and, when many comparisons are based on the same samples, the
odds that at least some of the "statistically significant" differences did arise
by chance are considerably greater.

It is also possible, on the basis of statistical evidence, to assert positively
that two or more groups are alike. With samples of the size with which we
were dealing, however, the risks of making such statements erroneously are so
great as to make them pointless.

APPENDIX K

Summary Tables from the Gang Study

TABLE K-1   *Heroin-Users in High- and Low-Use Gangs*

	HIGH-USE GANGS (67)	LOW-USE GANGS (27)	TOTAL (94)
TOTAL NUMBER OF CASES			
a. Percentage of users who took heroin mainly			
Intravenously	56	52	54
Subcutaneously	7	7	7
Nasally	27	30	28
Information lacking	10	11	11
b. Percentage who currently used heroin			
Once a day or more often	44	41	43
Three to six times a week	16	5	13
Twice a week or less often	28	36	30
Information lacking	12	18	14
(Total number of current users)	(58)	(22)	(80)
c. Percentage who recently decreased intake of heroin	24	11	20
Percentage who stopped use	15	11	14
d. Percentage who had been using heroin			
Less than one year	2	29	10
One year	18	7	15
Two years or more	76	45	67
Information lacking	4	19	8
e. Percentage who had been picked up by police in connection with narcotics	27	22	26
f. Percentage who had been institutionalized for drug offenses	12	19	14

g. Percentage who expressed concern to group worker about using drugs — 48 | 48 | 48

h. Percentage who made efforts to cut down or stop using — 56 | 56 | 56

i. Percentage who received medical attention for drug use — 19 | 22 | 20

j. Percentage who increased delinquency with onset or increase of drug use or decreased delinquency with decrease or cessation of heroin use — 41 | 30 | 37

k. Percentage who decreased time spent with club with onset of heroin use or increased with decrease or cessation of heroin use — 39 | 33 | 37

TOTAL NUMBER OF CASES — (67) | (27) | (94)

TABLE K-2   Users and Nonusers in High-Use, Low-Use, and Drug-Free Gangs
(Background and Behavior)

	HIGH-USE GANGS			LOW-USE GANGS			DRUG-FREE GANGS (71)	TOTAL (305)
	USERS (67)	NON-USERS (26)	TOTAL (93)	USERS (27)	NON-USERS (114)	TOTAL (141)		
TOTAL NUMBER OF CASES								
a. Age: Percentage eighteen and older	64	61	63	74	52	57	25	51
b. Education: Percentage completed fewer than four years High School	85	62	78	96	85	87	95	86
c. Work: Percentage not working	34	27	32	63	24	31	46	35
d. Delinquency: Percentage habitual delinquents	75	65	72	78	68	70	55	67
e. Percentage arrested for nondrug delinquency	66	46	61	85	58	63	42	57
f. Percentage who sold drugs	51	24	42	40	3	11	4	19
g. Percentage who recently increased amount of delinquency	27	0	19	22	9	11	8	13
h. Percentage who did not drink wine	53	58	54	15	31	28	14	33
i. Percentage who did not drink whiskey	37	50	41	15	30	27	15	29
j. Percentage with sexual aberration (homosexuality)	28	8	23	22	21	21	3	17

k. Percentage who spent little time with their gangs	16	23	18	41	16	21	4	16
l. Percentage leaders (top and secondary)	25	54	34	41	23	27	25	28
m. Percentage who lost leadership status	24	8	19	26	16	18	17	18
n. Percentage who lost leadership with onset of heroin use or gained it with decrease of heroin use	30	—	—	33	—	—	—	31
TOTAL NUMBER OF CASES	(67)	(26)	(93)	(27)	(114)	(141)	(71)	(305)

TABLE K-3   Users and Nonusers in High-Use, Low-Use, and Drug-Free Gangs
(Attitude toward Drug Use)

	HIGH-USE GANGS			LOW-USE GANGS			DRUG-FREE GANGS	TOTAL
	USERS (67)	NON-USERS (26)	TOTAL (93)	USERS (27)	NON-USERS (114)	TOTAL (141)	(71)	(305)
TOTAL NUMBER OF CASES								
a. Percentage who thought heroin use								
Worthwhile	22	4	17	26	2	6	1	9
OK if occasional	25	31	27	36	7	13	10	16
Opposed	19	46	27	19	62	54	34	41
Ambivalent	30	19	26	15	25	23	24	24
Information lacking	4	0	3	4	4	4	31	10
b. Percentage whose attitude to regular heroin-users was								
Hostile or derogatory	19	31	23	11	52	44	18	32
Tolerant	48	54	49	59	25	31	23	35
Ambivalent	28	15	25	26	18	19	28	23
Information lacking	4	0	3	4	6	6	31	11
c. Percentage whose attitude to occasional heroin-users was								
Hostile or derogatory	12	27	16	4	44	36	17	26
Tolerant	57	65	59	67	29	36	24	40
Ambivalent	28	8	23	22	21	21	28	23
Information lacking	3	0	2	7	6	6	31	11

d. Percentage who thought smoking marijuana is

Worthwhile	16	8	14	41	9	15	6	13
OK if occasional	22	35	26	30	19	21	7	19
Opposed	9	31	15	7	42	35	13	24
Ambivalent	9	19	12	7	19	17	15	15
Information lacking	43	8	33	15	11	11	59	29

e. Percentage whose attitude toward regular smokers of marijuana was

Hostile or derogatory	7	23	12	7	45	38	8	23
Tolerant	43	46	44	74	25	35	14	33
Ambivalent	7	23	12	4	19	16	20	16
Information lacking	42	8	32	15	11	11	58	29

f. Percentage whose attitude toward occasional smoking of marijuana was

Hostile or derogatory	7	19	11	7	35	30	7	19
Tolerant	43	58	47	74	32	40	15	36
Ambivalent	6	8	6	4	21	18	20	15
Information lacking	43	15	35	15	12	13	58	30
TOTAL NUMBER OF CASES	(67)	(26)	(93)	(27)	(114)	(141)	(71)	(305)

TABLE K-4 *Participation in Gang Activities by Users and Nonusers in High-Use, Low-Use, and Drug-Free Gangs**

	HIGH-USE GANGS			LOW-USE GANGS			DRUG-FREE GANGS	TOTAL
	USERS	NON-USERS	TOTAL	USERS	NON-USERS	TOTAL		
a. Percentage who participated in rumbles	56 (45)	62 (24)	58 (69)	40 (15)	61 (62)	57 (77)	58 (71)	58 (217)
b. Percentage who participated in robbery and burglary	57 (42)	7 (14)	45 (56)	48 (27)	32 (110)	35 (137)	13 (39)	34 (232)
c. Percentage who participated in vandalism and "hell-raising"	38 (42)	21 (14)	34 (56)	24 (21)	36 (87)	33 (108)	49 (71)	38 (235)
d. Percentage who participated in gang-organized sexual delinquency	45 (42)	21 (14)	39 (56)	17 (23)	13 (105)	13 (128)	10 (48)	19 (232)
e. Percentage who participated in active sports	26 (61)	57 (21)	34 (82)	30 (22)	54 (114)	50 (136)	65 (71)	50 (289)
f. Percentage who participated in gang dances	69 (67)	92 (26)	75 (93)	56 (18)	72 (89)	69 (107)	87 (71)	76 (271)
g. Percentage who participated in gang house parties	73 (47)	82 (17)	75 (64)	36 (22)	62 (98)	58 (120)	83 (71)	69 (255)

* Data are for gangs which engaged in the given activity. Since the N's vary with the number of gangs engaged in the activity, the N on which each percent-age is based is included in parentheses following the percentage figure.

TABLE K-5 *Youth Workers' Appraisals of High-Use, Low-Use, and Drug-Free Gangs*

	HIGH-USE GANGS	LOW-USE GANGS	DRUG-FREE GANGS	TOTAL
TOTAL NUMBER OF GANGS	(6)	(8)	(4)	(18)
a. Frequently in gang fights (once in three months or more often)	1	2	4	7
b. Frequently engaged in vandalism and "hell-raising" (once a month or more often)	2	4	2	8
c. Frequently conducted robberies and burglaries (twice a month or more often)	3	5	2	10
d. Frequently engaged in sexual delinquency (twice a year or more often)	1	4	3	8
e. Gambled frequently (once a week or more often)	1	5	3	9
f. Organized dances frequently (once a month or more often)	4	4	1	9
g. Organized house parties frequently (twice a month or more often)	2	4	2	8
h. Frequently engaged in active sports (once a week or more often)	2	4	3	9
i. Frequently watched sports events	3	5	2	10
j. Generally apathetic	2	3	0	5
k. "Cohesive"—none or only one of the major gang activities were done in cliques	1	3	3	7
TOTAL NUMBER OF GANGS	(6)	(8)	(4)	(18)

TABLE K-6 *Average Discrepancies between Self-Description and Various Ideals**

	NEGRO	PUERTO RICAN	CAUCASIAN	ALL
Users under 21	.417†	.362	.238	.339
Nonusers under 21	.361	.220	.218	.266
Adults using since before 21	.537	.333	.251	.374
Adults using since after 21	.252	.206	.204	.221
Nonusers over 21	.305	.124	.030	.153

* Adapted from Stanley Schiff, "A Self-Theory Investigation of Drug Addiction in Relation to Age of Onset" (New York University Graduate School of Arts and Science, doctoral dissertation, 1959), 66. There are twenty cases in each subgroup, or a total of 300 cases. Although we have included this table and the related discussion with the materials of the gang study, the study by Schiff had no connection with the latter.
† The higher the number, the smaller the average discrepancy.

APPENDIX L

Indexes of Family Influence

TABLE L-1   *Component Items of Index II*
                      Factors Conducive to Defective
                      Superego Functioning

	EARLY CHILDHOOD	RATIONALE*
15	Any mother figure a socially deviant or severe parental model	2
16	Any father figure a socially deviant or severe parental model	2
24	Overt threat of harsh punishment or loss of love used as form of discipline	3, 7
25	Parental standards either rigid or vague	4
3	Any mother figure passionate, objective, cool, or hostile in affection for boy (other-than-warm relationship)	5
4	Any father figure passionate, objective, cool, or hostile in affection for boy (other-than-warm relationship)	5
14	For a significant part of period, boy did not have father figure or mother figure in his life	1
	LATE CHILDHOOD	
3	Any mother figure passionate, objective, cool, or hostile in affection for boy (other-than-warm relationship)	5
4	Any father figure passionate, objective, cool, or hostile in affection for boy (other-than-warm relationship)	5
	ADOLESCENCE PERIOD	
24	Overt threat of harsh punishment or loss of love used as a form of discipline	3, 7
25	Parental standards either rigid or vague	4
	PRESENT	
15	Any mother figure a socially deviant or severe parental model	2

EARLY CHILDHOOD | RATIONALE*

16 Any father figure a socially deviant or severe parental model   2

PERIOD NOT SPECIFIED

1 Institutionalization of boy at any time in childhood   1, 3

17 Boy frustrated in his wishes, overindulged, or both   6

18 Boy experienced highly intense or extremely weak mother–son relationship or both   5

19 Boy experienced highly intense or extremely weak father–son relationship or both   5

20 Mother had indifferent attitude to the physical needs of boy (some or gross neglect as pattern)   3, 6

23 One parent attempted to subvert other's attempts at discipline   4

* See below.

Rationale for Composition of Index II
Factors Conducive to Defective Superego Functioning

For the purposes of this study, optimal superego functioning was defined as the operation of internalized moral standards which influence behavior in a realistic and socially acceptable manner and without a pervasive sense of guilt. Normal superego development was assumed to develop by identification with parent figures and the assumption of their moral standards as a result of childhood dependency and fear of loss of parental love. We have delineated two major types of defective superego functioning: (1) the superego that consists of poorly internalized standards and/or socially ineffective operation of these standards (the "weak" superego) and (2) overly strong, harsh, and punitive superego functioning.

Considering that either of these extreme kinds of superego would lead to difficulty of functioning in present-day American society, environmental influences toward one or the other or both are influences toward defective superego development. Separate subindexes (II-A and II-B) were developed to measure family experiences conducive to each of these two forms. The present index, however, attempts to measure the degree to which any of these experiences interfering with optimal superego development were present in the life of the boy.

Each of the family experiences listed in our index would tend to impair optimal superego functioning as described in the following paragraphs.

1. The absence of parental models interferes with the development of dependency and identification, thus lessening the opportunity for the taking-over of parental standards.
2. Deviant or severe parental models may lead to the internalization of these standards of morality by the child.

3. Harshness, chronic punishment, and lack of affection interferes with the development of dependency on parental love. This situation tends to prevent the internalization of parental standards and encourage a morality of expediency.

4. Rigidity of parental expectations leads to the incorporation of severe standards. If the parental standards for the boy are vague or inconsistent, this tends to lead to confusion about how he should act or to provocation as a way of extracting standards from his parent figures.

5. Overly strong dependency may lead to the incorporation of highly severe standards. On the other hand, insufficient dependency may result in a lack of motivation to retain the love of the parent by doing what he or she wants.

6. Chronic frustration of gratifications interferes with the development of dependency. Indulgence enhances childhood dependency and may result in a highly severe superego because of an intense fear of losing the love and services on which the child is dependent.

7. Frequent threats of loss of parental love may provoke strong guilt feelings in the child in reaction to ideas or acts of transgression. If the child is dependent on such love, this parental pattern tends to promote an overly strong superego.

TABLE L-2   *Component Items of Index II-A*
Factors Conducive to Overly
Strong and Severe Superego

EARLY CHILDHOOD	RATIONALE*
3 Any mother figure either passionate or warm in affection for boy	4
4 Any father figure either passionate or warm in affection for boy	4
15 Any mother figure a severe parental model	2
16 Any father figure a severe parental model	2
24 Threat of loss of love predominated as a form of discipline	3
25 Rigid parental standards for boy	2
LATE CHILDHOOD	
3 Any mother figure either passionate or warm in affection for boy	4
4 Any father figure either passionate or warm in affection for boy	4
ADOLESCENCE	
24 Threat of loss of love predominated as a form of discipline	3

	EARLY CHILDHOOD	RATIONALE*
25	Rigid parental standards for boy	2
	PRESENT	
15	Any mother figure a severe parental model	2
16	Any father figure a severe parental model	2
	PERIOD NOT SPECIFIED	
1	Institutionalization of boy any time after *early* childhood	1

* See below.

Rationale for Composition of Index II–A
Factors Conducive to Overly Strong and Severe Superego

The environmental prerequisites for the development of overly strong and severe superego functioning are similar to the requirements for an optimally functioning superego. These requirements are childhood dependency, fear of loss of parental love, and the consequent identification with parent figures and internalization of their moral standards. The difference in etiology is one of degree, in the extreme case resulting in excessive childhood dependency, a heightened fear of loss of parental love and consequent overidentification with parent figures, and the incorporation of inflexible standards of conduct.

Each of the family experiences listed in our index tend to exaggerate this normal development and produce an overly strong and severe superego. The rationale for each item is described in the following paragraphs.

1. Identification with rigid and authoritarian institutional standards leads, by a taking-over of the standards, to an overly severe and strong superego.
2. The pressure of severe parental models may lead to the internalization of rigid standards of morality.
3. A heightened fear of the loss of the love of parental figures provides motivation for the taking-over of parental standards of conduct to ensure against this loss.
4. Parental affection encourages dependency and the incorporation of parental standards in order to ensure against the loss of love.

TABLE L-3   *Component Items of Index II-B*
Factors Conducive to Weak
Superego Functioning

	EARLY CHILDHOOD	RATIONALE*
1	Boy institutionalized	1
3	Any mother figure cool or hostile to boy	1
4	Any father figure cool or hostile to boy	1

14	For a significant part of period, boy did not have father figure or mother figure in his life	1
15	Any mother figure an immoral model	2
16	Any father figure an immoral model	2
21	No clear parental roles in formation of discipline policy	3
22	Neither parent enforced discipline	3
25	Parental standards vague or inconsistent	3
24	Harsh punishment or its threat used as form of discipline	1

LATE CHILDHOOD

| 3 | Any mother figure cool or hostile to boy | 1 |
| 4 | Any father figure cool or hostile to boy | 1 |

ADOLESCENCE

21	No clear parental roles in formation of discipline policy	3
22	Neither parent enforced discipline	3
25	Parental standards vague or inconsistent	3
24	Harsh punishment or its threat used as form of discipline	1

PRESENT

| 15 | Any mother figure an immoral model | 2 |
| 16 | Any father figure an immoral model | 2 |

PERIOD NOT SPECIFIED

17	Boy frustrated in wishes and not overindulged	1
18	Boy experienced extremely weak mother–son relationship	1
19	Boy experienced extremely weak father–son relationship	1
20	Mother had indifferent attitude to physical needs of boy (gross neglect as pattern)	1
23	One parent attempted to subvert other's attempts at discipline	3
30	Impulse-orientation marked in mother figure	2
30	Impulse-orientation marked in father figure	2

* See below.

Rationale for Composition of Index II–B
Factors Conducive to Weak
Superego Functioning

This index was designed to measure family experiences that would interfere with the development of socially adequate internalized standards. Each of the listed experiences would:

1. discourage childhood dependency and identification with the parent;
2. encourage socially unacceptable behavior or discourage appropriate mechanisms of impulse control by the presence of bad potential models; or
3. make it difficult for the youngster to distinguish the parents' ideas of right and wrong.

An accumulation of such experiences would be expected to produce what we have defined as weak superego functioning.

TABLE L-4   *Component Items of Index III*
Factors Conducive to Inadequate
Male Identification

	EARLY CHILDHOOD	RATIONALE*
2	More than one mother figure present	1
4	Any father figure cool or hostile to boy	2
8	Father had unstable work history	2
12	Any father figure was subordinate adult in home	1
13	A mother figure was more important parent in boy's life	1
14	For a significant part of period, boy did not have father figure in his life	1
21	Mother figure made disciplinary policy	1
3	Any mother figure passionate in affection for boy	1
22	Discipline enforced primarily by mother figure	1
16	Any father figure a weak and immature personality	2
	LATE CHILDHOOD	
2	More than one mother figure present	1
4	Any father figure cool or hostile to boy	2
8	Father had unstable work history	2
12	Father was dominant adult in home	1
13	A mother figure was more important parent in boy's life	1
14	For significant part of period, boy did not have father figure in his life	1
3	Any mother figure passionate in affection for boy	1
	ADOLESCENCE	
21	Father figure made disciplinary policy	1
22	Discipline enforced primarily by mother figure	1
	PERIOD NOT SPECIFIED	
18	Boy experienced highly intense mother–son relationship	1
19	Boy experienced extremely weak father–son relationship	2

26	Mother discouraged "rough" companions	1
7	Boy was only son with two or more sisters	1
19	Father performed maternal functions	2

* See below.

Rationale for Composition of Index III
Factors Conducive to Inadequate Male Identification

Each of the items in this index would tend to hamper adequate masculine identification in one of two ways:

1. Dominance of females in the family environment and in the life of the boy tends to encourage dependency on and identification with females, the development of feminine tastes, style, orientations, and the like.
2. The presence of a weak, unstable, or hostile father figure may interfere with the ability of the child to form a dependency relationship with a male and to wholeheartedly identify with him. This situation (or the absence of male figures in his environment) diminishes the opportunities for the taking-over of masculine standards and behavior patterns.

TABLE L-5   *Component Items of Index IV*
Factors Hampering Development
of Realistic Aspirations with
Respect to Long-Range Goals

	LATE CHILDHOOD AND EARLY ADOLESCENCE	RATIONALE*
32	Mother had unrealistically high or low aspirations for boy	2
32	Father had unrealistically high or low aspirations for boy	2
	LATE ADOLESCENCE AND PRESENT	
32	Mother had unrealistically high or low aspirations for boy	2
32	Father had unrealistically high or low aspirations for boy	2
	PERIOD NOT SPECIFIED	
31	Status-orientation marked in mother figure	3
31	Status-orientation marked in father figure	3
33	Mother figure unrealistically optimistic, feels that life is a gamble, or does not concern herself with own future	1
33	Father figure unrealistically optimistic, feels that life is a gamble, or does not concern himself with own future	1
30	Impulse-orientation marked in mother figure	1
30	Impulse-orientation marked in father figure	1
34	Family feels inferior or superior to neighbors	3

* See below.

Rationale for Composition of Index IV
Factors Hampering Development of Realistic Aspirations with Respect to Long-Range Goals

This index was designed to measure the extent to which the parents of the boy had attitudes and goals deviating from those of realistically oriented middle-class persons. An item may be included in the index because the parental attitude is:

1. more characteristic of lower-class than middle-class orientation;
2. unrealistic and contrary to the usual middle-class attitude; or
3. an exaggeration of certain middle-class values at the expense of other middle-class values, such as the obtaining of gratification and satisfaction.

TABLE L-6   *Component Items of Index V*
Factors Encouraging Distrust of
Major Social Institutions

	LATE CHILDHOOD AND EARLY ADOLESCENCE	RATIONALE*
32	Mother had unrealistically low aspirations for boy	3
32	Father had unrealistically low aspirations for boy	3
	LATE ADOLESCENCE AND PRESENT	
32	Mother had unrealistically low aspirations for boy	3
32	Father had unrealistically low aspirations for boy	3
	PERIOD NOT SPECIFIED	
27	Mother did not trust authority figures	1
27	Mother tried to manipulate authority figures	1
27	Father did not trust authority figures	1
27	Father tried to manipulate authority figures	1
28	Mother aware of but made no use of organized community resources	2
28	Father aware of but made no use of organized community resources	2
33	Mother was unrealistically pessimistic or felt that life is a gamble	4
33	Father was unrealistically pessimistic or felt that life is a gamble	4

* See below.

Rationale for Composition of Index V
Factors Encouraging Distrust of Major Social Institutions

The following paragraphs describe how the parental characteristics included in this index may, by example, create distrust of major social institutions on the part of the boy.

1. Distrustful and/or manipulative attitudes by parents toward representatives of authority reflects a distrust of major social institutions. Such parental attitudes may encourage the development of similar attitudes in their children.
2. By example, parents who are aware of but do not make use of organized community resources encourage a similar attitude in their children. Such a pattern tends to breed distrust of such resources as possible avenues of gaining help when needed and of enriching life.
3. Unrealistic lack of parental aspirations for the boy may lead to a feeling that institutional and social arrangements prevent him from achieving what his interests and capacities allow.
4. Parental thinking about the future in unrealistic and pessimistic terms can lead to a basic attitude of distrust in the boy which may find expression in pessimistic and untrustful attitudes toward major social institutions. Seeing life as a gamble may lead to the attitude that a capricious fate determines our lives; a person cannot count on institutional arrangements, but should take his chances without any planning.

APPENDIX M
Possibility of Interviewer Bias

Although we could withhold the predictions and rationales from the interviewers, we could not conceal which families contained the addicts and which the controls. With this knowledge, biased interviewers could slant the data in accordance with their own expectations and prejudices—expectations which could well correspond to our own. They might, for example, pursue certain lines of information for one type of family, but not for the other. Accordingly, we did some elaborate checks on our interviewers to deal with this difficult methodological problem.

Before they started field work, each interviewer was asked to give her own predictions as to the differences that would be found between addicts and controls on the items covered in the questionnaire. Each interviewer was also asked to describe, by checking thirty-five rating scales, what she thought the mother of the addict would be like. From the rating scales, we obtained a measure of negative, hostile attitudes toward the mothers of the addicts.

After the data were collected, we compared the reports for families of addicts and families of controls of those interviewers whose expectations were similar to our predictions with those who had differing expectations. On the separate comparisons for each of the hypotheses and on a combined index of gross environmental pathology, there was no case of significant difference in the reports by the two classes of interviewers.

Similar comparisons were made of the results reported by interviewers who had differing initial attitudes toward the mother of the addict. An analysis of the ratings of mothers of addicts by the interviewers (prior to any actual contact with such mothers) showed that, as one might expect, none of our interviewers had favorable attitudes. There was, however, wide variation among the interviewers, ranging from a fairly neutral attitude to a very negative and hostile one. The interviewers were then divided into three groups: those with rather neutral attitudes, those with moderately negative ones, and those who pictured the mothers of addicts in strongly negative terms. A comparison of their reports on addicts and controls again showed no difference among the three types of interviewers.

We also used a combined design involving, at the same time, interviewer expectations and attitudes (four equal groups of interviewers—three above the median in attitude and above the median in agreement of their predictions with our own, three above the median in attitude and below the median in agreeing with us, etc.) with no change in result. There is good reason, therefore, to believe that the data were not influenced by the preconceptions or prejudicial attitudes of the interviewers.[1]

The statistical technique used was that of analysis of variance, which is one for testing the hypothesis that the average differences between two or more groups are no larger than can reasonably be expected by chance if these groups are random samples of the same population. The principles of the test are that scores can be divided into a number of components from which one can obtain independent estimates of the population variance and that the probability of discrepancies in these estimates can be assessed. The probabilities of ratios (referred to as F-ratios) of independent estimates of the population variance have been calculated (and tabled) on the basis of certain assumptions; but it is known that the test is quite rugged in that the probability estimates tend to remain accurate even when there is reason to believe that there are quite marked deviations from conditions assumed in the derivation of the probabilities of the F-ratios.

In the present application, we had, for any given index, an estimate of the population variance based on the average index differences for addict and control families (with the interviewer effects balanced out), another estimate based on the average index difference obtained by the various classes of interviewers (with the differences related to types of families balanced out); another estimate based on what are known as "interaction effects" (in the present instance, various types of interviewers reacting differently to the two types of families, i.e., an estimate based on the degree to which the average index differences between addict and control families differ for the types of interviewers); and, finally, an estimate based on the residual variance (i.e., on the index variance that remains after subtracting a component related to family-type differences, a component related to interviewer-type differences, and a component related to the interaction effect). The latter estimate was used as the denominator in computing three F ratios—one to assess the chance probability of getting differences comparable to that obtained between the addict and control families, one to assess the chance probability of getting differences comparable to that obtained between the classes of interviewers, and one to similarly assess the interaction effect.

When all the analyses of variance for each of the indexes and for the combined index of over-all environmental deprivation were assembled, we found that in no instance was there either a significant interviewer-type effect or a significant interaction between interviewer type and addict–control difference.

[1] Details of the checks on the possibility of interviewer bias are given in Robert S. Lee, "The Family of the Addict" (New York University Graduate School of Arts and Science, doctoral dissertation, 1957), pp. 133–149.

Index

abstinence period, need for, 360
abstinence syndrome, 25, 247; *see also* withdrawal symptoms or syndrome
academic achievement, 291
acceptance, by others, 257; rehabilitation and, 382; by self, 211, 257
activity changes, 166–168
activity and sports, versus drug use, 13, 184, 187
Adams, Walter A., 201 n., 210, 212, 214
adaptive changes, 365; addiction and, 227–228; at defense levels, 233–235; psychophysiological reaction and, 237–250; unconscious processes and, 235–236
addict(s), "acceptance" of, 211, 257, 382; adolescent, *see* adolescent addict; characteristics of, 6; childhood experience of, 254–255, 459–466 (*see also* childhood experience); court commitment of, 384; deliquent subculture of, 13; democracy of, 211–212; "down-and-out" stereotype of, 355; versus drug-users, 8–9, 19, 22–23; family background factors and, 251–275, 459–466; female, *see* female addict; "frantic-junkie" state of, 24, 163; as human being, 3; "hustling" of, 25; life style of, 162–168; loose meaning of term, 113 n., 377; medical assistance sought by, 18; money spent by, 163; number of, 7, 20, 29–37, 372; "old-timers" among, 21; passive personality of, 49; personality disorders of, 14–15; physician's relations with, 372–373; rehabilitation of, 324–327; self-commitment by, 22, 333, 384; types of, 27–28; work habits of, 358–359; *see also* addiction
addiction, adaptive changes and, 227–228; adolescent, *see* adolescent addict; alcoholism and, 280–281 (*see also* alcoholism); awareness and, 406;

cause of, 3, 22–23; compared to alcoholic intoxication and addiction, 234; compulsory therapy for, 332–333; as "contagious" disease, 328, 376; control and prevention of, 369–386; craving and, 27, 160, 237; crime and, 8–9, 41, 166–167, 327, 350, 359, 364; dependence and, 22–23, 246–248; "detached" discussion of, 4–5; as disease, 8–9, 16, 328–329, 333–334; versus drug use, 45 n., 60–61 (*see also* drug use); efforts to break habit in, 168–174; emotional state and, 243; "epidemic" of, 16; exaggerated dangers of, 327–330; fear of, 168; female, *see* female addict; heroin as source of, 151–152; home life and family background in, 13–14, 251–259, 459–466; as human suffering, 366; illegality of, 350–351, 371–375, 380; inducement as cause of, 5; and loss of interest in work, 358; meaning and varieties of, 22–29; misery and, 328; objective of treatment in, 14; pathology and, 20; personality and, 193–250; physiological dependence and, 27, 249–250, 360; prevention and treatment of, 369–386; process of, 149–176; proposed steps to alleviate, 323 ff.; recognition of, 24; repressive approach to, 327; as social problem, 363–368; stages in, 149–174; struggle to break habit in, 168–174; three dimensions of, 27; total involvement in, 26–27; treatment, prevention, and control of, 369–386; typology of, 28–29; unconscious symbolism in, 235–236; withdrawal symptoms as criteria of, 113, 248 (*see also* withdrawal symptoms); *see also* addict; drug-user
addiction-prone personality, 253–254, 380